LondonTown.com

London 2013 →

WELCOME TO 'London 2013 from LondonTown.com'.

Although buoyed by its own gold medal performance in staging the Summer Olympics, London in recent years has been obsessively innovating, bursting with confidence, and relentlessly growing - this is nowhere more evident than with its huge annual arts, entertainment and events calendar.

LondonTown.com will feature over 60,000 events during 2013; this book is our edit of this huge collection of the best that the events world has to offer in London throughout this year, but be sure to also sign up to the various newsletters featured throughout this book to stay informed and receive information on events that space prohibits us from featuring here.

To get started take five minutes now to read our preview of the exciting new openings, theatre, concerts, comedy, opera, talks, gigs, ballet, sport, food events, festivals of all kinds, exhibitions and anniversaries, coming up in the year ahead: **'Prologue 2013'** → 8.

Steven Potter, Editor
SP@LondonTown.com

Contents

London events in 2013

50	Ongoing events
66	January 2013
80	February 2013
96	March 2013
112	April 2013
128	May 2013
144	June 2013
160	July 2013
174	August 2013
184	September 2013
196	October 2013
208	November 2013
218	December 2013

London 2013 Features

8 **PROLOGUE: London in 2013**
London enters 2013 riding the crest of a wondrous wave as the capital continues its cultural boom

13 **WHAT'S NEW: Opening in 2013**
Additions include a new National Theatre venue and a fashion college in Soho

14 **London's Major Museums**
London's penchant for huge 'blockbuster' exhibitions continues alongside specialist shows

17 **The Shard**
London's tallest building opens its 72nd-floor viewing platform to the public

LondonTown.com

18 London Theatre Highlights
Leading Hollywood stars gather on the London stage for another bumper year

22 Talks of the Town
The great and the good share ideas, inform, animate and encourage debate

24 The Sporting Year 2013
There's no time for an Olympic hangover with a fixture-fuelled year of sporting showdowns

29 150 Years of the Tube
The world's first ever underground railway network reaches an historic milestone

30 Major Entertainment Venues
London has more multi-purpose arts and culture hubs than any other capital city in the world

33 London Design Festivals
London's quest for innovation, style and conceptual beauty shines through

34 Classical Music, Ballet and Opera in 2013
Birthday boys Britten, Wagner and Verdi are at the centre of another stellar year

38 Summer Music Festivals
The biggest bands in the business entertain the masses in parks and venues all over town

136

58

151

157

Contents continued

40 London's Fringe Theatres
Some of the best drama in town comes from these intimate spaces with small budgets but big ideas

42 Food Festivals
With so many gastronomic dates for the diary, London is a true foodie's delight

43 Film Festivals
London rolls out the red carpet for film fanatics in a variety of intriguing places

44 Major Art in 2013
From Lichtenstein to Lowry, Manet to Man Ray, the city's artistic palette is delightfully diverse

46 London Comedy
Stand-up comedian James Mullinger discusses who and what will make us all laugh this year

48 Quirky London Events
We Brits are an odd bunch - as reflected in some of the wackiest events around town

65 London's Dance Venues
From ballet to contemporary, street to ballroom, there's an eclectic range of dance venues on offer

79 Live Music Venues
Know your XOYO from your Cafe Oto as we plug our six best gig venues from around the capital

95 London Sporting Venues
The UK's two biggest stadia are located in London - as well as many a celebrated sporting arena

111 Comedy Clubs
Our nine favourite places where Londoners can nurse a pint, let their hair down and laugh

127 Weekly Markets
The best in unusual antiques, fresh flowers, second-hand clothes and vintage accessories

143 Golden Oldies
They say life starts at 40 - but for these musical stars of yesteryear, that's being way too generous

LondonTown.com

159 Kids Theatres
Whether your little ones are into puppets, plays or panto - there's so much to choose from

173 Re-opening the Olympic Park
Exactly a year after the London 2012 Opening Ceremony, parts of the Olympic Park reopen

183 London Lidos
Cool down in the summer with a plunge into one of our many public pools

195 Cabaret and Burlesque
Tassels, corsets and suggestive striptease - London has become a cheeky cabaret capital

207 Behind the Scenes
Some of London's most intriguing buildings and institutions are accessible by appointment only

217 London's Christmas Markets
Help fill those stockings with a trip to some of London's best festive markets in December

225 Christmas Ice Skating
There's nothing like taking to the ice to get into the Christmas spirit with a seasonal skate

226 London's Town Houses
London's stately homes offer a slice of living history and a steady flow of contemporary events

228 2013: Year of the Dead
Topical residents in London's famous 'Magnificent Seven' Victorian cemeteries

230 London's Lesser-Known Museums
Circumvent the mainstream blockbuster shows with a visit to one of London's hidden gems

233 2013 Anniversaries
From Sir Michael Caine to Jack the Ripper - London has its fair share of anniversaries and milestones

237 Index
242 Where to get this book

UPFRONT

THE LONDON YEAR

PROLOGUE 2013

From the 64,192 events scheduled for 2013 we've selected the best cultural, sporting and oddly eccentric happenings in London in 2013. Come on - experience more than your fair share.

BY STEVEN POTTER

THERE'S AS MUCH TO BE EXCITED ABOUT in the coming 12 months as there was this time last year - London is currently riding the crest of a wave as it enters a cultural, sporting and social boom. Sure, the Olympics and the Diamond Jubilee were the kind of events that will go down in history but London isn't resting on its laurels.

There are 64,192 events in London during 2013 that will be featured on LondonTown, from blockbuster art exhibitions, entertainment and new openings, to intimate talks, gigs and book signings.

2013 also is the year that the Olympic legacy starts to take shape. It's the first phase of the regeneration process that will transform the Olympic infrastructure from a private zone into state-of-the-art venues and, most importantly, new public places **01**. It's inspiring to witness the seismic changes to this area of east London.

Exactly a year after a parachuting James Bond and Her Majesty marked the start of 'London 2012', the former Olympic Park reopens as the Queen Elizabeth Olympic Park this July → 171. The beautiful Velodrome will soon after open its doors to aspiring Chris Hoys while the redeveloped Copper Box – which hosted handball during the Olympics – will become London's third biggest multi-purpose indoor arena. Stratford will have a new public green space the same size as Hyde Park.

Over a decade ago, the Millennium Dome was dismissed by all and sundry as an ugly, money-losing white elephant. Ten years later, the O2 Arena had established itself, possibly, as the world's most popular live music venue, playing host not only to rock and pop concerts, but also live comedy, circus acts and a huge range of sports – from tennis to ice skating. I was there with my family for the Olympics and we were genuinely impressed by the surroundings. It's a whole mini town down there; you can now even walk over the top of the roof, or arrive by Thames Cable Car, to take in the famous London skyline.

LondonTown.com   UPFRONT   9

If the much maligned Millennium Dome can become one of the biggest success stories of any modern city all over the world, then just think what can come of our Olympic Park. It's just one of the intriguing openings set for 2013 → 12 that will raise the bar once again for both Londoners and visitors alike.

The recently opened Duck & Waffle restaurant on the 40th floor of Heron Tower in the City is also an incredible experience. Looking down over the Gherkin and open 24 hours a day, this is a new experience hard to beat. But the boundaries are about to be pushed even further. As of 1st February this year, you'll be able rise to the 72nd floor of The Shard 14 to an observation deck significantly higher than anything else in London, and eat in two restaurants which put the lofty Duck & Waffle or Galvin at Windows in the shade → 17. From May, guests will also be able to reach for the stars in The Shard's luxury Shangri-La hotel. As it catches the sun and shines over the city like a beacon, Renzo Piano's iconic tower is already part of London folklore.

There are other new exciting buildings and developments, too. In autumn, the Guildhall School opens the 608-seat Milton Court Concert Hall → 201 while London's newest square opens in the shadow of King's Cross Station. The whole King's Cross area development is vast - the redevelopment around the canal and at the station will be astonishing 05, and Kings Place which will host its annual festival in September → 189 is consistent with the high quality of its entertainment, and representative of the new creative style that is being introduced into the area, which is now the new home to St. Martins College. Look at the example of the South Bank, which used to be a mess of concrete buildings in which people played violins. Now the Southbank Centre is one of the most vibrant entertainment centres → 30 in the world, while the whole area - from the London Eye to Tower Bridge - is London's most popular riverside hub.

Granted, the Olympics are over even if the legacy will live on. But sports fans in 2013 should continue to be excited → 24. Two finals stand out: Wimbledon → 157 - where for the first time since Fred Perry 77 years ago, surely Andy Murray has his best shot at delivering a home Grand Slam to the British public? - and the football Champions League → 140. Wembley Stadium becomes the first stadium in history to host the European Cup final twice in three years.

What's great about the final returning to Wembley is that it was a conscious decision on the part of UEFA to celebrate 150 years of the English Football Association's existence - just one of many massive mile-stones being commemorated this year in London. Also celebrating one and a half centuries is the capital's famous Tube network 06, which opened with the unveiling of the Metropolitan Railway from Paddington to Farringdon in 1863 → 29. We complain of the prices, but the enduring legacy of the world's first underground railway system is one of the secrets of London's greatness today.

The Tube's 150th birthday is but one of numerous anniversaries

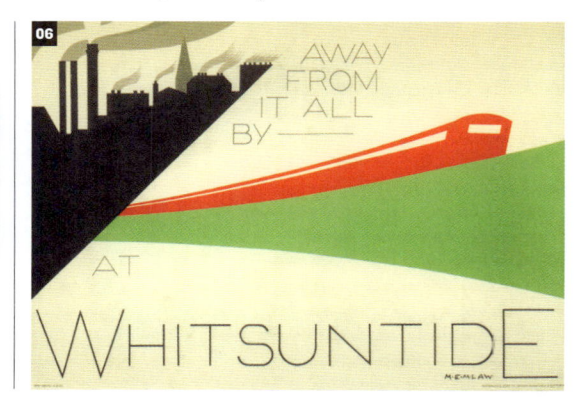

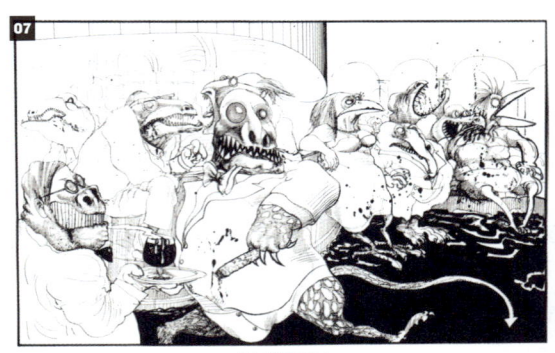

UPFRONT

highlighted in our special London Anniversaries feature → 233. There are also double centenaries for the composers Wagner and Verdi, and a single centenary for Benjamin Britten. The BBC Proms → 166 will be heavily weighted towards Britain's most influential composers, while Britten's operas 'Gloriana' → 154 and 'Death in Venice' → 152 and the moving 'War Requiem' → 214, are all performed in the wake of a 'Britten at 100' festival in February → 85.

Four decades of Sir Paul Smith are savoured at the Design Museum from November → 215 while the career of another famous knighted Londoner, Sir Michael Caine, is the focus of a four-month exhibition at the Museum of London to coincide with the actor's 80th birthday → 106. There's also a 77th birthday retrospective for the madcap British cartoonist **07** Ralph Steadman → 103.

Britain's biggest anniversary, however, is that of the Queen: last year may have been Her Majesty's official Diamond Jubilee, but 2013 actually marks 60 years since her Coronation - and there's a special four-day festival in the Gardens of Buckingham Palace in July paying tribute to her timelessness → 165. Who knows, maybe she'll be a great grandmother by then.

The Queen is also the subject of an ongoing exhibition at Windsor Castle which sees Andy Warhol's screenprint portraits of Elizabeth II displayed for the first time → 62. For fans of modern art and photography there's the Lichtenstein retrospective **02** at Tate Modern this spring → 92 as well as the Man Ray Portraits show at the National Portrait Gallery → 89 and Antony Gormley's sculptures at White Cube → 58. For the traditionalists there's the first ever major UK exhibition of the French painter Edouard Manet at the Royal Academy of Arts → 72, not to mention offbeat exhibitions of Whistler → 203 and Picasso' → 88 **09**.

'The Book of Mormon' **03** - from the creators of 'South Park' - is one of the big draws on the West End stage → 94, while for the children it's all about 'Charlie and the Chocolate Factory' → 156. Once again, London seems to be the heartbeat of world theatre, with top Hollywood stars coming to the capital to perform on stage → 18. Rupert Everett reprises his role as Oscar Wilde in 'The Judas Kiss' → 70, Helen Mirren will be 'The Queen' once again in 'The Audience' → 90; in 'Quartermaine's Terms', Rowan Atkinson → 76 returns to the stage for the first time since 'Oliver!', while James McAvoy renews his acquaintance with a king of Scotland in 'Macbeth' after a four-year break from the London stage → 87. Another excellent ongoing theatre initiative is the Michael Grandage season of five plays at the Noel Coward Theatre **11** : not only are there 100,000 tickets at just £10, the likes of Daniel Radcliffe → 150, Jude Law → 215, and Bond duo Ben Whishaw and Dame Judi Dench → 102 are all involved.

London continues to attract the biggest names in the music business to its summer festival **04** programme → 38. There's also a steady stream of 'golden oldies' swinging past - the likes of Clapton

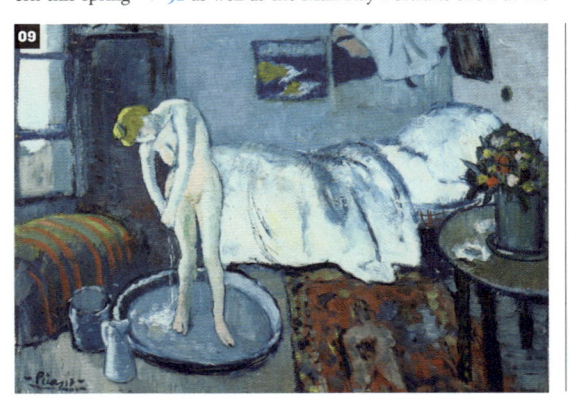

UPFRONT

→ 136, Springsteen 13 → 152, Knopfler → 141 and de Burgh → 124 - which we've clustered together in one spread → 143. Kraftwerk's eight live performances in the Tate's Turbine Hall → 84 promise to be an impressive experience, and there'll be a stream of acts like One Direction 12 at the O2. Yoko Ono curates this year's Meltdown Festival at the Southbank → 152 and Paloma Faith 10 brings some sassiness to the Apollo → 85. On the comedy stage, Eddie Izzard brings his new 'Force Majeure' tour to town → 134. Ballet fans are spoilt for choice again at The Royal Opera House and the Coliseum (ENO) 08 .

There's no doubt that London attracts the biggest cultural heavyweights from around the globe - and they all know that they're expected to be at their best. With expectations so high, there's simply no room for mediocrity. Yet it's not just about the huge and contrasting list of fresh, new events happening in 2013. There were some events I attended last year that I just cannot wait to happen again. Take the London Design Festival in September → 190, for example. It was a genuine inspiration fest last year - and it keeps going from strength to strength. The same could be said about London's continually excellent programme of talks and lectures → 22 which sees the great and the good gather to inform and inspire and share priceless ideas, often for free.

All over London there's a confidence and courageousness that belies the fact that we're still stuck in the woods of recession. Times are hard - and yet every day here in the capital there are innovative and inspirational works aplenty. Many of them are free. Yes, the London entertainment scene can be very commercial - but there's so much more simmering underneath the surface. We have more free museums and events here than anywhere else in the world. Anyone who is anyone wants to come to London to put on a show because to prove yourself, you have to conquer the current cultural capital of the world.

But despite all the grandeur, stars and bright lights, people still get a kick out of madcap goat races, pancake and pudding relays, clowns congregating in East End churches, soggy cricket games in February or Scotch egg cook-offs → 48. London is the capital of Great Britain and the British are crazy and weird. We jump into freezing lakes on Christmas Day 15 → 224 or take part in umbrella jousting on bicycles → 169. And if London reflects Britain's penchant for quirkiness it also underlines the strong community spirit that binds us all together in this multi-cultural city. There's an element of togetherness here in London, where thousands gather to watch films under the stars at Somerset House → 164 and even more line the banks of the river each year to watch two university crews race along the Thames → 110.

Tradition. Community. Innovation. Brilliance. These words all sum up London - and nowhere are they more apparent than 2013. Last year, during the Olympics, all eyes were on London. The great thing is that no one's yet to blink. ● *SP@LondonTown.com*

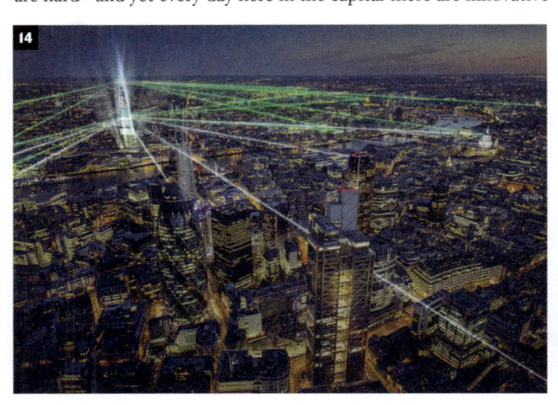

12 | UPFRONT | LondonTown.com

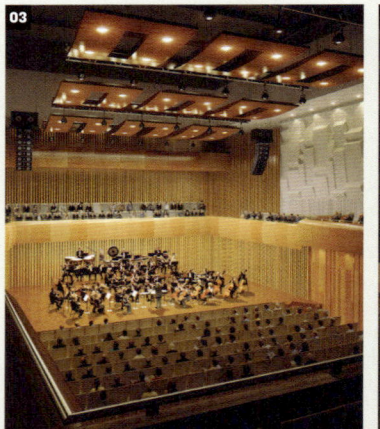

1. SERPENTINE SACKLER GALLERY © ZAHA HADID ARCHITECTS, 2. THE SHARD, COURTESY OF SELLAR PROPERTY GROUP 3. MILTON COURT CONCERT HALL, COURTESY GUILDHALL SCHOOL OF MUSIC & DRAMA 4. TOM FORD © S. BUKLEY

LondonTown.com UPFRONT 13

06

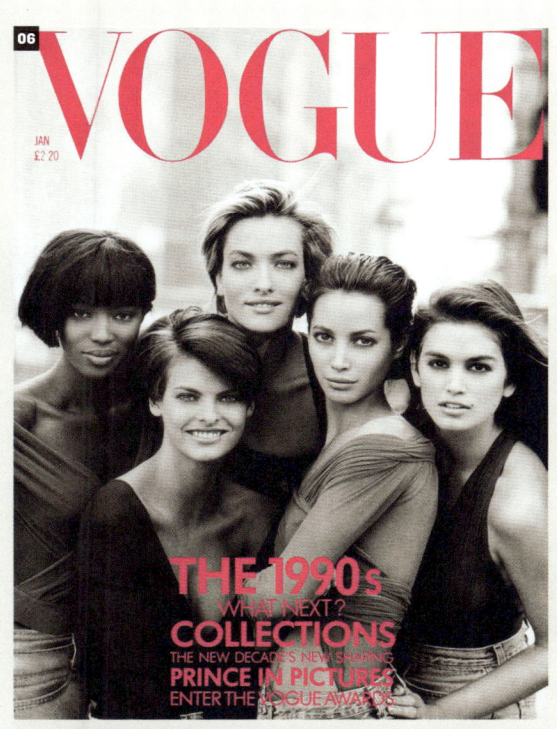

WHAT'S NEW IN LONDON

NEW IN 2013

London's highest public viewing platform, Condé Nast's first fashion college... *Francesca Young* on what's new in 2013

IT'S A FASHIONABLE START TO THE YEAR with the opening of the Condé Nast college in Soho in January **06**, followed by the first J.Crew store outside North America on Regent Street, and Tom Ford's store on Sloane Street **04**, both expected late in the year.

One of the biggest – certainly the tallest – openings of the year, The View from The Shard → **17 & 83** will welcome its first visitors on 1st February. The Shard's two new restaurants open in April **02**, one operated by Zuma, the other by the Aqua group, both promising all-day dining and quality cuisine. And from May, the Shangri-La, The Shard's 185-room hotel, launches with body contouring beds, spacious rooms and an infinity pool.

There will be more luxury hotels from André Balazs, the man behind The Mercer, The Standard and Château Marmont, who opens a hotel with just 26 suites in a former Marylebone fire station, and Nobu with its 143-room Ron Arad-designed hotel in Shoreditch. There are enticing new restaurant openings from Claude Bosi, Jason Atherton, Tom Aikens and – perhaps the most mouth-watering prospect – Keith McNally's Balthazar, which opens in Covent Garden in February.

Southwark Playhouse → **40** re-opens in larger premises on Newington Causeway in April. Also in spring, The Park Theatre opens in Finsbury Park, and the new £3.6 million 'Tiger Territory' → **110** opens at London Zoo. From April, The National Theatre opens The Shed → **126**, a temporary performance space designed by Haworth Tompkins, the firm behind the V&A's new Textiles and Fashion Study and Conservation Centre located within the grade II listed Blythe House building in Olympia, which opens in October.

The Science Museum's new purpose-built Media Space opens in June while the former Olympic Park re-opens as the Queen Elizabeth Olympic Park → **171** on 27th July **05**. The Pritzker Prize-winning architect of the Aquatics Centre (not due to re-open until 2014), Zaha Hadid, is also responsible for the Serpentine Gallery's new Sackler Gallery which opens in 2013 **01**.

In autumn, King's Cross Square opens at the front of King's Cross Station **07** offering stunning views of Lewis Cubbitt's Victorian station façade and across to St Pancras International. The Rambert Dance Company moves into its new Allies & Morrison-designed headquarters on the South Bank, and Milton Court Concert Hall → **201**, provides new facilities for the Guildhall School including a 608-seat performance hall **03**. Start filling your diary now.

WHAT'S NEW IN LONDON NEWSLETTER

→ To receive the What's New in London Newsletter send a blank email now to: **New@LondonTown.com**
PRIVACY PROMISE: We will never (and that means never) give your email address to anyone else. You mean too much to us.

MUSEUMS

MAJOR MUSEUMS

From 'blockbuster' exhibitions to specialist shows, there's something for everyone in London's main museums in 2013. *By Peter Watts*

EVERY YEAR, A LIST OF LONDON'S MOST POPULAR tourist attractions is published by the Association of Leading Visitor Attractions, and every year London's major museums – most of which are free – dominate the top ten.

Top of the pile is inevitably the British Museum 06 in Bloomsbury, which draws nearly six million people through its famous doors, often to see its legendary 'blockbuster' exhibitions. There are two of these in 2013. In spring, the museum holds 'Ice Age Art: Arrival of the Modern Mind' → 86, which will present some of the world's oldest sculptures and drawings alongside modern works by Henry Moore, Mondrian and Matisse to demonstrate how ancient art influences contemporary artists. Then comes 'Life and Death in Pompeii and Herculaneum' → 109, with 250 stunning finds from the Roman cities destroyed by Vesuvius in AD 79, the first exhibition on this subject in London in 40 years and one of the undoubted highlights of 2013. The museum will also be home to an exhibition on Shunga → 201, a type of Japanese erotic art, and on Colombian Gold → 189, as well as numerous smaller exhibitions, talks, screenings, tours and events. It's a popular place for good reason.

If you combine the visitors attending the three South Kensington museums – the V&A, Natural History Museum and the Science Museum – you'll find they are even more popular than the grand old BM.

The V&A in particular is famed for the quality, depth and charisma of its exhibition programme. This spring it launches 'David Bowie Is...' → 108 – costumes, artwork, photographs and handwritten lyrics that celebrate the pop icon's influence in fashion, sound, graphics, theatre and film 01. Almost as glamorous is 'Treasures of the Royal Court: Tudors, Stuarts and the Russian Tsars' 07 → 105, which looks at some of the incredible items traded between Britain and Russian in the 16th century. The V&A celebrates summer with 'From

Club To Catwalk' → 171, a look at London fashion in the 1980s, and ends the year with 'Pearls' → 192, a stunning study of spectacular jewellery from the Roman Empire to the present day.

Across the road from the V&A is the Natural History Museum, housed in its glorious neo-Gothic cathedral. It will spend 2013 commemorating the centenary of the death of scientist Alfred Russel Wallace, who is often overlooked as the co-discoverer of evolution, having published a paper on the theory with Charles Darwin a year before the publication of *On the Origin of Species*. There will be a monthly lecture series about Wallace, and a new Wallace Discovery Trail to see some of Wallace's most important specimens.

The NHM's major exhibition for 2013 is 'Extinction: Not The End Of The World' → 86, which examines the role extinction plays in evolution and looks at endangered species. A huge attraction every year is its 'Wildlife Photographer of the Year' → 206 exhibition, and in 2013 they will also be holding another photographic exhibition, 'Genesis' → 119, featuring the work of renowned photographer Sebastião Salgado.

Last of the South Ken big three is the Science Museum, whose major exhibition is winter's look at the 'Large Hadron Collider' 05 → 213, the remarkable invention in Geneva which is attempting to recreate the Big Bang in one of the greatest scientific endeavours of our time. There will also be continuing exhibitions on pain relief, codebreaker Alan Turing and the BBC's 90 years of public broadcasting → 64. A new Media Space also opens in June and begins with 'Revelations: Experiments in Photography' → 158, an exhibition that will explore contemporary artists' responses to scientific photography from 1850 to 1920.

Across London from South Kensington is the Design Museum, the UK's only collection devoted to contemporary design and architecture. They kick off spring with 'Designs of the Year 2013' 08 → 109, a showcase of the world's best designs in architecture, digital, fashion, furniture, graphics, transport and product. Summer brings an exhibition curated by Edward Barber and Jay Osgerby → 133, who designed the 2012 Olympic torch and whose exhibition looks at everyday objects from a tennis ball to the £2 coin. The year ends with a landmark exhibition on British designer Paul Smith → 215, whose career has spanned 40 years and has resulted in an iconic, colourful but very English brand of fashion 02. The exhibition will examine Smith through the different stages of the production of a catwalk collection, showing how decisions are made and where Paul Smith the man and Paul Smith the brand connect.

Another British icon getting the exhibition treatment in 2013 is Michael Caine 04, whose 80th birthday is marked by a display at the Museum of London focusing on key moments in his life → 106. Caine was born in London and the exhibition promises to explore how his upbringing as a rebellious working-class Londoner influenced his career. Later in the year, the museum will hold a major exhibition on the Cheapside Hoard → 205, a priceless cache of 16th-century jewels and gemstones discovered in a cellar in 1912. These remarkable treasures will be displayed in their entirety for the first time since their discovery.

The Museum of London Docklands, a beautiful collection of material related to East London and the Thames, celebrates its 10th birthday in 2013. It will do so with a programme of events – including an evening that celebrates British seafood, from the oyster to jellied eels, and a cycling tour of the East End art scene – as well as a photographic exhibition, 'Estuary', which looks at the outer limits of the Thames, the eastern wilderness where the river meets the North Sea.

London, in fact, boasts one of the world's great museums devoted to the sea, the National Maritime Museum in Greenwich. 'Turner & The Sea' → 216, which closes in April 2014, offers the chance to examine JW Turner's dramatic paintings of water, something that preoccupied him throughout his life. Summer brings 'Visions of The Universe' → 158, a fascinating look at the way artists and photographers depict the universe, from early drawings inspired by the imagination to cutting-edge photographs from the Hubble telescope. A new permanent gallery, 'Nelson, Navy, Nation', looks at the 18th-century British Navy and Lord Admiral Nelson. Another new permanent exhibit is 'The Great Map' → 110, which will bring the museum's largest open space to life with an interactive world map that visitors can use to discover more about some of the most famous, infamous and exciting events in Britain's rich maritime history.

Up the hill from the National Maritime Museum is the Royal Observatory, a wonderful collection of clocks and telescopes with amazing views over the Thames. It also holds exhibitions, and 2013 brings 'Alien Revolution' → 110, a small exhibition that looks at the way aliens have been portrayed in art and literature. It forms part of the Observatory's 'Alien Season' that includes planetarium shows, public talks, special events, workshops, cult classic sci-fi movie screenings and courses. The year ends with the always stunning 'Astronomy Photographer of the Year' competition 04 → 59, which celebrates the best in astrophotography from around the world with remarkable images from space.

The British Library has only started putting on exhibitions in recent years, but they've already produced some memorable and thought-provoking ones on big themes. 'Propaganda: Power and Persuasion' → 137 looks at the use of state propaganda in modern times through posters, films, cartoons and textbooks, and promises to be a detailed and absorbing look at a thorny topic. The year will end with a major exhibition on The Georgians → 216, timed to commemorate 300 years since George I ascended the throne. If you prefer something more light-hearted, the BL's smaller gallery has exhibitions including 'Murder In The Library', a celebration of crime fiction with some luridly appealing covers, and a display of Children's Literature at the end of the year.

Finally, one of London's most popular museums, the Imperial War Museum, is getting a complete refurbishment and will be closed for the first six months of the year. It reopens in July with a cracking family exhibition, 'Horrible Histories: Spies' → 168, which looks at the world of spies and spying from the inimitable 'Horrible Histories' team. There will also be exhibitions on the Architecture of War, looking at how war affects the way people live, and regular screenings of Omar Fast's film, 'Five Thousand Feet Is The Best', about drone operators in Pakistan and Afghanistan. ●

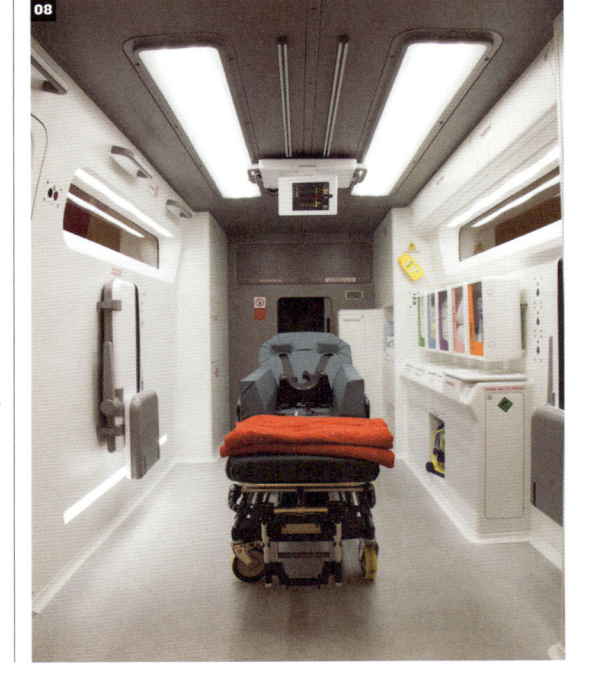

LondonTown.com   UPFRONT   17

ARCHITECTURE

THE VIEW FROM THE SHARD

London's highest public viewing platform. *By Francesca Young*

LONDON HAS A NEW LANDMARK. With its steeple-shaped spire piercing the London skyline The Shard is hard to ignore. Designed by Italian architect Renzo Piano – best known for creating Paris's Pompidou Centre in collaboration with Britain's Richard Rogers – the mixed use building is a 'vertical city', including offices, homes, restaurants and a hotel.

Although officially launched last year, 2013 will be the year we get to 'know' the new building which, at a vertigo-inducing 1,016ft (309.6m), is the tallest in Western Europe. And it's not just the office workers and millionaires who own the plush apartments (Europe's highest homes – yours for £30 to £50 million) who'll get to explore it.

Firstly, there will be a public viewing platform. When it officially opens on Friday 1st February 2013, The View From The Shard will become the highest public platform in the city – almost twice the height of any other previously available in London – 68 to 72 floors up on the tallest building in the European Union.

For the majority, The View will be the most accessible part. At £24.95 a ticket is not cheap, but the 244 metre (800ft) ascent in a high speed lift will surely be worth it. Arriving at Level 69 the unrivalled 360 degree view stretching 64km (40 miles) over the city is revealed. Ascend to Level 72, the highest public level of The Shard and you'll be exposed to the elements with the sounds of the city around you.

Secondly, there's the deluxe 202-room Shangri-La Hotel, occupying floors 34 to 52 of the spire and due to open in spring 2013. For those who can afford it, a stay at the hotel will be the height of luxury in more ways than one: the lobby is the same height as the London Eye.

Double rooms, at 42 metres square, will be among the largest in London and come complete with LCD TVs, hi-fi equipment and body-contouring beds. The public areas and restaurants will make maximum use of their panoramic views and there's even a glass-enclosed winter garden, but we suspect the best bit will be the indoor infinity swimming pool and luxury spa.

A third chance for members of the public to explore The Shard will be the three restaurants within it. In addition to the restaurant run by the Shangri-La, there will two further destination restaurants. Between levels 31 and 33, overlooking a triple-height atrium and open for all-day dining, will be two separate restaurants run by Zuma founders Arjun Waney and Rainer Becker, and David Yeo's Aqua Restaurant Group. ●

SHARD FACTS:

- Standing at a lofty 309.6 metres (1,016ft) tall, The Shard is the highest building in Western Europe
- Covered in 11,000 panes of glass
- Viewing platform is located on floors 68, 69 and 72
- Platform is 244m (800ft) above one of the greatest cities on earth
- The highest habitable floor of The Shard is 259.9m (853ft) up
- Renzo Piano's Shard has 72 floors
- Steel frame of The Shard weighs 11,836 tonnes
- 800 separate pieces of steel make up the spire
- Gross floor area of The Shard is 31.4 acres
- The Shard has 5 escalators or, if you prefer, 306 flights of stairs
- Shangri-La at The Shard will be one of London's premium hotels

UPFRONT   LondonTown.com

THEATRE

THEATRE HIGHLIGHTS FOR 2013

A deliciously diverse year on the stage sees a cluster of Hollywood A-Listers flock to London's Theatreland. *By Rachel Halliburton*

01

THE ARRIVAL OF 'CHARLIE AND THE CHOCOLATE FACTORY' → 156 this summer in a production directed by Sam Mendes is not the only reason this year's theatre looks like a sweetbox 10 . Worries that London might suffer the equivalent of a cultural famine in 2013 after the theatrical and artistic glut surrounding the Olympics should be allayed by a line-up including Judi Dench, Helen Mirren, Daniel Radcliffe, Rowan Atkinson, and Jude Law.

If you're looking for a challenge – the equivalent of toffee for the brain – the big classics include 'Henry V' → 215 and 'Sweet Bird of Youth' → 149. Should you prefer the citric tang of new writing then there's 'Chimerica' → 137 directed by wunderkind Rupert Goold, or 'The Audience' → 90 by Peter 'Frost/Nixon' Morgan. And if you just want the suck-it-and-see of bold experimentalism, then a new site specific work at Somerset House 'In the Beginning Was The End' kicks off the theatrical year → 77.

It's not just post-Olympic exuberance but post-Jubilee exuberance that's making itself felt, since an obsession with royalty forms a significant strand of West End programming. 'The Audience' → 90, which promises to be a highlight, reunites Helen Mirren 04 and Peter Morgan after their Oscar-winning collaboration in 'The Queen'. Here Mirren reprises her role as Elizabeth II – she has confessed she was initially reluctant, but was understandably won over by the artistic team. Stephen 'Billy Elliot' Daldry directs an evening that examines the monarch's relationship with her different prime ministers – Robert Hardy plays Churchill, while Haydn Gwynne plays Thatcher. At time of going to press, it wasn't known if Blair would feature, but hopes must be high that he will, and if so that Michael Sheen will rise once more to the challenge.

At the end of the year Jude Law becomes the latest actor to take on the challenge of playing 'Henry V' → 215, in the final play of the season launched by the Michael Grandage Company in December 2012. When artistic director Sam Mendes left the Donmar Warehouse (Off West End) in 2002 he seemed like an impossible act to follow, but Grandage presided over a golden era that saw the Donmar expand its territory into the West End. Now he in turn has handed over the Donmar, and this year will preside over five productions at the Noel Coward theatre 02 that will reach out to young audiences by offering more than 100,000 tickets at £10. In 'Privates on Parade' → 60, which opened at the end of 2012, national treasure Simon Russell Beale plays the cross-dressing Captain Dennis. This is succeeded by Judi Dench and Ben Whishaw - M and Q respectively from 'Skyfall' - combining their considerable forces for 'Peter and Alice' → 102, a new play by John Logan. Logan imagines what happened when Alice Liddell Hargreaves (the inspiration for 'Alice Wonderland') met Peter Llewellyn Davies (ditto for 'Peter Pan') at the opening of an exhibition.

The fictional Peter Pan may never have grown up, but 'Harry Potter' star Daniel Radcliffe continues to do all he can to earn adult credentials, and in the third play in Grandage's season stars in 'The Cripple of Inishmaan' → 150. Before rounding off the season with 'Henry V', Grandage extends what will no doubt be a lamentable British summer with 'A Midsummer Night's Dream' → 188. With tongue-in-cheek perversity, this kicks off on September 7 and will hopefully raise temperatures with the double act of 'Little Britain''s David Walliams as Bottom and the West End's 'Legally Blonde' star Sheridan Smith as Titania.

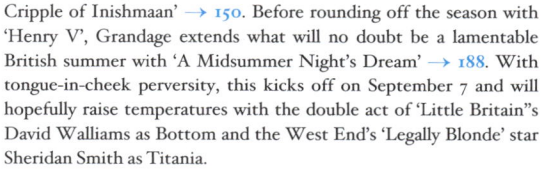

Despite his disastrous 'Don Giovanni' at the Met in New York in 2011, back in London many see Grandage as the director with the Midas touch. But there's plenty of competition out there, not least from Rupert Goold, whose Headlong company continues to break boundaries with its bold intellectual leaps and stunning coups de theatre. This year he presents 'Chimerica' → 137 at the Almeida, a new play by Lucy Kirkwood whose title is inspired by the term coined by historian Niall Ferguson and Moritz Schularick for the prickly yet symbiotic relationship between China and the US. There's also a lot of excitement surrounding 'Anna Karenina' director Joe Wright's theatrical debut with the nineteenth-century classic 'Trelawny of the Wells' → 90 at the Donmar this February. Just to prove he's not scared of making the transition from screen to stage, he's also going to direct Chiwetel Ejiofor in 'A Season in the Congo' → 164 at the Young Vic in July.

There's no shortage of exciting female British directors either, not least Josie Rourke who is the latest artistic director of the Donmar.

UPFRONT

This April she brings 'The Weir' → 121 back to London theatre, the hugely successful Conor McPherson play which looks at Irishmen in a pub swapping ghost stories, only to be upstaged by the woman they are trying to impress. At the Young Vic 07, Carrie Cracknell revives her sexy, passionate production of 'A Doll's House' → 116. And Marianne Elliott, who won the 2011 Tony Award for Best Direction of a Play for 'War Horse' 14 (still playing at the New London Theatre), now takes on Tennessee Williams' 'Sweet Bird of Youth' → 149, which will star Kim Cattrall as fading Hollywood star Alexandra del Lago.

Will there ever be a Shakespeare backlash? Not imminently it would seem - last year new research commissioned by the Royal Shakespeare Company and the British Council proved that he is the world's most studied author. As well as the appearances of his work in Grandage's season, there will be a high-profile production of 'Much Ado About Nothing' → 188 at the Old Vic, reuniting James Earl Jones and Vanessa Redgrave following the success of 'Driving Miss Daisy'. Adrian Lester, who formerly played the first black Henry V at the National Theatre (spot that royal theme again?) will also play 'Othello' → 126, again at the National.

If there's a theatrical obsession with power in the form of royalty, there's an equal obsession with the satirisation of power. In April, Cheek By Jowl – arguably one of the world's most influential theatre companies – brings its production of Alfred Jarry's excoriating 'Ubu Roi' → 118 (loosely based on 'Macbeth') to the Barbican. Antony Sher, who was such a defining theatrical villain in 'Richard III' at the Barbican in 1985 takes on the role of a much more minor dictator in German writer Carl Zuckmayer's 'The Captain of Kopenick' → 77. This is at the Nationale 03, which also revives its highly successful 'This House' → 93, a new play by James Graham that puts the microscope on the Palace of Westminster during Britain's winter of discontent in 1974.

As if to remind us of the power that might have been, 'The Book of Mormon' → 94 – by 'South Park' creators Trey Parker and Matt Stone, and 'Avenue Q' writer Robert Lopez – finally arrives from Broadway 01. This promises to be that Holy Grail for West End producers, the musical for people who don't even like musicals. Not that there's a shortage of those who do – and there's plenty to keep them happy too, not least 'A Chorus Line' → 84, which director Bob Avian is reviving in the West End for the first time since the original in 1976. 'Once: The Musical' → 104 based on the Oscar-winning film of the same name also transfers from Broadway. It's 'Charlie and the Chocolate Factory' → 156 though which promises to be the major attraction, and with Sam Mendes at the helm, fresh from breaking UK box office records with 'Skyfall', hopes will be as high as the potential sugar rush.

There's no shortage of display and spectacle in many of these productions, but an equally important function of theatre is to provide a public space where you can experience private, intimate emotions. This January former Royal Court director Ian Rickson will direct a cracking cast - Kristin Scott Thomas, Rufus Sewell, and Lia Williams 06 – in Harold Pinter's achingly erotic 'Old Times' → 71. In April Krister Henriksson – who plays Wallander in the lauded Swedish TV series – plays the title role in 'Doktor Glas' → 120, a play about a doctor who falls in love with the wife of a corrupt clergyman. The revival of Peter Nichol's devastating drama about infidelity, 'Passion Play', allows director David Leveaux and actress Zoe Wanamaker to collaborate for the first time since their award-winning 'Electra' in 1997. And in January Rupert Everett 11 and the rising Freddie Fox remind us of what happens when private emotions are forced into the public arena, as they play Oscar Wilde and Lord Alfred Douglas in David Hare's 'The Judas Kiss' → 70.

Casting a comedian in the lead often acts as a magnet for people who don't normally go to the theatre. So 2013 promises plenty of initiates, starting in January with Rowan Atkinson's 08 appearance in 'Quartermaine's Terms' → 76 by Simon Gray, directed by Richard Eyre. Lee Evans and Sheila Hancock star in gangster comedy 'Barking in Essex' → 188 while Felicity Kendal 13 graces the West End in Alan Ayckbourn's 'Relatively Speaking' → 136. The play that kicked off at the National in 2011 with James Corden in the lead - 'One Man, Two Guvnors' 12 - continues to be seen by many as the funniest play in the West End. A rather more subtle comedy, 'The Curious Incident of the Dog In the Night-Time' → 100 makes its transfer from the National to the Apollo Theatre in March 09.

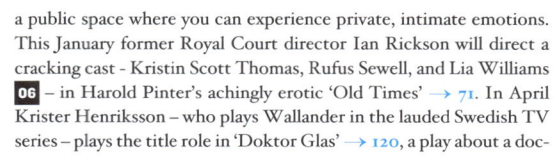

The huge importance of site specific theatre in London over the last decade means that any survey of what's on in 2013 would be incomplete without looking at what's happening in less conventional spaces. From April, during the refurbishment of its Cottesloe space, the National has announced that it is opening 'The Shed' → 126 at the front of its building, a temporary structure to celebrate new and challenging theatre. In January it is also backing the extraordinarily accomplished dreamthinkspeak theatre company, as it creates an apocalyptic installation piece 05 at Somerset House 'In The Beginning Was The End' → 77. This promises to combine Leonardo-inspired hydraulics with a blend of film, installation, and live performance. If it's only half as beautiful and ingenious as the works they've created in the past, it will still be a great way to whet your appetite for an infinitely varied year. ●

> " 'Charlie and the Chocolate Factory' promises to be the major attraction ... with Sam Mendes at the helm"

LONDON'S BEST

TALKS

TALKS OF THE TOWN

The great and the good hold court in London.

ON ANY GIVEN NIGHT IN LONDON there will be a wonderful range of inspirational talks or stimulating seminars given by top figures – be they industry specialists, famous actors or literary giants.

You see, the capital has a magical pull for those seeking thought-provoking and intimate salon-style events, with people flocking to the capital from far and wide to share their ideas.

London has always been renowned for its educational institutions, but now there's an increasing trend for small independent hubs aimed at challenging open-minded people outside the framework of everyday working life and giving their brains a thorough work-out.

Take the School of Life in Bloomsbury, for instance. Founded in 2008 by the philosopher Alain de Botton, this hive of adult learning has been described as "an apothecary for the mind" by Monocle magazine.

The truth is that London is constantly thinking, talking, listening, inspiring and trading ideas. The great and the good come to the city every week and give talks in small rooms or large lecture halls, mingle with the crowd, interact, encourage debate and answer questions.

These challenging, ad hoc public events are on the rise as thinking becomes more of a favoured pastime. What's more, some of the talks are so niche and under-attended you often get the impression that you're experiencing a one-to-one tutorial with a celebrity thinker.

It's quite exhilarating brushing shoulders with famous people and hearing their take on topical issues or unknown specialist subjects. More and more Londoners are realising that a good night out doesn't have to entail booze or being boisterous - it doesn't even have to involve established art forms such as the theatre, cinema or a gallery. ●

SCHOOL OF LIFE'S SUNDAY SERMONS
Conway Hall, WC1R 4RL
An alternative to Sunday morning church, these topical sermons of enlightened thought invite maverick cultural figures to preach persuasive polemics with peculiar passion.

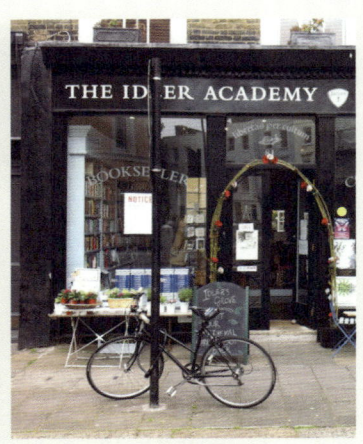

IDLER ACADEMY
81 Westbourne Park Road, W2 5QH
A school of "philosophy, husbandry and merriment", the Idler bookshop and coffeehouse promotes "freedom through education" for loafers who (quite rightly) see learning as a distinct pleasure.

5X15
*The Tabernacle, W11 2AY
(and various venues)*
Ingenious in its stimulating simplicity, five speakers in a range of venues recount tales of passion, obsession, achievement and adventure with just two rules: no scripts and only 15 minutes each.

TELL SERIES
London Business School, NW1 4SA
These intimate fortnightly Talks on Entrepreneurial Leadership at LBS are open to anyone and include a lecture from a guest speaker followed by a moderated Q&A session and a networking reception.

DON'T FORGET
BE BRILLIANTLY INFORMED: SIGN UP TO LONDONTOWN.COM NEWSLETTERS
WHAT'S NEW | GIGS | TALKS | WEEKENDS | TOURS | COMEDY | CLASSICAL | CABARET
THEATRE | DANCE | FOOD EVENTS | SPORT | SUMMER | CHRISTMAS

LondonTown.com   LONDON'S BEST   23

THE RSA
Off The Strand, WC2N 6EZ
Encouraging a principled, prosperous society and the release of human potential, the RSA promotes ideas and actions for a 21st century enlightenment with a series of talks by guest speakers.

D&AD
Logan Hall, WC1H 0AL
The British Design & Art Direction aims to inform, educate and inspire those who work in and around the creative industries, and holds regular President's Lectures with key figures.

TED
Various venues in London
The worldwide Technology, Entertainment and Design movement holds up to three conferences a week where guest speakers have 18 minutes to share "ideas worth spreading".

LAST TUESDAY SOCIETY
11 Mare Street, E8 4RP
Devoted to decadence, dandyism and exploring the esoteric, literary and artistic aspects of life in London, the Hendrick's Lecture Series covers offbeat subjects such as taxidermy and mask making.

BISHOPSGATE INSTITUTE
230 Bishopsgate, EC2M 4QH
This hive of ideas and debate, learning and enquiry promotes independent thought with a regular series of evening talks and lectures, including historical and literary events, and local community chats.

BRUNEL UNIVERSITY PUBLIC LECTURES
Uxbridge, UB8 3PH
Regular evening open lectures in the Hamilton Centre of the west London university explore a range of topics geared towards science, the environment and technology, with three guest speakers.

LONDON TALKS NEWSLETTER
→ To receive the London Talks Newsletter from LondonTown.com send a blank email now to: **talks@londontown.com**
PRIVACY PROMISE: We will never (and that means never) give your email address to anyone else. You mean too much to us.

SPORT

THE SPORTING YEAR 2013

Forget London 2012 and the sporting successes of last year -
there's much more to be excited about in a fixture-fuelled 2013. *By Felix Lowe*

THE OLYMPIC PARTY HAS LEFT OUR BACK GARDEN but London is still the place for sport. Highlights this year include another Champions League final at Wembley, an Ashes Test series, a new major professional cycling road race, Andy Murray's latest assault on SW19 and not one, but two, NFL International Series games.

No Olympic hangover

The legacy of the track and field will live on as world-class athletics returns to London with the British Athletics GP at Crystal Palace in July → 170. Last year Mo Farah won the 5,000m event here with relative ease as he stepped up his preparations ahead of an Olympics that would see him secure two Gold medals. This is the only two-day Diamond League event on the circuit and it's also the final athletics event of the season - with day two on Saturday coinciding with the first anniversary of London 2012.

Exactly one year after a parachuting James Bond and the Queen marked the start of the Games, the redeveloped Queen Elizabeth Olympic Park is unveiled → 173. The Velodrome and redeveloped Copper Box arena will open their doors, while 250 acres of beautifully landscaped parkland will be made available to the public. One weekend later (3rd & 4th August), Britain's biggest cycling festival will feature amateur and professional races that start in the Park. The Ride-London Classic → 177 will be the biggest one-day race in Britain and will attract some of cycling's best pro riders - including, we hope, Mark Cavendish and Tour de France champion Bradley Wiggins.

Hyde Park has been selected to host the eighth and final leg of the 2013 ITU World Triathlon Series following the success of the Olympic events last summer → 188. All eyes will be on the Serpentine as the public cheer on the brilliant Brownlee brothers, who picked up Gold and Bronze back in August.

Football: Celebrating 150 years

The Football Association reaches an important milestone in 2013 with a series of mouth-watering fixtures lined up to commemorate its 150th anniversary. Besides the ongoing World Cup 2014 qualifying campaign (with group games against Moldova → 187, Montenegro → 202 and Poland → 203), England have two special international friendlies at Wembley lined up against Brazil in February → 84 and Scotland in August → 178.

Wembley will also host its usual cup competitions: the FA Cup Semi-Finals → 119 and Final → 134, Capital One Cup Final → 94, Johnstone's Paint Trophy Final → 117, FA Vase → 132 and FA Trophy → 108, as well as the Football League and Championship Playoff Finals → 137, and the season curtain-raiser, the Community Shield → 178.

But London's major football event for 2013 is the final of the Champions League → 140. History will be made as Wembley becomes the first stadium in the world to host the European Cup final twice in three years as UEFA also doffs its cap to the FA's special anniversary. In 2011 Barcelona comfortably beat Manchester United in the Wembley final despite a brilliant goal by Wayne Rooney 01; perhaps this time, we'll get a British winner? Both Chelsea and Manchester City fell at the first hurdle, but United, Arsenal and Celtic enter the new year still in with a shout.

Wembley: Not just the beautiful game

Once a year Wembley is overtaken by scantily clad cheerleaders, giant buckets of fizzy pop, shoulder pad-wearing hulks and ample ad breaks for the annual NFL International Series game 04. But not this year; no, in 2013 'American Football' (as we Brits quaintly call it) touches down for double the fun in front of more than 80,000 fans. For the first time in history we have two Sunday afternoon regular-season NFL games coming to London, with the Minnesota Vikings hosting six-time Super Bowl winners Pittsburgh Steelers in September → 194 and the Jacksonville Jaguars taking on the San Francisco 49ers in October → 206.

Wembley will also be in action for one of the biggest fixtures in the rugby league calendar, the RFL Challenge Cup Final in August → 180, as well as the inaugural International Stadium Poker Tour earlier in the summer → 142. Nearby Wembley Arena 02 also hosts the showpiece showdown of the British Basketball calendar in April: the Playoff Final → 125.

Rugby: Six Nation Army

It's another busy year for Stuart Lancaster's England at Twickenham, with home Six Nations clashes against Scotland → 84, France → 93 and Italy → 103. On the same Saturday in May as the Champions League final, the Aviva Premiership Rugby Final takes place in front of 82,000 fans → 140, while Harlequins will swap their Stoop Stadium for Twickenham against as-yet-unknown opponents in the annual Big Game on the last Saturday of the year → 224. The Marriott London Sevens also features the 16 best international teams in the fast-moving format of the game over one weekend in May → 134.

Cricket: Ashes to Ashes

Following winter tours to India and New Zealand, England's busy year continues with home series against New Zealand and Australia. Alastair Cook's side play the first of two Tests against the Kiwis at Lord's in mid-June → 136 before returning to the same venue for the first of three ODIs on the last day of the month → 142. The ICC Champions Trophy - a knock-out competition featuring the world's top eight one-day international sides - gets under way with West Indies taking on Pakistan at the Oval on 7th June → 148. There follows three other group games at the Oval - including England's clash with Sri Lanka → 151 - ahead of one semi-final clash on 19th June → 154 before the final, which is played at Edgbaston in Birmingham.

After two Twenty20 games at the Oval against New Zealand in late June → 156, the focus moves onto the main cricketing event of the summer: the Ashes 03. Australia's touring side will attempt to emerge victorious in cricket's oldest rivalry after two consecutive series defeats at the hands of England. The second Test starts at Lord's on 18th July → 167 just four days after the series opener at Trent Bridge, while the final Test is played at the Oval from 21st August → 179. Two T20 and five ODI series matches against Australia all take place outside the capital - before England head Down Under in November to defend what they hope will be a third successive Ashes series win.

Tennis: Murray's moment

Andy Murray came of age last year, avenging his heart-breaking Wimbledon 07 final loss to Roger Federer with an Olympic gold after defeating the Swiss maestro in straight sets on Centre Court. Murray then became the first British man to win a Grand Slam singles title since 1936 when he defeated Novak Djokovic in five sets in the US Open. Expectations will once again be high for Murray as he bids to end Britain's 77-year wait for a Wimbledon winner → 157. But Federer will target a record eighth victory, while in the women's game Serena Williams will eye a sixth SW19 title → 164.

The Queen's Club Championships takes place earlier in June and sees many of the world's best grass-court players fine-tuning ahead of Wimbledon → 150. Later in November, the world's eight best men's players descend upon the O2 Arena for the ATP World Tour Finals → 212, last year won by Djokovic. As well as tennis, London's most important indoor arena hosts an array of contrasting sports throughout the year, including NBA London Live in January → 72 and Premier League Darts in May → 136.

In December, the major tennis stars of yesteryear gather at the Royal Albert Hall for the annual Masters Tennis tournament → 221, the highly entertaining season-ending event of the ATP Champions Tour which usually features the likes of John McEnroe, Tim Henman and Goran Ivanisevic.

Rowing and running

Organisers of the annual Boat Race **05** will hope that Australian anti-elitism protesters keep out of the water and steer clear of the oars when Oxford and Cambridge come head to head on 31st March → 110. The Light Blues eventually won last year's controversial race and now lead the Dark Blues by 81 wins to 76. A week earlier, some 420 crews take part in the Head of the River Race → 107 on the same stretch of water, only in reverse.

More people have walked on the moon than have successfully rowed around Great Britain's coastline - and the GB Row 2013 → 147, the world's richest rowing race, looks to overturn that striking anomaly. The 2,000-mile race - expected to attract 15 crews - starts on 1st June at Tower Bridge. Less gruelling but still tough enough to be described as rowing's equivalent of the London Marathon, the Great River Race → 188 takes place one week later as numerous crews cover the 21 miles between the London Docklands and Ham.

The rowing season concludes with one of Britain's most famous summer sporting fetes, the Henley Royal Regatta → 164, which runs for five days in early July. It's a picnic-'n'-Pimm's extravaganza that attracts hordes of Tim Nice But Dims from the upper echelons of English society, who flock to the riverside village in boaters and pink trousers to watch international crews battle it out on the Thames.

As usual, London's runners have a vast array of events to choose from with the return of the London Marathon → 122, the Bupa London 10,000 → 141, the British 10K London Run → 167, the Royal Parks Foundation Half Marathon → 202 and Run to the Beat → 206.

Horseplay: Plenty of polo

Four major horse racing festivals take place annually at the racecourses that surround London. The Derby Festival → 142 at Epsom Downs in early summer centres around one of the oldest and greatest horse races in the world; later in June, the five-day Royal Ascot → 153 attracts all the biggest names in the racing fraternity - plus some outrageous hat designs on Ladies' Day; in July **08**, Glorious Goodwood → 172 brings some of the nation's finest thoroughbreds (horses and humans) to what King Edward VII described as "a garden party with racing tacked on" while on Boxing Day festive punters flock to the Winter Festival to watch the King George VI Chase → 224.

International Polo at the O2 in April → 121 and Polo in the Park in Fulham's Hurlingham Park **06** in June → 149 both return. And finally, fans of jumping and dressage will make their annual festive pilgrimage to the London International Horse Show, which runs for seven days in December at Olympia → 223. Whatever sport you're into, in water, on horseback or under your own steam, you can see world class athletes cross swords in London in 2013 ●

UPFRONT

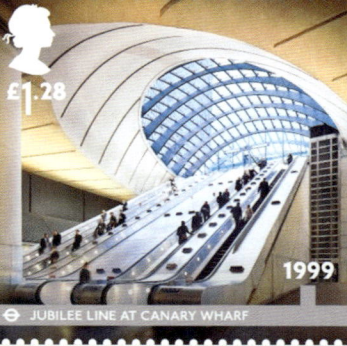

LondonTown.com

> HISTORY

150 YEARS OF THE TUBE

The world's oldest underground railway is still going strong, says *Francesca Young*

HARD TO BELIEVE IT NOW, but the first train to travel on London's famous underground system was powered by steam. Next time you're somewhere between Paddington and Farringdon just think, that's where, one hundred and fifty years ago, the first steam train made its virgin voyage under the streets of London.

On Saturday 10th January 1863 the first public passengers queued up to travel the three and a half miles underground from Paddington to Farringdon aboard gas-lit wooden carriages hauled by steam locomotives. Described by The Illustrated London News as 'the most stupendous engineering undertaking yet achieved in the railway world', it was the birth of the world's first underground train system - a system which now carries an estimated 3.5 million people per day.

In 2013 London celebrates its pioneering subterranean train system with a series of special events. Steam and heritage train outings, talks, tours, a large scale poster art exhibition and theatrical events in the disused Aldwych tube station are all part of the celebrations marking the 150th Anniversary of the London Underground.

On Sunday 13th and 20th January 2013, passengers (who have bought tickets allocated by ballot) can take a nostalgic trip and travel via steam, once again, through the tunnels of the Metropolitan line between Paddington and Farringdon – now part of the Circle and the Hammersmith & City Line – in an 1892 carriage pulled by the Met Locomotive No. 1 which has been painstakingly restored especially for the occasion. It will be the first steam passenger journey to travel on the Underground network since 1905.

For a really in-depth look at the last 150 years of Underground history, immerse yourself in the book 'Underground – How the Tube shaped London', a 286-page tome put together in a lively and informative way by David Bownes, Oliver Green and Sam Mullins. All three authorities on the Underground will host a series of illustrated talks at the London Transport Museum's Cubic Theatre in Covent Garden between January and March 2013.

David Bownes opens the series on Monday 21st January with his talk on 'The Underground Pioneers', beginning with the first day, 10th January 1863, when nearly 40,000 people queued up to be the first to travel underground. He follows the birth of the fledgling network right up until a shady American entrepreneur, Charles Tyson Yerkes, created the Underground Electric Railways Company of London (UERL) in 1902, which later became the Tube.

The following month, on 25th February, Oliver Green, head curator at the London Transport Museum from 2001 to 2009, considers 'The Rise and Fall of London', examining how the world's greatest urban public transport system was developed and extended in the 1920s and '30s until the outbreak of war in 1939.

Sam Mullins, Director of the London Transport Museum since 1994, will be giving the third and final talk, 'Out of Chaos' on Monday 25th March, in which he focuses on the last fifty years from the building of the Victoria line in the 1960s right up to the travel challenges of the 2012 Olympics.

There are further discussions on the history and use of the Underground at the Centre for Metropolitan History, Institute of Historical Research, one of the world's leading centres for the study of the history of London and other cities. Anyone with an interest can buy tickets to take part in the two-day conference on 17th and 18th January at Senate House, University of London, in Bloomsbury.

From 1908, under the direction of Frank Pick, the Underground began to commission poster art and became well known for its outstanding poster designs – a reputation which continues to this day. It is this heritage which is celebrated in the London Transport Museum's major exhibition, 'Poster Art 150: London Underground's Greatest Designs' → 93. Visitors to the exhibition will be asked to choose their favourite from a selection of 150 posters that showcase the very best poster art, with contributions from the likes of Man Ray, and the most popular poster will be revealed at the end of the exhibition.

There will be special behind the scenes events at the museum's Depot in Acton – which is usually closed to the public – when it opens for two weekends in April and October. The Acton open days will give visitors the chance to learn more about the restoration of old rolling stock including the Metropolitan Railway Jubilee Carriage No. 353, a wooden four-wheeled first class carriage built in 1892, in use for the first time since 1940. Met Loco No. 1, the restored 1898 engine which will be the showpiece of the heritage days on Sunday 13th and Sunday 20th January, will be covering visitors in clouds of steam, with information about its return to the tracks, 150 years after it first took passengers underground.

The disused Aldwych tube station, the only stop on the now-defunct Strand branch of the Piccadilly Line and closed for the last 18 years, will be opened again, in May and June, for an immersive art event. And, if you want something to help you remember the 150th anniversary, commemorative stamps are being issued by the Royal Mail revealing the timeline of the Tube, from the opening of the Metropolitan railway in 1863 to Sir Norman Foster's modern Canary Wharf station, opened in 1999. ●

ENTERTAINMENT

MAJOR ENTERTAINMENT CENTRES

London has more arts and culture hubs than any other capital city. *By Felix Lowe*

IT'S NO SURPRISE THAT LONDON is often called the cultural capital of the world. Given the peerless array of historic and iconic entertainment centres across the city it's a hard task singling out the very best.

Imagine London as a chess board whose pieces are those major venues that give London its cultural trailblazing reputation. There are all manner of pawns dotted around the city, excellent venues in their own right, but often serving just one purpose and moving in one direction. What we're interested in outlining here are the kings, queens, bishops, rooks and knights of London's entertainment scene – establishments that move in a variety of ways and deliver both consistently and commercially.

Take the Royal Albert Hall 09, for instance. Well worthy of its regal status, the eye-catching Grade I-listed giant oval amphitheatre presides over Kensington Gardens and is one of London's most versatile venues. Classical music, rock concerts, jazz, opera, dance, theatre, circus acts, banquets, balls, awards ceremonies and even sporting events such as Masters Tennis → 221 all take place in the RAH, perhaps best-known for the world famous BBC Proms series → 166 & 192 that features more than 100 classical concerts over two months every summer.

Much to the delight of the traditionalists, the RAH can hardly be described as cutting-edge. For pushing the boundaries, while maintaining a constant high level of both classic and conventional events, Londoners have two cultural heavyweights in the Southbank and Barbican centres.

Perched beside the Thames near Waterloo Station, the Southbank Centre 07 may not display the same architectural elegance at the Royal Albert Hall (the '60s 'brutalist' concrete structure is not to everyone's taste) but it sure makes up for it with a diverse programme of events that covers virtually every art form.

The Royal Festival Hall is the Centre's main stage, offering classical and orchestral music, world music events and even electronic outings; Queen Elizabeth Hall and the Purcell Room host regular recitals, dance performances and choral concerts; the Hayward Gallery consistently exhibits important and influential artists and collections, while the British Film Institute – which sponsors the annual London International Film Festival → 43 & 202 – is a mecca for movie buffs of all genres and ages.

Often seen as the Southbank's principal rival, the Barbican has been described by the Queen (no less) as "one of the wonders of the modern world". Granted, the multi-faceted performance and arts venue may not be London's prettiest building, but its archaic futurist style is quite intriguing. Situated in an area badly bombed during World War II and open 363 days a year, it offers the most diverse programme of any London venue.

Barbican Hall 08 is home to the London Symphony Orchestra, while the Barbican Theatre, previously home to the Royal Shakespeare Company, welcomes top international productions. There's a second theatre called The Pit, three cinema screens, the Barbican Art Gallery, the new-commission Curve gallery, and a host of smaller exhibition spaces within its labyrinthine corridors.

London's biggest purpose-built concert hall since the Barbican makes up part of the new award-winning Kings Place 02 complex at King's Cross. While it still has a lot of ground to catch up on its older, more illustrious competitors, Kings Place is a growing hub for music, art, dialogue and food, and is fast gaining a reputation as one of the city's best new performance venues. Two orchestras – the London Sinfonietta and the Orchestra of the Age of Enlightenment – are based here in the stunning wood-lined 420-seat auditorium. There are also two art galleries and some appealing public spaces, which become heavily animated during the annual Kings Place Festival → 189. The venue also boasts invaluable media contacts: it shares a building with the new offices of the arts-heavy Guardian and Observer newspapers.

Lambasting the ill-fated Millennium Dome was one of the things papers like the Guardian did best – and who would have thought that a project so reviled as this New Labour own-goal would go on to become one of London's most versatile venues? Attracting the biggest bands and singers on the globe, the O2 Arena in Greenwich 10 is now officially the world's busiest music arena. And it's not just music concerts from the likes of Pink → 124, One Direction → 92 and Plan B → 87 taking centre-stage: the cavernous venue, which can sit up to 20,000 per gig, this year hosts some of the funniest comedians in the business, including Eddie Izzard → 134 and Micky Flanagan → 139. The O2 also hosts numerous sporting events – from indoor International Polo → 121 to the annual ATP World Tour Finals → 212 – and it was one of the main London 2012 venues outside the Olympic Park.

Before the rise of the O2, London's biggest arena was at the opposite end of town. Built in 1934 and originally housing a swimming pool that was used during the 1948 Olympics, Wembley Arena is a large and versatile venue that still hosts big-name pop and rock concerts, some of the UK's best-known comedians, TV shows such as 'X Factor', 'Dancing on Ice' and 'Strictly Come Dancing', and an array of sporting events, from boxing to basketball → 125. During London 2012, Wembley Arena hosted the Olympic badminton and rhythmic gymnastics competitions.

Next door, the recently refurbished Wembley Stadium 06 welcomes its second Champions League Final in three years this May → 140. The 90,000-capacity venue not only hosts all of England's home games, the FA Cup Semi-Finals and Final → 134, and Playoff games → 141, it also hosts the rugby league Challenge Cup final → 180, two annual NFL International Series games → 194, 206, and a cluster of concerts from top music acts. Playing catch-up in this respect is Arsenal's Emirates Stadium, London's biggest club stadium, which now welcomes major bands such as Muse → 140 and Green Day → 147.

When it comes to classical music, opera, ballet and dance, London is teeming with specialist multi-purpose venues. The traditionalists have the ornate Grade II-listed London Coliseum 01 in the West End, home of the English National Opera, as well as the palatial Royal Opera House 03, which rises above Covent Garden, and through several reconstructions (the latest in the '90s) has welcomed major stars of the classical music world since 1858.

A short bus ride away from the West End, Sadler's Wells in Clerkenwell 04 has a balanced mix of both contemporary and classic performances. It's the home of Matthew Bourne's ground-breaking ballet company, New Adventures, and is also universally accepted as London's go-to venue for dance.

Finally, a round-up of London's best multi-purpose venues wouldn't be complete without a nod to one of the capital's most accessible (and central) open playgrounds: Hyde Park 05. More than just a vast green space free for all to roam, Hyde Park is one of London's primary outdoor music venues, hosting each summer the Wireless Festival → 39, 'Hard Rock Calling' → 38, the popular Proms in the Park event → 188 and, returning for a second time this year, a BBC Radio 2 Live event → 194.

Blur played here as part of their reunion in 2009 and also headlined an Olympic closing concert last August, adding to a list of the park's illustrious performers through the years that includes Pink Floyd, Queen, Luciano Pavarotti and Elvis Costello. Every winter, the area of the park near the Serpentine Lake holds the festive 'Winter Wonderland' → 213, while Hyde Park and the boating lake will also host the 2013 ITU World Triathlon Finals → 188 on the top of a successful showing in the Olympics. ●

LondonTown.com   LONDON'S BEST   33

DESIGN FESTIVALS

Showcasing an impressive degree of talent, these intriguing annual style symposiums celebrate the creative flair found within London, says *Vicki Forde*

01

LONDON DESIGN FESTIVAL 03
14th – 22nd September 2013
Various venues
This ambitious project incorporates hundreds of events and designers for nine days of design events

TENT 02
19th – 22nd September 2013
Old Truman Brewery, London E1 6QL
Taking place during the London Design Festival, this impressive show displays the very latest interior products

DESIGNJUNCTION 03
19th – 22nd September 2013
The Sorting Office, 21-31 New Oxford Street, London WC1A 1BA
Aiming to inspire visitors from across the globe, designjunction incorporates both creative and commercial designs

CLERKENWELL DESIGN WEEK
21st – 23rd May 2013
26 St. John's Ln., London EC1M 4DA
This three-day festival of installations, workshops, product launches and debates celebrates contemporary design

GRAND DESIGNS LIVE
4th – 12th May 2013
ExCel Exhibition Centre, One Western Gateway, London E16 1XL
Design guru Kevin McCloud returns with 500 exhibitors to help inspire visitors to create their dream home

100% DESIGN
18th – 21st September 2013
Earls Court Exhibition Centre, Warwick Road, London SW5 9TA
The UK's first contemporary design event is devoted to the latest product launches, ideas, designs and technology

02   **03**

LONDON DESIGN NEWSLETTER
→ To receive the London Design Newsletter from LondonTown.com send a blank email now to: **design@londontown.com**
PRIVACY PROMISE: We will never (and that means never) give your email address to anyone else. You mean too much to us.

UPFRONT

LondonTown.com

CLASSICAL

CLASSICAL MUSIC, BALLET AND OPERA IN 2013

It's not so much Back to the Future as Back to Futurism this year, says *Rachel Halliburton*

01

THREE MAJOR CELEBRATIONS OF MUSIC from the first part of the twentieth century - 'The Rest Is Noise' → 74, 'Dancing Around Duchamp' → 89, and 'A String of Rites' 14 → 118 – will immerse audiences in the thrilling turbulent atmosphere that heralded the avant-garde. For those more guarded about their avants, it's also the centenary of Benjamin Britten 11, whose aversion to much of the experimentalism surrounding him attracted scorn in his lifetime. Today however, he is the most performed British composer worldwide. That will be marked not just by the performance of all his works across the UK (including his 14 operas) and a central position in this year's Proms, but also by the Royal Mint's release of a new coin bearing his image.

'Why did the Holocaust change the course of music for ever? How did America, through the CIA, become the biggest funder of avant-garde composers?' These are just two questions posed by Jude Kelly, artistic director of the Southbank Centre, in her introduction to 'The Rest Is Noise' festival. When the music critic of the New Yorker Alex Ross published his book of the same name in 2008, he instantly spawned a devoted following with his brilliant analysis of the cataclysmic cacophonous century into which he had been born. This, then, is the ultimate tribute, a season of talks, concerts, films and art installations, kicking off with the London Philharmonic Orchestra's performance of Strauss's 'Salome' 12 and bringing audiences right up to the last millennium. En route you can tune in to such delights as 'Zeitgeist: Dance of the Machines' – an adventure into Paris featuring pianola, aircraft propellers and electric bells; Kurt Weill's 'The Threepenny Opera' conducted by Vladimir Jurowski; the festival's featured artist, Canadian soprano Barbara Hannigan singing Schoenberg, Alma Mahler, and Berg; and Messiaen's 'Quartet for the End of Time' performed by the Capuçon Brothers, pianist Denis Kozhukin and clarinettist Jorg Widmann.

LondonTown.com   UPFRONT   35

In pleasing counterpoint to this season is the Barbican's 'Dancing Around Duchamp', dedicated to the French artist who famously detonated his first piece of controversy at the New York Armory Show in 1913 with his painting 'Nude Descending A Staircase'. This cross-disciplinary celebration will include two dance works. Legendary choreographer Merce Cunningham's 'Rain Forest' will be performed by the Rambert Dance Company, while the electrically exciting Richard Alston Dance Company will recreate extracts from Cunningham's repertoire in 'Event'. Composer John Cage will also feature – not least in a talk given by director Robert Wilson who will give Cage's talk on 'Nothing', famously based on musical principles **01**.

It's unlikely that the multi-disciplinary exuberance surrounding the performance of avant-garde music will lead to the sacrifice of a virgin – say – on the South Bank. But there will be plenty of tributes to the piece of music that evokes this, Stravinsky's 'The Rite of Spring'. In February it will be performed by the London Philharmonic Orchestra, while later in the year Sadler's Wells will introduce 'A String of Rites', three works inspired by this radical moment in the history of both music and ballet. At the wildly beating heart of the season is choreographer Akram Khan's 'iTMOi **03** ('In The Mind of Igor') → 142, which bravely bypasses Stravinsky's own music to celebrate him with a new work by Nitin Sawhney, Jocelyn Pook and Ben Frost. Kicking off the Sadler's Wells celebrations, Michael Keegan Dolan will recreate his Olivier-nominated version of 'The Rite of Spring' → 118, while in June 'RIOT Offspring' → 149 brings together four choreographers, a full orchestra, and 80 non-professional dancers to examine links between 2011's London riots and the uprisings caused by Stravinsky in 1913. Back in the Southbank, on 31st May, the UK première of 'The Oracle' by Australian choreographer Meryl Tankard adapts the first performance of Nijinsky's original choreography for Stravinsky's classic.

Yet another champion of the avant-garde is celebrated in the City of London Sinfonia's Poulenc Festival in April. It will take place in a number of venues close to the City, culminating in the performance of his fantastic Organ Concerto and 'Gloria' at Southwark Cathedral. In the same month, admired Finnish soprano Karita Mattila performs his 'Banalités' as part of her recital at the Wigmore Hall. Although Poulenc was French, in a neat piece of circularity he was first published in London because Stravinsky was a fan of his early work.

There's also a link with Britten, since in 1945 the English composer and Poulenc performed together in the latter's 'Concerto for Two Pianos and Orchestra'. It's rather pleasing that there's an overlap in festivals for all three, though the festival dedicated to Britten ("Britten at 100', already underway) is by far the largest. The many highlights include ENO's staging of his final opera 'Death in Venice' → 152 at the Coliseum in June, the Royal Opera House's production of his 'Gloriana' → 154 – composed to mark Queen Elizabeth II's coronation in 1953 and directed here by Richard Jones – and the BBC Symphony Orchestra's performance of his 'War Requiem' → 214 at the Royal Albert Hall in November. His work will also, as previously mentioned, form a central strand to the BBC Proms → 166 which runs from 12th July to 7th September. And Kings Place presents 'Britten at 100' → 85 from 7th-9th February, and among other concerts featuring his work the Barbican will put on a dedicated weekend in early November.

Several anniversaries mark the living as well as the dead, not least the 40th birthday of dynamic Cuban ballet dancer Carlos Acosta **08**. Among several appearances, this February he will play the Greek god of music in George Balanchine's 1928 ballet, 'Apollo', at the Royal Opera House. A more specific celebration of his birthday comes in July with 'Carlos Acosta: Classical Selection' → 172 at the Coliseum, in which he will perform a programme of classical and neo-classical works with some of his former dance collaborators. The Barbican kicks off the year with a celebration of 'Sir Colin Davis at 85'. He will conduct the London Symphony Orchestra in the Mozart 'Requiem', various Schubert symphonies, and Britten's 'Turn of the Screw'. Pioneer of the period instrument movement, Sir John Eliot Gardiner will conduct the LSO playing Stravinsky for his 70th birthday concert in April, while Valery Gergiev, principal conductor of the LSO, will mark his comparatively youthful 60th year at the Barbican in May.

All conductors have their followers, especially Venezuelan Gustavo Dudamel, who shot to fame when he started conducting the Simon Bolivar Symphony Orchestra, which famously rescued some of Venezuela's most deprived children, giving them instruments in return for their weapons. This March he brings the Los Angeles Philharmonic to the Barbican for their first residency as Barbican International Associate. That other firebrand conductor - who's been burning for much longer than Dudamel but shows no signs of burning out – Sir Simon Rattle comes to the Royal Festival Hall with the Orchestra of the Age of Enlightenment to perform Mozart's last three symphonies.

There are a lot of exciting premieres this year, not least the arrival of Philip Glass's 2011 opera 'The Perfect American' **04** → 148, a controversial portrait of Walt Disney, at the London Coliseum this June. The ENO also presents Michel van der Aa's new 'Sunken Garden' → 119 – a collaboration with David 'Cloud Atlas' Mitchell – and Carrie Cracknell's new take on 'Wozzeck' → 135. Outside 'The Rest Is Noise' festival, the South Bank Centre's London Sinfonietta presents Steve Reich's 'Radio Rewrite' → 100, inspired by two Radiohead Songs. (Reich will also take part in every music student's favourite, his 'Clapping Music', in the same concert.) The Royal Opera House will present the UK première of British composer George Benjamin's 'Written on the Skin' → 102. Benjamin collaborated with leading playwright Martin Crimp on this work, and it will be directed by the much lauded, intellectually rigorous Katie Mitchell. Another première, though admittedly three hundred and twenty years after it was first written, is French composer Marc-Antoine Charpentier's 'Medea' → 90, which receives its first full UK staging this February back at the Coliseum.

From Bach to Bausch, from Romanticism to Minimalism... If music be the food of love, let's face it, 2013's going to be an orgy.

Those in search of something completely different might be intrigued by the arrival of Canadian company RUBBERBANDance Group, who combine ballet with hip hop. They will appear at the Purcell Room in May with their UK première of 'Gravity of Center' 10, a piece of dance inspired by the collapse of Lehman Brothers. For more classic experimentalism, the Tanztheater Wuppertal Pina Bausch → 88 brings two of the late choreographer's rarely performed works to Sadler's Wells, 'Two Cigarettes In The Dark' 09 and 'Vollmond' ('Full Moon') 06 to mark the company's 40th anniversary. In the same month Ballet Black → 94 – the company that works with black and Asian dancers – presents a season of new choreography at the Royal Opera House. Choreographer Wayne McGregor's new work 'Raven Girl' → 139 will be presented there in May – his first narrative ballet, it will be based on a graphic novel by Audrey Niffenegger, who wrote 'The Time Traveler's Wife'.

All this, and so much more, as the cliché goes. As ever London will also be catering to more traditional tastes with a huge range of established talent. Pianist Andras Schiff will complete his cycle of Beethoven Sonatas at Wigmore Hall, culminating in an extraordinary demonstration of stamina on his 60th birthday in December with a performance of the 'Diabelli Variations' and the 'Goldberg Variations'. And Lang Lang 02 → 214 will be performing Mozart and Chopin at the Royal Albert Hall in November. At Kings Place, which continues to earn its credentials as one of London's most exciting new venues, there will be 'Bach Unwrapped' 05, a year-long series featuring more than 70 concerts, events, and study days. At the Royal Opera House there's a new staging of Verdi's 'Nabucco' 13 → 110 by Daniele Abbado, the English National Ballet 07 perform 'Swan Lake' in the round at the Royal Albert Hall → 151, and 'West Side Story' makes a triumphant return to Sadler's Wells → 178. From Bach to Bausch, from Romanticism to Minimalism, there's something to satisfy all tastes this year in London. If music be the food of love, let's face it, 2013's going to be an orgy. ●

MUSIC

SUMMER MUSIC FESTIVALS

Tessa Edmondson on why London is the summer music festival capital

Festivals come and go quicker than you can get your wellies on these days, with many succumbing to the tempestuous British weather, others becoming victims of the dreaded recession, and some never really getting off the starting blocks (need we mention the disastrous opening of last year's Bloc?). With so many festivals dropping like flies, it's tricky to know which one is best to invest in. So here's our pick of the best summer music festivals in 2013 that will guarantee you don't get Glasto-envy.

A few tried and tested favourites are the Victoria Park regulars, Field Day → 140 and Lovebox → 168. Known for fashion conscious attendees and lively line-ups of established and emerging acts, you can expect a mixed bill of musical genres ranging from folk right through to electro and hip-hop.

If you like your festivals to come with big names and even bigger performances you can't beat Hard Rock Calling. Nominated for the Best Major Festival in the UK, it consistently makes history by attracting pop and rock icons to Hyde Park and last year featured unforgettable performances from Paul Simon and Bruce Springsteen.

If traipsing around a field in a waterproof poncho or queuing endlessly for a portaloo isn't your idea of a good time, try one of the many indoor festivals taking place in London this year. Bushstock is the brainchild of indie record label Communion Records and takes place in a variety of intimate venues around Shepherd's Bush. Or sign up to the incredible iTunes gigs taking place under the cover of the iconic Roundhouse roof → 163.

Finally, those after something fresh should try the brand-spanking new festival courtesy of Mercury prize winning band The xx, who are hosting a Night + Day of their favourite bands at the spectacular National Trust-owned Osterley Park mansion. ●

FIELD DAY
25th May 2013
Victoria Park E3
The East London favourite returns with a top-notch line-up of electro, dance and folk acts for its annual day of fashionable frolicking in Victoria Park

HARD ROCK CALLING
July - TBC
Hyde Park W2
Last year the police pulled the plug on The Boss and Paul McCartney, but that doesn't stop this central festival being one of the best in the UK

LOVEBOX
19th-21st July 2013
Victoria Park E3
Camp, colourful and crazy. Lovebox brings some carnival spirit to East London with three hedonistic days of massive pop, rock and dance acts

SOUTH WEST FOUR
24th-25th August 2013
Clapham Common SW4 9DE
House and techno fans make the most of the August bank holiday with bass-fuelled two-day marathon of cutting-edge electro and dance music

DON'T FORGET
BE BRILLIANTLY INFORMED: SIGN UP TO LONDONTOWN.COM NEWSLETTERS
WHAT'S NEW | GIGS | TALKS | WEEKENDS | TOURS | COMEDY | CLASSICAL | CABARET | THEATRE | DANCE | FOOD EVENTS | SPORT | SUMMER | CHRISTMAS

UPFRONT

NIGHT + DAY
23rd June 2013
Osterley Park and House TW7 4RB
Taking place in Portugal, Berlin and London. Mercury Prize-winners The xx gather together some of their favourite bands for a spectacular one day show

APPLE CART
June - TBC
Victoria Park E3
Family friendly and full of foodie delights, the Apple Cart is a calmer alternative to some of London's hectic high-energy festivals

WIRELESS
July - TBC
Hyde Park W2
An unbeatable bill of international stars play to crowds of more than 20,000 over three days in the heart of London. Rihanna and Jessie J starred last year

BUSHSTOCK
1st June 2013
4 Shepherds Bush venues
Hosted by record label Communion, this one-day festival takes over four West London venues with their best live music acts

ITUNESFESTIVAL
July - TBC
Roundhouse, Camden NW1 8EH
The legendary Chalk Farm Road venue hosts a month-long festival of free gigs, featuring a consistently brilliant line-up of popular current acts

SUMMER SERIES
July - TBC
Somerset House, Strand WC2R 1LA
The intimate atmosphere and the fantastic acoustics in the Somerset House courtyard make this one of the most memorable summer events

LONDON MUSIC FESTIVALS NEWSLETTER

→ To receive the London Music Festivals Newsletter send a blank email now to: **festivals@londontown.com**
PRIVACY PROMISE: We will never (and that means never) give your email address to anyone else. You mean too much to us.

THEATRE

LONDON FRINGE THEATRE VENUES

With small budgets and big ideas, these intimate spaces create extraordinary theatre.

TUCKED AWAY IN UNUSUAL PLACES – above or below a pub, in a former church or a converted paint factory – London's fringe theatres may be harder to find than their West End counterparts but they are home to hidden treasures. "London's fringe theatre has never been this good," ran The Guardian's headline at the beginning of 2012 and 2013 looks set to reinforce that feeling of optimism.

The Finborough 03, the Tricycle and the Bush Theatre 01 are just a few of London's well established fringe theatres which consistently produce excellent theatre and that's set to continue in 2013. Added to these are newcomers The Print Room, The Yard and the New Diorama, and in spring 2013 the purpose-built The Park adds to that list.

Opening in a converted 1960s office block next to Finsbury Park tube station, The Park, designed by David Hughes Architects, will provide two performance spaces – a two-tiered theatre seating 200 and a smaller space with seating for 90, plus a cafe and bar.

Notting Hill newcomer The Print Room launches a new space, The Print Room Balcony in January 2013 with Ivy and Joan while in the main theatre the year begins with the world première of 'Flow', a dance show staged in the round, with design by Tom Dixon.

Another must-visit venue for fans of fringe, the Southwark Playhouse, moves to new, larger premises while its usual home in London Bridge is renovated. When it re-opens in April 2013 on Newington Causeway, SE1, the new venue, which will increase capacity by more than a third, will have a 240-seat main house and a 120 capacity studio as well as its own cafe and rehearsal rooms.

It's all change at The Almeida in Islington 02, where Kevin Spacey and Cate Blanchett have graced the stage, when Michael Attenborough, the theatre's artistic director for the past 11 years, steps down in spring 2013. His final season will include Henry James' 'The

Turn of the Screw' → 73 and the world première of Lucy Kirkwood's 'Chimerica' → 137, co-produced with Rupert Goold's respected Headlong theatre company.

Wilton's music hall 04 reaches a significant milestone with its restoration project at the end of January and its production of 'The Great Gatsby' → 91, which sold out in May 2012, returns in February as their opening production after the auditorium is repaired.

One of the few fringe theatres in central London, the Jermyn Street Theatre has been enjoying a recent resurgence and was named as fringe theatre of the year 2012 by industry publication The Stage. Michael Gambon and Eileen Atkins starring in Trevor Nunn's production of 'All That Fall' 05 was a highlight of last year's programme and 2013 begins with toe-tapping musical 'Gay's The Word'.

The Off West End Theatre Awards – affectionately known as the Offies – are another good indication of where to find the best of the fringe. Last year, the Finborough Theatre → 100 won five prizes at the Offies in the same year it won the Peter Brook Empty Space Award for the second time. The Landor, a theatre above a pub in Clapham known for its musical productions, was another big winner.

If you're a fan of musicals, The Menier Chocolate Factory is another fringe venue lauded for its productions. Other theatres making a name for themselves by specialising in certain areas include the Tricycle Theatre in Kilburn which stands out for its political productions, The Orange Tree in Richmond, a theatre in-the-round which is well suited to the new, neglected and re-discovered works it specialises in, and the Soho Theatre on Dean Street which is often host to experimental theatre and well known comedy acts who appear here before their nationwide tours.

In its Downstairs space, a small studio with a capacity of around 80, the Hampstead Theatre has been hosting a programme of new writing. To date, two Downstairs productions have transferred elsewhere and, this year, Amelia Bullmore's 'Di and Viv and Rose' → 73 will be the first to go to the theatre's main space with Tamsin Outhwaite, Gina McKee and Anna Maxwell Martin making up an all-star cast.

At the Hampstead Theatre last year Rupert Everett gave "the performance of his career" (The Guardian) in 'The Judas Kiss' which transfers to the West End at the beginning of 2013 → 70, but catching a show like this at a smaller venue makes it so much more special. In February, James McAvoy, star of 'Atonement' and 'The Last King of Scotland', swaps the big screen for the small stage, playing another Scottish king when he appears in Macbeth → 87 at the intimate Trafalgar Studios.

But however enticing a Hollywood star on stage may be, the true appeal of the fringe is not about big names in bright lights – if you want that, go to the West End. These smaller venues, typically run on an increasingly short shoestring, are all about nurturing new talent, and giving experimental innovators a stage. Without the fringe we have no theatre. ●

LONDON'S BEST

LondonTown.com

FOOD FESTIVALS

Indulging in both sweet and savoury, these gastronomic events provide a treat for all palates and underline just why London is a foodie's heaven

MADE IN BRITAIN MARKET
7th-9th June
Southbank Centre
Mouth-watering food from top British producers

TASTE OF CHRISTMAS
6th-8th Dec (TBC)
ExCeL
All-star line-up gives Christmas a gourmet makeover

TASTE OF LONDON
20th-23rd June
Regent's Park
Vast outdoor food festival celebrates its 10th year

CHEESE AND WINE FESTIVAL
26th-28th Apr & 11th-13th Oct
Southbank Centre
A celebration of the perfect gastronomic pairing

LONDON COFFEE FESTIVAL
25th-28th Apr
Old Truman Brewery
Three-day event embraces London's vibrant coffee scene

FOODIES FESTIVAL
25th-27th May
Hampton Court Palace
Seasonal food and drink, tastings, and hourly demos

BBC GOOD FOOD SHOW
15th-17th Nov
Olympia
'Great British Bake Off', 'Saturday Kitchen' and 'MasterChef'

CHOCOLATE FESTIVAL
22nd-24th Mar & 13th-15th Dec
Southbank Centre
Celebration of chocolate with tastings and masterclasses

CRAFT BEER FESTIVAL
22nd & 23rd Feb
Old Truman Brewery
Independent beer producers, street food, bands and DJs

FEAST
Summer (TBC)
Unusual locations
Chefs from HIX, St John, Hawksmoor & Moro take part

FOODIES FESTIVAL
27th-29th July
Battersea Park
Sample food from top restaurants and meet Michelin-starred chefs

LONDON RESTAURANT FEST.
1st-15th Oct (TBC)
Various Venues
A city-wide celebration of eating out

LONDON FOOD NEWSLETTER

→ To receive the London Food Newsletter from LondonTown.com send a blank email now to: **food@londontown.com**
PRIVACY PROMISE: We will never (and that means never) give your email address to anyone else. You mean too much to us.

LONDON'S BEST

FILM FESTIVALS

From cinematic blockbusters to cult classics and intriguing shorts, London is constantly rolling out the red carpet for the silver screen

BANFF MOUNTAIN FILM FESTIVAL 01
21st Feb – 1st March 2013
Union Chapel, London N1 2UN
This collection of adventure, action and environmental films creates an adrenaline-packed programme

LONDON INDIAN FILM FESTIVAL
18th – 25th July 2013
BFI Southbank, London SE1 8XT
Celebrate 100 years of Indian cinema with a varied programme from the world's most prolific film producing nation

PORTOBELLO FILM FESTIVAL
29th August – 15th September 2013
Westbourne Studios, London W10 5JJ
Created in 1996, the Portobello Film Festival aims to provide a platform for exciting new film makers

BICYCLE FILM FESTIVAL
3rd – 6th October 2013
Barbican Centre, London EC2Y 8DS
Originating in New York in 2000, the BFF is now a firm fixture in the London calendar and returns for its tenth season

INTERNATIONAL ANIMATION FESTIVAL
25th October – 3rd November 2013
Barbican Centre, London EC2Y 8DS
This creative showcase dispels the myth that animation is little more than cartoons for children

RAINDANCE FILM FESTIVAL
25th September – 6th October 2013
Apollo Piccadilly, London SW1Y 4LR
Still going strong after more than 20 years, this indie event boasts feature films and cutting-edge documentaries

LOCO: LONDON COMEDY FILM FESTIVAL
24th – 27th January 2013
BFI Southbank, London SE1 8XT
Lift your January blues with laughs courtesy of these playful, provocative and passionate films

LONDON SHORT FILM FESTIVAL 2013
4th – 13th January 2013
ICA, London SW1Y 5AH
Edgy line-up of the most crazy, avant-garde films the industry has to offer, accompanied by live music and awards

THE TIMES BFI LONDON FILM FESTIVAL
9th – 24th October 2013
BFI Southbank, London SE1 8XT
Hollywood players and indie film makers flock from around the globe to enjoy this festival's extensive programme

---

LONDON FILM NEWSLETTER

→ To receive the London Film Newsletter from LondonTown.com send a blank email now to: **film@londontown.com**
PRIVACY PROMISE: We will never (and that means never) give your email address to anyone else. You mean too much to us.

UPFRONT

LondonTown.com

ART

MAJOR ART

From Lichtenstein to Lowry and Manet to Man Ray, London's galleries are putting on a glorious palette of exhibitions in 2013. *By Omer Ali*

THE DOMINANCE OF THE BLOCKBUSTER SHOW continues unabated in 2013: big-name draws this year include Roy Lichtenstein, Johannes Vermeer, Egon Schiele, Paul Klee, LS Lowry – even David Bowie. London's art scene is also due its first big shake-up for many decades when Tate Britain restores the chronological hang for its collection of work from 1540 to the present day.

The blockbusters kick off at the Royal Academy with the first major UK exhibition of French Impressionist Edouard Manet's portraiture and scenes of modern life → 72. And photography gets in on the act in Greenwich, where the National Maritime Museum hosts over 100 original landscape prints by US pioneer Ansel Adams → 63 until 28th April.

French photographer Henri Cartier-Bresson's 01 influence is in the spotlight at Somerset House until 27th January → 56, while the V&A celebrates new photography from the Middle East → 63. The camera is also key at the Saatchi Gallery's wide-ranging survey of new Russian art → 63 and features alongside videos in Tate Modern's 'A Bigger Splash' → 62, which focuses on the relationship between painting and performance since 1950.

In late January, recent work by German photographer Juergen Teller → 76 goes on show at the ICA, before the National Portrait Gallery presents the first major retrospective of Man Ray's 02 photo portraiture → 89. Meanwhile, Tate Britain hosts the first substantial display of late work by modernist Kurt Schwitters → 78, who fled Nazi Germany only to be interned as an 'enemy alien' in Britain, before settling in Cumbria.

Perhaps inspired by its successful 2006 retrospective of Dan Flavin, the Hayward Gallery features his work in its introduction to light sculptures and installations → 78, which also includes pieces from Olafur Eliasson and Jenny Holzer. New work by another artist recently celebrated by the Southbank venue – Antony Gormley – can be seen at White Cube Bermondsey until 10th February → 58, while

UPFRONT

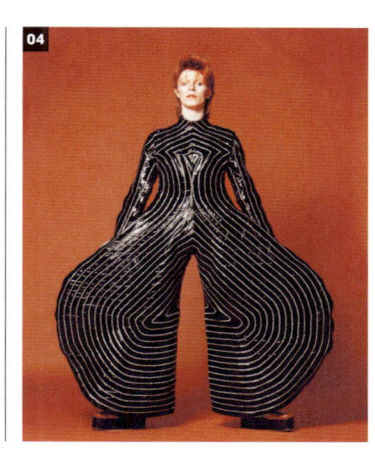

Roy Lichtenstein → 92 is the subject of a major retrospective at Tate Modern, the US pop artist's first since a Hayward show 10 years ago.

Also in February, the Barbican mines the links between Marcel Duchamp → 89, famous for his found objects, and four Americans: composer John Cage, choreographer Merce Cunningham, and artists Robert Rauschenberg and Jasper Johns. At the same gallery before 3rd March, Random International's installation → 61 allows visitors to control rain. Be prepared to queue.

Bowie mania descends on the V&A from March 04, when more than 300 outfits, handwritten lyrics, instruments, photographs, videos and film from the pop star's archive go on show → 107.

For real Renaissance men, the Queen's Gallery pays tribute to northern artists of the 15th and 16th centuries, including Albrecht Dürer, Hans Holbein the Younger and Lucas Cranach the Elder → 63, until 14th April. And the National Gallery showcases 16th-century Italian painter Federico Barocci's 03 appreciation of human form, and sense of harmony and colour, in altarpieces and devotional works never before seen outside Italy → 94.

'Looking at the View' → 87 at Tate Britain examines the changing way more than 50 British artists, including Tracey Emin and JMW Turner, have tackled landscape. The display, taken from the Tate's collections, serves as prelude to the chronological rehang of its galleries to be unveiled in May covering 500 years of work; it devotes special areas to William Blake, Henry Moore and, of course, Turner. From June, the gallery also pairs artists Patrick Caulfield and Gary Hume → 148 before it becomes the first major London museum to mount an exhibition of LS Lowry's 05 landscapes since the hugely popular Lancashire artist's death in 1976 → 156.

British artists also feature in 'A Crisis of Brilliance' → 151, Dulwich Picture Gallery's survey of such contemporaries as CRW Nevinson, Stanley Spencer, Mark Gertler and Dora Carrington, from their time at the Slade School of Art to their responses to the First World War.

You'll no doubt need to book ahead when the National Gallery brings works by the incomparable Dutch artist Johannes Vermeer → 156 and his contemporaries to London. They're coupled with rare musical instruments and songbooks to showcase the rich musical life of the Netherlands in the 17th century.

Soon after its annual summer exhibition kicks off, the Royal Academy travels to Mexico → 165 for work by Diego Rivera, Tina Modotti and Edward Weston, among others, before it embarks on a hugely ambitious survey of Australian art – the first here for more than 50 years.

Tate Modern promises a series of premieres across the year, including the UK debut of pioneering Lebanese abstract artist Saloua Raouda Choucair → 120, a substantial solo show for US-born contemporary artist Ellen Gallagher → 131, plus the first full-scale exhibition in Britain of Latin American artist Mira Schendel → 193. Then there's the first British retrospective in more than a decade for German artist Paul Klee → 203, from 15th October.

Another of autumn's highlights is the National Gallery's look at the art of portraiture in Vienna → 202 from the turn of the 20th century, featuring work by Gustav Klimt, Oskar Kokoschka and Egon Schiele. Also in October, the Royal Academy showcases Honoré Daumier → 205 and Dulwich Picture Gallery hosts American artist James Whistler's paintings of Chelsea and the River Thames → 203 from his first arrival in the capital in 1859. If all this makes you hungry to invest, art fairs will be unavoidable mid-month as PAD London → 204 descends on Mayfair while Frieze London → 204 takes over Regent's Park. ●

PERFORMANCE

LONDON COMEDY

London-based stand-up comedian *James Mullinger* talk us through his highlights of hilarity for the coming 12 months

01

02

MICKY FLANAGAN IS THE LATEST COMIC to be promoted to arena status but surely the most well deserved. A circuit legend for a decade before becoming a national treasure, Flanagan is possibly the only comedian to reach this level of success without a single person resenting him. Having tested out new material at the Leicester Square Theatre, Flanagan **07** takes his 'Back In The Game' → 139 tour to Wembley Arena and the O2, and it's sure to be as insightful and hilarious as anything he's done. If you only go to one comedy show in 2013, make sure this is it.

Also hitting the arena stage is the peerless Eddie Izzard **04**, who is taking on another world record having recently run 41 marathons in 53 days. This time he'll be using transport but the feat is no less impressive. 'Force Majeure' → 134 the biggest international stand-up tour of all time, taking in 25 countries around the world. From Cardiff to Kathmandu, Moscow to Mumbai - Eddie is leaving no stone unturned. 20 UK arena dates include two at Wembley Arena in May and one at the O2 in June. Undoubtedly one of the world's greatest living stand-up comedians, Izzard's show is sure to be unadulterated genius. The tour will be legendary. Be a part of it.

There are few stand-ups willing to be quite as honest about their own failings as Russell Kane **02**, who tours the UK in 2013 with as-yet-unconfirmed dates in London over the summer. Despite hitting the big time following his well-deserved Edinburgh win in 2010, Kane has resisted the urge to become sanitised. His show, 'Posturing Delivery', is about masculinity and Kane's own insecurities, infused with manic streams of consciousness.

Harry Hill **03** upset everyone by quitting his popular 'TV Burp' at its peak this year, but the big-collared buffoon is back with a long awaited return to stand-up. Hill's masterstroke is that he lost none of his zaniness with mainstream success. His act may not have evolved in 20 years in show business, but then it hasn't needed to. There aren't many acts you can say that about. His new show, 'Sausage Time' → 108, is likely to be the funniest thing you'll see all year.

Talking of sausages - this year Richard Herring 01 revives his seminal show, 'Talking Cock' → 119. This reworked version is even better than the 2002 original, Herring having grown as a performer in the past decade. Thought-provoking, profoundly honest and hysterically funny, Herring's unmissable riposte to 'The Vagina Monologues' comes to the Bloomsbury Theatre for two nights in April.

Without question the most exciting act on the comedy circuit right now, Nick Helm's 06 shows are unlike any other. Brooding, boisterous, bursting with vicious energy but above all hysterically funny, his increasingly impressive live shows boast everything from sing-alongs and games of Russian Roulette with orange fizzy pop.

Remarkably, Helm finds pathos amongst the madness and the result is an exhilarating and refreshing stand-up performance like no other. In a circuit crawling with Russell Howard wannabes, Helm is a revelation. And you can find him playing London clubs a few nights each week - and at the Udderbelly comedy festival on the South Bank → 118.

Believe it or not, I'm a former Women's Studies student whose first full-length solo show was titled 'James Mullinger is The Bad Boy of Feminism'. As such, I cannot write about the 2013 comedy scene in London without mentioning one of my favourite women stand-ups on the circuit.

In the wake of 'The Sarah Millican Television Programme' being commissioned for a second series on BBC 2 and her second live DVD breaking records for a female comic, Millican's 05 brand new stand-up tour, 'Home Bird' → 213, is as inviting a proposition as it's possible to imagine.

Every bit as charming, filthy and loveable as she was on the circuit, Millican is now a bona fide superstar but unlike, say, John Bishop, she hasn't gone all 'celebrity' on us. This home bird is keeping it real. My prediction for 2014? She will be the UK's first female comic to sell out an arena.

And finally, being the self-confessed 'Bad Boy of Feminism' as I am, I'd like to mention a fundraiser gig that I'm organising for Eaves, a London-based charity that provides support to vulnerable women who have experienced violence. 'Stand Up For Women' → 72 takes place on Monday 14th January at the Bloomsbury Theatre and features the best the UK comedy circuit has to offer (as well as me as MC).

For just £15 you can catch 'Live At The Apollo' star Sara Pascoe, 'The Office''s Robin Ince, bestselling author and star of 'Mock The Week' Shappi Khorsandi, truly brilliant Mary Bourke, Edinburgh darlings Max and Ivan, 'Have I Got News For You' panellist Shazia Mirza, oddball anti-comic Ed Aczel and Children's BBC Presenter Ed Petrie making a rare return to his stand-up roots. Blow away those January blues with an incredible night of laughs for a truly amazing cause. ●

LONDON'S BEST

LondonTown.com

QUIRKY EVENTS

Britain's famous sense of humour is celebrated in a raft of madcap events that take place across London each year

GREAT SPITALFIELDS PANCAKE RACE
Old Truman Brewery
Tuesday 12th February
Pancake enthusiasts race in fancy dress

FOOLS CHARITY CRICKET MATCH
Bank of Eng. Sports Ground
Sunday 24th February
Winter cricket for a good cause

OXFORD VS CAMBRIDGE GOAT RACE
Spitalfields City Farm
Sunday 31st March
Forget the boats and focus on goats

LONDON NAKED BIKE RIDE
Central London
Saturday 8th June
For those who think Lycra is unsightly

LORDS V COMMONS TUG OF WAR
Westminster College Garden
Tuesday 11th June
Parliamentary pull for charity

THE CHAP OLYMPIAD
Bedford Square Gardens
Saturday 20th July
Celebrating buffoonery and dandyism

SCOTCH EGG CHALLENGE
The Ship
Tuesday 17th September
Leading chefs work their Scotch magic

GREAT GORILLA RUN
Tower Bridge
Saturday 21st September
A day of serious monkey business

GREAT CHRISTMAS PUDDING RACE
Covent Garden Piazza
Saturday 7th December
Puddings and plates for eggs and spoons

LONDON EVENTS NEWSLETTER

→ To receive the London Events Newsletter from LondonTown.com send a blank email now to: **events@londontown.com**
PRIVACY PROMISE: We will never (and that means never) give your email address to anyone else. You mean too much to us.

Before you book your London hotel, visit the **London HotelMap**™ at LondonTown.com

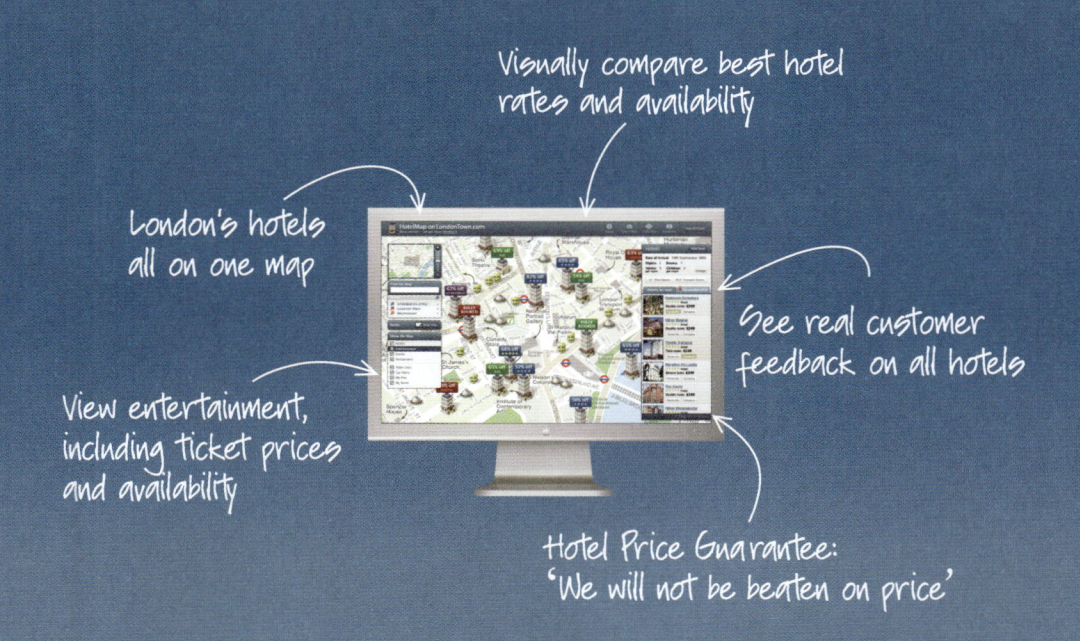

Visually compare best hotel rates and availability

London's hotels all on one map

View entertainment, including ticket prices and availability

See real customer feedback on all hotels

Hotel Price Guarantee: 'We will not be beaten on price'

www.londontown.com/hotels

**FREEPHONE
0800 LONDON**
0800 566 366

LondonTown.com™
Your Best Friend in London™

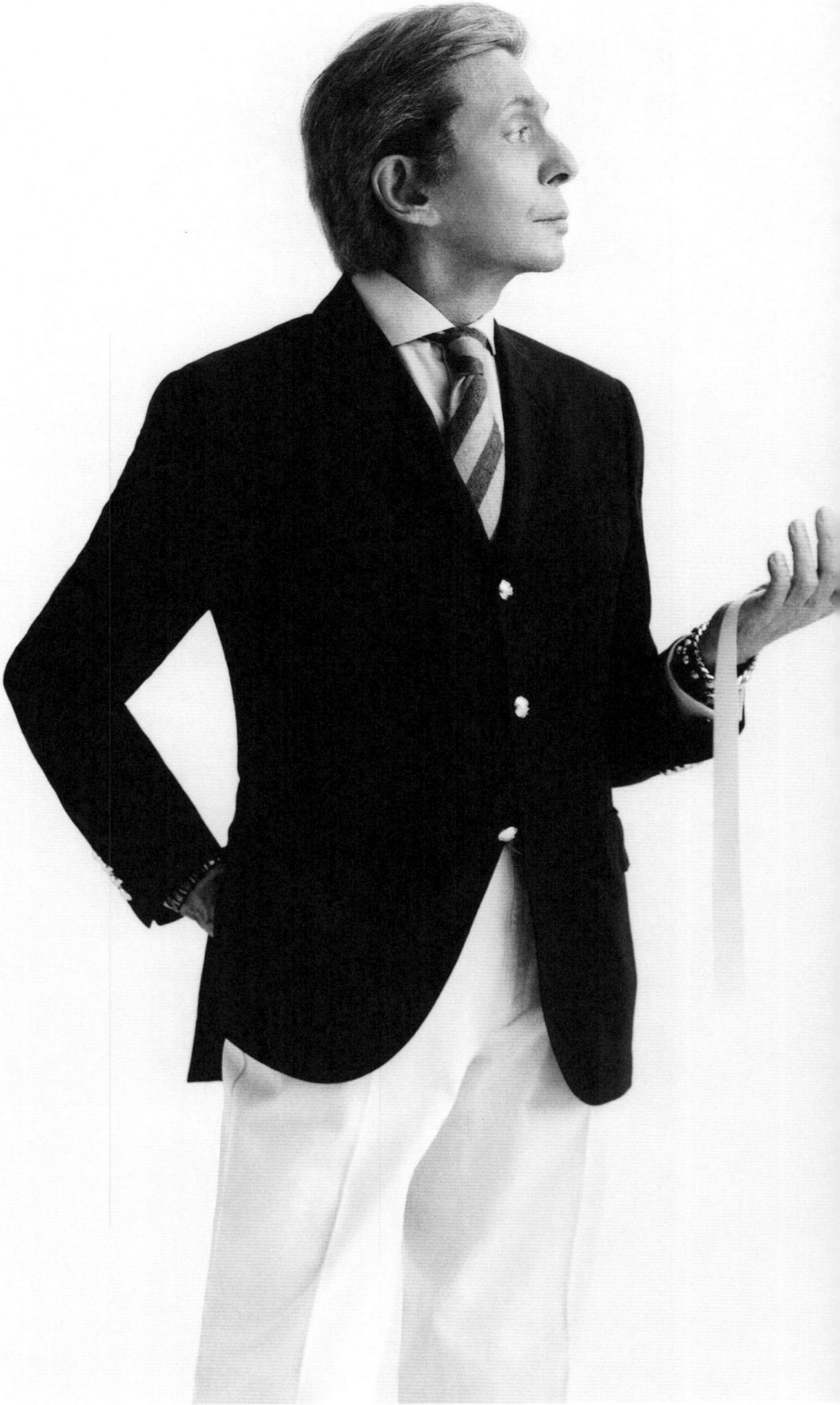

As we enter 2013, a number of great events are already under way across the capital, including Somerset House's stunning showcase of Valentino…

PAGE 61

ONGOING

Before you book your London hotel, visit the **London HotelMap**™ at LondonTown.com

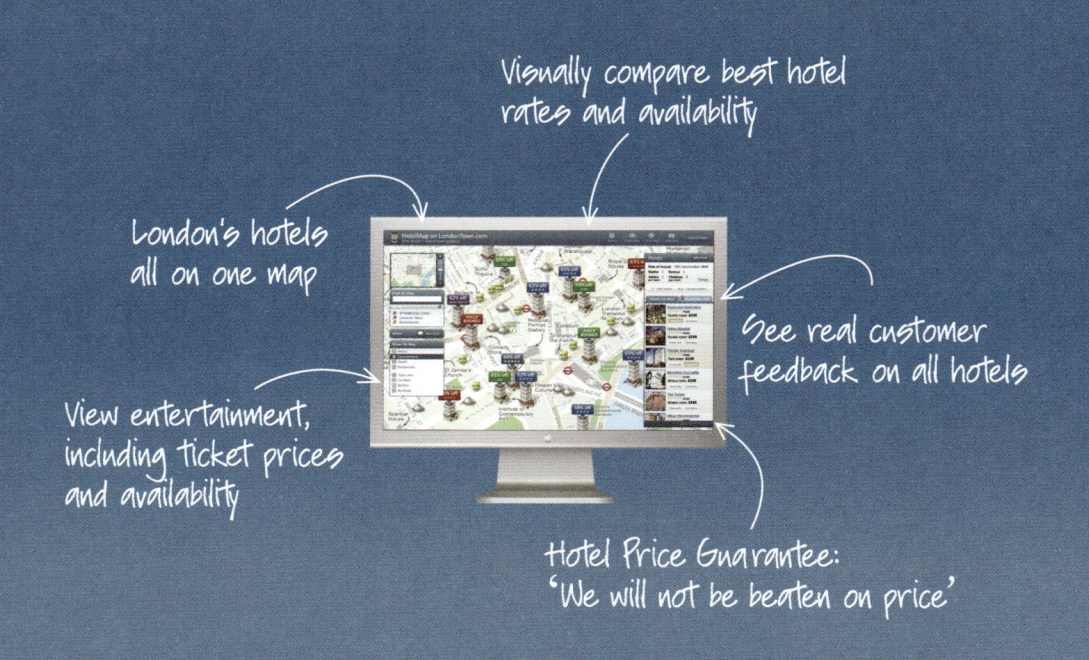

Visually compare best hotel rates and availability

London's hotels all on one map

See real customer feedback on all hotels

View entertainment, including ticket prices and availability

Hotel Price Guarantee: 'We will not be beaten on price'

www.londontown.com/hotels

FREEPHONE
0800 LONDON
0800 566 366

LondonTown.com
Your Best Friend in London™

LondonTown.com

ONGOING 2013

53

PICK

ART

Marilyn Monroe: A British Love Affair

Until 24th March 2013
National Portrait Gallery, St Martin's Place, London WC2H 0HE

PAGE 62

Ending in January 2013

English National Ballet: The Nutcracker
Until 5th January 2013
English National Opera, London Coliseum, London WC2N 4ES
Unless your name's Ebenezer Scrooge, this glittering production of E.T.A. Hoffman's 'The Nutcracker' cannot fail to revive your Christmas spirit. As sure as putting up fairy lights, filling Christmas stockings and having too much mulled wine at the office party, watching Clara dance in front of the Christmas tree is a truly festive thing to do - and if you missed it before the big day, then here's your chance before the decorations come down on the Twelfth Night. It's hard to imagine a production more indulgently sumptuous than Wayne Eagling's choreography to Tchaikovsky's famous score. From the heart-warming family party of the opening scene to the appearance of the magical kingdom, the action beckons you in.

Ballgowns: British Glamour Since 1950
Until 6th January 2013
Victoria and Albert Museum, London SW7 2RL
The revamped fashion gallery at the V&A reopened last spring with the exhibition 'Ballgowns: Sixty Years of British Glamour'. Events such as the recent Royal Wedding proved how a nation can become fixated on one item: a dress. This event showcases and celebrates some famous ball gowns worn by celebrities including Princess Diana, Kate Moss and Elizabeth Hurley over the past sixty years. With designers Stella McCart-

ONGOING 2013

Bob Willoughby's photo of James Dean studying a script is on display in The Silver Age of Hollywood

ney, Alexander McQueen and Gareth Pugh all having their creations displayed, this is a revival of fashion history and the opportunity to see these fashion masterpieces up close and personal.

Renaissance To Goya: Prints and Drawings From Spain

Until 6th January 2013
British Museum, Bloomsbury, London WC1B
This "triumphant" (The Standard) exhibition sets out to challenge the perception that the seventeenth century Spanish artist, Francisco de Goya, was operating as a 'lone genius'. It does this by placing him within the context of scientific, social and artistic developments occurring in Spain and Europe at the time. With the building of Philip II's monastery of the Escorial near Madrid foreign artists arrived in Spain creating a rich exchange of ideas. Works by influential visitors such as the Italians Pellegrino Tibaldi and Federico Zuccaro, and the Flemish printmaker Pedro Perret, are displayed alongside pieces by native talents including Diego Velazquez, Alonso Cano, Bartolome Murillo, and Jusepe de Ribera. The last part of the exhibition is devoted to Goya and his contemporaries, including the Tiepolo family who arrived in Madrid from Italy in the 1760s, worked for Charles III, and whose etchings revolutionised printmaking in Madrid.

Josiah McElheny

Until 12th January 2013
White Cube, Mason's Yard, London SW1Y 6BU
Josiah McElheny's third exhibition at the White Cube galleries, 'Interactions of the Abstract Body', showcases glass sculptures inspired by 20th century artists and designers, and the Italian architect, glass and furniture maker Carlo Scarpa. The New York-based artist uses the installations to examine how fashion and modernism have intersected and influenced one another.

The Silver Age of Hollywood

Until 13th January 2013
Proud Chelsea Gallery, King's Road, Chelsea, London SW3
Credited with inventing the photo journalistic motion picture still, Bob Willoughby was the first outside photographer to be hired by a studio specifically to take publicity images. With this all-areas access to Hollywood's elite, he became known for his artfully informal pieces. 'The Silver Age of Hollywood' displays intimate behind the scenes photos from films such as 'The Graduate', 'Rebel Without a Cause', 'My Fair Lady' and 'Ocean's Eleven'. It showcases some of Willoughby's most evocative images, including a striking image of James Dean studying a script, a beautiful Natalie Wood caught off guard and a meditative Jane Fonda as she practises her lines. The exhibition also includes Willoughby's first photograph of Audrey Hepburn, a snapshot of a pre-Bond Sean Connery and an image of Frank Sinatra a year before he married Mia Farrow.

Digital Crystal: Swarovski

Until 13th January 2013
Design Museum, 28 Shad Thames, London SE1 2YD
The meaning of memory in the digital age is explored in the Design Museum's 'Digital Crystal' exhibition, a display which includes the works of 15 leading figures in design who have been commissioned by Swarovski crystal in the past decade. Internationally renowned artist, architect and designer Ron Arad is just one of the designers taking part. Through Ron Arad's 'Lolita' chandelier anyone anywhere in the world can take part in the exhibition using Twitter or texting; their message appearing in the 1000 LEDs hidden in the crystals of the chandelier.

Pre-Raphaelites: Victorian Avant-Garde

Until 13th January 2013
Tate Britain, Millbank, London SW1P 4RG
The Tate has brought together a collection of over 150 pieces of art showcasing the very best of the rebel Pre-Raphaelite movement from the mid-nineteenth century, who overturned orthodoxy and set the tone for avant-garde modernism.

ONGOING 2013

Paintings, sculpture, photography and applied arts will sit alongside rare masterpieces including Ford Madox Brown's controversial 'Work (1852-1865)', and Philip Webb and Burne-Jones's 'The Prioress's Tale' wardrobe of 1858. Don't miss this final chance to view work from Britain's original modern art movement.

Richard Hamilton: The Late Works
Until 13th January 2013
National Gallery, Trafalgar Square, London WC2N 5DN
A little more than a year on from his death, a retrospective of major paintings by the artist Richard Hamilton is on display at the National Gallery, including his unfinished work based on Honoré de Balzac's short story, 'Le Chef-d'oeuvre inconnu'. The influential British artist always had close ties to the National Gallery and this display marks the first substantial exhibition since his passing and includes a selection of never before seen masterpieces featuring computer generated images overworked with paint.

Everything Was Moving: Photography from the '60s & '70s
Until 13th January 2013
Barbican Centre, Silk Street, London EC2Y 8DS
Presenting a major survey of the photographic medium during a period of rapid social change, this intriguing exhibition features more than 400 images taken by some of the most widely acclaimed photographers from across the globe. With works dating back to the Cultural Revolution, the striking display gives visitors a unique opportunity to browse through some of the most astounding shots taken by the likes of William Eggleston and Graciela Iturbide.

Cabaret
Until 19th January 2013
Savoy Theatre, Strand, London WC2R 0ET
Welcome back to the Cabaret, old chum, as the king of musicals is revived at the Savoy Theatre complete with a sparkling new cast and a repertoire of classic showtunes. Since its Broadway première in 1966 the show has collected an astonishing number of awards, including seven BAFTAs, eight Oscars and 13 Tonys. 'Cabaret' never fails to attract famous faces to the roles and this production continues the tradition with Will Young playing the Emcee and 'Eastenders' star Michelle Ryan starring as Sally Bowles. Director Rufus Norris's production of the musical written by John Kander and Fred Ebb, features timeless tunes such as 'Maybe This Time' and 'Willkommen'. So take a trip back to 1930s Berlin and visit the famed Kit Kat Klub for some good old fashioned decadence.

The Master and Margarita
Until 19th January 2013
Barbican Theatre, Silk Street, London EC2Y 8DS
Following its successful season back in 2012, Simon McBurney's award-winning theatre company Complicite returns to the Barbican with a new adaptation of Mikhail Bulgakov's classic Soviet satire. In the novel 'The Master and Margarita' there are two plot lines, one following the last few days in the life of Jesus Christ, the other the chaos of Moscow, satirising the Soviet system and bureaucracy. While Pontius Pilate argues with Jesus about the nature of human worth, Satan comes to save the world. 'Happy-Go-Lucky' actress Sinead Matthews, who is no stranger to the stage, takes on the role of Margarita, opposite Paul Rhys.

Seduced by Art: Photography Past and Present
Until 20th January 2013
National Gallery, Trafalgar Square, London WC2N 5DN
"Exquisite and astounding" (The Guardian), 'Seduced by Art' brings together early and contemporary photography and discusses how the influences of the early pieces are reflected in the more recent images. Leading photographers Tom Hunter, Thomas Struth, Craigie Horsfield, Sam Taylor-Wood and Beate Gütschow all have work displayed - each of these photographers trace their sources back to the nineteenth century or perhaps even older historical art traditions. The exhibition will also map the development of photography from the nineteenth century onwards, representing the progression in subjects such as still life, landscape and social portraiture.

William Kentridge: I Am Not Me, The Horse Is Not Mine
Until 20th January 2013
Tate Modern, 25 Sumner Street, London SE1 9TG
The South African artist William Kentridge is a "brilliant draughtsman" (The Guardian) whose eight channel video installation is projected across the walls of the Tate Modern Tanks exhibition space on a continuous loop to create an immersive audio visual environment. When Kentridge delivered his theatrical monologue 'I Am Not Me, the Horse Is Not Mine' in New York in November 2009, drawing a crowd of close to four hundred people, The New Yorker saw it as a mark of "how influential Kentridge's work has become since 1997". This is a must-see exhibition and, according to The Guardian, "a meditation on the dreams and failures of the Russian revolution".

'Lady Lilith' by Dante Gabriel Rossetti at the Tate Britain → 54

ONGOING 2013

Flame and water pots: prehistoric ceramic art from Japan
Until 20th January 2013
British Museum, Bloomsbury, London WC1B
Pots from one of the oldest ceramic cultures in the world, dating from the Middle Jomon period, 3500-2500 BCE, are displayed. Featuring three flame and water pots from ancient Japan, the exhibition looks at the imagery and symbolism on the pots, attempting to provide an insight into their mysterious cultural past, and demonstrates how Jomon pots have been an inspiration to today's Japanese culture.

Matthew Bourne's Sleeping Beauty
Until 26th January 2013
Sadler's Wells Theatre, Rosebery Avenue, London EC1
The famous ballet 'Sleeping Beauty' hits the London stage in Matthew Bourne's re-imagining of the iconic classic. The choreographer is renowned for his revolutionary adaptations of classic works and this production of Tchaikovsky's 1889 ballet is no different: the heroine of the piece, Aurora, wakes up in 2011 and, in a radical twist on the original tale, doesn't fall in love at first sight. Bourne describes the modern age that she wakes up in as "a world more mysterious and wonderful than any fairy story". He has also produced modern versions of 'Swan Lake' and 'Nutcracker!' and the 'Sleeping Beauty' revival will be part of the 25th anniversary of his company.

Fuerzabruta
Until 26th January 2013
Roundhouse, Camden Town, London NW1 8EH
Once its multimillion pound refurbishment was complete, the Roundhouse was reopened in 2006 in spectacular fashion. Its opening show 'Fuerzabruta' - meaning brute force - impressed London and was extended due to popular demand; now it's returning for a strictly limited four week period. With incredible visual effects - including its iconic image of a man bursting full throttle through a series of walls and a scene of a watery world suspended just inches above the audience – it is an all-encompassing theatrical experience that engulfs the audience and all their senses. As well as the visual effects, it also includes impressive acrobatic stunts and is a show that "leaves you dazzled by its physical bravura and technical skill" (The Guardian).

Hollywood Costume
Until 27th January 2013
Victoria and Albert Museum, London SW7 2RL
John Travolta's white three-piece suit worn in the classic 1977 film 'Saturday Night Fever' is among the iconic outfits from the silver screen displayed at the V&A in 'Hollywood Costume', which celebrates some of the best loved American film characters from over a century of film making. Dorothy's glittering red shoes and gingham pinafore dress are displayed alongside Audrey's little black dress from 'Breakfast at Tiffany's' and Johnny Depp's slightly less chic Jack Sparrow ensemble. This is the first time these costumes will all be seen together and it offers a rare chance to soak up some Hollywood glamour. The exhibition also includes film clips, projections and never before seen interviews with Hollywood designers, directors and stars including Robert de Niro and Meryl Streep.

Cartier-Bresson
Until 27th January 2013
Somerset House, Strand, London WC2R 1LA
Ten previously unseen Henri Cartier-Bresson images feature in this Somerset House exhibition on the emergence of colour photography. It's well-known that Cartier-Bresson was disparaging towards colour in photography but, as this exhibition demonstrates, his criticisms of the medium spurred on a new generation, determined to overcome the obstacles and prove him wrong. Curated by William A. Ewing, the free display in the Terrace Rooms and Courtyard Rooms features over 75 works by 15 modern day photographers including Carolyn Drake, Andy Freeberg, Ernst Hass, Fred Herzog and Alex Webb, and illustrates how photographers working in Europe and North America adopted and adapted what Cartier-Bresson referred to as 'the decisive moment' to their work in colour.

Antony Gormley's solid iron blocks are on display at his Model exhibition at White Cube → 58

ONGOING 2013

Tim Walker: Storyteller
Until 27th January 2013
Somerset House, Strand, London WC2R 1LA
Striking images by fashion photographer Tim Walker drawn from the pages of some of the world's leading magazines are displayed at Somerset House alongside a selection of the extraordinary props and models he uses. Giant grotesque dolls for Italian Vogue and an almost life-size replica of a Spitfire fighter plane are among the props on show. The exhibition is also accompanied by a series of events - including a rare opportunity to hear Tim Walker in conversation with Gentlewoman editor-in-chief Penny Martin - that reveal the influences and stories behind his work.

William Klein/Daido Moriyama
Until 27th January 2013
Tate Modern, 25 Sumner Street, London SE1 9TG
The 'William Klein/Daido Moriyama' exhibition at Tate Modern will explore the relationship between the work of William Klein (b.1928) and Daido Moriyama (b.1938). With Klein being one of the 20th century's most important photographers and film makers and Moriyama emerging from the 1960s Provoke movement in Japan, this exhibition will observe the use of film and photography in urban experience and political protest. The display will cover New York and Japan as it traces the influence of Klein's 1956 photo-book, 'Life is Good and Good For You in New York' and Moriyama's 'Another Country in New York'. Vintage images from New York, Tokyo and Paris will also be displayed.

The Mikado
Until 31st January 2013
English National Opera, London Coliseum, London WC2N 4ES
Gilbert and Sullivan's comic opera 'The Mikado' returns to the London Coliseum having first graced the famed West End theatre's stage in 1986. Satirically transposing the topsy-turvy orientalism of the Town of Titipu to the ever so slightly seedy opulence of a typical English 1930s seaside hotel, this revival of a modern musical masterpiece stars Robert Murray and Mary Bevan as Nanki-Poo and Yum-Yum (both new to the roles), with Richard Suart celebrating his 25th anniversary as the resplendent Ko-Ko (the pathological list-maker Lord High Executioner), Richard Angas back as the amiably grotesque Mikado and Donald Maxwell playing Poo-Bah (the Lord High Everything Else). Elaine Tyler-Hall directs Jonathan Miller's inspired, much-loved and hilarious ENO production of one of the most frequently played musical theatre pieces in history.

Ending in February 2013

The Karl Ferris Psychedelic Experience
Until 3rd February 2013
Proud Camden, Stables Market, London NW1
"You're doing with photography what I'm doing with music – going far out beyond the limits and blowing minds". These were the words Jimi Hendrix used to describe the work of Karl Ferris. Principle innovator of psychedelic aesthetic photography, Ferris was renowned for his promo shots of the British rock elite of the '60s and '70s.

Karl Ferris' album cover to Jimmy Hendrix's 'Are You Experienced' record

Following a centre fold spread in The Sunday Times, his flamboyant photography and unique technique fast attracted attention and he soon became the go-to for psychedelic fashion features, magazine covers and record album covers. With works such as the infamous Jimi Hendrix 'Are You Experienced' album cover, he helped craft the public images of Hendrix, Donovan, Eric Clapton, Cream and The Hollies. This exhibition showcases many of the album covers and promo shoots, as well as kaleidoscopic shoots for Vogue, Harper's Bazaar and The Beatles' Apple Boutique.

Royal Philharmonic Orchestra Resident Season
Until 7th February 2013
Cadogan Hall, London SW1X
The Royal Philharmonic Orchestra concludes its resident season at the renowned venue with a dazzling programme of Shostakovich, Sibelius, Prokofiev and Mussorgsky. Dmitry Yablonsky conducts, with Farhad Badelbeyli on piano.

Julius Caesar
Until 9th February 2013
Donmar Warehouse, Covent Garden, Earlham Street London WC2H 9LX
Phyllida Lloyd directs an all-female production of William Shakespeare's 'Julius Caesar' starring Dame Harriet Walter as Brutus at Covent Garden's Donmar Warehouse. Lloyd previously worked at the Donmar in 2005 on a production of Schiller's 'Mary Stuart', in which Dame Harriet also appeared. The pair had previously teamed up in the original London production of the classic West End musical 'Mamma Mia!'. Shakespeare's classic study of power charts the bloody fall of the Roman emperor Julius Caesar and deals with a terrible trio of conspiracy, assassination and retribution. This intriguing all-female cast also includes recent Ian Charleson award-winner Cush Jumbo as Mark Anthony, Jenny Jules as Cassius, Jade Anouka as Calpurnia and Frances Barber in the title role.

Twelfth Night
Until 10th February 2013
Apollo Theatre, Shaftesbury Avenue, London W1D 7EZ
The Apollo Theatre welcomes back Mark Rylance for one of Shakespeare's most beloved comedies. The actor returns to the Bankside theatre to star in an all-male award-winning production of 'Twelfth Night' by Original Practices. Rylance plays Olivia in the production, reviving a role he took on ten years ago when the show premièred in 2002. With a celebrated cast in some of Shakespeare's most loved roles you can expect comedy, cruelty and plenty of cross-dressing in this bittersweet production about two teams battling within the house of Olivia. On the one hand, the lovesick lord Orsino plots against the heart of indifferent Olivia; on the other, a vexed alliance of servants scheme against her steward Malvolio (portrayed deliciously by Stephen Fry).

Richard III
Until 10th February 2013
Apollo Theatre, Shaftesbury Avenue, London W1D 7EZ
Acclaimed actor Mark Rylance reprises his celebrated role of 'Richard III' - the determined Duke of Gloucester - who battles ruthlessly to reach his place on the throne. Heartlessly betraying anyone that comes between him and the crown - including the king, the king's son, his two brothers and his defenceless nephews (the legendary Princes in the Tower) – Richard III is truly Shakespeare's most despicable bad guy: a scheming, Machiavellian hunchback who is arguably one of the most villainous characters in history. Ten years have passed since Rylance last played the charismatic villain, a role he took on during his time as Artistic Director of the Globe. This current revival adheres to the Original Practices - meaning it will be performed by an entirely male cast - as it would have been in Shakespearean times. Clothing, music, choreography and settings are approached as if it were being performed in 1593.

Antony Gormley: Model
Until 10th February 2013
White Cube, Bermondsey, London SE1 3TQ
In this major new collection of works, the British sculptor - best known for his vast public sculpture in Gateshead, the 'Angel of the North' - explores our perceptions of architecture through the body and of the body through architecture. Human in form and made from 100 tonnes of sheet steel, the centrepiece is both a sculpture and a building. Visitors to the exhibition pass through the work, entering from the foot before being guided through its dark inter-connected internal chambers by direct and indirect light reflecting onto its structure. The gallery also displays a selection of Gormley's new sculptures built of solid iron blocks and various working models displayed on a series of tables, all showcasing Gormley's unique exploration of the body as a site of transformation.

The Magistrate
Until 10th February 2013
National Theatre: Olivier Theatre, South Bank, London SE1 9PX
Considering his taste for smoking, gambling, port and women, it's hard to believe

Mario Testino: British Royal Portraits
Until 3rd February 2013
National Portrait Gallery, St Martin's Place, London WC2H 0HE

THE OFFICIAL ENGAGEMENT portraits of the Duke and Duchess of Cambridge taken by Mario Testino are among the eight photographs of the Royal Family by the Peruvian photographer which are shown together for the first time in this free exhibition. All of the images were taken between 2003 and 2010 and include official commissions as well as personal photographs. Visitors can see the princes' official Christmas card from 2004 and the image taken to mark Prince Henry's 21st birthday, shown alongside a portrait of HRH The Prince of Wales and The Duchess of Cornwall, commissioned by British Vogue in 2006.

that Cis Farringdon is still in his teens. And that's because he's not. His mother chopped off five years from her real age and her son's when she married the Magistrate, Posket. This Victorian comedy by Arthur Wing Pinero, starring American screen and stage actor John Lithgow, is given a musical revival by Timothy Sheader.

Uncle Vanya
Until 16th February 2013
Vaudeville Theatre, The Strand, London WC2R 0NH
Christopher Hampton's adaptation of Anton Chekhov's comic tale 'Uncle Vanya' at the Vaudeville stars Ken Stott, Samuel West and Anna Friel, and is directed by Lindsay Posner. Chekhov's masterpiece takes place on the rural estate of an elderly professor, who is visiting from the city with his younger, glamorous second wife Yelena (Friel). This ribald study of ennui in the provinces involves an eternally frustrated love triangle between Yelena and two friends - estate manager Vanya (Scott), brother of the professor's late first wife, and the local doctor, Astrov (West). Throw in Sonya, the professor's daughter from his first marriage, who is smitten with Astrov, and the professor's proposed sale of the estate, and a farcical crisis pervades the stage. Blending sparkling wit and earthly humour, 'Uncle Vanya' is one of the most celebrated comedic studies of the trials and tribulations of the human condition.

Astronomy Photographer of the Year
Until 17th February 2013
Royal Observatory Greenwich, National Maritime Museum, Greenwich SE10 9NF
The winning images of the Astronomy Photographer of the Year competition are presented in a free exhibition at the Royal Observatory Greenwich which showcases some incredible images of the sky, from within our solar system and far into deep space. The winning entry for 2012 by Martin Pugh shows the M51 - The Whirlpool Galaxy, a stunning image of the archetypal spiral galaxy, pictured along with finalists for all the categories: 'Earth and Space', 'Our Solar System, Deep Space', and the Young Astronomer Photographer of the Year which was won by 15-year-old Jacob von Chorus from Canada. Winning entries have come from all around the world with more images entered than ever before.

Taylor Wessing Photographic Portrait Prize
Until 17th February 2013
National Portrait Gallery, St Martin's Place, London WC2
Showcasing the work of the most talented professional photographers, photography students and gifted amateurs across the world, the Taylor Wessing Photographic Portrait Prize regularly attracts around 6,000 entries by over 2,500 photographers who compete for the prestigious prize, not to mention the £12,000 which goes to the winner. The exhibition is an annual fixture and a highlight of the arts calendar in London with approximately 60 works selected from the thousands of submissions. The exhibition is recommended for its mix of themes, styles and approaches to the contemporary photographic portrait. In 2012, first prize was awarded to Jordi Ruiz Cirera, a 28-year-old Spanish photographer living in London, for a photograph he took of a 26-year-old woman from Bolivia whose shyness in front of the camera speaks of her religious beliefs.

Ian Hamilton Finlay
Until 17th February 2013
Tate Britain, Millbank, London SW1P 4RG
Regarded as one of the most unique artists of the twentieth century, renowned concrete poet Ian Hamilton Finlay juxtaposes neon, wood, stone and bronze sculptures against printed works in this free exhibition. Tate Britain shines a light on some of his most prolific artworks, concentrating on Finlay's alternative to a neo-classical idiom and his word and image-combined metaphoric sculptures.

Women in Focus
Until 17th February 2013
Museum of London, 150 London Wall, London EC2Y 5HN
Best known for her street photography and portraiture, Dorothy Bohm has been taking snapshots of the women of London for over two decades now and the resulting collection is now exhibited at the Museum of London. The photographs capture various female subjects in a style that contrasts them with their capital city surroundings, with shop windows, magazine pictorials, advertising billboards and artworks becoming the backdrops, highlighting the relationship between feminine portrayals and the realities of womanhood.

Project Space: Objects in Mirror are Closer than they Appear
Until 17th February 2013
Tate Modern, 25 Sumner Street, London SE1 9TG
An exploration of the multi-layered relationship between the moving image, narrative and perception, 'Objects in the Mirror' questions the paradoxical demands that cinema places upon its viewers. Looking at the logic of storytelling and the role our imagination plays in constructing a narrative, the exhibition sets out to blur the margins between depiction and deception. On show in the Project Space (formerly the Level 2 gallery) of Tate Modern, presentation highlights includes a viewing of the Mano de Boer film 'Dissonant', video work by Jan Mancuska and the video installation 'Powerchord Skateboard 2006', by Sherif El-Azma.

The Effect
Until 23rd February 2013
National Theatre, South Bank, London SE1 9PX
Actress and singer Billie Piper makes her debut at the National Theatre in this "clinical romance" by 'Enron' playwright Lucy Prebble. 'The Effect' is a drama on sanity, neurology, love and the limits of medicine, and reunites Prebble with director Rupert Goold, who was also at the helm in 'Enron' - the award-winning play based on the 2001 scandal that led to the bankruptcy of the major American energy company. Piper (who cut her acting teeth with 'Doctor Who' and who starred in ITV's critically acclaimed 'Secret Diary of a Call Girl', which was also written by Prebble) was last seen on the stage

Privates On Parade at the Noel Coward Theatre

in Neil LaBute's 'Reasons to be Pretty' at the Almeida, in which BBC Radio 4 described her as "fantastic, completely brilliant". Both funny and moving, this vibrant theatrical exploration into the human brain via the human heart also stars Tom Goodman-Hill, Anastasia Hille and Jonjo O'Neill.

Death: A Self Portrait
Until 24th February 2013
Wellcome Collection, London NW1 2BE
Death is the somewhat sombre subject of the Wellcome Collection's latest exhibition which showcases 300 works assembled by Richard Harris, a former antique print dealer based in Chicago. Rare prints by Rembrandt, Durer and Goya are among the items displayed which include anatomical drawings, plaster-cast bones and human remains. The exhibition is divided into five themed areas including violent death which invites the viewer to address the horrors of war and death on a mass scale. A programme of events and talks which tie in with the exhibition help to open up a "more serious conversation about the subject of death that we need to have in our society" - which was Richard Harris's original intention in creating his collection.

Family Matters: The Family of British Art
Until 24th February 2013
Tate Britain, Millbank, London SW1P 4RG
Part of Tate Britain's BP British Art Displays, this exhibition looks at how family life has been portrayed in British art over 400 years. It includes public displays of genealogy, depictions of private relationships, idealised visions of domesticity and images of the fragmented reality that can sometimes be family life. Displaying work by artists such as Bill Brandt, David Hockney and Michael Andrews, it represents families as a vision of strength, a fragile unit and a depiction of questionable values.

Breaking the Ice: Moscow Art 1960s-80s
Until 24th February 2013
Saatchi Gallery, Chelsea, London SW3 4SQ
Displaying 'non-conformist art' made in Soviet-era Russia, this group exhibition features work from artists such as Eric Bulatov, Grisha Bruskin, Boris Orlov and Francisco Infante. The duo Vitaly Komar and Alexander Melamid also feature heavily, "from their early, deliberately slapdash satires of Soviet propaganda to a later group of Nostalgic Socialist Realist Paintings, scorning the approved aesthetic style and the imagery of the Soviet state" (The Evening Standard). With around 200 works on display, the exhibition is an engaging account of Moscow art between the '60s and '80s.

Ending in March 2013

Privates on Parade
Until 2nd March 2013
Noel Coward Theatre, St Martin's Lane, London WC2N 4AU
Simon Russell Beale stars in Michael Grandage's production of 'Privates on Parade', Peter Nichols's Second World War-set comedy, the first of five plays to be staged by the director at the Noel Coward Theatre for the following 15 months for which over 100,000 tickets are on offer for a mere £10. The well respected actor, who recently starred as Timon of Athens at the National Theatre, plays the flamboyant Captain Terri Dennis who heads up the Song and Dance Unit while performing in the manner of Marlene Dietrich, Vera Lynn and Carmen Miranda. Set against the backdrop of the Malaysian campaign at the end of the Second World War, this award-winning comedy follows the trials of the recently-arrived Private Steven Flowers who discovers it takes more than a uniform to maketh the man.

Kiss Me, Kate
Until 2nd March 2013
The Old Vic, London SE1
The acclaimed director Trevor Nunn directs a rebooted version of Cole Porter's dazzling Broadway classic 'Kiss Me, Kate' at the Old Vic. The famous show within a show revolves around the production of a musical staging of Shakespeare's 'The Taming of the Shrew' and the comical conflict both on - and off - stage between the show's director, producer and star, and his leading lady (who happens to be his ex-wife). Throw in gun-toting gangsters, reckless gamblers, sparring actors and romantic tussles, and you get this timeless, exuberant, Tony Award-winning hit. Alex Bourne, David Burt, Clive Rowe, Hannah Waddingham and Adam Garcia all star in this wonderfully choreographed classic.

Unexpected Pleasures
Until 3rd March 2013
Design Museum, 28 Shad Thames, London SE1 2YD
This temporary jewellery exhibition invites us to consider the pleasures of wearing such personal adornment and examines the meanings associated with these portable designs. Curated by Melbourne jeweller Dr Susan Cohn, 'Unexpected Pleasures' showcases work by David Watkins, the designer behind the medals for the London 2012 Olympics, and other UK talents including Wendy Ramshaw,

ONGOING 2013

best known for her geometric designs, and Hans Stofer; a turbine engineer before training as a jeweller and silversmith.

Aspen Magazine
Until 3rd March 2013
Whitechapel Gallery, London E1
All 10 complete sets of the cult 1960s publication are on display in this exhibition. Each distinctive issue of this rarely seen magazine was produced by a different editor and designer, who took complete creative control. It included contributions by artists, writers and musicians such as Peter Blake, William S. Burroughs, John Cage, Ossie Clark, Marcel Duchamp, David Hockney and Lou Reed. This exhibition will showcase Andy Warhol and David Dalton's pop art issue, recordings by Yoko Ono and John Lennon, and a psychedelic issue edited by Angus MacLise, the original Velvet Underground drummer.

Halfway to Paradise: The Birth of British Rock
Until 3rd March 2013
Victoria and Albert Museum, London SW7 2RL
Photographs of the musicians who led the way in British Rock in the 1950s and 1960s are displayed in a free exhibition at the V&A's Theatre and Performance Galleries. 'Halfway to Paradise' explores the exceptional work of Harry Hammond, the music photographer who took pictures for the influential music magazine New Musical Express (NME). He documented the emergence of rock 'n' roll in post-war Britain capturing images of the most influential musicians from Roy Orbison and Ella Fitzgerald to Cliff Richard and Shirley Bassey. The display features more than 60 portraits, behind the scenes insights and performance shots including iconic images of the Beatles from the 1960s.

Wildlife Photographer of the Year
Until 3rd March 2013
Natural History Museum, Cromwell Road, London SW7
The stunning Veolia Environnement Wildlife Photographer of the Year exhibition at the Natural History Museum shows new perspectives of familiar creatures and quirky corners of nature. Animals, insects, plants and landscapes are captured brilliantly across a number of categories in what must be one of the most colourful and heart-warming collections of images on display in the capital. The high profile competition is the most prestigious and successful event of its kind in the world (the pictures tour the globe once the London exhibition winds down in spring). It is open to amateur and professional photographers and each year a panel of wildlife and photography experts scrutinise around 30,000 entries from a global pool for their composition and originality.

Valentino: Master of Couture
Until 3rd March 2013
Somerset House, Strand, London WC2R 1LA
This major exhibition celebrating the life and work of Valentino gives a rare insight into the secretive world of Italian couture. A stunning showcase of over 130 exquisite haute couture offerings, the exhibition includes designs worn by famous beauties including Jackie Kennedy Onassis, Grace Kelly, Sophia Loren and Gwyneth Paltrow. Visitors can view photographs from the designer's personal archive, walk the catwalk lined with couture gowns and discover the world of couture craftsmanship. The creation of the wedding dress worn by Princess Marie Chantal of Greece is used to illustrate the painstaking work of les petit mains who hand sew extraordinary garments like these. Through films showing behind-the scenes access to the Valentino atelier and a virtual museum, visitors are fully immersed in Valentino's world.

rAndom International: Rain Room
Until 3rd March 2013
Barbican Centre, Silk Street, London EC2Y 8DS
An immersive, interactive installation by art studio rAndom International, exploring the notion of water as an increasingly scarce resource, fills the Barbican's Curve gallery. Visitors can simply watch or opt to walk through the perpetual rainfall - trusting that they won't get wet. The 'Rain Room' art work invites us to consider the role played by technology in the harnessing of precious natural materials. On four Sundays during the exhibition, dancers will perform a new short piece created by choreographer Wayne McGregor, Artistic Director of Random Dance, to a score by Max Richter who previously collaborated with McGregor and artist Julian Opie when he wrote the score to the 2008 'Infra' as part of a Royal Ballet commission.

Focus: Charles Harrison as Curator
Until 10th March 2013
Tate Britain, Millbank, London SW1P 4RG
Despite refusing to acknowl-

David Hockney makes A Bigger Splash at Tate Modern → 62

edge himself as an artist, Charles Harrison became a leading figure of the British art world in the late '60s and '70s. Art historian, editor, creator and member of the artist collective 'Art & Language', he sought to give priority to the concept, process and activity over the finished piece of work. This display will examine his previous exhibitions and recognise his experimental approach, as well as his development from scholarly historian to curator.

Marilyn Monroe: A British Love Affair

Until 24th March 2013

National Portrait Gallery, St Martin's Place, London WC2
To mark the 50th anniversary of Marilyn Monroe's death, the National Portrait Gallery is staging a free display of photographs documenting the actress's connections with Britain. Photographs and magazine covers, vintage prints and film stills trace the transformation of the global star from popular pin-up to acclaimed actress between 1947 and 1962. In 1956 Monroe spent four months in Britain for 'The Prince and The Showgirl', and photographs by Larry Burrows for 'Life' magazine are included in the exhibition. Pictures of Monroe in a yellow bikini, and her meeting the Queen are shown along with those taken by Cecil Beaton and a photograph of British pop artist Pauline Boty pictured in front of her Monroe painting.

Ending in April 2013

A Bigger Splash: Painting After Performance Art

Until 1st April 2013

Tate Modern, 25 Sumner Street, London SE1 9TG
The Tate Modern takes a close look at the vibrant relationship between performance and painting with their new exhibition, 'A Bigger Splash'. A diverse range of art genres will be contrasted and considered using the notion that the canvas is a stage on which a gestural or theatrical act takes place. Jackson Pollock and David Hockney will be among the artists included in the exhibition, alongside face and body artists Cindy Sherman and Jack Smith, the paintings of the Vienna Actionists and Nikki de St Phalle's 'Shooting Pictures'. This insightful collection provides a chance to look at established works and also to explore the work of new emerging artists whose approach is influenced by these historical sources.

Mughal India: Art, Culture And Empire

Until 2nd April 2013

British Library, London NW1
More than 200 paintings and artefacts documenting the entire period of the Mughal Empire, which at its peak spread from Kabul in the northwest and covered most of the South Asian subcontinent, are displayed in this major exhibition. Taking place at the British Library, it will be the first ever exhibition to document the entire period, from the 16th to the 19th centuries. Among the 200 exquisite objects on display, Bahadur Shah II's crown, a page from the imperial manuscript 'Akbarnama' and a portrait of Prince Dara Shikoh will feature.

People

Until 2 April 2013

National Theatre, South Bank, London SE1 9PX
Frances de la Tour, Linda Bassett and Selina Cadell star in

The Queen: Portraits of a Monarch

Until 9th June 2013
Windsor Castle, Windsor SL4 1NJ

ANDY WARHOL'S SCREEN-PRINTED PORTRAITS of Her Majesty, recently acquired for the Royal Collection, are displayed for the first time here at Windsor Castle. Queen Elizabeth II is one of the most depicted women in the world and the exhibition presents a selection of official, commissioned and formal portraits of the Queen, brought together from a number of royal residences. As well as the 1985 works by Warhol, part of his 'Reigning Queens' portfolio - sprinkled with crushed glass which sparkle like diamonds - there are paintings by well-known artists for whom she has sat including Cecil Beaton, Pietro Annigoni and Lucian Freud (Above). Some of the works are accompanied by reflections from the artists who give a personal insight into the challenge of portraying such a universally renowned face.

Nicholas Hytner's production of Alan Bennett's drama. When Dorothy contemplates having a sale, a chance to release all her wonderful treasures onto the open market, there is one aspect to consider: the horrifying thought of opening her beloved stately home to the public. Will the end result be worth inviting all these people to traipse through her house?

Light From The Middle East: New Photography
Until 7th April 2013
Victoria and Albert Museum, London SW7 2RL
More than 90 photographs by 30 artists from 13 countries are on display at the first major museum exhibition of contemporary photography from and about the Middle East. Documenting and responding to changes in the social and political landscape of the region over the last 20 years, the exhibition features images by Newsha Tavakolian, Hassan Hajjaj and Nermine Hammam whose recent work includes the series 'Uphekka' created after the revolution in Egypt. Hammam reworks photographs of Egyptian soldiers taken during the 2011 protests in Tahrir Square, Cairo, and transports them to multi-coloured landscapes far removed from their original location.

The Northern Renaissance: Durer to Holbein
Until 14th April 2013
Queen's Gallery, Buckingham Palace, London SW1A 1AA
The less publicised Northern Renaissance is the subject of an exhibition displaying more than 130 fine works from the 15th and 16th centuries at the Queen's Gallery at Buckingham Palace. While the Italian Renaissance gets all the press, northern Europe was undergoing its own dramatic changes at the time. Albrecht Durer and Hans Holbein the Younger, two heavyweights of the time are allocated a gallery each and represented by a number of works. Highlights include Durer's woodcut of an Indian rhinoceros, and Holbein's preparatory drawings which are displayed alongside the finished oil portraits. Lucas Cranach the Elder, an influential figure in Dutch art, was creating mythological paintings while Pieter Bruegel the Elder's 'The Massacre of the Innocents' transforms a biblical scene to a contemporary setting. The exhibition may be "something of a jumble" but it is "a jumble of the highest quality art" (The Telegraph).

Doctors, Dissection and Resurrection Men
Until 14th April 2013
Museum of London, 150 London Wall, London EC2
Following the 2006 finding by archaeologists of a burial ground at the Royal London Hospital, Whitechapel, this major show offers an insight into 19th century dissection. It features animal and human remains, drawings, models and original artefacts, revealing the relationship between surgeons interested in anatomical studies, the resurrection men who supplied them and the demand for corpses.

Modern British Childhood 1948-2012
Until 14th April 2013
V&A Museum of Childhood, London E2 9PA
Using clothing, photography, film, artworks, television programmes and more, this exhibition is an exploration of the history and transformation of childhood in Britain between the 1948 and 2012 London Olympic Games. Aspects such as poverty and politics will also be considered to examine the themes of children being the centre of family life, technology in childhood and children's lives being more structured.

Ansel Adams: Photography from the Mountains to the Sea
Until 28th April 2013
National Maritime Museum, Greenwich, SE10 9NF
More than 100 of Ansel Adams's photographs documenting the natural landscapes of America are put on display. Best known for capturing mountains and parklands, this exhibition is a rare snapshot into his lifelong fascination with the dynamic qualities of water, featuring dramatic images of waterfalls, rapids, geysers, rivers, ponds and ice.

Focus: Frank Bowling
Until 30th April 2013
Tate Britain, Millbank, London SW1P 4RG
Having encountered abstract painting when he moved to New York in 1966, Frank Bowling became increasingly interested in the effects that could be created by paint. This led to his experimentation with poured paintings. Pouring paint directly onto the canvas, sometimes from as high as two metres, Bowling discovered this innovative style that saw the paint freefall onto the canvas and, as a result, boasted a unique action painting. Part of the Tate's BP British Art Displays.

Ending in May 2013

Gaiety Is The Most Outstanding Feature Of The Soviet Union: Art From Russia
Until 5th May 2013
Saatchi Gallery, Chelsea, London SW3 4SQ
This large survey explores the recent history of Russia, including the crumbling of the Soviet Union and the years of Perestroika, and features works by 18 contemporary artists including Janis Avotin, Dasha Fursey, Irina Korina, Roman Savchenko and Sergei Vasiliev who photographed the tattoos of prison inmates in Russia. A second exhibition, 'Breaking the Ice: Moscow Art, 1960-80s', a group exhibition of 'non-conformist art' made during Soviet-era Russia, also runs at the Saatchi gallery until 24th February 2013.

Oskar Fischinger
Until 12th May 2013
Tate Modern, 25 Sumner Street, London SE1 9TG
German film maker Oskar Fischinger pioneered abstract musical animations and created dynamic new possibilities for cinema. With one of his more notable projects being his work on Walt Disney's remarkable 1940 movie 'Fantasia', Fischinger used experimental techniques in an attempt to push aside narrative and instead focus on the scale, motion, rhythm and colour of cinema. Reconstructing his performances from around 1926, this installation at Tate Modern sees the Fischinger films transferred to high definition and digitally restored with, for the first time, the magic of added colour.

ONGOING 2013

Dancers perform in the 'Rain Room' at the Barbican → 61

The Voice of the BBC: 90 Years of Public Broadcasting
Until 14th May 2013
Science Museum, South Kensington, London SW7
On 14th November 1922, the BBC broadcast its first transmission, an event marked 90 years on by the Science Museum which displays part of the 2LO transmitter originally located in Marconi House. Before each show the presenter would announce, 'This is 2LO, London Broadcasting Station calling!' Though the 2LO transmitter was replaced in 1925 it symbolises the creativity of the early days of broadcasting. Visitors to the exhibition can also see the Babble Machine which explores the sound of early radio.

Ending in June 2013

Codebreaker: Alan Turing's life and legacy
Until 30th June 2013
Science Museum, South Kensington, London SW7
Celebrating the centenary of the birth of the British codebreaker, Alan Turing, the Science Museum shows that there's more to this pioneering figure than maths. At the heart of this free exhibition of interactive displays, personal recollections and historic imagery is the Pilot ACE computer, the most significant surviving artefact relating to Turing's ground-breaking design. Bletchley Park and World War II are brought to life.

Ending September 2013

The Bloomberg Commission: Giuseppe Penone: Spazio di Luce
Until 1st September 2013
Whitechapel Gallery, London E1 7QX
Italian artist Giuseppe Penone has spent the last 45 years examining modern society's complex relationship with nature. His current installation at the Whitechapel Gallery continues this concept with a huge bronze tree that has been hollowed out and displayed in sections. The piece was made by casting a real tree, which was then chopped up, destroyed and is now only traceable through the art. "The result is eerie and magnificent, a gnarled, complex, strange object. Life's ramifications are suggested by proliferating boughs." (The Guardian)

The Art of Seeing Nature
Until 22nd September 2013
Victoria and Albert Museum, London SW7 2RL
Following the cleaning of Constable's full-size oil sketches for 'The Hay Wain' and 'The Leaping Horse' which hang in the British Museum, visitors are invited to a free exhibition which not only reveals the colours John Constable intended but also examines the work which goes into their conservation. The South Kensington museum has an unrivalled collection of the artist's work and displays 49 of his oil sketches in the room next door. See both displays to follow the development of his style from early studies to sketches rapidly painted in the open air, leading to his expressive late works.

Research on Paintings: technical art history and connoisseurship
Until 22nd September 2013
V&A, South Kensington, London SW7 2RL
Using 11 case studies, the V&A offers an insight into the way in which art historians establish the nature and origins of oil paintings. A two year project saw 200 of the museum's paintings re-attributed or re-identified. Through the free exhibition 'Research on Paintings' we get a behind-the-scenes look at the documentary research and technical analysis which goes into such an undertaking.

Ending December 2013

Matilda The Musical
Until 22nd December 2013
Cambridge Theatre, Earlham Street, London W1D 7DY
The Royal Shakespeare Company's record breaking musical adaptation of Roald Dahl's celebrated children's book 'Matilda' has been such a success since transferring to the West End from Stratford that it has been extended right through 2013. Winner of seven Olivier Awards in 2012 - including Best New Musical - Dennis Kelly's musical (with music and lyrics by Tim Minchen) tells the story of five-year-old bookworm Matilda who overcomes family and school obstacles (in the form of the cruel headmistress Miss Trunchball) and helps her teacher Miss Honey reclaim her life.

DANCE VENUES

Whether you're big on ballet, wild on waltz or fanatical about foxtrot, London's vast array of dance venues offer a rich programme of events

TRINITY LABAN
King Charles Court, London SE10 9JF
This music and dance school in Greenwich hosts regular performances from both students and staff

SADLER'S WELLS
Islington, London EC1R 4TN
Also home to the Lilian Baylis Theatre, this favourite offers the best in national and international dance

PEACOCK THEATRE
Portugal Street, London WC2A 2HT
Part of the Sadler's Well sphere, the Peacock's innovative dance programme boasts West End appeal

ROYAL OPERA HOUSE
Covent Garden, London WC2E 9DD
A beacon of modern theatre design, the imposing ROH stages a steady flow of high-quality performances

LONDON COLISEUM
Covent Garden, London WC2N 4ES
One of the capital's grandest theatres, the Coliseum's splendour is matched by the ENO's impressive programme

THE PLACE
Bloomsbury, London WC1H 9PY
London's specialist venue for contemporary dance unites training, creation and performance

SOUTHBANK CENTRE
South Bank, London SE1 8XX
The largest single-run arts centre in the world offers a range of dance events throughout the year

BARBICAN CENTRE
Silk Street, London EC2Y 8DS
Located in the heart of the City, this multi-faceted performing arts centre hosts diverse dance productions

SIOBHAN DAVIES STUDIOS
Elephant and Castle, London SE1 6ER
Opened in 2006, these studios offer a broad spectrum of dance events, classes, workshops and exhibitions

---

LONDON DANCE NEWSLETTER

→ To receive the London Dance Newsletter from LondonTown.com send a blank email now to: **dance@londontown.com**
PRIVACY PROMISE: We will never (and that means never) give your email address to anyone else. You mean too much to us.

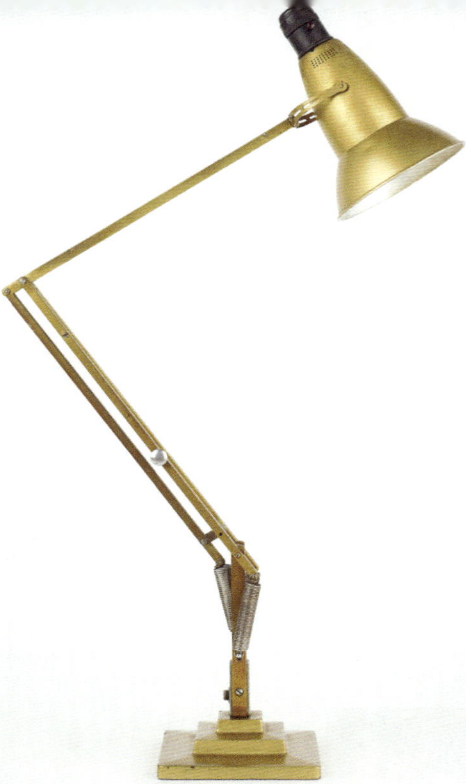

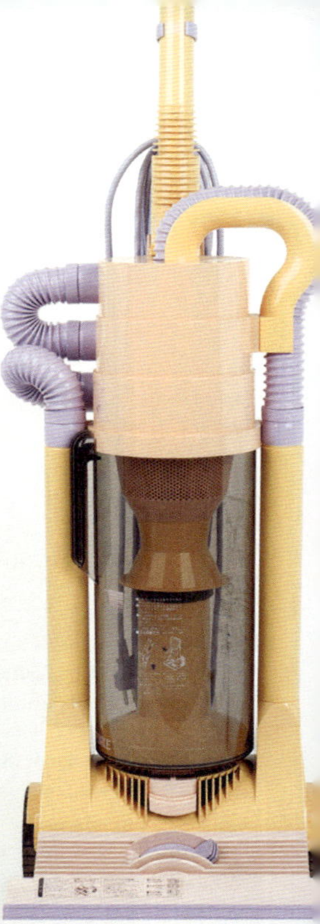

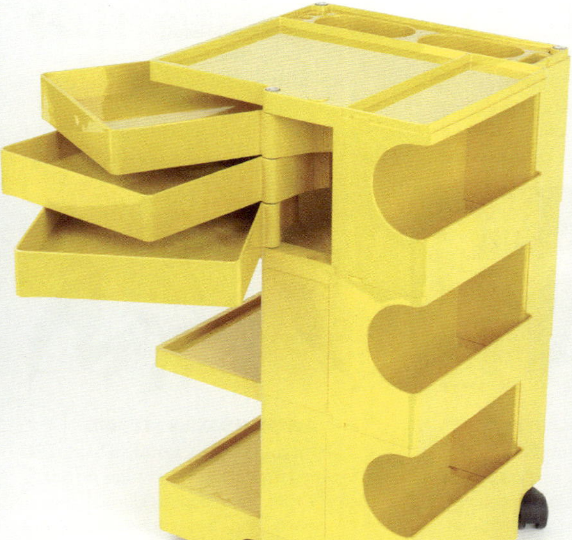

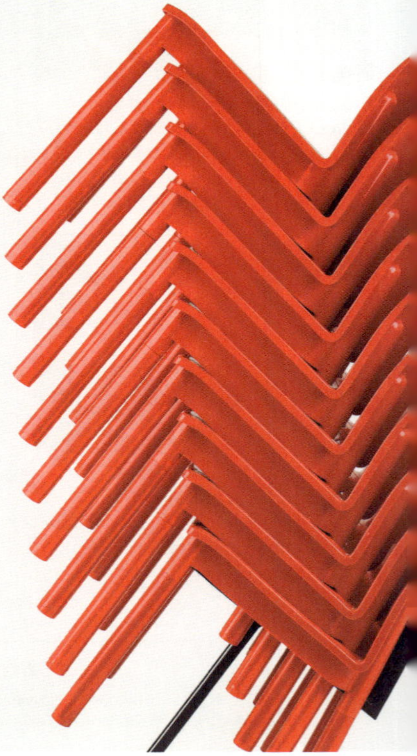

An action-packed January boasts Cirque de Soleil acrobatics, Manet's deft paintwork and the Design Museum's opening shows...

PAGE 78

JANUARY

WHAT'S ON WHERE IN JANUARY

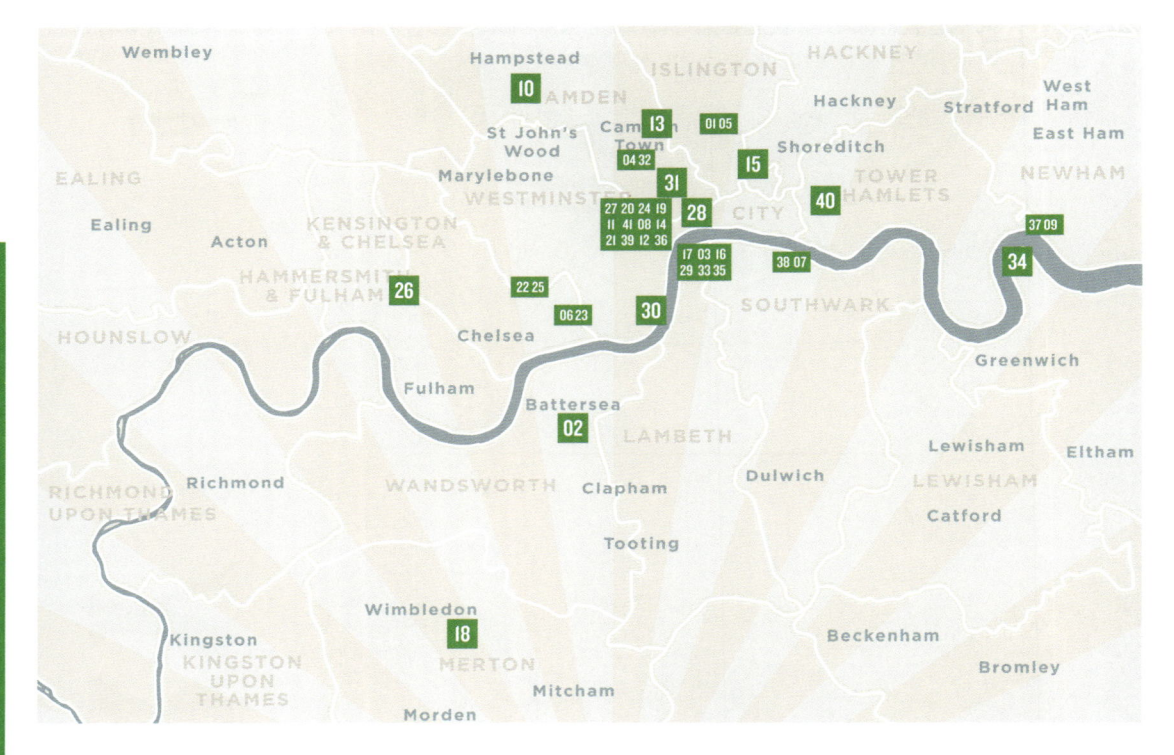

01 Almeida Theatre Page 74	**13 Kings Place** Page 76	**25 Science Museum** Page 71	**37 Trinity Buoy Wharf** Page 75
02 Battersea Arts Centre Page 69	**14 London Coliseum (ENO)** Page 70	**26 Shepherd's Bush Empire** Page 73	**38 Unicorn Theatre** Page 75
03 BFI Southbank Pages 71 & 76	**15 LSO St Luke's** Page 73	**27 Soho Theatre** Pages 75 & 77	**39 White Cube Mason's Yd** Page 74
04 Bloomsbury Theatre Pages 72 & 77	**16 Lyttelton Theatre** Page 75	**28 Somerset House** Page 77	**40 Whitechapel Gallery** Page 73
05 Business Design Centre Page 72	**17 Olivier Theatre** Page 77	**29 Southbank Centre** Pages 71 & 74	**41 Wyndhams Theatre** Page 76
06 Cadogan Hall Page 78	**18 New Wimbledon Theatre** Page 75	**30 Tate Britain** Page 78	
07 Design Museum Page 78	**19 Peacock Theatre** Page 77	**31 The Cartoon Museum** Page 70	
08 Duke of York's Theatre Page 70	**20 Phoenix Theatre** Page 77	**32 The Foundling Museum** Page 76	
09 ExCeL Exhib Centre Pages 71 & 73	**21 Royal Academy of Arts** Page 72	**33 The Hayward Gallery** Page 78	
10 Hampstead Theatre Page 73	**22 Royal Albert Hall** Page 70	**34 The O2 Arena** Pages 72 & 74	
11 Harold Pinter Theatre Page 71	**23 Royal Court Theatre** Page 71	**35 The Young Vic** Page 77	
12 Inst. Contemporary Arts Pages 69 & 76	**24 Royal Opera House** Page 74	**36 Trafalgar Studios** Page 70	

JANUARY 2013

PICK

DANCE

The Sleeping Beauty

9th – 19th January 2013
English National Opera, London Coliseum, London WC2N 4ES

PAGE 70

3rd – 19th
A Very Old Man With Enormous Wings
3rd – 19th January 2013
Battersea Arts Centre, Lavender Hill, London SW11 5TN
Gabriel Garcia Marquez's magical tale is brought to life in a spellbinding collaboration between the Little Angel puppet theatre and storytelling masters, Kneehigh. This "rewarding, mature show" is "quietly charming and visually ravishing" (The Guardian), a treat for both children and adults. The beautifully crafted puppets and wondrous design stand out in a modern fable about fame and fortune, miracles that soar, and how quickly everything can come down to earth with a bump.

4th - 13th
London Short Film Festival
4th – 13th January 2013
Various venues
The London Film Short Festival, the première UK showcase for cutting edge UK independent film, celebrates its 10th anniversary in 2013 and so expect a bumper programme of daring cross-arts shorts from the very best of the country's raw talent. Described by The Guardian as "the best short film festival in the world", LSFF is renowned for its crazy, avant garde and challenging offerings in an array of venues across town – including the ICA, Curzon Soho, Hackney Picturehouse, Roxy Bar and the Cine Lumiere. This really is a buzzing, edgy and often decadent event from start to finish, accompanied by training sessions, drunken bashes, live music and awards.

JANUARY 2013

From 5th
Cirque de Soleil – Kooza
5th January – 14th February 2013
Royal Albert Hall, London SW7
The Montreal-based troupe has made the Royal Albert Hall something of a home-from-home and they return again to the iconic venue for their new show, 'Kooza'. Praised as a return to form and simplicity, 'Kooza' has a retro feel and combines two circus traditions - acrobatics and clowning. Otherworldly, mystical, garishly colourful and intimate, 'Kooza' tells the story of the Innocent, a loner in search of his place in the world. There are thrills, chills and surprises galore as the contortionists, trapeze artists and acrobats test the limits of human performance – most notably with the show-stopping Wheel of Death. The Innocent's journey brings him into contact with a whole raft of characters such as the Trickster, the Pickpocket and a life size Bad Dog.

From 7th
Flook – and Humph too!
7th January – 10th March 2013
Cartoon Museum, 35 Little Russell Street, London WC1
The work of Wally Fawkes or 'Trog' as the cartoonist for the Daily Mail, Punch, the Observer and the Sunday Telegraph was known, is displayed at this exhibition. As well as creating the comic strip character 'Flook', he drew cartoons of 'Humph' – Humphrey Lyttelton, the famous voice of BBC radio programme 'I'm Sorry I Haven't a Clue' who was also Wally's close friend, a fellow jazz musician and cartoonist. Cartoons by both are displayed until 10th March.

9th - 19th
The Sleeping Beauty
9th – 19th January 2013
ENO, London Coliseum, London WC2N 4ES
An enchanted world of castles and curses, forests and fairies returns to the West End with a new awakening of 'The Sleeping Beauty'. When an evil witch places a curse upon Princess Aurora, it dooms her to a premature death on her 16th birthday. The kind Lilac Fairy succeeds in counteracting this curse and instead sends the Princess into a deep sleep for a hundred years; but, in a fateful twist, only the touch of true love's kiss can save her. Will Prince Charming awaken her in time? With choreography by Kenneth MacMillan, beautiful costume design from Nichols Georgiadis and some of Tchaikovsky's best loved ballet music, including 'Rose Adagio' and the music for 'Once Upon a Dream' in Disney's 'Sleeping Beauty', this revival of the classic tale is set to be spellbinding.

From 9th
The Judas Kiss
9th January – 6th April 2013
Duke of York's Theatre, London WC2N 4BG
Rupert Everett reprises his role as Oscar Wilde, alongside rising star Freddie Fox as Lord Alfred Douglas, as David Hare's 1998 play transfers to the West End following an acclaimed run at the Hampstead Theatre last year. Neil Armfield's revival of 'The Judas Kiss' focuses on two pivotal points in Oscar Wilde's final years - the eve of his arrest at Cadogan Hall and a night in Naples after his release from prison - and is a tale of betrayal, downfall and sacrifice for love. Convinced by his petulant lover, Lord Alfred, ever romantic Wilde decides against fleeing the country and instead remains to face arrest and a journey to self destruction. Following two years of imprisonment, Wilde reunites with Lord Alfred and is struck by yet more heartbreak.

From 10th
Silence of the Sea
10th January – 2nd February 2013
Trafalgar Studios, Whitehall, London SW1A 2DY
Anthony Weigh adapts 'Silence of the Sea' by Vercors for the Trafalgar Studios this January. When a German soldier is billeted to a home occupied by an old Frenchman and his niece, they are powerless to turn him away so they use silence as a weapon. Resisting acknowledgement of the officer, they are fighting their own battle against the German occupiers. However, the officer is in fact dreaming of brotherhood between the French and Germans. This powerful drama examines the dilemmas of both sides and highlights the testament that the original novel gives to the power of the human spirit.

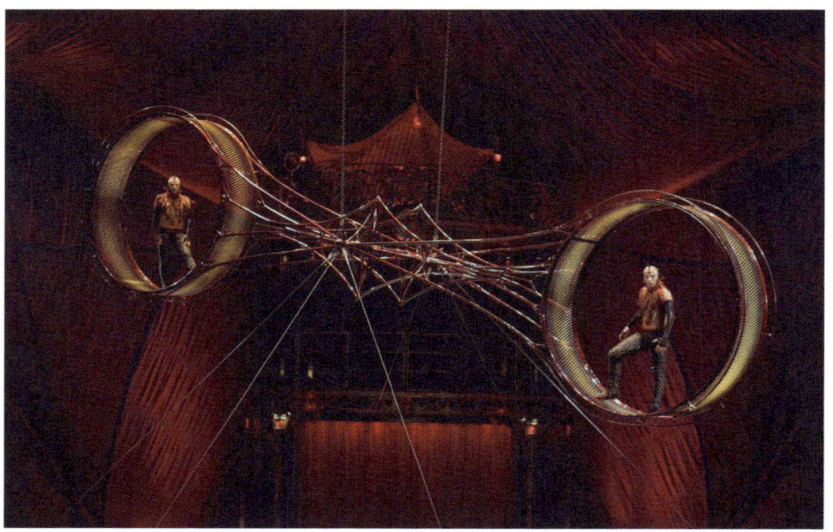

10th – 27th
London International Mime Festival

Acrobatic performance and the art of clowning are championed in Cirque de Soleil's 'Kooza' at the Royal Albert Hall

JANUARY 2013

10th - 27th January 2013
Southbank Centre, Barbican Centre, Royal Opera House and various venues
If you thought mime was all about white-faced clowns continually plagued by invisible glass and very strong winds, this will make you think again. Taking place at top arts venues across London - including the Barbican, Jacksons Lane, Roundhouse, and the Southbank - the festival brings contemporary visual arts from around the world to London. It's packed with some of the freshest and most inventive physical theatre, dance, circus, puppetry and live art. Selected highlights include: the Israeli artist, Amit Drori, who takes the audience on a journey to an imaginary 'Savanna'; aerial specialists Ockham's Razor who return with 'Not Until We Are Lost'; and Chinese-born puppeteer Yeung Fai who presents 'Hand Stories', a show that covers more than half a century of Chinese history.

From 11th
No Quarter
11th January – 9th February 2013
Upstairs Royal Court Theatre, Sloane Square, London SW1W 8AS
Robin looks for sanctuary in the remote family homestead and in his music in Polly Stenham's new play 'No Quarter' which opens in the Jerwood Theatre upstairs at Royal Court Theatre on 11th January 2013. But everything around him is crumbling and he wonders what the cost will be to save it all. Tom Sturridge, Maureen Beattie and Zoe Boyle (who played Lavinia Swire in TV drama 'Downton Abbey'), appear in the drama which is directed by Jeremy Herrin. It will be a homecoming of sorts for playwright Polly Stenham whose debut play 'That Face', written when she was just 19, received its world première in 2007 at the Royal Court. Its subsequent transfer to the Duke of York's made her the youngest playwright on the West End since Christopher Hampton in 1966.

12th
The First Doctor: An Unearthly Child
Saturday 12th January 2013
BFI Southbank, Belvedere Road, London SE1 8XT
'Doctor Who' marks its 50th anniversary in November 2013 and the BFI starts its countdown to this landmark with a Saturday afternoon screening of the first ever episode of the BBC science fiction drama. William Hartnell stars in the title role in this opening story from 1963 which introduces the Doctor, his fantastic time machine - the Tardis - and his first human companions, Ian and Barbara. The screening will be followed by a guest Q&A.

12th – 20th
London Boat Show
12th - 20th January 2013
ExCeL London Exhibition Centre, Royal Victoria Dock, London E16 1XL
Ahoy there! London's biggest exhibition of boats and water crafts of all kinds returns - featuring 500 exhibitors showcasing anything from 1.4-metre sailing dinghies to 37-metre tri-deck motor yachts. Visitors can also take part in a range of thrilling watersports activities such as kayaking, windsurfing and wakeboarding in a special Action Pool. With displays ranging from indoor canoeing to sailing, tall ships, historic vessels and a marina full of some of the largest exhibitor boats in production (at the Royal Victoria Dock), it's set to be an action-packed event with all hands on deck - if that kind of thing floats your boat. The event coincides with The London Bike Show, The Outdoors Show and The Active Travel Show and one ticket gets you into all four.

From 12th
Old Times
12th January – 6th April 2013
Harold Pinter Theatre, Panton Street, London SW1Y
Rufus Sewell, Kristin Scott Thomas and Lia Williams play Kate, Anna and Deeley in 'Old Times', Harold Pinter's emotionally wrought three-hander directed by Ian Rickson which plays at the London theatre recently renamed after the playwright. Set in a farmhouse, married couple Deeley and Kate chat about an impending visit from Kate's old friend and roommate Anna, whom they haven't seen for 20 years. But as the three old friends recall their early days in London and reminisce, underlying sexual tensions re-ignite. In an unusual twist, Kristin Scott Thomas and Lia Williams alternate the roles of Anna and Kate so leading man Rufus Sewell will be kept on his toes.

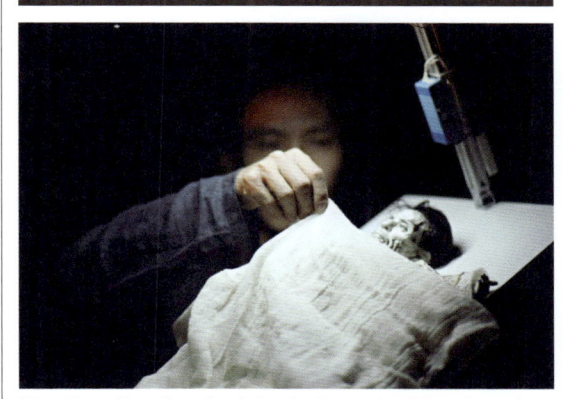

'Hand Stories' is performed at the London International Mime Festival

From 12th
Science Night
12th January – 7th December 2013
Science Museum, South Kensington, London SW7
Youngsters aged 7 to 13 sleep over at the Science Museum where they can experience exciting hands-on workshops and 3D films while sleeping among the museum's amazing exhibits. It will all be under the watchful eye of experienced staff who will make your visit fun and educational, and then steer you towards a tasty breakfast in the morning. Science Nights in 2013 are on 12th January, 20th April, 18th May, 6th July, 12th October and 7th December.

From 12th
RAF Photographer of the Year
12th January – 30th April 2013
RAF Museum, Grahame Park Way, London NW9 5L
The Royal Air Force Photographer of the Year competi-

tion has run for 23 years, in recognition of the skills and talent of the Royal Air Force photographers, and from January 2013 you can see the shortlisted images at the Royal Air Force Museum in north west London. 'The Milestones of Flight' exhibition features photographs taken by serving personnel, giving the public behind the scenes access to the lives of the RAF, both at home and in the field, with the images beamed onto glass panels.

14th
Stand Up For Women
Monday 14th January 2013
Bloomsbury Theatre, 15 Gordon Street, London WC1
Beat the January blues with a star-studded comedy line-up in support of Eaves, the women's support charity. Brought together by self-proclaimed feminist, writer and comedian James Mullinger, the likes of Shappy Khorsandi ('Live At The Apollo'), Isy Suttie ('Peep Show'), Sara Pascoe ('The Thick of It') and Shazia Mirza ('Have I Got News For You') join an incredible cast of comedians that also includes the bafflingly brilliant anti-comic Ed Aczel.

16th - 20th
London Art Fair
16th-20th January 2013
Business Design Centre, Islington, London N1 0QH
Now in its 25th year, the London Art Fair shows no signs of losing its cutting edge. Whether you're buying or just looking you'll have over a hundred of London's best galleries to look through. The stunning works on display cover the last 100 years or so of British art. With prices going as low as £20 it's an interesting exhibition for the amateur collector as well as the professional. There are two additional shows within the show: 'Art Projects', showcasing galleries from the UK, New York, Germany and Ireland and 'Photo50', where 50 contemporary photographs from the UK and international galleries are featured in a curated exhibition - this year Nick Hackworth, director of Paradise Row takes the helm.

17th
NBA London Live 2013
Thursday 17th January 2013
The O2 Arena, Greenwich, London SE10 0DX
The New York Knicks and the Detroit Pistons head to London to play a regular season game as the NBA London Live returns to the O2. This is the second time in three seasons that the NBA has headed to London. Last year's scheduled match-ups between the Orlando Magic and the Nets fell victim to the NBA lockout - so London's basketball fans should be well up for this one. Three-time NBA champions Detroit Pistons have a new coach in Lawrence Frank but the young and inexperienced team are in a state of flux and playing their debut game on European soil. Two-time winners the Knicks boast prolific scorers Carmelo Anthony and Tyson Chandler from the Olympic Gold medal-winning US squad.

From 17th
Sinéad O'Connor
Thursday 17th January 2013
Saturday 15th February 2013
Wednesday 27th March 2013
LSO St Luke's, London EC1V 9NG | Royal Albert Hall, London SW7 2AP | Barbican Centre, London EC2Y 8DS

From 26th
Manet: Portraying Life (PICK)
26th January - 14th April 2013
Royal Academy of Arts, Burlington House, London W1J 0BD
BEHOLD THE FIRST MAJOR UK exhibition of portraiture by the famous French painter Edouard Manet, featuring more than 50 paintings together with pastels and photographs which provide an insight into Parisian society in the 19th century. By arranging portraits thematically, into family, friends, status portraits and genre scenes, the exhibition examines the relationship between Manet's portrait painting and his scenes of modern life. Highlights include 'The Luncheon' which depicts Leon, the son of Manet's wife; 'Mme Manet in the Conservatory'; 'Berthe Morisot with a Bouquet of Violets', on loan from the Musee d'Orsay in Paris; and an early version of 'Le Dejeuner sur l'herbe'. His 1862 painting, 'Music in the Tuileries Gardens', is another hugely popular work and was his first major piece depicting modern city life, in which the band plays to a fashionable crowd - a gathering of Manet's literary friends and theatrical acquaintances.

The Glenageary-born singer-songwriter performs alt-pop and new wave folk-rock with her 7-piece band on her 'Crazy Baldhead' tour. O'Connor hit the height of fame in the '80s with heartfelt classics like the lovelorn ballad 'Nothing Compares 2 U', and now presents her latest works from a career spanning 25 years. Praise for her latest album, 'How About I Be Me (And You Be You)', shows a welcome return to form: "The Irish songbird's best album in years" notes the BBC, and "feisty, fresh and confident" writes The Independent.

17th – 20th
The Outdoors Show | The London Bike Show | The Active Travel Show
17th - 20th January 2013
ExCeL London Exhibition Centre, Royal Victoria Dock, London E16 1XL
All three shows coincide with The London Boat Show at the ExCeL Centre and one ticket gets you into all four. More than just a giant shopping opportunity, each exhibition showcases the latest equipment, hosts talks by experts in the field and gives visitors a chance to participate in outdoors activities. At The Active Travel Show you can get professional advice on how to plan a year out, the best ways to stay safe while abroad, and there's even a chance to take on the indoor climbing wall.

From 17th
Di and Viv and Rose
17th January – 23rd February 2013
Hampstead Theatre, Eton Avenue, London NW3 3EU
Di, Viv and Rose all met when they were 18 at university. They lived together, which was intense but fun, and they became a force not to be messed with. Together they felt unassailable. Fast forward a few years and life has thrown them some hurdles - what will these traumatic events do to their friendship? This witty play from Amelia Bullmore first took to the stage last year in the smaller downstairs theatre and now, due to its resounding success, it's back to be showcased on the main stage – the first play to see such a transfer. Starring Anna Maxwell Martin, Gina McKee and Tamzin Outhwaite; directed by Anna Mackmin.

From 17th
Gerard Byrne: A State of Neutral Pleasure
17th January – 8th March 2013
Whitechapel Gallery, London E1 7QX
With Irish artist and film installation specialist Gerard Byrne, you're never sure what you're going to get. Previous subjects include the Loch Ness Monster, the possible location of Beckett's 'Waiting for Godot' and the history of Minimalist art. This free exhibition at the Whitechapel once again sees Byrne explore the way we understand the present by revisiting the past, through a range of investigations spanning sexual politics and the actual production of the art object.

From 18th
Alt-J (∆)
18th & 19th January 2013
O2 Shepherd's Bush Empire, London W12 8TT
16th & 17th May 2013
O2 Academy Brixton, London SW9 9SL
With their infectious genre hopping tunes, Alt-J fast became one of the most successful British bands of 2012. Their debut album 'An Awesome Wave' – a result of five years' work recorded while at university - won the Mercury music prize, they've played sold-out shows in the US and have charted in numerous European countries with their wonderfully complex singles 'Tessellate' and 'Matilda'. The Cambridge-based band have re-branded guitar music, offering a hybrid of electro-rock and indie-pop, as well as being influenced by hip hop and trip hop. Success seems to be snowballing for Alt-J, and 2013 is set to be another promising year.

From 18th
The Turn Of The Screw
18th January – 16th March 2013
Almeida Theatre, Islington, London N1 1TA
A new governess arrives to look after Miles and Flora in the stage adaptation of Henry James's late 19th-century ghost story 'The Turn Of The Screw', and she soon learns to care deeply for her two wards. Figures start to appear in the darkness, the house is haunted, and the governess must protect the children against these worrying dangers. The spooky

Mercury winners Alt-J play at Shepherd's Bush and Brixton

tale, adapted by Rebecca Lenkiewicz, is directed by Lindsay Posner and stars Anna Madeley as the governess. Gemma Jones plays the housekeeper, Isabella Blake, Emilia Jones and Lucy Morton share the role of Flora, and 16-year-old Laurence Belcher plays her brother Miles.

From 18th
Kris Martin

18th January – 16th March 2013
White Cube, Mason's Yard, London SW1Y 6BU
Belgian conceptualist Kris Martin questions the notion of time and our desire with objects and interventions designed to provoke a state of mind. For instance, in 2007 he quite literally brought London's most famous art fair, Frieze, to a standstill when he announced a minute's silence over the microphone in a bid to draw the entire crowd's attention to the present moment. This latest exhibition of Martin's work at White Cube's Mason's Yard gallery furthers his on-going interest in themes of destiny, chance, time and material transformation.

From 19th
Onegin

19th January – 8th February 2013
Royal Opera House, Covent Garden, London WC2E 9DD
John Cranko's adaptation of Alexander Pushkin's verse-novel 'Eugene Onegin' will once again take to the stage this year. Having choreographed the dances for Tchaikovsky's opera 'Onegin' in 1952, Cranko then created a distinctive version of Pushkin's work for the Stuttgart Ballet in 1965. The three act ballet of the same name uses powerful duets and an eclectic range of dance forms - folk, modern, ballroom and acrobatic - to showcase the turbulent relationship between Eugene Onegin, Tatyana, her sister Olga and Olga's fiancé. Accompanied by Kurt Heinz Stolze's unique arrangement of Tchaikovsky's music, the piece is emotionally charged and showcases technical finesse.

From 19th
The Rest is Noise

19th January – 9th June 2013
Southbank Centre, London SE1 8XX
One of the Southbank Centre's most ambitious classical music projects to date, 'The Rest is Noise' is a year-long festival that takes audiences on a chronological journey through music in the 20th century. Based on the 2007 book by Alex Ross, the series will bring the book to life through concerts, performances, films, talks and debates. The backbone of the festival will be provided by the London Philharmonic Orchestra, who will play more than 30 concerts to help with the storytelling and dramatisation of the most important musical, political and social moments of the 20th century. Jude Kelly, the Southbank Centre's Artistic Director, describes the festival as viewing 20th century music "through the prism of history with its revolutions and counter-revolutions, its major moral and philosophical upheavals around race, gender, faith, political credo and pacifism – and its new relationship to technology and artistic democracy."

20th
Donny and Marie

Sunday 20th January 2013
The O2 Arena, Greenwich, London SE10 0DX
Singing siblings Donny and Marie Osmond bring their Las Vegas live show to London with this one night only performance at the O2 Arena to kick off a mini UK tour in celebration of five decades in the business. Backed by eight dancers and a nine piece band, the duo will run through a medley of unforgettable hits - including classics such as 'One Bad Apple', 'Paper Roses', 'Love Me For A Reason' and 'Crazy Horses'. Together, the Osmonds have recorded more than 70 albums and have topped the charts worldwide. They have also done wonders for the dental and tanning industries - not to mention, in all likelihood, Hollywood's big suppliers of Botox.

21st - 26th
Rocky Horror Show 40th Anniversary Tour

21st - 26th January 2013
New Wimbledon Theatre, 93 The Broadway, London SW19
6th - 11th May 2013
Richmond Theatre, The Green, Surrey TW9 1QJ
Sharpen your stilettos for the rockiest ride of your life as the

Johan Kobborg and Alina Cojocaru take to the Royal Opera House stage in 'Onegin'

world's favourite musical comedy returns to the stage with a 40th anniversary UK tour starring the 'X Factor''s Rhydian and 'Emmerdale''s Roxanne Pallett. First performed in 1973 at the Royal Court Theatre, Richard O'Brien's famous musical - whose central character is a mad cross-dressing scientist - ran for almost 3,000 performances before closing in 1980 and features timeless classics such as 'Sweet Transvestite', 'Damn It Janet' and the pelvis-thrusting 'Time Warp'.

From 21st
Alexei Sayle

21st January – 9th February 2013
Soho Theatre, 21 Dean Street, London W1D 3NE
The father of modern comedy, Alexei Sayle, returns with his first full length solo stand-up show in over 16 years. A key component in the alternative comedy circuit of the '80s, Sayle is just as much at home as a cynical political comic as he is performing physical comedy in the tradition of Spike Milligan and Monty Python. Renowned for his absurd and surreal riffs, Sayle promises a calmer second incarnation and comes to the Soho Theatre on the back of a sell-out tour of small UK venues testing out new material. "Still gobby and engagingly self-deprecating," says the Evening Standard, while The Times praises the loudmouth Liverpudlian for his "rare and wonderful" comic control.

From 22nd
Port

22nd January – 7th February 2013
National Theatre: Lyttelton, South Bank, London SE1
Award winning playwright Simon Stephens is producing plays like there's no tomorrow. With 'The Curious Incident of the Dog in the Night-Time', 'Morning', 'A Doll's House' and 'Three Kingdoms' all taking to the stage last year, his Pearson Award-winning play 'Port' now comes to the National Theatre. Set between 1988 and 2002 and inspired by Stephens' childhood in Stockport, 'Port' starts with a pivotal moment when a young brother and sister are abandoned by their mother and left with a drunk of a father. Celebrating courage and the human spirit, it follows them over a 13 year period in the deprived shadows of Manchester.

From 23rd
Silent Opera

23rd January – 10th February 2013
Trinity Buoy Wharf, Docklands, London E14 0JY
Much like the silent disco concept, Silent Opera is an immersive experience in which spectators don a pair of wireless headphones and are allowed to roam freely through the performance space, following the story and creating their own bespoke theatrical experience. Following the successes of Puccini's 'La bohéme' and Purcell's 'Dido and Aeneas', both performed in the tunnels beneath Waterloo station, Silent Opera's next project is a run of Monteverdi's 'L'Orfeo' at Trinity Buoy Wharf in East London, which tells the story of the mournful Orpheus travelling to the underworld to retrieve his beloved Eurydice after her untimely death. Further interactive innovations sees one audience member per night given the choice between two different endings. This is opera as you've never seen, heard or experienced it before.

PICK

From 30th
A Thousand Slimy Things

30th January - 7th February 2013
Unicorn Theatre, Southwark, London SE1

Based on Samuel Taylor Coleridge's poem 'The Rime of The Ancient Mariner', this play for children takes you on a mythical imaginary adventure on the high seas. 'A Thousand Slimy Things' opens at a beautiful wedding and all seems well, until the Ancient Mariner begins to tell you his story with words full of dread. Your mood changes from impatient to intrigued, fascinated to fearful as this tale of doom and destruction takes you into the gloomy depths of your imagination. Will you be brave enough to let go and follow him? Will this Gothic adventure change you forever? Suitable for children aged 10 and up, The Guardian described the play as "a distinctive mix of storytelling, physical theatre and live music".

JANUARY 2013

From 23rd
Juergen Teller: Woo
23rd January – 17th March 2013
Institute of Contemporary Arts (ICA), The Mall, London SW1Y 5AH
German-born photographer Juergen Teller, who has lived and worked in London since 1986, is the subject of a major solo exhibition at the ICA which opens in January 2013. Considered one of the most important photographers of his generation, Teller has seen success in both the commercial and art world. For the past fourteen years, Teller has been working with Marc Jacobs on his advertising campaigns and this exhibition takes visitors on a tour through his landmark fashion and commercial photography from the '90s. Alongside images of celebrities including Lily Cole, Kate Moss and Vivienne Westwood are more recent landscapes and family portraits.

From 23rd
Quartermaine's Terms
23rd January – 13th April 2013
Wyndham's Theatre, Charing Cross Road, London WC2H
Rowan Atkinson was last seen on stage in 2009 with his Olivier-nominated portrayal of Fagin in 'Oliver!'. The actor will now return to the West End to star in Simon Gray's 'Quartermaine's Terms'. A tragedy set in a 1960s English language school, it tells a moving account of several years in the lives of a seven teachers. Predominantly focusing on St John Quartermaine, an agreeable but hopeless teacher played by Atkinson, the quintessentially British drama takes a comical yet serious view of the teachers' stories and their tendency to treat Quartermaine as an agony uncle. However, despite being part of the furniture, his job is put under threat after the arrival of a new school Principal.

24th - 26th
London A Cappella Festival
24th - 26th January 2013
Kings Place, 90 York Way, London N1 9AG
Curated by five-time Grammy Award-winning vocal group the Swingle Singers and showcasing some of the best choral, jazz, contemporary and beatbox ensembles, the annual festival offers an eclectic assortment of music that ranges from choral masterpieces to extraordinary beatbox and Nordic folk to retro pop. The line-up includes The Magnets, an all-male group that boasts razor sharp harmonies and slick vocal stunts; The King's Singers, Grammy award-winners that have enjoyed global success for more than forty years; and Finnish triple platinum recording group Rajaton, who have proved to be a favourite of the 'A Cappella' Festival. The event will also see the hosts, Swingle Singers, celebrate their 50th anniversary.

24th - 27th
LOCO: London Comedy Film Festival
24th - 27th January 2013
BFI Southbank and selected cinemas, London SE1 8XT
A playful, provocative, pioneering and passionate programme of comedy films hits the Southbank to lift the January blues. Spread over four days at the BFI and selected cinemas across London, 'LOCO' celebrates Britain's great tradition of cinematic comedy with screenings of a number of humorous movies and a range of workshops and events all aimed at kick-starting the next generation of British comedy film talent. Last year's screenings included 'The Muppets', the gory yet laughable 'Shaun of the Dead' and classics from Buster Keaton and Charlie Chaplin. All screenings contain an interactive element with the aim of being mischievous as well as educational.

From 25th
Fate, Hope & Charity
25th January - 19th May 2013
Foundling Museum, 40 Brunswick Square, London WC1N 1AZ
A heart-wrenching selection of coins, jewellery, buttons, poems and playing cards left as identifying tokens by destitute mothers when they placed their unwanted babies at the Foundling Hospital in the 18th century.

From 25th
Feast
25th January – 23rd February 2013
Young Vic, 66 The Cut, London SE1 8LZ
Directed by award-winning director Rufus Norris, who is known for 'Cabaret', 'London

Anthony McCall's 'You and I Horizontal' is on display at the Hayward Gallery's Light Show → 78

JANUARY 2013

Road' and Olivier-nominated 'Vernon God Little', 'Feast' is an epic Young Vic and Royal Court co-production. Written by five playwrights across the world - Yunior Garc a Aguilera (Cuba), Rotimi Babatunde (Nigeria), Marcos Barbosa (Brazil), Tanya Barfield (US) and Gbolahan Obisesan (UK) – it takes a journey through Nigeria in the 1700s, the Americas and London in 2013, and explores Yoruba culture and religion. When a family are on their way to dinner, three sisters are separated at a crossroads. With an immense amount of courage, mischief and resilience, the sisters' spirits enable them to survive.

27th
The NATYS (New Act of the Year)
Sunday 27th January 2013
Bloomsbury Theatre, 15 Gordon Street, London WC1H 0AH
Twelve new acts are given five minutes to work their magic in the annual final to crown comedy's New Act of The Year (NATYS). Now in its 30th year, this comedy showcase and awards event comes to the Bloomsbury Theatre for the first time and promises a wide variety of performers - from stand-up to sketch shows, singers to surrealist and spoofs. Previous finalists included the likes of Russell Brand, Harry Hill, Ed Byrne, Lee Mack, Tim Vine, Micky Flannagan, Jack Whitehall, Simon Amstel, Rhod Gilbert and last year's winner Patrick Cahill. Fancy your chances? Auditions and heats for the 2014 competition will be held in December 2013 at Brixton's Rich Mix Arts Centre.

From 28th
In the Beginning was the End
28th January – 30th March 2013
Somerset House, Strand, London WC2R 1LA | King's College, Covent Garden London WC2R 2LS
A promenade performance exploring the subterranean passages and hidden spaces of Somerset House and King's College, this is the first chance audiences have to experience a new work by acclaimed site-responsive theatre company dreamthinkspeak since the sell-out success of their 2004 show 'Don't Look Back'. Through their signature mix of film, installation and live performance, a vision of the world on the verge inspired by the apocalypse - is it on the brink of collapse or rebirth? - is revealed.

From 29th
The Captain of Kopenick
29th January - 4th April 2013
National Theatre: Olivier Theatre, South Bank, London SE1 8XZ
Fifteen years of being trapped in a cell have passed and, stuck in a bureaucratic maze, petty criminal Wilhelm Voight wanders 1910 Berlin desperately searching for identity papers and an honest job. Instead, he comes across an olary uniform in a fancy dress shop and discovers that with his disguise people are only too willing to comply with his every command. What doors will this new-found power open for the ex-convict? Ron Hutchinson's English version of Carl Zuckmayer's satirical play comes to the National Theatre this January and sees Antony Sher take the title role.

Argentinian dance company Tango Fire return to the West End

From 30th
Tango Fire: Flames of Desire
30th January – 24th February 2013
Peacock Theatre, Holborn, London WC2A 2HT
Argentina's hottest dance company Tango Fire returns to the West End with its latest dance production 'Flames of Desire'. Having wowed audiences in 2011 with their speedy footwork and hypnotic moves, the Buenos Aires beauties are returning to put on another spectacular show. Made up of ten world class dancers, the production showcases both group numbers and duets, starting out with traditional dances performed in 1940s costumes and then progressing into impressive acrobatic tango show-dances. With the line-up including four world tango champions and Quarteto Fuego, the company's quartet of musicians, the show is a sexy and mesmerising performance.

From 30th
LIFT
30th January – 24th February 2013
Soho Theatre, London W1D
The uncomfortable silence, unnatural proximity to strangers and fear of eye contact are just a few factors that can make a lift journey unbearably awkward. Yet, when eight people get into one of the lifts at Covent Garden tube, and we are privy to everything they are thinking, including the revelations of their deep secrets, it doesn't take long before we realise that they are all connected. This world première of new musical 'LIFT', from the book by Ian Watson and with original music from Craig Adams, will delve into love, life and loss all within a seemingly normal London lift.

From 30th
Midnight Tango
30th January – 2nd March 2013
Phoenix Theatre, Charing Cross Road, London WC2H
Vincent Simone and Flavia Cacace from BBC's 'Strictly Come Dancing' star in this dance-narrative extravaganza set in a Buenos Aires bar but performed in London's West End. 'Midnight Tango' has enthralled audiences on a record-breaking UK tour and Simone and Cacace are joined by ten of the finest tango dancers in the world as they throw down some

JANUARY 2013

Jane Birkin sings Gainsbourg classics at Cadogan Hall

intoxicating tango rhythms in front of a captivated crowd. Co-produced by acclaimed choreographer Arlene Phillips, 'Midnight Tango' tells the story of a young couple as they meet in a late night bar, dance and fall in love right before the audience's eyes. Allow yourself to be entranced by this dazzling tale of rhythmic passion and romance.

From 30th
Light Show
30th January – 21st April 2013
The Hayward Gallery, Belvedere Road, London SE1
Exploring the powerful effect of light and the way in which it can affect our state of mind, this exhibition displays artworks from the 1960s onwards including pieces by Olafur Eliasson, Anthony McCall and Conrad Shawcross. Visually stimulating artworks as well as rarities not seen for decades are brought under one roof, including intangible sculptures and installations that use light to create atmospheric works in which you can move around. A sensory experience that enables visitors to experience light in all its forms, whether relating to colour, duration, shadow, intensity and projection, as well as our perceptual phenomena surrounding light.

From 30th
United Micro Kingdoms (UmK) - A Design Fiction
30th January – 28th April 2013
Design Museum, 28 Shad Thames, London SE1 2YD
The Design Museum begins its 2013 programme with an exhibition which presents a fictional future for the United Kingdom, as imagined by Dunne & Raby, a London based design studio established in 1994 by Anthony Dunne and Fiona Raby. The duo - both professors: Dunne at the Royal College of Art in London; and Raby at the University of Applied Arts in Vienna - use 'live laboratories' to challenge the way we live. Everything from industrial design to transport systems, science and politics is used to provoke debate about the potential of design.

From 30th
Schwitters in Britain
30th January – 12th May 2013
Tate Britain, Millbank, London SW1P 4RG
The late work of Kurt Schwitters, a significant figure in European Dadaism, comes under the spotlight in the first major exhibition to examine the artist, who was forced to flee Nazi Germany. The exhibition focuses on Schwitters' British period, from his arrival in Britain as a refugee in 1940 until his death in Cumbria in 1948. The works, which show traces of the impact of his exile, number over 150 collages, assemblages and sculptures, many shown in the UK for the first time in over 30 years.

From 30th
Extraordinary Stories about Ordinary Things
30th January – 31st December 2013
Design Museum, 28 Shad Thames, London SE1 2YD
The anglepoise lamp is just one of the archetypal designs celebrated in this collection display devoted to contemporary design and architecture. Other everyday items such as the post box and the London 2012 logo are presented as examples of extraordinary design and emblems of modernism in an exhibition which offers a snapshot of modern day design. Sections include 'National Identity', 'Plastics and Modernism' as well as 'Style Through The Decades', featuring fashion from the '70s to the '90s, from Carnaby Street to the Kings Road.

31st
Jane Birkin
Thursday 31st January 2013
Cadogan Hall, 5 Sloane Terrace, London SW1X 9DQ
The English actress and singer makes a rare London appearance performing the songs of her late partner Serge Gainsbourg. Initially scheduled for last October, this special concert is a reinterpretation of the late Gainsbourg's repertoire performed by his muse with a group of four Japanese musicians with whom Birkin first performed in Japan in 2011, soon after the tragic tsunami that shocked the world. Featuring classic Gainsbourg songs such as 'Requiem Pour Un Con', 'Comic Strip', 'Amour Des Feintes' and 'Do Di Dah', this poignant and celebratory concert comes alive with the musical versatility of the Japanese quartet, pays homage to one of music's most iconic figures and showcases the remarkable talent that is the effortlessly gamine Birkin.

LONDON'S BEST

LIVE MUSIC VENUES

Tucked away in tiny basements, converted warehouses and cavernous chapels… London's music venues come in all shapes and sizes. By *Vicki Forde*

XOYO
32-37 Cowper Street, Shoreditch EC2A 4AP
This Old Street basement club is one of the best places to catch big-name DJs, dance acts and breakthrough bands

UNION CHAPEL
Compton Avenue, Islington N1 2XD
The Islington Chapel is easily one of the most enchanting music venues in London, with unrivalled acoustics and a brilliant roster of bands

CAFÉ OTO
18-22 Ashwin Street, E8 3DL
Dalston's café/creative haven doubles up as an evening music venue, attracting some of the best experimental acts and contemporary jazz musicians

ROUNDHOUSE
Chalk Farm Road, NW1 8EH
Tons of big-name acts, plus a programme dedicated to nurturing fresh young talent, are all housed under the famous Roundhouse roof

KOKO
1A Camden High Street, NW1 7JE
Located in an old theatre, KOKO is a Camden institution offering a mixture of live bands and club nights underneath its trademark art deco chandeliers

HOOTANANNY
95 Effra Road, Brixton, SW2 1DF
A spiritual home for London's reggae, rock and world music fans, this lively Brixton bar is bursting with atmosphere

LONDON LIVE MUSIC NEWSLETTER

→ To receive the London Gigs Newsletter from LondonTown.com send a blank email now to: **gigs@londontown.com**
PRIVACY PROMISE: We will never (and that means never) give your email address to anyone else. You mean too much to us.

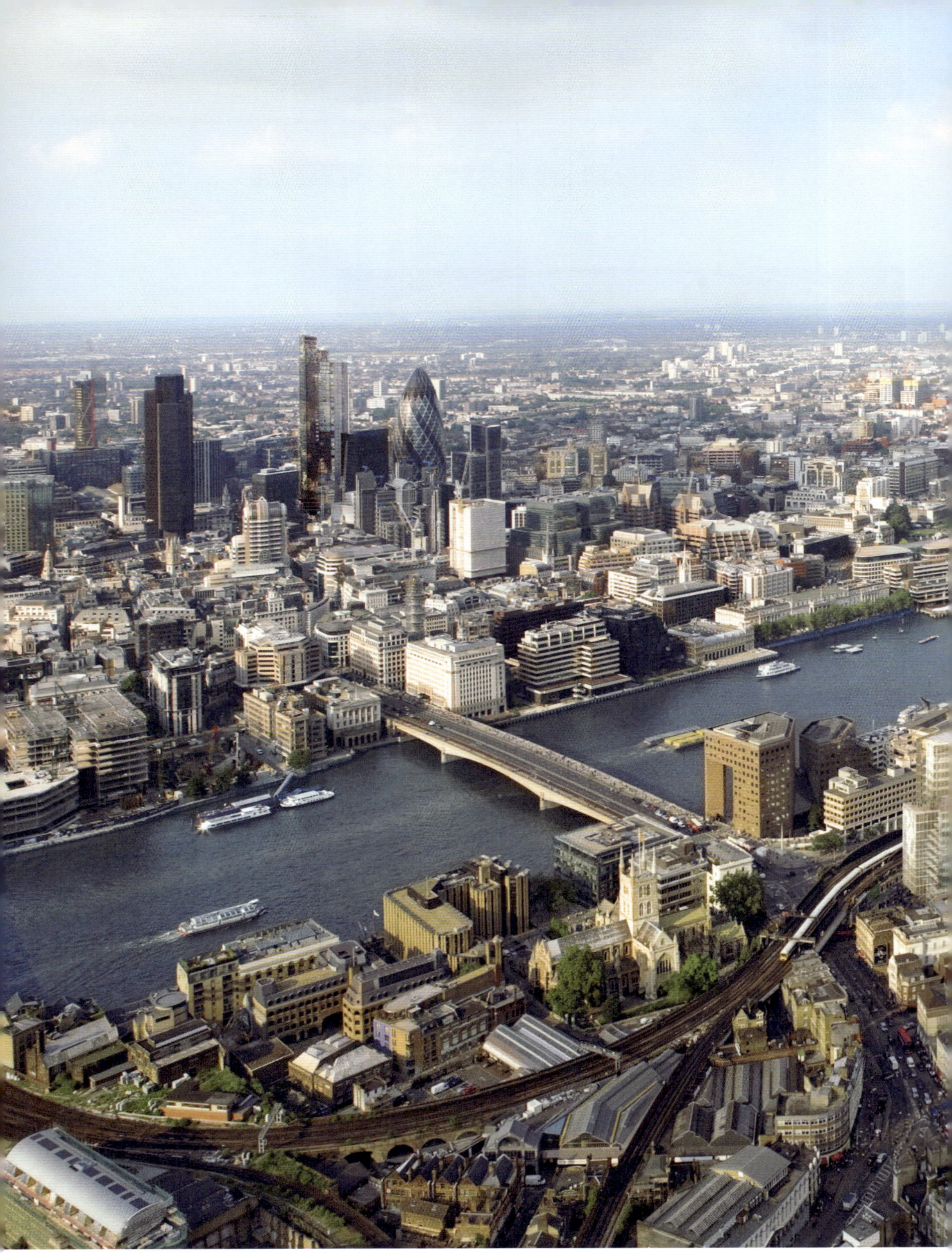

81

February welcomes Lichtenstein and Man Ray to London, plus sees the Shard's vertiginous viewing platform open…

PAGE 83

FEBRUARY

WHAT'S ON WHERE IN FEBRUARY

LondonTown.com

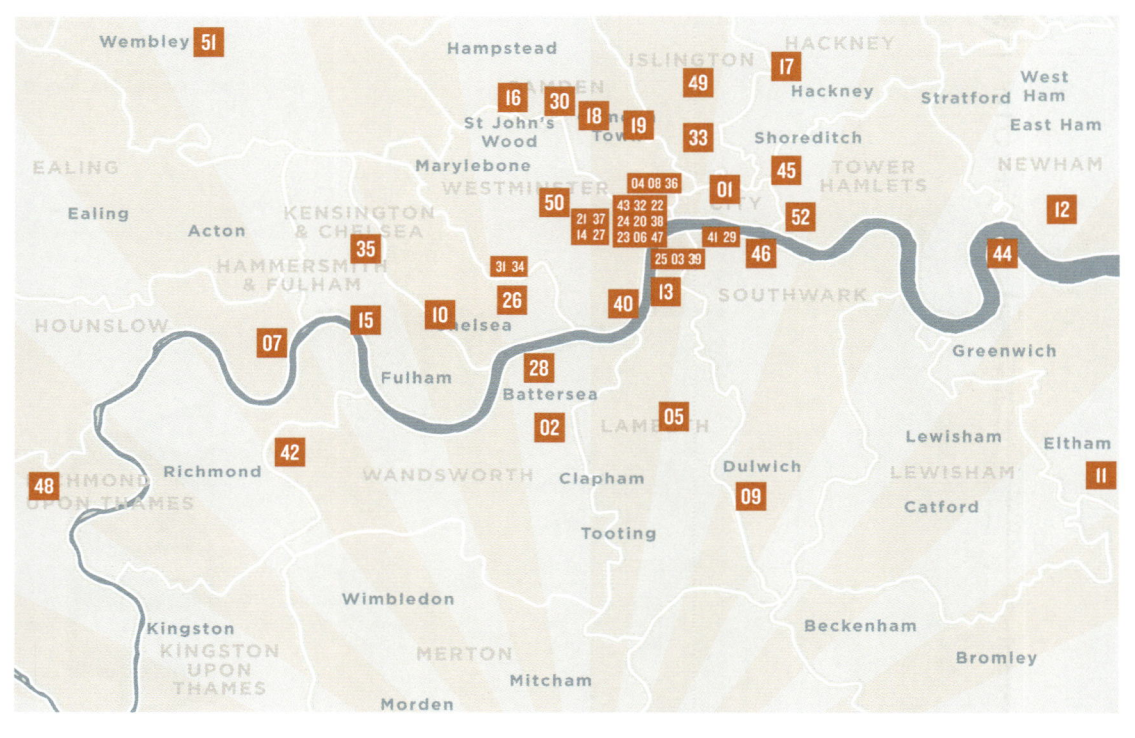

01	**Barbican Art Gallery** Pages 88 & 89
02	**Battersea Arts Centre** Page 90
03	**BFI Southbank** Pages 87 & 91
04	**British Museum** Pages 85 & 86
05	**Brixton Academy** Page 86
06	**Charing Cross Hotel** Page 83
07	**Chiswick House** Page 91
08	**Conway Hall** Page 87
09	**Dulwich Picture Gallery** Page 85
10	**Earls Court** Page 92
11	**Eltham Palace** Page 91
12	**ExCeL** Page 93
13	**Garden Museum** Page 88
14	**Gielgud Theatre** Page 90
15	**Hammersmith Apollo** Pages 85, 88 & 91
16	**Hampstead Theatre** Page 94
17	**Holy Trinity** Page 84
18	**Jazz Cafe** Page 88
19	**Kings Place** Page 85
20	**London Coliseum (ENO)** Pages 84, 90 & 94
21	**London Palladium** Page 84
22	**Transport Museum** Page 93
23	**National Gallery** Page 94
24	**National Portrait Gallery** Page 89
25	**Olivier Theatre** Page 93
26	**Natural History Museum** Page 86
27	**Prince of Wales Theatre** Page 94
28	**Pump House Gallery** Page 84
29	**Rose Theatre** Page 86
30	**Roundhouse** Page 86
31	**Royal Albert Hall** Pages 73 & 92
32	**Royal Opera House** Page 94
33	**Sadler's Wells Theatre** Page 88
34	**Serpentine Gallery** Page 88
35	**Shepherd's Bush Empire** Page 94
36	**John Soane's Museum** Page 90
37	**Soho Theatre** Page 91
38	**Somerset House** Pages 88 & 89
39	**Southbank Centre** Pages 84, 86, 87 & 88
40	**Tate Britain** Page 87
41	**Tate Modern** Pages 84 & 92
42	**Bank of England Sports Ctr** Page 94
43	**The Donmar Warehouse** Page 90
44	**The O2 Arena** Pages 87, 91 & 92
45	**The Old Truman Brewery** Page 87
46	**The Shard** Page 83
47	**Trafalgar Studios** Page 87
48	**Twickenham Stadium** Pages 84 & 93
49	**Union Chapel** Page 92
50	**Wallace Collection** Page 85
51	**Wembley Stadium** Pages 84 & 94
52	**Wilton's Music Hall** Page 91

PREVIOUS PAGE: THE SHARD, COURTESY OF SELLAR PROPERTY GROUP

LondonTown.com **FEBRUARY 2013** 83

PICK

"WHY, BRAD DARLING, THIS PAINTING IS A MASTERPIECE! MY, SOON YOU'LL HAVE ALL OF NEW YORK CLAMORING FOR YOUR WORK!"

ART

Lichtenstein: A Retrospective

21st February – 27th May 2013
Tate Modern, 25 Sumner Street, London SE1 9TG

PAGE 92

From 1st
The View From The Shard
The Shard, 96 Tooley Street, London SE1 2TH
London will look like a city in miniature from the viewing platform at the top of the tallest building in Western Europe when it opens in February 2013. Lifts will transport members of the public from ground level to The View From The Shard, on floors 68 to 72 of The Shard which at 309.6 metres (1,015 foot) tall towers over London Bridge and its neighbouring buildings offering exceptional views of the city stretching for 40 miles. That means - on a really good day - you can see the sea at Southend in Essex to the east and as far as Reading in Berkshire to the west.

From 1st
Faulty Towers: The Dining Experience
1st February – 21st December 2013
Charing Cross Hotel, The Strand, London WC2N 5HX
Combine a meal out, the bright lights of the West End and a bellyful of laughs with this globetrotting production featuring the neurotic Basil Fawlty, his domineering wife Sybil and the ever-suffering but equally hopeless Manuel. Described by The Daily Telegraph as a "two-hour eat, drink and laugh sensation", 'Faulty Towers: The Dining Experience' returns for matinee and evening performances at the fictional Torquay Suite Theatre following a successful two-month run before Christmas. Inspired by the much loved TV programme starring John Cleese, the show starts as the audience waits to be seated and then hurtles along for three courses of fully immersive, highly interactive,

FEBRUARY 2013

site-specific comedy theatre. All conversations welcome at the dinner table - just don't mention the Germans...

2nd
RBS 6 Nations: England v Scotland
Saturday 2nd February 2013
Twickenham Stadium, London TW1 1DZ
Stuart Lancaster's England get their Six Nations campaign underway with this home clash against Scotland at Twickenham - and morale will be sky high after the December rout of New Zealand. In the corresponding fixture last year, England edged the Scots 13-6 at Murrayfield to win the coveted Calcutta Cup. It was the first of five successive defeats for Scotland, who ended the tournament rock-bottom on zero points. England missed out on the Grand Slam after losing to the all-conquering Welsh side at home with Wales going on to become the fourth side in as many years to win the Six Nations trophy.

From 2nd
La Traviata
2nd February – 3rd March 2013
English National Opera, London Coliseum, London WC2
Giuseppe Verdi's bicentenary is celebrated with Peter Konwitschny's new production of 'La Traviata', one of the most consistently loved of all operas. Verdi's music takes audiences to the heart of Violetta's world as the famed courtesan gives up her wild lifestyle for love and makes the ultimate sacrifice. There's romance, there's tragedy, there's even a scandal - the portrayal of a 'fallen' heroine would have been shocking to the première audiences of 1853. Both old hands and opera virgins will be reaching for the tissues at the ENO's Coliseum as Violetta sings her way to the heart-rending end of Act 3, while the celebrated Brindisi drinking song of Act 1 never fails to bring the roof down. Sung in Italian with English subtitles.

From 2nd
A Chorus Line
2nd February – 13th July 2013
London Palladium, Soho, London W1F 7TF
After much speculation, it was finally announced that Michael Bennett's Tony Award-winning production of 'A Chorus Line' is coming to London's West End this year. Returning to London for the first time since 1975, the show will take to the stage at Andrew Lloyd Webber's world-famous London Palladium. Directed by Bob Avian, it takes a behind-the-scenes look at auditions for a new Broadway musical and, through a spectacular blend of song, dance and drama, tells the stories of the auditionees and what has moulded them into the aspiring dancers they are today. The West End production will be a tribute to late composer Marvin Hamlisch, who wrote the music, and who passed away in August 2012.

3rd
Grimaldi Clowns' Church Service
Sunday 3rd February 2013
Holy Trinity Church, Beechwood Rd, London E8
London's most peculiar church service takes place on the first Sunday of February each year as hordes of clowns congregate at Dalston's Holy Trinity Church. Now in its 67th year, the annual Clowns' Church Service remembers the great Georgian gagster Joey Grimaldi, the inventor of the modern clown, who died in 1837. Around 60 clowns, harlequins, jesters and pierrots of all shapes and sizes assemble in a colourful mass of big feet, rubber noses, curly wigs, whoopee cushions and painted faces to pay their respects to Grimaldi and to light a candle for contemporary clowns who have died over the last 12 months. The service is followed by a clown show for children in the church hall.

4th
Chris Addison: The Time is Now, Again
Monday 4th February 2013
Queen Elizabeth Hall, Southbank Centre, London SE1
If you missed it the first time around, Chris Addison brings his twice extended, critically acclaimed tour to Queen Elizabeth Hall for one night only. The 41-year-old star of 'The Thick of It' and 'Mock the Week' has perfected his sharp brand of observational middle class comedy to a tee and pulls no punches as he wades through a wide subject matter ranging from the Royal Family to the desirability of tattoos. Vociferous, cerebral, topical and often sparklingly original, Addison's show asks how our prejudices and views affect the way we look at the world, and is brimming with amusing anecdotes. Best enjoyed with a glass of wine, not beer.

6th
International Friendly: England v Brazil
Wednesday 6th February 2013
Wembley Stadium, Wembley, London HA9 0WS
The Football Association's 150th anniversary celebrations kick off with this mouth-watering midweek friendly clash between England and Samba stars Brazil at Wembley. England have not beaten Brazil in eight meetings since 1990, when a Gary Lineker goal was enough to give the home side a 1-0 win at Wembley. The last time the two sides faced each other at the spiritual home of English football, in 2007, a Diego header in injury time salvaged a draw for Brazil after John Terry had put Steve McClaren's side ahead after the break. Six years on, and it's all change as Roy Hodgson's new-look side continue to find their feet ahead of the 2014 World Cup.

6th - 14th
Kraftwerk
6th – 14th February 2013
Tate Modern, London SE1
German electronic music group Kraftwerk play eight live performances in Tate Modern's imposing Turbine Hall between 6th and 14th February 2013. Each performance will feature one of their albums in full, and will be performed in order of release, starting with arguably their most famous album, 'Autobahn' (1974). The £60 tickets for the series of gigs by the influential Kraut rock pioneers, their first London dates since 2004, are expected to sell out fast.

From 6th
Participatory Photography Commission: BBKP
6th February – 7th April 2013
Pump House Gallery, Battersea Park, SW11 4NJ
Art collective BBKP are the creative juices behind the an-

Kraftwerk take the Autobahn all the way to Tate Modern → 84

nual Participatory Photography Commission at Battersea Park's Pump House Gallery. Renowned for their wry humour and oddball projects, the quartet - Nathan Birchenough, Nicolas Brown, Craig Kao and Savvas Papasavva - were present at the gallery throughout the autumn to encourage the public to get involved with their artistic experiments. The resulting new works form the centrepiece of this two-month exhibition at the small yet intriguing gallery, which is housed in the former Victorian water tower that once supplied water to the lakes and cascades of Battersea Park.

From 6th
Murillo at the Wallace Collection: Painting of the Spanish Golden Age
6th February – 12th May 2013
Wallace Collection, Hertford House, London W1U 3BN
With its free display, 'Murillo at the Wallace Collection: Painting of the Spanish Golden Age', the Wallace Collection ties in with the exhibition, 'Murillo and Justino de Neve: the Art of Friendship' being held at the Dulwich Picture Gallery at the same time. The Wallace Collection display reunites paintings by the seventeenth-century Spanish artist Bartolome Esteban Murillo, a key protagonist of Spain's Golden Age, not seen together in over two hundred years. The collection put together by the 4th Marquess of Hertford includes eight Murillo masterpieces as well as several works by his workshop and associates, Francisco Meneses Osorio and Juan Simon Gutierrez.

From 6th
Murillo and Justino de Neve: the Art of Friendship
6th February – 19th May 2013
Dulwich Picture Gallery, London SE21 7AD
'Murillo and Justino de Neve: the Art of Friendship' brings together a group of late works by the seventeenth-century Spanish artist, Bartolome Esteban Murillo, in an exhibition shown at the Museo del Prado in Spain in the summer of 2012. From February 2013 London's Dulwich Picture Gallery, which holds an important group of works by the artist, hosts the exhibition which examines the artist's friendship with Justino de Neve, canon of Seville cathedral. The display of seventeen paintings, five of which have been specially restored for this event, ranges from religious and devotional works to portraits, allegories and the only known miniature attributed to Murillo. It is the first major exhibition on the artist since 1982 and runs at the same time as the free display, 'Murillo at the Wallace Collection'.

7th
Paloma Faith
Thursday 7th February 2013
Hammersmith Apollo, London W6 9QH
Since coming onto the scene in 2009, former burlesque dancer Paloma Faith has made a name for herself in both music and acting, as well as being known for her quirky personality and unique sense of fashion. Her debut album 'Do You Want the Truth or Something Beautiful?' was certified Platinum and produced five singles. After announcing in 2010 that she had started to shape her second album, it wasn't until 2012 that Faith released 'Fall to Grace'. With the album's initial single 'Picking up the Pieces' being her highest charting song to date and the album reaching number two in the UK albums chart – second to Gary Barlow's Diamond Jubilee record – the soul singer is now coming to London for one night to perform tracks from this latest album.

7th - 9th
Britten at 100
7th – 9th February 2013
Kings Place, 90 York Way, King's Cross, London N1
To mark the centenary of the birth of one of the finest and most influential composers of the past century, Kings Place is holding a three-day 'Britten at 100' special. Three concerts on consecutive evenings see Benjamin Britten's own works placed alongside music by some of the composers he most admired (such as Schubert and Fauré), his contemporaries (including Finzi, Tippett and Grace Williams) and a handful of present-day British composers who carry on the song-writing tradition with which Britten is so closely associated.

From 7th
In Search of Classical Greece: Dodwell & Pomardi
7th February – 28th April 2013
British Museum, Bloomsbury, London WC1B
A selection of 70 highly finished watercolours, sepia drawings and pen-and-ink sketches by the classical scholar Edward Dodwell and the Italian artist Simone Pomardi are grouped together in an exhibition that examines the motivation for travel as well as its cultural consequences. Inspired by the journey the pair made through Greece in 1805-6 during the age of Enlightenment, these intriguing travel drawings range from beautiful rural landscapes to the striking antiquities of Greece, and include five vast panoramas measuring up to four metres in length.

From 7th
Ice Age Art: Arrival of the Modern Mind
7th February – 26th May 2013
British Museum, Bloomsbury, London WC1B

Landscapes are savoured at the Tate's 'Looking at the View' → 87

Discover masterpieces from the last Ice Age drawn from across Europe in an exhibition 40,000 years in the making. Some of the world's oldest known sculptures, drawings and portraits - including a bison sculpted from mammoth ivory about 20,000 years ago - will be presented alongside modern works by Henry Moore, Mondrain and Matisse, to explore art as a form of communication and worldly understanding.

From 7th
Playing Cards 1: Spades
7th February – 2nd March 2013
Roundhouse, Camden Town, London NW1 8EH
A deck of cards and the games played with them can represent rules, skills, symbols, mythologies, signs and characters. Using this concept, international director and theatrical master Robert Lepage has created a quartet of plays that focus on the meaning behind the cards; each play is shaped around one suit and what that suit represents. 'Playing Cards 1: Spades' will be the first in the series and, exploring the theme of war, will juxtapose two desert cities at the time when the United States invaded Iraq. Based in Las Vegas, a caricature of the Western World and its values, it delves into a world of illusions, escape and private battles with a heavy dose of sex, drugs, violence and politics. Bets are on as to how the story will play out in Sin City.

From 7th
The Vortex
7th February – 9th March 2013
Rose Theatre, Kingston KT1
Described as "un peu shocking", 'The Vortex' was Noel Coward's first great success. Its dark plot focuses on drug abuse among the upper classes and a tense relationship between Florence, a highly-sexed mother and Nicky, her cocaine addicted son. With Nicky struggling to deal with his cocaine addiction, the resentment he has for his mother and her extramarital affairs is on the verge of an explosive climax. Coward wrote the character of Nicky with the intention of casting himself and, like Coward, he was homosexual – a fact that had to be subtly conveyed due to attitudes at the time. Brimming with controversial topics, the notoriety attracted large audiences and encouraged the move from a small theatre to a West End stage. Now, after numerous successful revivals, 'The Vortex' is set to take the stage once more.

8th
An Evening with Rolf Harris
Friday 8th February 2013
Royal Festival Hall, Southbank Centre, London SE1 8XX
Multitalented Aussie Rolf Harris has been adopted by Britain and become legendary for his artwork, TV presenting, and silly songs, not forgetting his love of the wobble board. This February, the eccentric entertainer will be stopping by the Southbank Centre's Royal Festival Hall for an evening of unique family entertainment. The audience can expect plenty of sing-along opportunities as he'll be performing classic songs 'Stairway to Heaven', 'Tie me Kangaroo Down, Sport', 'Sun Arise' and 'Two Little Boys'. He'll also paint live on stage, be joined by a seven-piece band and play possibly one of the biggest didgeridoos in the world. Strewth, now that's what you call a variety show!

8th
Two Door Cinema Club
Friday 8th February 2013
O2 Academy Brixton, London SW9 9SL
Saturday 27th April 2013
Alexandra Palace, London N22 7AY
Northern Irish indie band Two Door Cinema Club revelled in success after their 2010 debut album 'Tourist History' achieved platinum status in the UK and Ireland, was awarded the Choice Music Prize and sold over 1 million copies worldwide. With the pressure on to record that 'difficult second album', they released the highly anticipated 'Beacon' in 2012. Recorded in LA with acclaimed producer Jacknife Lee, this album showcased a more mature sound for the collective and, as described by the BBC, "takes all the greatest components of its predecessor, armour-plates them and gears itself up for a much more immediate impact". With two successful albums under their belt, the trio are coming to London twice in 2013 to perform for their ever-growing fan base.

From 8th
Extinction: Not the End of the World?
8th February – 8th September 2013
Natural History Museum, Cromwell Road, London SW7 5BD
Ninety nine per cent of all species to have graced the Earth are extinct - does that mean we are fighting a lost cause? Asking whether extinction could mean a new start as opposed to an irrevocable end, this highly topical exhibition uses the latest scientific findings to study the real risks to today's endangered species. Will the tiger and orang-utan soon go down the same road as the dodo and the dinosaurs - or can we solve the enigma of extinction? Using astonishing images, real specimens and interactive installations, this Natural History Museum exhibition brings to life lost species such as giant deer, eerie insects and super-sized birds, and tells the remarkable stories of the survivors of mass extinctions.

FEBRUARY 2013

9th
Doctor Who: Tomb of the Cybermen
Saturday 9th February
BFI Southbank, Belvedere Road, London SE1 8XT
The BFI continues its monthly countdown to November's 50th anniversary of 'Doctor Who' with a Saturday afternoon screening of the episode that most ardent fans cite as the true zenith of the Cybermen - the Doctor's most persistent enemies alongside the infamous Daleks. 'Tomb of the Cybermen' (1967) gave fans of the BBC science fiction drama the first taste of the show's second Doctor, Patrick Troughton, who reinvented the character as a mischievous and witty soul with unexpected steel beneath his apparent bonhomie. 'Who' addicts will delight in this episode, which delivers some key strands within the over-arching mythology of the show. The screening will be followed by a guest Q&A.

9th
Plan B
Saturday 9th February 2013
The O2 Arena, Greenwich, London SE10 0DX
Plan B, aka Ben Drew, has become much more than an east London rapper. Aside from his third studio album 'Ill Manors', Drew has released a film of the same name, starred in the remake of 'The Sweeney', supported his community at the BBC Radio 1 Academy and set up a charity. His debut album 'Who Needs Actions When You Got Words' was critically acclaimed but it took his 2010 work 'The Defamation of Strickland Banks' to boost his status. With soulful songs 'She Said' and 'Stay Too Long', the multiplatform star attracted a greater audience and gained top ten hits. However, his latest album offers political, heavy hip hop aimed at educating listeners on "David Cameron's broken Britain". Described by NME as "a one-man iPod shuffle", Plan B will stop by the O2 to perform his broad spectrum of musical offerings.

Sunday 10th February
CHINESE NEW YEAR (YEAR OF THE SNAKE)

From 9th
Macbeth
9th February – 27th April 2013
Trafalgar Studios, 14 Whitehall, London SW1A
Scottish actor James McAvoy, who has enjoyed big screen success with 'Atonement' and 'The Last King of Scotland', stars as Macbeth in a new season at Trafalgar Studios, called 'Trafalgar Transformed', directed by Jamie Lloyd. The pair previously worked together when McAvoy last appeared on stage in 2009 in (the Olivier Award nominated) 'Three Days of Rain' at the Apollo Theatre which Lloyd also directed. For this production to be played in the round Shakespeare's darkest tale is played out in a dystopian Scotland brutalised by war. Design for all the plays in Jamie Lloyd's season is by Soutra Gilmour, who won the 2012 Evening Standard Award for Best Design.

10th
The School of Life Sunday Sermon: Hussein Chalayan on Fitting In
Sunday 10th February 2013
Conway Hall, Bloomsbury, London WC1R 4RL
By his own account, British designer Hussein Chalayan has never quite fitted in and he has chosen this as the topic of his School of Life Sunday Sermon on 10th February 2013. In this sermon at Conway Hall the designer who famously made fashion from furniture will share the projects that he calls his 'life studies' which he makes to help him understand the world. One such study investigates how national events transform our personal identities while another changes disgust to an appreciation of beauty. A revealing insight into the mind of one of the brightest creative talents working in the fashion industry today.

11th – 24th
Imagine
11th – 24th February 2013
Southbank Centre, London SE1
Take the kids to the Southbank Centre during the February half-term and treat them to 'Imagine', the annual children's literature festival that pulls words off the page. With two weeks' worth of activities, there's a huge amount of literary events to choose from including readings, storytelling, beat-boxing and poetry. Children will even get a chance to run the festival during Kids Takeover, have the opportunity to feature in performances and play alongside the Philharmonic Orchestra. As well as appearances by leading children's writers, there's comedy, poetry hopscotch, music and magic for all ages.

Tuesday 12th February
PANCAKE DAY (SHROVE TUESDAY)

12th
The Great Spitalfields Pancake Race
Tuesday 12th February 2013
The Old Truman Brewery, Brick Lane, London E1 6QL
In celebration of Shrove Tuesday, pancake enthusiasts leg it down Dray Walk at The Old Truman Brewery near Brick Lane with a frying pan and a slab of batter for a relay race with a difference. All participants need for The Great Spitalfields Pancake Race is a team of four spirited souls dressed up in wacky costumes and armed with frying pans (pancakes are provided). Heats kick off at 12.30pm, followed by the finals and ceremonial prize-giving (for the winners: an engraved frying pan, of course). There's an award for the best-dressed team too so pick a theme and don the appropriate garb - however ridiculous. It's a really eccentric occasion made only better by the wandering clowns and string band playing in the background.

From 12th
Looking at the View
12th February – 2nd June 2013
Tate Britain, Millbank, London SW1P 4RG
Through its free exhibition, 'Looking at the View', Tate Britain invites visitors to contemplate landscapes and the way artists have influenced our view of them over the last 300 years. Featuring works by artists as diverse as Tacita Dean, Julian Opie and JMW Turner, this exhibition, which consists entirely of works from the Tate collection, presents works from a sizeable stretch of time, drawing surprising parallels in the way artists have looked at the scenery that surrounds them.

FEBRUARY 2013

13th
Little Mix
Wednesday 13th February 2013
Hammersmith Apollo, London W6 9QH
Since becoming the first ever group to win the 'X Factor', Little Mix have been working hard to ensure they don't fall under the same umbrella as many previous unsuccessful winners. They seem to have succeeded with this mission so far as their winner's single 'Cannonball' topped both the UK and Irish singles charts, followed by another number one with 'Wings'. Their third single 'DNA' offered a more mature sound, showing potential growth for the foursome. With their debut studio album released in November 2012, they are now embarking on their first UK tour.

13th
Brendan Cole Licence to Thrill
Wednesday 13th February 2013
Barbican Hall, Silk Street, London EC2Y 8DS
After his successful 2012 tour, 'Live and Unjudged', Brendan Cole is back to thrill audiences once more but this time he has a licence to do so. Known to be one of the most charismatic 'Strictly Come Dancing' professionals, 'Licence to Thrill' is set to be another dazzling show from the television star. With six world-class dancers and a 14 piece orchestra in tow, plus the musical direction of Barry Robinson, this 2013 tour will incorporate classical ballroom with feisty Latin dance and will offer music from across the ages to create an enjoyable show for everyone. A message to all daughters out there: lock up your mothers - Brendan's back.

13th
Salif Keita
Wednesday 13th February 2013
Royal Festival Hall, Southbank Centre, London SE1
This year, the London Jazz Festival invites Salif Keita, known as 'The Golden Voice of Africa', to perform. Returning to London for the first time in two years, Keita is at the forefront of modern Malian music and has a distinctive musical voice. He combines rock, funk and jazz with West African griot traditions. The Evening Standard describes his voice as "grainy and searing tenor, its power continues to drop jaws, cause goosebumps".

From 13th
Rosemarie Trockel: A Cosmos
13th February – 7th April 2013
Serpentine Gallery, Kensington Gardens, London W2 3XA
"An elegant, mind-expanding refusal of the standard big-game retrospective," is how The New York Times described 'Rosemarie Trockel: A Cosmos' when it appeared in the city's New Musuem in October 2012. London's Serpentine Gallery now hosts the exhibition, juxtaposing works created in the last 30 years by this mid-career German artist with a range of objects and artworks created by others with whom she feels an affinity. Knitted paintings, often considered her signature style, are displayed along with ceramics and zoological specimens as well as artefacts by fellow artists including outsider artists like Morton Bartlett, James Castle and Judith Scott.

Thursday 14th February
VALENTINE'S DAY

From 14th
Floriculture – Flowers, Love and Money
14th February – 28th April 2013
Garden Museum, Lambeth, London SE1 7LB
Beginning in 17th century Covent Garden, 'Floriculture' tells the story of the cut flower trade from those early times, when the central London square was a flourishing fruit and veg market, to today's blooming £64 billion industry. The perfect way to spend Valentine's Day, the exhibition at the Garden Museum includes paintings which reveal the art of floristry and their symbolism. Not just pretty to look at, flowers play an important role in marriage, funerals and are often loaded with meaning. Examples used to illustrate changing tastes in floral design include the 1961 marriage of the Duke and Duchess of Kent and Shane Connolly's floral creations for the Duke and Duchess of Cambridge's wedding in 2012.

14th - 16th
Jocelyn Brown
14th – 16th February 2013
Jazz Café, Camden Town, London NW1 7PG
North Carolina acid jazz soul vocalist Jocelyn Brown returns to her favourite London haunt, Camden's Jazz Café, to head up three nights of dance classics. Best known for her '80s anthem 'Somebody Else's Guy', Brown is one of the world's most popular session queens and has collaborated with the diverse and contrasting talents of Luther Vandross, Better Midler, John Lennon, Quincy Jones and Michael Jackson (to name but a handful). The soul diva's immortal line "I've got the power" was sampled from her 1986 dance hit 'Love's Gonna Get You' by the electronic group Snap! for their worldwide hit, 'The Power', making Brown's powerful voice instantly recognisable to clubbers the world over.

14th – 25th
Tanztheater Wuppertal Pina Bausch
14th – 25th February 2013
Sadler's Wells, Rosebery Avenue, London EC1R 4TN
The late Pina Bausch's Tanztheater Wuppertal returns to London after last summer's critically acclaimed World Cities 2012 season with two rarely performed works from the German choreographer's outstanding canon. 'Two Cigarettes in the Dark' (1985) looks at the monotony of life, while 'Vollmond' ('Full Moon') from 2006 sees Bausch create a completely unique world for the dancers on stage. If you missed these "inspired and committed dancers" (The Telegraph) last summer then this is an ideal opportunity to put things straight.

From 14th
Becoming Picasso – Paris 1902
14th February – 26th May 2013
The Courtauld Gallery, Strand, London WC2R 1LA
The year is 1901 and the 19-year-old Pablo Picasso is a relatively unknown artist outside Barcelona. All this was about to change as this Courtauld Gallery exhibition reveals. Focusing on the remarkable story of the Spanish artist's breakthrough year, 'Becoming Picasso' gives visitors an opportunity to experience the artist's very first masterpieces which mark the beginnings of his famous 'blue period'. On

24th June 1901, Picasso's first major exhibition opened at a gallery on rue Lafitte in Paris, marking the beginning of Picasso's meteoric rise to becoming one of the greatest artists of the 20th century.

From 14th
Dancing around Duchamp
14th February – 9th June 2013
Barbican Centre, Silk Street, London EC2Y 8DS
This spring, the Barbican celebrates Marcel Duchamp with 'Dancing Around Duchamp', a major cross-arts season which explores the work of the famous French Surrealist artist, his precursors, collaborators and those he influenced in music, dance, theatre, film and art. At the heart of the season is an exhibition at the Barbican Art Gallery, 'The Bride and the Bachelors: Duchamp with Cage, Cunningham, Rauschenberg and Johns', which features over 90 artworks, including some of Duchamp's readymades and iconic works by Jasper Johns and Robert Rauschenberg.

From 14th
The Bride and the Bachelors: Duchamp with Cage, Cunningham, Rauschenberg and Johns
14th February – 9th June 2013
Barbican Art Gallery, Barbican Centre, EC2Y 8DS
'The Bride and the Bachelors: Duchamp with Cage, Cunningham, Rauschenberg and Johns' explores Marcel Duchamp's American legacy by tracing his relationship to four great modern artists – composer John Cage, dancer and choreographer Merce Cunningham, and visual artists Robert Rauschenberg and Jasper Johns.

15th - 19th
London Fashion Week
15th - 19th February 2013
Somerset House, Strand, London WC2R 1LA
Alongside New York, Paris and Milan, London Fashion Week is one of the world's leading designer fashion showcases and it takes place in February and September at Somerset House. It features 200 of the industry's most creative designers and businesses, in the UK and internationally, with catwalk shows, exhibitions and award ceremonies. The Exhibition at Somerset House houses over 100 ready-to-wear and accessory designers and includes The Estethica stand which highlights the best in fair-trade and ethical design, while the NEWGEN stand (sponsored by TOPSHOP) picks out the finest up-and-coming designers. Over 5,000 visitors - fashion buyers, press and photographers - are expected and while events tend to be invite-only you can still spot top models and designers around town while it's on.

From 15th
Medea
15th February - 16th March 2013
English National Opera, London Coliseum, London WC2N 4ES
This winter, the English National Opera will be showing the first-ever UK staging of Charpentier's dramatic full-scale opera 'Medea'. One of the most disturbing of all the Greek myths, 'Medea' delves into the troubling world of a barbarian sorceress who has been banished, betrayed and besieged. Feeling lost and desperate, she uses witchcraft to poison her faithless lover

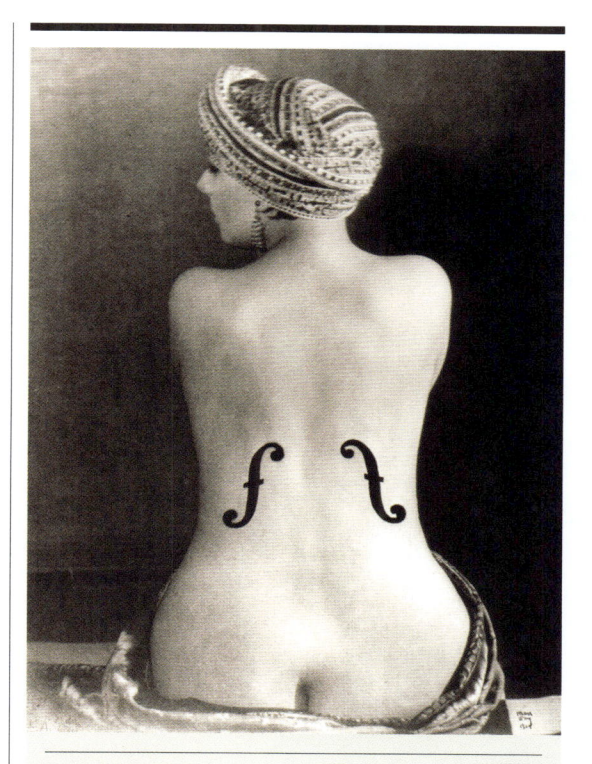

From 7th
Man Ray Portraits **PICK**
7th February - 27th May 2013
National Portrait Gallery, St Martin's Place, London WC2H 0HE

OVER 150 VINTAGE Man Ray prints, including works never before exhibited in the UK such as studies of the American impersonator, high wire performer, and trapeze artist Barbette, Catherine Deneuve and Ava Gardner, can be seen at the National Portrait Gallery. 'Man Ray Portraits', the first major museum retrospective of the artist's photographic portraits, highlights the role Man Ray played in the Dada and Surrealist movements and examines his friendship with French artist Marcel Duchamp. Featuring photographs taken between 1916 and 1968, the exhibition shows Man Ray's revolutionary photographic techniques such as solarisation - evident in his own 'Self-Portrait with Camera' - and experiments with colour in the 1950s. The exhibition reveals the wide variety of his subjects - famous stars, friends, lovers and contemporaries - and closes with his 1968 portrait of film star Catherine Deneuve in which she wears the twisted gold 'lampshade' earrings the artist designed.

and anyone he holds dear to him – even those who are also dear to her. Opera director David McVicar returns to the ENO to take on this thrilling piece that, with its daring and psychological complexity, was incomparable to anything of its day.

From 15th
Trelawny of the Wells
15th February – 13th April 2013
Donmar Warehouse, Covent Garden, London WC2H 9LX
BAFTA award-winning film director Joe Wright, known for 'Pride and Prejudice', 'Atonement' and 'Hanna', will make his theatre directing debut this year as he directs Arthur Wing Pinero's 'Trelawny of the Wells' at the Donmar Warehouse. Josie Rourke, the Donmar's artistic director as of 2012, describes the play as Pinero's love letter to theatre and says: "it feels very apt that having grown up in a theatre, Joe should be directing 'Trelawny of the Wells'". The play is an 1898 comic piece that tells the story of Rosie Trelawny, the shining star of a theatre company who gives it all up for love. However, once married, she is left with the stark reality of a life away from her beloved melodramas and recapturing her vivacious persona becomes something of a challenge. Wright will take on 'A Season in the Congo' at the Young Vic later in the year.

From 15th
Master Drawings Uncovered: Piranesi's Paestum Drawings
15th February - 18th May 2013
Sir John Soane's Museum. Holborn, London WC2A 3PA
For the first time, Giovanni Battista Piranesi's fifteen highly resolved preparatory drawings of the three great Doric temples in Paestum, Sicily, are shown together in a focused exhibition which considers them as great works of art in their own right, as well as examining how they revolutionised architects' and artists' understanding of early Greek Classical architecture.

From 15th
The Audience
15th February – 15th June 2013
Gielgud Theatre, Shaftesbury Avenue, London W1D 6AR
Following her Oscar-winning performance in the 2006 film 'The Queen', Helen Mirren is to reprise her role as Queen Elizabeth II in Peter Morgan's play 'The Audience'. For the past sixty years, private meetings have taken place between the Queen and each of her Prime Ministers. With an unspoken rule of utmost privacy, they provide a time for confession, advice and consoling – sometimes resulting in heated discussions and maybe even some teasing. The contract of this silence is about to be broken for the world première of this drama as the content, tone and the Queen's thoughts are to be imagined for a series of pivotal meetings - ranging from Churchill to Cameron.

16th & 17th
Alan Davies: Life is Pain
16th & 17th February 2013
Hammersmith Apollo, London W6 9QH
After a decade away from stand-up, the comedian, writer and actor Alan "Jonathan Creek" Davies continues his UK tour with these back-to-back weekend performances. Straightforward, autobiographical and brimming with "blokey-fogeyish

From 14th
The Paper Cinema's Odyssey
PICK
14th February – 9th March 2013
Battersea Arts Centre, Lavender Hill, London SW11 5TN

HOMER'S CLASSIC IS VIVIDLY brought to life by The Paper Cinema with beautiful illustrations, live animation and masterful puppetry in "a delicately executed piece which is bound to delight" (The Telegraph). Follow the trials and tribulations of Odysseus during his seemingly interminable journey back to Ithaca following the Fall of Troy, through high seas and supernatural obstacles. Featuring the Cyclops, the Sirens and the slaying of the suitors, this is a truly original portrayal of these timeless gods, men and monsters, set against a wonderful live score.

bewilderment" and "droll close-to-home riffs about parenting" (The Telegraph), this nostalgic show sees the affable Davies plough through a raft of contrasting topics including the language employed by fellow Essex men, the imminent end of the world, social media, the London riots and his upbringing, touching even on the effect of his mother's death when he was six. During his absence from stand-up, Davies became a regular on the Stephen Fry-fronted 'QI'. Reviews of 'Life is Pain' seem to be pretty unanimous: the dunce from 'QI' is in fact QE - Quite Entertaining.

16th - 18th
BFI Future Film Festival
Saturday 16th – Monday 18th February 2013
BFI Southbank, Belvedere Road, London SE1 8XT
The 6th BFI Future Film Festival returns to the Southbank this February with a long-weekend of workshops, masterclasses, networking opportunities, screenings and Q&As designed to inspire and develop your film knowledge and skills. Saturday focuses on fiction, Sunday is all about animation, and Monday delves into documentary. Young film makers are invited to submit their short films in each category for consideration at the Future Film Awards - the best will be shown in front of a panel of industry experts who will offer their advice and feedback. For anyone looking for a leg-up into the film business - whether you're advanced or a beginner, a writer or a producer - this a must. "With our film industry crumbling before us, this festival is more important than ever," says the Guardian.

From 16th
Camellia Festival
16th February - 17th March 2013
Chiswick House & Gardens, Burlington Lane, London W4 2RP
The Chiswick House camellia collection, housed in the spectacular conservatory, is a national treasure and the oldest in the Western world. Guests can also celebrate these beautiful blooms in the newly restored nineteenth-century Italian Garden, which was replanted in 2012. Known as the queen of the winter flowers, the camellias at Chiswick bring a burst of glorious colour to season - from pinks to reds, whites to stripes.

17th
Great Hall Sleepover
Sunday 17th February 2013
Eltham Palace, Court Yard, Eltham, London SE9 5QE
Families are invited to spend an exclusive evening in the magical Eltham Palace, the childhood home of Henry VIII. Enjoy a hearty supper, a late-night tour and a storytelling session before bed, and then a full English breakfast the next morning. Steeped in history, Eltham Palace is one of London's secret wonders, a captivating blend of 1930s art deco decadence and classic medievalism.

From 19th
Bitch Boxer
19th February – 9th March 2013
Soho Theatre, London W1D
Fighting fit from sell-out shows at the Edinburgh Fringe, this one-woman show certainly packs a punch. Chloe from Leytonstone, East London, is like most 21-year-olds: she loves singing along to Rihanna, winding her dad up and cherry Sambuca.

Comedian Alan Davies performs on the Hammersmith Apollo stage → 90

Oh, and she's a boxer. Down the road in Stratford, women step into the Olympic ring for the very first time. With London 2012 acting as an inspiring backdrop, Chloe trains for the fight of her life - just when she's left winded by two life-changing events. "Sweat-slick and tough, yet sweet and gifted with terrific timing," says The Times.

20th
The BRIT Awards 2013
Wednesday 20th February 2013
The O2 Arena, Greenwich, London SE10 0DX
The biggest music event in Britain's calendar, The Brit Awards are returning to the O2 Arena for 2013. As usual, the ceremony will feature a host of the year's most successful artists all hoping to get their hands on a Brit Award trophy. Last year saw Ed Sheeran pick up two awards: Best British Male Solo Artist and Best British Breakthrough Act. Further winners included One Direction for Best British Single, Coldplay for Best British Group and Emeli Sandé was the Critics' Choice. Chart sensation Adele also claimed two awards: Best British Female Solo Artist and the prestigious Mastercard British Album of the Year. This year, Mercury Prize winners Alt-J are tipped to feature heavily on the nominations list after their debut album 'An Awesome Wave' has reaped success. However, it's questionable whether James Corden will be invited back after cutting short Adele's speech last year.

From 20th
The Great Gatsby
20th February - 30th March 2013
Wilton's Music Hall, Graces Alley, London E1 8JB
To celebrate the re-opening of the wonderful Wilton's Music Hall following much-needed repairs, Peter Joucla's Tour de Force Theatre production of 'The Great Gatsby' returns to the enchanting East End venue for a six-week run. The immersive adaptation of F. Scott Fitzgerald's great American novel was a sell-out success during its first run last May, described by The Telegraph as "an unashamed nostalgia party for a world we never knew". The audience are encouraged to dapperly dress in their '20s best for this night of jazz, glitz and Prohibition-themed decadence at the Wilton's speakeasy. There's

no better way to get geared up for the belated summer release of Baz Luhrmann's 'The Great Gatsby' movie.

From 21st
Banff Mountain Film Festival World Tour
21st February - 1st March 2013
Union Chapel, Compton Terrace, London N1 2UN
The most breath-taking and inspiring collection of adventure, action sports and environmental films returns to the UK for a fourth adrenaline-packed year in 2013. The bumper week-long London leg of the annual Banff Mountain Film Festival World Tour comes to the Union Chapel for seven nights of mind-blowing films, shorts and documentaries paying homage to the great outdoors. Showcasing remote landscapes, vibrant cultures and extreme sports such as hiking, biking, skiing, climbing, paragliding and kayaking, the festival draws on some of the world's best film makers and accomplished outdoor heroes to celebrate the wonders of the natural world through film. Suitable for dreamers, adventurers, environmentalists and anyone prone to wanderlust, this festival basks in exhilarating imagery from some of Earth's last great wild places.

From 21st
Carmen
21st February - 3rd March 2013
Royal Albert Hall, Kensington Gore, London SW7 2AP
The very essence of Spain and the secrets of Seville are served up in this acclaimed in-the-round production of the world's most popular opera. Raymond Gubbay's take on Bizet's 'Carmen' returns to the Royal Opera House for a limited run of 14 performances, telling the story of a captivating love triangle between Carmen, a fiery gypsy girl, her hapless prison guard Don Jose, and the glamorous bullfighter Escamillo. Brimming with passion and jealousy, Bizet's rich and timeless score contains some of opera's finest and most recognisable arias - including 'Song of the Toreador' and 'Flower Song'.

From 21st
Lichtenstein: A Retrospective
21st February – 27th May 2013
Tate Modern, 25 Sumner Street, London SE1 9TG
In 1964, Lichtenstein became the first American to exhibit at the Tate Gallery, and in 2013 the American pop artist reunites with the London gallery for the first time since it staged his 1968 show when people were queuing round the block. Tate Modern reveals the pop artist's hidden side in 'Lichtenstein: A Retrospective', "the biggest Lichtenstein show since the Guggenheim staged a retrospective in 1993 when the artist was still alive" (The Guardian). Alongside instantly recognisable pop art images - including 'Whaam!', one of the most popular artworks at Tate Modern - are less well-known early abstract expressionist paintings which may take visitors by surprise. The scale of his work is sometimes overwhelming; take the enormous 1988 version of the 'Laocoon'; or 'Interior With Waterlilies', painted in 1991, which is a vast painting at more than four metres wide and approximately three metres high. Queues are likely, once again, for this Lichtenstein exhibition which shows works from private collections, some of which usually hang in collectors' bedrooms, alongside monumental paintings, comic book art, sculptures, abstracts and close to 50 works on paper taken from 70 boxes of works to which curators have never before been given access.

22nd
Bloc Party
Friday 22nd February 2013
Earls Court Exhibition Centre, London SW5 9TA
Following a two-year hiatus to focus on side projects, British band Bloc Party reformed in 2011 and finally released their fourth studio album in 2012. Aptly named 'Four' the album title represents both the placement in the band's discography and the four year gap since their last album. Established as an indie rock band, the four-piece experimented with R&B styles for their second album 'A Weekend in the City' while also incorporating electronic music. Having always indulged in guitar rock, they have stepped away from electro and moved back to their original roots for this fourth album. The BBC states: "Bloc Party sounds full of potential where just four years ago they sounded depleted. Indeed, Four may be 2012's most exciting guitar album." The London-based four-piece will stop by Earls Court this February to perform new tracks as well as from their previous records.

From 22nd
One Direction
22nd – 24th February 2013
The O2 Arena, Greenwich, London SE10 0DX
1st – 5th April 2013
The O2 Arena, Greenwich, London SE10 0DX
They've conquered the UK, cracked America and invaded girls' hearts worldwide, now British boy band sensation One Direction are coming to London for eight nights as part of their 2013 world tour. With the 'X Factor' a distant memory, the five heartthrobs have exploded ontp the music scene since their infectious 2011 debut single 'What Makes You Beautiful'. They've also won several awards and released two studio albums – the first of which was the UK's fastest selling debut album of 2011. Whether it's for their musical talents or simply their boyish good looks, it can't be denied that the five-piece are currently winning the popularity contest in the music industry.

23rd
Example
Saturday 23rd February 2013
Earls Court Exhibition Centre, London SW5 9TA
Electronic hip hop, house and grime at Earls Court Exhibition Centre from the chart-topping London-based rapper and singer-songwriter Example, born Elliot John Gleave, in support of his newest album 'The Evolution Of Man'. After a quiet period surrounding his first record, Example shot to fame in 2009 with his second album 'Won't Go Quietly' and has since released 2011's 'Playing In The Shadows', which went to number one in the UK album charts. He has collaborated with artists such as Professor Green, Wretch 32, Giggs and Calvin Harris. Expect the crowd to be wowed by popular tracks such as 'Kickstarts', 'Changed The Way You Kiss Me' and 'Stay Awake'.

23rd
RBS Six Nations: England v France

Saturday 23rd February 2013
Twickenham Stadium, London TW1 1DZ
England take on France in the third round of the Six Nations tournament at Twickenham with the visitors eager to avenge last season's narrow 24-22 defeat at the Stade de France last year. This will be Stuart Lancaster's England's second home game of the tournament and it comes two weeks after what will no doubt be a fiercely contested game against Ireland at the Aviva Stadium in Dublin. Games between England and France are traditionally ferocious affairs - and the French will be looking to bounce back after finishing last year's tournament in lowly fourth place.

23rd & 24th
London Super Comic Convention

23rd & 24th February 2013
ExCeL Centre, London E16
The London Super Comic Convention brings the US comic convention to London. A vast number of US and UK creators will be attending, turning the ExCeL Centre into heaven for any lover of comic books. With fanatics invited to dress up as their favourite characters, and the chance to get comics signed by artists and writers, this two-day event will be bringing comic books to life. Creators attending the event include living legend Neal Adams, responsible for rescuing Batman from the campy TV show of the '60s and transforming him into his present persona; J Scott Campbell, known for his exceptional work on the cover of 'The Amazing Spider-man'; and Simone Bianchi, who found his big break in 2004 when he worked on Grant Morrison's 'Seven Soldiers: Shining Knight'. There will, of course, also be the chance to purchase new comic books to enhance any collection.

From 23rd
This House

23rd February – 8th April 2013
National Theatre: Olivier Theatre, South Bank, London SE1 8XZ
The country faces an economic crisis and there's a hung parliament. If you are a sick MP you're still expected to make your way through the lobby to cast your vote. There are fist fights a-plenty in the Westminster bars, and the parties' whips bend the rules, but not all the time. Following a successful run at National Theatre's Cottesloe, James Graham's 1974-set drama now transfers to the Olivier.

24th
Capital One Cup Final

Sunday 24th February 2013
Wembley Stadium, Wembley, London HA9 0WS
Although often treated by top Premier League managers as a chance to give their reserve team a run-out, the Football League Cup has been won by the likes of powerhouses Manchester United, Chelsea, Tottenham Hotspur and Liverpool in recent years - underlining Sir Alex Ferguson's claim that the trophy is still "a pot worth winning". Liverpool are the current holders, having beaten Championship side Cardiff City on penalties last year after a thrilling 2-2 draw

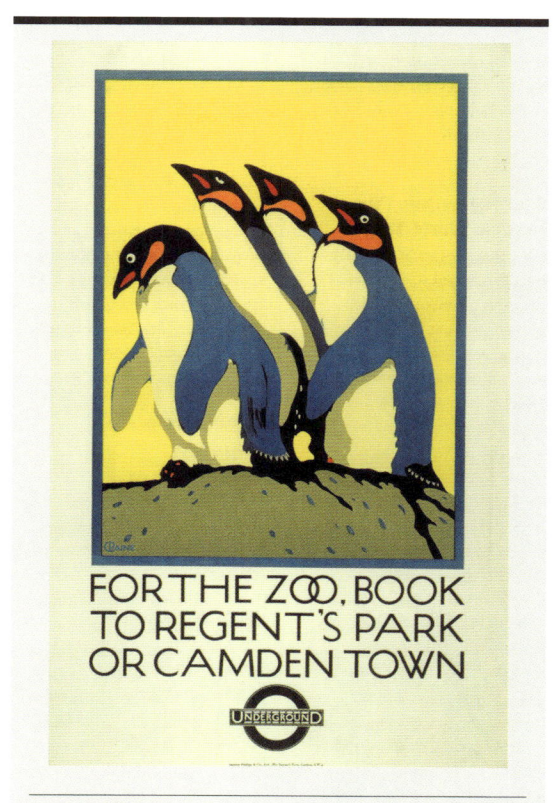

From 15th
Poster Art 150: London Underground's Greatest Designs

PICK

From 15th February 2013
London Transport Museum, Covent Garden, London WC2E 7BB

THE LONDON UNDERGROUND is not only famous for its ingenious concept and operation but also the artwork that features on the tunnel walls. Since its first graphic poster commission in 1908, the London Underground has commissioned countless outstanding poster designs and has become a pioneering patron of poster art. 'Poster Art 150' will exhibit 150 of the best designs – chosen by an independent panel – that have been displayed over the years. Well-known pieces such as Man Ray's 'Keeps London Going' pair will feature alongside lesser-known works. Visitors will be asked to vote for their favourite piece and the most popular one will be revealed at the end of the exhibition.

FEBRUARY 2013

at Wembley Stadium. Funnily enough, it was a missed penalty by Cardiff's Anthony Gerrard - cousin of Liverpool captain Steven - which sealed the win for the Reds in front of 89,000 fans.

24th
The February Fools Charity Cricket Match
Sunday 24th February 2013
Bank of England Sports Ground, Priory Lane, London SW15 5JQ
A cricket match between celebrities in February does admittedly sound rather foolish - but it's all in the name of charity and good fun. Played at the resplendent Bank of England Sports Ground in Roehampton, this annual clash usually sees TV darling Chris Tarrant and Sky Sports presenter Max Rushden captain the 'Luvvies XI' and 'Broadcasting XI' with guaranteed play - whatever the weather. Last year, the actor Jim Carter (Mr Carson from 'Downton Abbey') and John Altman ("Nasty" Nick Cotton from 'Eastenders') bowled the first balls while journalist Damian Radcliffe was man of the match for the winning Broadcasters team. It's free admission for spectators with auctions, a raffle, book stall and children's lucky dip raising money for the Twickenham-based David Adams Leukaemia Appeal Fund in aid of The Royal Marsden Hospital.

From 25th
The Book of Mormon
25th February – 5th May 2013
Prince of Wales Theatre, Coventry Street, London W1D 6AS
The creators of 'Southpark', Trey Parker and Matt Stone, have turned their satirical eyes to the cheery world of musicals. With a helping hand from the composer of 'Avenue Q' (Robert Lopez), this ballsy comedy has collected an obscene amount of Tony Awards and lands in London at the Prince of Wales Theatre in 2013. The plot follows two fresh-faced young Mormon Missionaries who find themselves posted to Uganda; humour ensues as they follow their faith through some fairly trying situations.

From 25th
The Barber of Seville
25th February - 17th March 2013
English National Opera, London Coliseum, London WC2N 4ES
It's been two centuries since 'The Barber of Seville' made its première - and Rossini's masterful prequel to 'The Marriage of Figaro' remains as popular as ever. This 25th anniversary ENO revival sees conductor Jaime Martin making his operatic debut, adding a suitably Hispanic touch to the tuneful, ironic and uproariously funny production. Bronze-voiced baritone Benedict Nelson stars as Figaro, charismatic soprano Lucy Crowe returns as the feisty Rosina, while Andrew Shore reprises his "classic portrayal" (The Guardian) of Doctor Bartolo.

27th & 28th
Jake Bugg
27th & 28th February
O2 Shepherd's Bush Empire, London W12 8TT
At the tender age of 18, Jake Bugg has already firmly established himself as an incredibly talented songwriter. Having rejected his friends' proposition to audition for 'Britain's Got Talent', stating "it doesn't seem genuine", Bugg proceeded to go it alone and his determination paid off. The singer/songwriter's self-titled debut album draws on his experiences from growing up in Clifton, the UK's former largest housing estate, and offers some poignant and wistful lyrics. NME gave the album an impressive review and described it as "...rife with uncommon wit, insight and melody". Having already found fans in Noel Gallagher and The Stone Roses, Bugg's future is looking bright. The young star will be stopping by Shepherd's Bush Empire this February to showcase his talents.

From 27th
Ballet Black
27th February – 6th March 2013
Royal Opera House, Covent Garden, London WC2E 9DD
When envisioning a ballet dancer most people will likely draw upon an image of a girl who resembles an English Rose. Stepping away from this stereotype, Ballet Black is a professional ballet company dedicated to international dancers of black and Asian descent. Aiming to bring ballet to a more culturally diverse audience, their intention is to see an increase in the number of black and Asian dancers in mainstream ballet companies and, as a result, reduce the need for their company.

From 27th
Barocci: Brilliance and Grace
27th February – 19th May 2013
National Gallery, Trafalgar Square, London WC2N 5DN
Sixteen spectacular altarpieces by Italian artist Federico Barocci go on display at the National Gallery in an impressive collection of works by the late 16th century artist who once created a fresco for the Casino of Pope Pius IV at the Vatican. 'Barocci: Brilliance and Grace' gives visitors a chance to see his important altarpieces, devotional paintings and portraits alongside preparatory drawings and oil sketches. Barocci, a native of Urbino in central Italy, is best represented by his Marchigian altarpieces, including the famous 'Entombment' from Senigallia on Italy's Adriatic coast and 'Last Supper' from Urbino Cathedral, which are being shown outside Italy for the first time.

From 28th
Longing
28th February – 13th April 2013
Hampstead Theatre, Eton Avenue, Hampstead, London NW3 3EU
Hoping for a pleasant break from his life in Moscow, Kolia visits his oldest friends on their estate in the country. Upon arrival, the comedy of provincial life unravels around him and he is caught amongst false expectations, missed opportunities and unspoken passions. Adapted by the award-winning novelist William Boyd ('Any Human Heart', 'Restless', 'Waiting for Sunrise'), the play is based on two short stories by Anton Chekhov and delves into the familiar and unfamiliar aspects of nineteenth century Russian life. 'Longing' will see Nina Raine return to the Hampstead Theatre following her critically acclaimed transfer to the West End for 'Jumpy' and 'Tribes'. The cast for 'Longing' will be announced in January 2013.

LONDON'S BEST

SPORTS VENUES

Sports fans are spoiled for choice in London, home to the two biggest stadia in the UK as well as numerous other sporting arenas

LORD'S CRICKET GROUND
St John's Wood, NW8
Spiritual home of English cricket with a stunning Victorian pavilion and futuristic media centre

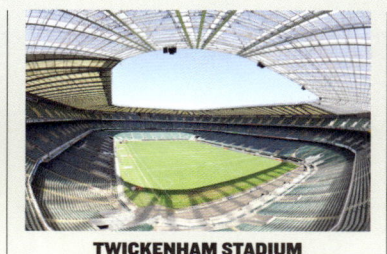

TWICKENHAM STADIUM
Twickenham, TW1
Atmospheric home of English rugby is London's second biggest stadium with a capacity of 82,000

KEMPTON PARK
Sunbury-on-Thames, TW16
Closest racecourse to London hosts the prestigious King George VI Chase meet on Boxing Day

ALL ENGLAND CLUB
Wimbledon, SW19
Home of the world-famous Wimbledon championships, the only Grand Slam tournament played on grass

HYDE PARK
London, W2
Iconic Royal Park hosts annual triathlon, running and half marathon events throughout the summer

EMIRATES STADIUM
Islington, N5
State-of-the-art (but trophyless) 60,365 capacity stadium has been Arsenal FC's home since opening in 2006

THE OVAL
Kennington, SE11
Home of Surrey County Cricket Club, the Oval traditionally hosts the fifth and final Test in Ashes series

WEMBLEY STADIUM
Wembley, HA9
The refurbished 90,000-capacity home of the England national football team is renowned for its 134-metre-high arch

THE O2 ARENA
Greenwich, SE10
Indoor arena hosts ATP World Tour tennis finals, NBA basketball, gymnastics, polo and darts

LONDON SPORT NEWSLETTER

→ To receive the London Sport Newsletter from LondonTown.com send a blank email now to: **sport@londontown.com**
PRIVACY PROMISE: We will never (and that means never) give your email address to anyone else. You mean too much to us.

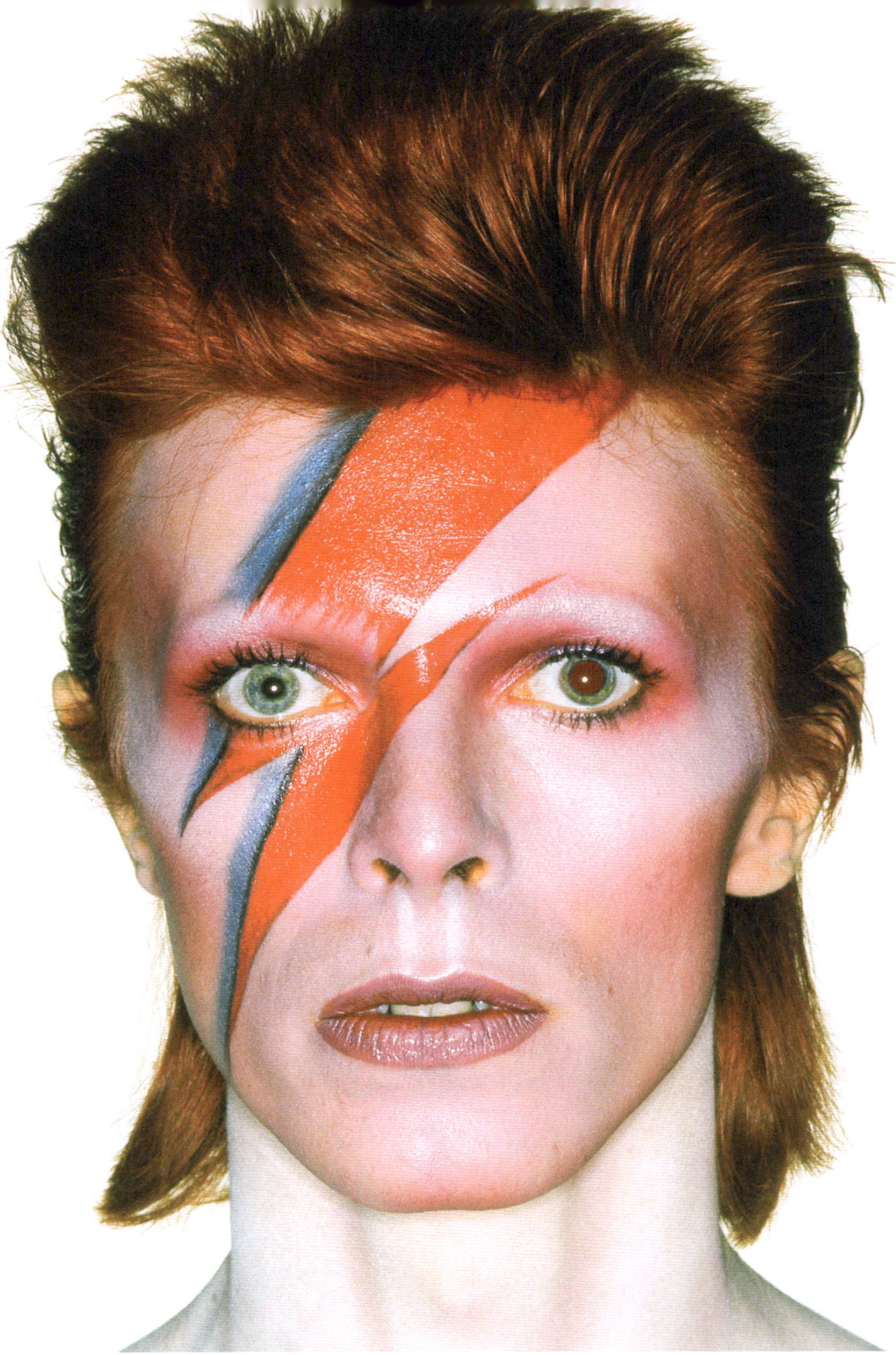

97

Two of London's most famous sons - Michael Caine and David Bowie - stand tall as the capital comes alive with the sounds of spring...

PAGE 108

MARCH

WHAT'S ON WHERE IN MARCH

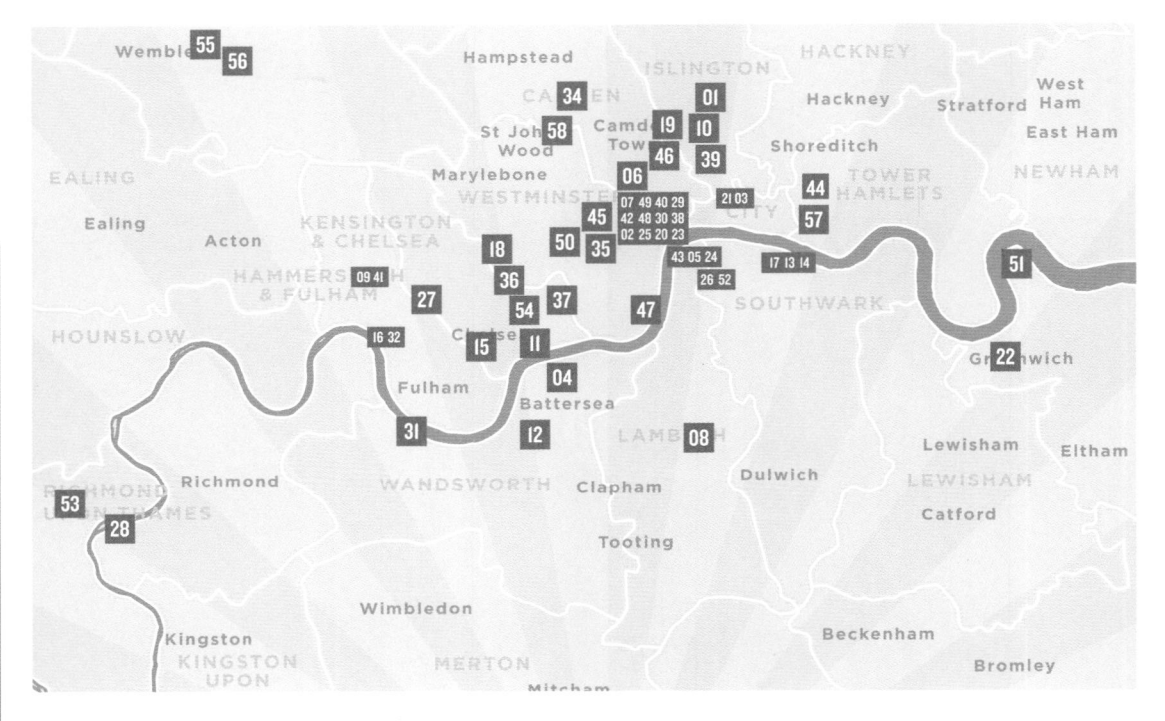

01	**Almeida Theatre** Page 107
02	**Apollo Theatre** Page 100
03	**Barbican Centre** Pages 73 & 100
04	**Battersea Park** Page 101
05	**BFI Southbank** Page 104
06	**Bloomsbury Theatre** Page 108
07	**British Museum** Page 109
08	**Brixton Academy** Pages 99 & 101
09	**Bush Theatre** Page 106
10	**Business Design Centre** Page 106
11	**Chelsea Old Town Hall** Page 104
12	**Clapham Grand** Page 109
13	**Design Museum** Page 109
14	**Fashion Museum** Page 107
15	**Finborough Theatre** Page 100
16	**Hammersmith Apollo** Page 109
17	**HMS Belfast** Page 104
18	**Kensington Gardens** Page 102
19	**Kings Place** Page 102
20	**London Coliseum (ENO)** Page 106
21	**Museum of London** Page 106
22	**National Maritime Msm** Page 110
23	**National Portrait Gallery** Page 102
24	**Lyttelton Theatre** Page 110
25	**Noel Coward Theatre** Page 103
26	**Old Vic Theatre** Page 102
27	**Olympia** Page 102
28	**Orleans House Gallery** Page 102
29	**Peacock Theatre** Page 109
30	**Phoenix Theatre** Page 104
31	**Putney Bridge** Pages 107 & 110
32	**Riverside Studios** Page 101
34	**Roundhouse** Page 104
35	**Royal Academy of Arts** Page 105
36	**Royal Albert Hall** Page 102
37	**Royal Court Theatre** Page 101
38	**Royal Opera House** Pages 100, 102, 104 & 110
39	**Sadler's Wells Theatre** Page 104
40	**Shaftesbury Theatre** Page 101
41	**Shepherd's Bush Empire** Pages 101 & 103
42	**Soho Theatre** Pages 103 & 108
43	**Southbank Centre** Pages 100 & 107
44	**Spitalfields City Farm** Page 110
45	**St George's Church** Page 103
46	**St Pancras Int Station** Page 99
47	**Tate Britain** Page 104
48	**The Borderline** Page 108
49	**The Cartoon Museum** Page 103
50	**The Grosvenor Chapel** Page 107
51	**The O2 Arena** Pages 103 & 107
52	**The Young Vic** Page 101
53	**Twickenham Stadium** Page 103
54	**V&A Museum** Pages 105 & 108
55	**Wembley Arena** Page 103
56	**Wembley Stadium** Page 108
57	**Whitechapel Gallery** Page 106
58	**ZSL London Zoo** Page 110

MARCH 2013

PICK

DANCE

Alice's Adventures in Wonderland

15th March - 13th April 2013
Royal Opera House, Covent Garden, London WC2E 9DD

PAGE 104

1st
Kaiser Chiefs
Friday 1st March 2013
O2 Academy Brixton, London SW9 9SL
Following a two-year break from the limelight, the Kaiser Chiefs returned in 2011 with their controversial fourth studio album. 'The Future is Medieval' was released in a unique way that allowed fans to buy it directly from their website, selecting 10 of 20 available songs to create their own personalised compilation. Followed by a later official release that featured one previously unavailable track, it begged the question: was this an ingenious marketing move or a scam to tell twice the number of albums? Having promoted the album - renamed 'Start The Revolution Without Me' for the US market - with a North American tour, they're now coming to the Brixton O2 Academy as part of their UK tour.

1st – 20th
Tiger Tracks
1st - 20th March 2013 & Gala Dinner 21st March 2013
St Pancras International, St Pancras Renaissance Hotel, London NW1 2QP
'Tiger Tracks' invites visitors to St Pancras International to walk on the wild side with tiger themed activities including music, entertainment and a photographic exhibition for three weeks in March 2013. Many of the bars, restaurants and shops at the magnificent train station are taking part so look out for promotions and events that all the family can take part in. The event culminates with an exclusive champagne reception and black tie Gala dinner at the 5 star St Pancras Renaissance

Hotel on 21st March - attended in previous by celebrities like Joanna Lumley, Jimmy Choo and Alistair McGowan. Your £300 ticket gets you a champagne reception, dinner and entertainment as well as the satisfaction that you're supporting a good cause - saving the wild tiger. And if you want to see these big cats in real life, visit the new 'Tiger Territory' which opens at London Zoo this month.

From 1st
The Curious Incident of the Dog in the Night-Time
From Friday 1st March 2013
Apollo Theatre, Shaftesbury Avenue, London W1D 7EZ
Following a successful run at the National Theatre last summer, Simon Stephens' adaptation of 'The Curious Incident of the Dog in the Night-Time' is transferring to the Apollo Theatre. Marianne Elliott directs this adaptation of the mystery murder novel, which is written from the perspective of a 15-year-old boy with an autistic spectrum condition, working with a cast that includes Niamh Cusack, Luke Treadaway, Sophie Duval and Matthew Barker. Rising star Treadaway reprises the title role having appeared on film as the star of David Mackenzie's 'You Instead' and in Joe Cornish's 'Attack the Block', and on stage in 'War Horse' and 'Saint Joan', alongside Anne-Marie Duff.

From 2nd
Wonder: Art and Science on the Brain
2nd March – 8th April
Barbican Centre, Silk Street, London EC2Y 8DS
'Wonder' brings together two of London's great cultural institutions, the Barbican and the Wellcome Trust, for the first time. Exploring what happens when art and neuroscience collide, the month-long event features special lectures by mathematician Marcus du Sautoy and outspoken comedienne Ruby Wax, a film season exploring mental health and a Barbican Weekender on Brain Waves which includes creative events for all ages. What happens when art and science combine? We get a rich season of events – including dance, theatre, music and art – that explore, and are inspired by our most intriguing organ, the human brain.

From 2nd
Tosca
2nd March – 20th July 2013
Royal Opera House, Covent Garden, London WC2E 9DD
It is doubtful that Jonathan Kent's 'Tosca' will ever escape the shadow of its predecessor at the Royal Opera House - Franco Zeffirelli's 1964 'Tosca' had a 40-year run, which is a pretty good innings - but this production has qualities of its own. Puccini's opera overflows with dangerous passions and the darkest crimes as it twists and turns its way through a doomed love affair and, in Kent's production, an "unnerving" (The Guardian) atmosphere pervades the action. Paul Brown's designs, sitting between a backdrop of politically-charged Rome and sinister imagery, play a part in this but it is Puccini's theatrical score, capturing Tosca's light-hearted first entrance and then plunging to the dark depths of Scarpia's evil, that releases the tension.

3rd – 19th
Laburnum Grove
3rd – 19th March 2013
Finborough Theatre, West Brompton, London SW10
Laburnum Grove is a quiet residential address in one of the newer north London suburbs. Living there is George Radfern, an upstanding respectable citizen and householder who takes pleasure from simple things. However, when his greedy in-laws and daughter's obnoxious boyfriend try to leech money from him, he makes a surprising confession. Written by J.B. Priestley, this comedy delves into the greed and dishonesty that lurks within suburban England. Directed by Oscar Toeman, it is the first London revival of the play in nearly 40 years.

4th – 10th
Women of the World Festival
4th – 10th March 2013
Southbank Centre, London SE1 8XX
Celebrating International Women's Day (8th March), the Women of the World Festival (WOW) is back in full force at the Southbank Centre for 2013. The festival was originally launched by Jude Kelly, Southbank Centre's Artistic Director, following the criticisms she received as a woman new to the role: "I created WOW to celebrate the formidable power of women to make change happen, to remind us of our history and to encourage men to add their support as we aim to achieve a fairer world." The one-week festival boasts a programme of gigs, films, comedy, classical music, theatre and poetry. There will also be the chance to join in debates, networking, mentoring, workshops and free participatory events.

5th
Radio Rewrite
Tuesday 5th March 2013
Royal Festival Hall, Southbank Centre, SE1 8XX

The Affordable Art Fair returns to Battersea this spring → 101

The world première of a new work by master of minimalism Steve Reich is unveiled at the Royal Festival Hall this spring. Inspired by Reich's meeting with Radiohead guitarist Jonny Greenwood, 'Radio Rewrite' re-imagines two Radiohead songs – 'Everything in its Right Place' from 'Kid A' and 'Jigsaw Falling into Place' from 'In Rainbows'. These songs provide some of the harmonic and melodic material for the new piece, which is performed by the London Sinfonietta and is scored for flute, clarinet, two vibraphones, two pianos, a string quartet and an electric bass. Around 20 minutes in length, 'Radio Rewrite' is performed alongside Reich's legendary 'Clapping Music' and other pieces from the American composer's repertoire.

5th – 7th
Of Monsters and Men
5th – 7th March 2013
O2 Shepherd's Bush Empire, London W12 8TT
With their simple guitar plucks and soothing harmonies, Icelandic six-piece Of Monsters and Men are gradually captivating audiences around the world. Comparable to British band Mumford and Sons, the sextet sing in English and have reaped success from their debut album 'My Head is an Animal', which topped the charts of their homeland and numerous European countries back in 2011, and reached number six in the US Billboard chart a few months later. Finally released in Britain in 2012, it then peaked at number three in the UK album chart. Their musical offerings may not be ground-breaking but they are undeniably alluring.

From 6th
Burn the Floor
6th March – 1st September 2013
Shaftesbury Theatre, London WC2H 8DP
Guest starring Robin Windsor and Kristina Rihanoff from 'Strictly Come Dancing', and featuring a strong cast of 16 world class dancers, 'Burn the Floor' is ballroom at its best. Choreographed by Australian Jason Gilkison (former World Champion Latin and Ballroom dancer), the globe-trotting show features a spectacular blend of Latin and Ballroom routines. Originally put together for Elton John's 50th birthday celebrations in 1997, 'Burn the Floor' had its first public showing two years later. All aspects of ballroom dancing are here from the elegance of the Viennese waltz to the sensual samba, from the tango to the mambo, the cha-cha to the Charleston.

7th - 10th
Affordable Art Fair Battersea
7th - 10th March 2013
Battersea Park, Albert Bridge Road, London SW11 4NJ
Over 100 galleries exhibit a huge array of affordable contemporary art in Battersea Park for the biannual Affordable Art Fair which has become a well-loved institution on London's art scene. Showing original paintings, prints, sculpture and photography all under one roof, it's an event that strips away the pretension of the art world and gives buyers a chance to pick up some really great work at fair prices, ranging from £40 to £4,000 (last year, around £4.5m exchanged hands). A fun, family day out, it's accessible to connoisseurs and the merely curious. There's a free crèche, artist-led workshops, informal talks and tours, and a specialist exhibition showcasing work by new artists.

7th - 9th
Sigur Ros
7th - 9th March 2013
Brixton Academy, 211 Stockwell Road, London SW9 9SL
Sigur Ros, the four-piece from Reykjavik, Iceland, led by singer Jonsi Birgisson, play three nights at London's Brixton Academy as part of a European tour. Renowned for their wonderfully atmospheric music, expect sweeping and classically influenced post-rock and ambient music from their back catalogue of greatest hits as well as new tracks from their latest album, 'Valtari'. The support act is Blanck Mass, the solo project of young British musician Benjamin John Power, whose music featured in the London Olympics Opening Ceremony.

From 7th
Mies Julie
7th March – 19th May 2013
Riverside Studios, Hammersmith, London W6
Internationally acclaimed director Yael Farber sets her contemporary reworking of August Strindberg's 'Miss Julie' in the remote Eastern Cape Karoo. This explosive revival focuses on one night that is intriguingly both brutal and tender as it explores sexual drama and class politics after apartheid. The play delves into the haunting and violent, the intimate and epic as the two main characters, John and Mies Julie, have a deadly battle over power, sexuality and memory.

7th – 28th
Above Me the Wide Blue Sky
7th – 28th March 2013
Young Vic, Waterloo, London SE1 8LZ
Following their previous Young Vic production 'On Ageing', performance company Fevered Sleep are back with their latest offering. 'Above Me the Wide Blue Sky' is a multi-screen installation that delves into our relationship with the ever changing world and how we are linked with nature. Staged with a sound-scape of birdsong, electronic music and a new score for string quartet, it will weave together images, movement and sound with stories of love, loss and belonging.

From 7th
George Catlin: American Indian Portraits
7th March – 23rd June 2013
National Portrait Gallery, St Martin's Place, London WC2H 0HE
For the first time in history, George Catlin's whole body of American Indian Portraits are displayed together outside America, with over 50 offerings giving great insight into the indigenous people and their ways of life. Between 1796 and 1872, Pennsylvanian-born artist Catlin is known to have made five trips to the western region of the United States in order to create what is now one of the most prominent and extensive recordings of the native people.

From 7th
Fischli/Weiss: Rock on Top of Another Rock
7th March 2013 – March 2014
Kensington Gardens, London W2 3XA
'Rock on Top of Another

MARCH 2013

Rock' is the first and only public sculpture by Swiss artists Fischli and Weiss to be commissioned in the UK. Located in Kensington Gardens, the unique sculpture is a representation of the earliest and most basic types of monument from around the world. Formed of two glacial igneous granite boulders, it shows one rock balanced precariously on top of the other and is visible from a number of viewpoints across the park. The aim was to create a piece that is initially startling but also fits both locally and historically with its surroundings.

8th March
Three Cane Whale
Friday 8th March 2013
Kings Place, 90 York Way, King's Cross, London N1
Alex Vann, Pete Judge and Paul Bradley are Three Cane Whale, a multi-instrumental acoustic trio who hail from Bristol. Their debut album, recorded live in an 18th century Bristol church, was chosen by Cerys Matthews as one of her 'Top Five modern folk albums' (Sunday Telegraph). Alex plays mandolin, bowed psaltery, music box and something called a 'zither', Pete is a dab hand on the trumpet, harmonium, lyre, glockenspiel and dulcitone, while Paul plays acoustic guitar and miniature harp. Together they create "elegant and atmospheric" music, says The Guardian.

8th & 9th
Singin' In The Rain: Live in Concert
8th & 9th March 2013
Royal Albert Hall, Kensington Gore, London SW7 2AP
One of the world's most adored musical films is given a unique cinematic makeover at the Royal Albert Hall this spring featuring a live orchestral accompaniment by the Royal Philharmonic Concert Orchestra. Celebrating the 60th anniversary of 'Singin' In The Rain', this European première of the original 1952 American musical follows in the footsteps of 'The Lord of the Rings' trilogy, 'The Matrix' and 'West Side Story', all of which have enjoyed sold-out live orchestra screenings at one of London's most magical settings. Audiences can enjoy all the classics from the original film, including 'Broadway Rhythm', 'Should I?', 'Make 'Em Laugh and', of course, the title track, 'Singin' In The Rain'. These back-to-back performances are followed later in the year by a live orchestral rendition of Disney's 'Fantasia' in October.

8th – 10th
Move It
8th – 10th March 2013
Olympia, London W14 8UX
Whether you want to be a ballerina or learn how to dance like a 'Strictly Come Dancing' star, 'Move It' has all the dances covered. In fact, there are around 250 dance classes you can take part in, covering everything from the bunny hop to hip hop. If that sounds a bit too energetic, you can always see how it's meant to be done with performances from 1,500 dancers representing groups as diverse as the English National Ballet and the Urban Strides. There's something for all levels from beginners to the serious professional, including seminars on nutrition and how to do a good audition.

From 8th
The Winslow Boy
8th March – 25th May 2013
Old Vic Theatre, The Cut, London SE1 8NB
Award-winning theatre director Lindsay Posner comes to The Old Vic to direct Terence Rattigan's 1946 play 'The Winslow Boy'. The plot is set in Edwardian England and is based on the true story of a young naval cadet whose wrongful conviction for the theft of a five-shilling postal order sparked a media storm and debate that went all the way to the House of Commons.

8th – 22nd
Written on Skin
8th – 22nd March 2013
Royal Opera House, Covent Garden, London WC2E 9DD
After a well-received première at the 2012 Festival d'Aix-en-Provence, George Benjamin's 'Written on Skin' arrives at the Royal Opera House for an eagerly anticipated run. Set in 13th-century Provence, the story follows the Protector, who invites a scribe into his home and commissions a manuscript. However, when the scribe gets too close to the Protector's wife, an unimaginably violent tale runs its course. The story of love, passion and violence is given a unique contemporary twist as it is narrated by three angels who are in the present day. Benjamin's score is "more impassioned, more sensuously beautiful and, at times, more fiercely dramatic than anything he has written before" (The Guardian).

9th
Holi Hindu Festival
Saturday 9th March 2013
Orleans House Gallery, Riverside, Twickenham TW1
Spring is on its way and the Holi Hindu festival of Colour - a vibrant and playful celebration - will be welcoming it in style. Taking place in the grounds of Orleans House Gallery, and extending to Twickenham town centre, the colours of spring will be bursting into action with promenade performers, street theatre, music and an Indian market. With the tradition being for man and nature to throw off the gloom of winter and rejoice in the colours of spring, the customary coloured powders will be on hand ready to be thrown amongst the crowds.

From 9th
Peter and Alice
9th March – 1st June 2013
Noel Coward Theatre, St Martin's Lane, London WC2N 4AU
Dame Judi Dench stars as Alice Liddell Hargreaves in 'Peter and Alice', a new play by American playwright John Logan - his first since 'Red', which went on to win six Tony Awards in 2010. The second of five plays which are part of the Michael Grandage season at the Noel Coward Theatre, 'Peter and Alice' imagines a chance meeting between Alice in Wonderland and Peter Pan who here becomes Peter Llewelyn Davies, played by Ben Whishaw. Set in the 1930s, the drama unfolds as Alice attends the opening of a Lewis Carroll exhibition, and meets Peter in a Charing Cross Road bookstore.

Sunday 10th March 2013
MOTHER'S DAY

10th & 29th & 30th
Olly Murs
Sunday 10th March 2013
Wembley Arena, London HA9 0DH

'Steadman at 77': retrospective for British cartoonist

29th & 30th March 2013
The O2 Arena, Greenwich, London SE10 0DX
Olly Murs is yet another act to have spawned from the 'X Factor' and has since journeyed on the road to success. Crediting his career to 'Right Place, Right Time', the title of his chart topping third album, Murs has established himself as a singer-songwriter, sold out arena tours and turned his hand at TV presenting. As part of his 2013 tour, Murs will be performing three times in London and, if you're lucky, he might split his trousers mid-performance again. He will also be accompanying Robbie Williams on his 'Take the Crown' tour later in the year.

10th
RBS 6 Nations: England v Italy
Sunday 10th March 2013
Twickenham Stadium, London TW1 1DZ
In last year's match against Italy at the Stadio Olimpico in Rome, England relied largely on the boot of Owen Farrell as they limped past their opponents 19-15 in true underwhelming fashion. With Stuart Lancaster now settled as England coach, this third and final home game at Twickenham should be relatively straight-forward for England as they bid to win back the Six Nations crown from Wales. The game comes a fortnight after England's home game against France and one week ahead of their final game of the tournament against the Welsh at the Millennium Stadium in Cardiff.

11th & 12th
Lianne La Havas
11th & 12th March 2013
O2 Shepherd's Bush Empire, London W12 8TT
The soulful voice of Lianne La Havas has gradually been acquiring more and more fans. From being invited to "hang out and play guitar" with Prince at his home in Minneapolis, flown to Milan by Tom Ford to perform at the launch party for his 'Noir' fragrance and graced by a surprise appearance from Stevie Wonder at one of her gigs, the London-born singer has attracted some serious attention. Now, promoting her debut album 'Is Your Love Big Enough?', the Mercury Prize-nominated artist embarks on her biggest UK headline tour to date.

From 11th
London Handel Festival
11th March – 16th April 2013
St George's Church Hanover Square, Mayfair, London W1S 1FX & various venues
The London Handel Festival has been running for 25 years, celebrating Handel's music at venues across London with an extensive six-week season of concerts, talks and walks. Venues include the delightful St George's Church in Mayfair, Handel's own parish church, where the Handel Singing Competition and dozens of intimate performances take place. This year's programme includes a performance by the winner of last year's singing competition, Ukrainian Anna Starushkevych, who became the first mezzo-soprano to win the award. Collaborations with the Royal College of Music and the London Handel Players continue in 2013 with the latter joined by special guest Francis Colpron on recorder.

12th – 30th
Dirty Great Love Story
12th – 30th March 2013
Soho Theatre, London W1D
Following rave reviews while on show at the 2012 Edinburgh Festival Fringe, 'Dirty Great Love Story' returns to the Soho Theatre for a highly anticipated three-week run. The award-winning romantic comedy tells the story of Rich and Kate, who are both eager for some romancing. After spending a drunken night together, the unlikely lovers struggle to avoid each other and become bound by an unexpected turn of events. Packed with a series of laugh-out-loud moments, the production fuses poetry and prose, asking the big question: are they really right for each other? Co-written and performed by Richard Marsh and Katie Bonna, this very human story strikes all the right chords.

From 12th
Steadman at 77
12th March – 21st July 2013
The Cartoon Museum, 35 Little Russell Street, London WC1A 2HH
British cartoonist Ralph Steadman, best known for his work with 'Fear and Loathing...' author Hunter S. Thompson has illustrated such classics as 'Alice in Wonderland', 'Treasure Island' and 'Animal Farm'. The illustrator, who starred in 'For No Good Reason', a

documentary made about his laudable life and career which premièred at the 2012 London Film Festival, is the subject of a retrospective exhibition, 'Steadman at 77', at the London Cartoon Museum in 2013.

From 12th
Tate Britain Commission: Simon Starling
12th March – 20th October 2013
Tate Britain, Millbank, London SW1P 4RG
The Turner Prize winning artist Simon Starling has been selected to create a major new project for the 2013 Tate Britain Commission. Winning the Turner Prize in 2005 with 'Shedboatshed' - in which he dismantled a wooden shed on the banks of the river Rhine, created a boat and sailed it down the river before reassembling it in a museum - Starling is tasked with creating a new piece for the Tate's Duveen Galleries which should address the heritage of the space as a sculpture gallery.

13th – 17th
Chelsea Antiques Fair
13th – 17th March 2013
Chelsea Old Town Hall, London SW3 5EE
The Chelsea Antiques Fair has been a popular annual fixture on the Kings Road since 1950, catering for all sorts of budgets – from £20 to tens of thousands of pounds. The antiques are presented against the gilded opulence of Chelsea Town Hall, with its marble columns, chandeliers and original oil paintings. The fair has a host of specialist dealers, and a quick browse will reveal 19th and early 20th century porcelain and pottery, fine gem set jewellery, oak furniture, silverware, Chinese antiquities, art deco furniture, fine maps and prints, Persian carpets and rare glassware and much, much more.

14th – 24th
BFI London Lesbian & Gay Film Festival
14th – 24th March 2013
BFI Southbank, Belvedere Road, London SE1 8XT
Showcasing the best in new queer film and video, the BFI London Lesbian & Gay Festival returns for its 27th year. The third largest film festival in the UK, the LLGFF festival sees hundreds of film makers, cast, crew and more than 250,000 visitors flock to the city. The programme boasts around 250 feature films, shorts and documentaries, as well as plenty of events and club nights.

15th
The Stranglers: Feel It Live Tour
Friday 15th March 2013
Roundhouse, Chalk Farm Road, London NW1 8EH
Britain's most successful punk rock band drop into the Roundhouse as part of an extensive UK tour. Fans feared the worse when The Stranglers' frontman Hugh Cornwall quit back in 1990, but the progressive punk outlaws refused to lie down. Having re-signed to EMI in 2004, the veteran four-piece are enjoying a renaissance halcyon era with whippersnapper 48-year-old Baz Wayne taking over singing duties for the last three studio albums alongside original members Jet Black, JJ Burnel and Dave Greenfield. Having garnered a total of 24 Top 40 hits over four decades, The Stranglers have withstood the test of time, and are taking to the stage on the back of their critically acclaimed album, 'Giants'. Support comes from the reformed alternative rock band, The Godfathers.

15th – 27th
Flamenco Festival London 10th Anniversary
15th – 27th March 2013
Sadler's Wells, Rosebery Avenue, London EC1R 4TN
Foot-stamping and skirt-swirling drama returns to Sadler's Wells for the 10th anniversary of the annual Flamenco Festival. Brimming with raw energy and hot-blooded passion, the art of flamenco will be displayed on one very colourful stage by world class dancers from across Spain. From traditional performances inspired by flamenco's gypsy roots to the contemporary artists taking the form in whole new directions, this festival is set to be more flamboyant than ever with eight magnificent productions in the main house and two special performances in the Lilian Baylis Studio.

From 15th
Alice's Adventures in Wonderland
15th March -13th April 2013
Royal Opera House, Covent Garden, London WC2E 9DD
The Royal Ballet stages a stunning version of Lewis Carroll's fantastical tale which returns to the Royal Opera House following its well received 2011 world première. Christopher Wheeldon's 'Alice's Adventures in Wonderland' combines elaborate costumes, projections and backdrops with inventive props and music by Joby Talbot. Praised for its theatrical effects, all of Carroll's famous characters through the looking glass are portrayed in incredibly inventive ways. Although the story has been tweaked, beginning with a party in Oxford held by Alice's parents, children will enjoy the engaging show and atmospheric music and will recognise the twitchy White Rabbit, a tap dancing Mad Hatter, a sinuous caterpillar and The Queen of Hearts.

16th
Once
Saturday 16th March 2013
Phoenix Theatre, Camden, London WC2H 0JP
Having taken Broadway by storm, winning eight awards at the 2012 Tony Awards including Best New Musical and Best Actor, the musical 'Once' comes to London's Phoenix. Based on the 2006 Irish musical film of the same name, it has been brilliantly adapted by Enda Walsh and retains much of the film's original Grammy nominated soundtrack written by Glen Hansard and Marketa Irglova. It tells the story of an Irish busker and a young Czech mother who connect over their shared love of music and develop an unexpected friendship which then becomes a complicated romance.

16th & 17th
75th anniversary of the launch of HMS Belfast
Saturday 16th & Sunday 17th March 2013
HMS Belfast, London SE1
Sunday 17th March 2013, St Patrick's Day, marks 75 years since HMS Belfast was first launched in 1938. Now the floating military museum located on the River Thames, between Tower Bridge and London Bridge, is a reminder of the role of the Royal Navy ships during the Second World War. During

the weekend of 16th and 17th March, there will be a series of special events and activities (free with admission) to mark this monumental occasion.

From 16th
George Bellows (1882-1925)

16th March – 9th June 2013
Royal Academy of Arts, Burlington House, London W1J 0BD

In the spring, the Royal Academy of Arts stages the first ever UK retrospective for American Realist painter George Bellows, who would probably be regarded as one of the greatest of all American artists, had he not died in 1925, aged 42. He left behind a remarkable body of work for so short a career and this exhibition includes approximately 50 paintings, 20 drawings, and 20 lithographs out of the hundreds he left behind. Visitors to the exhibition are invited to explore the principle themes of Bellows's work - urban life in New York among them, evident in his better-known boxing paintings and his images of the excavation and construction of Pennsylvania Station.

From 16th
Music Hall: Sickert and the Three Graces

16th March 2013 – 5th January 2014
Victoria & Albert Museum, South Kensington, London SW7 2RL

The Bedford Music Hall in Camden Town, famous as a haunt for the Camden Town Group of artists headed by Walter Sickert, comes under the spotlights in 'Music Hall: Sickert and the Three Graces'. This free exhibition within the Victoria & Albert Museum's Theatre and Performance Galleries explores the vibrant world of the Edwardian Music Hall through paintings by W.R. Sickert, a new play by award-winning playwright Tanika Gupta as well as playbills, programmes and music sheets from the V&A's collection.

Sunday 17th March 2013
St Patrick's Day

19th – 23rd
Rutherford and Son

19th – 23rd March 2013
Rose Theatre, Kingston KT1

Portraying an Edwardian family on the brink of collapse, 'Rutherford and Son' is a gripping drama set to take the stage at the Rose Theatre. Dictatorial patriarch John Rutherford is oblivious to any hopes or feelings that his family members have and will sacrifice happiness for his one focus: the success of the family firm. The family members are enduring a control freak of a father, an unreachable milestone with the business and a home that resembles a prison, yet they still have dreams. With Northern Broadside's Artistic Director, Barrie Rutter, taking the role of John Rutherford, this drama lives up to the company's trademark gritty style.

20th – 24th
Birmingham Royal Ballet – Aladdin

20th – 24th March 2013
English National Opera, London Coliseum, London WC2N 4ES

The London Coliseum is transformed into a magical Arabian world as this tale of love, sorcery and triumph is brought to life through David Bintley's choreography and music by Carl Davis. When Aladdin has

From 9th
Treasures of the Royal Courts: Tudors, Stuarts and the Russian Tsars

PICK

9th March - 14th July 2013
Victoria and Albert Museum, London SW7 2RL

ARMOUR, TEXTILES AND AN extraordinary display of silver are among more than 150 objects in 'Treasures of the Royal Courts: Tudors, Stuarts and the Russian Tsars'. Riches from the royal courts from Henry VIII to Charles II and from Ivan the Terrible (Ivan IV) to the early Romanovs are gathered together from several state collections to create a narrative. At the heart of the exhibition, which marks the 400th anniversary of the Romanov dynasty, is a showcase of spectacular British and French silver given to successive Russian Tsars. Some would have been melted down for money had they remained in Britain or France.

a run-in with the Palace guards he is suddenly caught up in a whirlwind of adventure, love at first sight, unbelievable riches and, of course, the notorious magic lamp. This adaptation of the story returns to its original narrative, with its background in 'The 1001 Arabian Nights' and links to ancient Chinese stories, but is still recognisable as Aladdin deals with all the power, and trouble, that the lamp brings him.

20th – 24th
Country Living Magazine Spring Fair
20th – 24th March 2013
Business Design Centre, Islington, London N1 0QH
As daffodils and snowdrops push through the ground, spring takes charge and urges us to shake off the shackles of winter and make a change. The Country Living Magazine Spring Fair is full of ideas for sprucing up your home and wardrobe, and also encourages visitors to try their hand at something new. There will be over 400 exhibitors, many attending for the first time, as well as free workshops with the price of entry that include hat making, wire jewellery making, appliqué and biscuit decorating. The Country Living Theatre is another source of hands-on ideas as experts give talks on flower arranging, jam making and other home crafts. Be sure to leave time to browse the many stalls packed with cushions, fabrics, clothes, bags, jewellery, housewares and more.

From 20th
Max Mara Art Prize for Women
20th March – 7th April 2013
Whitechapel Gallery, London E1
This biannual prize at the Whitechapel Gallery has been celebrating the aesthetic and intellectual contribution that women artists bring to contemporary art for over five years. Winning artists are presented with a unique opportunity to develop a new project during a fully funded six-month residency in Italy. Here, Laure Prouvost, the fourth winner of the prize, presents a body of short films and installations developed during her residency. Referencing Roman murals and the pleasures of Italy, Prouvost connects language and understanding, playing on the historic idea of visiting the Mediterranean for inspiration. The exhibition includes presentations by a shortlist of this year's entrants who talk through their plans should they be chosen for the prize.

From 20th
Three Birds
20th March – 20th April 2013
Bush Theatre, 7 Uxbridge Road, London W12 8LJ
Winner of 2011's Bruntwood Prize for playwriting, 'Three Birds' is a dark comic tale from Janice Okoh. When Tiana, Tionne and Tanika are left home alone, the three siblings take different paths in keeping themselves entertained. Tiana holds it together with the aid of housework and homework, Tionne starts to get experimental and Tanika chooses the route of rebellion. All seems okay until the outside world starts to interfere and the three are prepared to do anything to keep their secret safe from the adults pressing in. Directed by Sarah Frankcom, it's a tale of childhood, family and fantasy.

From 13th
Michael Caine (PICK)
13th March - 14th July 2013
Museum of London, 150 London Wall, London EC2Y 5HN
AS SIR MICHAEL CAINE CELEBRATES his 80th birthday, the Museum of London reflects on the life of the prolific actor and iconic Londoner. Born in Southwark on 14th March 1933 as Maurice Mickelwhite, Caine burst into the limelight as a soldier in Zulu before taking on myriad roles from Alfie through to Alfred. Renowned for his distinctive cockney accent and famous for blowing the bloody doors off, Caine was voted London's favourite Londoner in 2008 and said in his acceptance speech: "If you're born in London you're one of the luckiest people on earth. This is a city that I will love to the day I die and I'm so proud to be a Londoner." This exhibition focuses on key moments in both Caine's personal life and his career as an actor and explores how his background as a rebellious working-class Londoner influenced his path to stardom.

From 21st
The Low Road
21st March – 27th April 2013
Downstairs, Royal Court Theatre, Sloane Square, London SW1W 8AS
Bruce Norris's 'The Pain and the Itch' was the first play that Dominic Cooke, Artistic Director of the Royal Court Theatre, directed in his inaugural season. Therefore, it is very apt that his final directing project as Artistic Director will be another of Bruce Norris's works. 'The Low Road' will take to the stage in the downstairs theatre this spring and tells the story of a young entrepreneur who sets out on a quest for wealth with priceless ambition and a purse of gold. Previous collaborations from Norris and Cooke include the multi award-winning 'Clybourne Park' which saw Norris receive a Pulitzer Prize and the Tony Award for Best Play, and Cooke nominated for an Olivier Award.

From 21st
Before The Party
21st March – 11th May 2013
Almeida Theatre, Islington, London N1 1TA
Based on a short story by Somerset Maugham, Rodney Ackland's 'Before The Party' finds humour in the wake of the Second World War at the expense of the socially aspirational Skinner family. Rarely staged - this production is the first one mounted in over 25 years - this is Ackland's first play at the Almeida and forms part of Michael Attenborough's final season at the Islington theatre. In post-war Britain rationing is still in place but the Skinner family won't let a little nuisance like that get in the way; they've got a party to go to. With daughter Laura returned from Africa, widowed but not alone, the unsavoury underbelly of upper middle class life is about to be exposed. Matthew Dunster directs.

22nd & 23rd
The Script
22nd & 23rd March 2013
The O2 Arena, Greenwich, London SE10 0DX
The rise to success has hardly been a slow burner for Irish rock band The Script. Despite two of the three members – Danny and Mark – originally struggling to find musical recognition, they soon found themselves admirers in the form of U2 and the rollercoaster began from there. Since their chart-topping eponymous debut album in 2008, the trio have released two more successful albums, played stadium shows with the likes of U2, Take That and Paul McCartney, and sold millions of records worldwide. Now they're coming to London's largest music venue for two nights as part of their '#3' world tour.

22nd – 24th
The Chocolate Festival
22nd – 24th March 2013
Southbank Centre, London SE1 8XX
Just in time to stock up for Easter, The Chocolate Festival returns with plenty more chocolatiers and artisan delights to tickle your taste buds. It features stands from award-winning chocolatiers such as William Curley, Damian Allsop, Paul Wayne Gregory and Co-Couture, plus the attendance of renowned and new chocolate companies. Demonstrations, tastings and talks will take place in the main marquee, where attendees can learn about the health benefits of chocolate, how to include chocolate in savoury dishes as well as tutored tastings. And, as always, there will be dozens of stalls all showcasing chocolate and chocolate products.

From 22nd
Kaffe Fassett - A Life in Colour
22nd March – 29th June 2013
Fashion and Textile Museum, Bermondsey Street, London SE1 3XF
The colourful world of the American-born artist Kaffe Fassett is celebrated at the Fashion and Textile Museum where the work of one of the great practitioners of contemporary craft goes on display. This exhibition, 'Kaffe Fassett - A Life in Colour', is the first in London since Fassett's retrospective at the Victoria and Albert Museum in 1988, the year he designed a gold medal-winning garden for the Chelsea Flower Show. The museum hosts a special installation featuring over 100 works, including 9-feet-wide knitted shawls, patchwork fabrics, yarns and knits as well as items especially created for this show and not seen in public before. You can also get all 'touchy-feely' with the textiles through a 'feeling' wall that uses touch to help explore the fabrics on display.

23rd
Messiah Anniversary Concert
Saturday 23rd March 2013
Grosvenor Chapel, South Audley Street, Mayfair W1
Say 'Hallelujah' to Handel with this one-off springtime performance by the Pegasus Choir marking the 270th anniversary of the London première of the Baroque composer's great oratorio 'Messiah'. Drawn from the King James version of the Bible and the Book of Common Prayer, and with a verbal text provided by Charles Jennens, 'Messiah' is Handel's most famous creation and amongst the most popular works in Western choral literature, presenting Jesus' life and its significance according to Christian doctrine.

23rd
Head of the River Race
23rd March 2013
Mortlake to Putney
The Head of the River Race is one of the classic races on the rowing calendar, a warm up for the Oxford vs. Cambridge Boat Race that follows the same course backwards, from Mortlake to Putney Bridge along the Thames. There are 420 crews in all, rowing down the 4.25 mile course, testing their willpower and teamwork in this uniquely macho sport. It is also a particularly nice stretch of the river, so even if you are not that excited by rowing, this is a really nice spot to enjoy a walk or a pint and watch the boats glide past - hopefully the tides will dictate that the race coincides nicely with an early pub lunch, but you'll have to book early if you want a seat that faces the river.

From 23rd
David Bowie Is
23rd March – 28th July 2013
Victoria and Albert Museum, London SW7 2RL
More than sixty flamboyant stage costumes worn by pop icon David Bowie can be seen

Fan-tastic: Edinburgh star Doctor Brown soloes in Soho

at this major retrospective of the musician and actor's career. Featuring lyrics, instruments, photographs and videos, 'David Bowie Is' showcases outlandish costumes including 1970s Ziggy Stardust bodysuits and the Union Jack coat designed by Bowie and Alexander McQueen for the 1997 'Earthling' album cover. The exhibition follows the young David Robert Jones, born in Brixton in 1947, on the artistic journey he makes in becoming David Bowie, the stage name he officially adopted in 1965. More than just a songwriter, Bowie was involved in designing the costumes, stage sets and album artwork and was truly innovative with his 1972 creation of alien alter ego Ziggy Stardust. His role in film and on stage is celebrated in the final section through an immersive audio-visual space with footage of music videos, live tours and films including 'Labyrinth' and 'Basquiat'.

24th
The FA Trophy Final
Sunday 24th March 2013
Wembley Stadium, Wembley, London HA9 0WS
Two teams from the lower echelons of League football come head to head in the final of this knock-out cup competition previously reserved for semi-professional sides. The holders are York City, who beat Newport County 2-0 last year, while former Northern Ireland international Martin O'Neill, in his first managerial role, led Wycombe Wanderers to two FA Trophy wins back in the early '90s.

From 25th
Doctor Brown, Befrdfgth
25th March – 20th April 2013
Soho Theatre, London W1D
Doctor Brown, the star of last year's Edinburgh Festival, brings his highly rated and confusingly titled 'Befrdfgth' to London's Soho Theatre. Mime acts may have been all the rage at Edinburgh but the silent creation from American Phil Burgers trumped the lot of them, picking up the Foster's Edinburgh Comedy Award and leaving behind a wake of raucously amused festival-goers. London audiences can expect plenty of absurd visual humour and hysterical clowning about from the "part mime artist, part lord of misrule" (The Guardian). If you think mime is something of a tired genre, then this is the show that will change your mind forever.

26th
Joe Bonamassa
Tuesday 26th March 2013
The Borderline, Soho, London W1D 4JB
American blues rock guitarist and singer Joe Bonamassa plays four nights in different iconic London venues on the back of his 11th studio album, 'Driving Towards the Daylight', which peaked at #2 in the UK charts in spring 2012. Starting at the intimate Borderline and ending four days later at the magical Royal Albert Hall (Saturday 30th March), the internationally renowned guitarist will also drop into the Shepherd's Bush Empire (27th March) and Hammersmith Apollo (28th March) on his whistle-stop tour of the capital. The 35-year-old from upstate New York has been playing the guitar since the age of four, opened for B.B. King at the age of 12 and at 14 formed a band with Miles Davis' son. That's quite some résumé from "the new messiah for guitar music lovers" (The Sun) who has fast forged a reputation as "the pre-eminent blues-rock guitarist of his generation" (The Guardian).

26th
An Audience With Mr Nice
Tuesday 26th March 2013
Bloomsbury Theatre, 15 Gordon Street, London WC1H 0AH
Howard Marks, the legendary Mr Nice, brings his hazy one-man show 'An Audience With Mr Nice' to the Bloomsbury to raise money for the homeless charity Crisis. Born in 1945 in a small Welsh coal-mining village, Marks cheated and crammed his way through a physics degree from Oxford University before dabbling in teaching and post-graduate philosophy. In his time, Marks has worked with the British Secret Service and been connected with the Mafia, IRA, MI6 and CIA. Drug trafficking saw him banged up for seven years in the States before Marks wrote his best-selling autobiography following his release in 1995. His critically acclaimed live show sees the 67-year-old cult figure discuss his life as a marijuana smuggler and his views on drug use and legalisation.

26th
Harry Hill's Sausage Time
26th March & 11th April 2013
Hammersmith Apollo, London W6 9QH
The madcap star of the award-winning 'TV Burp' is back with a banger! Once described as "Ronnie Corbett

possessed by the ghost of Salvador Dali", Harry Hill is one of comedy's most instantly recognisable (not to mention baffling) figures. The bespectacled baldy's new live show, 'Sausage Time', promises incontrovertible proof that God exists. The self-styled floppy-collared loon is joined by his band, The Harry's, and his son from his first marriage, Gary, who is gifted a debut stand-up spot following his ribald turn as Alan Sugar in 'TV Burp'. There's also a section dedicated exclusively to Tongans, a chance to catch up on Harry's Nan's latest ailments and meows from the legendary Stouffer the Cat. As sure as pork and lamb are the main two chops, there'll also be expert-whistler-of-chart-hits grandson Sam and his all-singing, all-dancing finale. Also, we presume, some sausages.

From 27th
English National Ballet 2 – My First Cinderella

27th March – 7th April 2013
Peacock Theatre, Holborn, London WC2A 2HT
English National Ballet have partnered with English National Ballet School to produce the My First series: a number of special performances introducing younger audiences to ballet through the magic of fairy tales. 'Cinderella', the charming tale of rags-to-riches, is narrated and accompanied by music from Prokofiev. Tormented by her evil stepsisters, Cinderella dreams of the day she can escape and attend the Prince's enchanting ball. One night, when she's been abandoned for yet more cleaning, Cinderella is visited by her Fairy Godmother and her dreams begin to come true.

28th – 31st
The London International Ska Festival

28th – 31st March 2013
Various London venues
Back for its 25th anniversary, this four-day festival invites more than 40 acts to perform across multiple London venues in celebration of all things ska. With a variety of guests, including a number of Jamaican legends, the festival spans across all eras of the music genre. From '60s Jamaica through to the '70s and late '80s revivals, visitors can expect music from all its influences including the original American rhythm and blues, The Specials 2 Tone era and Madness – who were responsible for bringing ska into the mainstream. Embracing these influences, the line-up boasts the likes of Lynval Golding from The Specials, Rico Rodriguez, USA ska pioneers The Toasters and The Sidewalk Doctors.

From 28th
Life and Death in Pompeii and Herculaneum

28th March – 29th September 2013
British Museum, Bloomsbury, London WC1
This spring, the British Museum stages a major exhibition on 'Life and Death in Pompeii and Herculaneum', an examination of two very different cities in the Bay of Naples, both buried by an eruption of Mount Vesuvius in 79 AD. Displaying over 250 objects, many of which have never before been seen outside Italy, the museum conveys what every day Roman life was like nearly 1700 years ago. Objects from Herculaneum, a small seaside town, include wooden furniture carbonised by the high temperatures of the

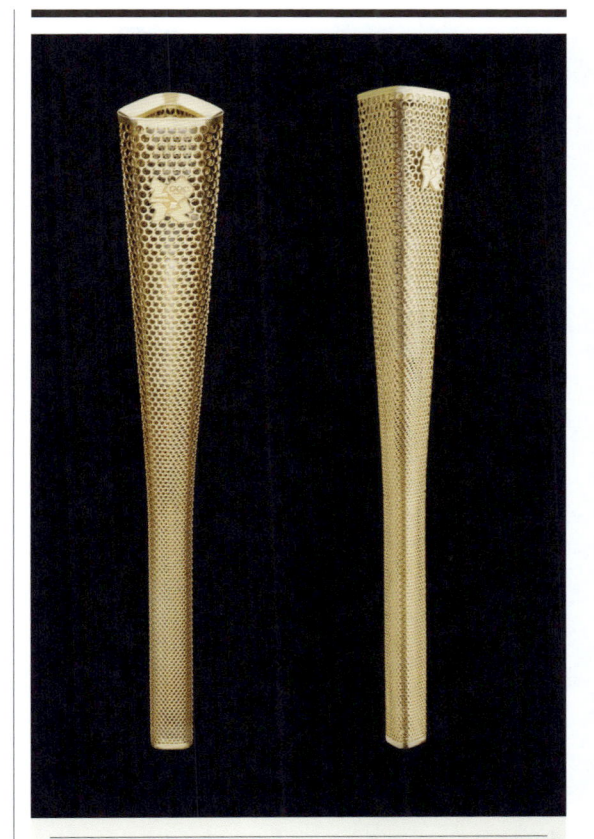

From 20th
Designs of the Year 2013

PICK

20th March - 7th July 2013
Design Museum, 28 Shad Thames, London SE1 2YD
A DISPLAY OF OBJECTS competing for the Design Museum's Designs of the Year awards, this exhibition is the result of a search for the most innovative designs of the year. Billed as 'the Oscars of the design world', beautifully designed pieces cross a whole range of categories including architecture, fashion, furniture and transport. A high profile judging panel decides the best entries in each of the seven categories and one overall winner who is announced to the public on 17th April 2013. Contenders will be hoping to take the mantle from last year's winners, Edward Barber and Jay Osgerby, who were awarded the prize for their design of the London 2012 Olympic Torch.

ash and a baby's crib that still rocks on its curved runners. From Pompeii, the industrial hub of the region, we have a beautiful wall painting of the baker, Terentius Neo and his wife, who appear as equal partners, in business and in life. Other fascinating objects include sculpted marble reliefs, carved ivory panels and casts showing the Pompeii victims forever suspended in their last moments. An intriguing insight into the daily life of the Roman Empire.

From 30th
Nabucco
30th March – 26th April 2013
Royal Opera House, Covent Garden, London WC2E 9DD
"With this opera, it can truly be said that my artistic career began" were the words of Giuseppe Verdi following the success of 'Nabucco'. Having fallen into despair after the failure of his second opera, Verdi vowed never to compose another piece. However, he was convinced by Bartolomeo Merelli, manager of La Scala Milan, to work on 'Nabucco' and its resounding success led to his fame. With a romantic and political plot, 'Nabucco' is set against the background of the plight of the Jews as they are assaulted and exiled by the Babylonian King. This revival is based in the second half of the 20th century and uses large-scale video projections to accompany the action on stage.

31st
The Boat Race: Oxford v Cambridge
Sunday 31st March 2013
Putney Bridge to Chiswick Bridge, southwest London
This year's Boat Race will struggle to repeat the drama of last year's, where a rogue swimmer - later jailed for six months for causing a public nuisance - was almost decapitated by an oar belonging to the Oxford crew. Following a re-start, Cambridge won the race - but to muted celebrations after the Dark Blues' bow man collapsed from exhaustion. One of London's oldest sporting events nevertheless returns in 2013 as England's two elite universities take to the water in a gruelling four-mile rowing race between Putney Bridge and Chiswick Bridge in southwest London. Around a quarter of a million fans are expected to line the Thames for the 159th annual Boat Race in which Oxford (with 76 wins) will look to close in on the Light Blues of Cambridge (81 wins). The start is scheduled for 4.30pm.

31st
Oxford v Cambridge Goat Race
Sunday 31st March
Spitalfields City Farm, Buxton Street, London E1
The stakes are high as Oxford and Cambridge once again come head-to-head in a nail-biting and highly competitive race. No, this isn't the famous Boat Race but the equally prestigious (okay, maybe not quite) Oxford vs. Cambridge Goat Race. Two feisty goats - one named Oxford, the other named Cambridge - embark on the sixth annual race, which takes place at Spitalfields City Farm on the same day as the Boat Race. Last year, Bramble the Golden Guernsey made it four in a row for Cambridge in front of 1,700 fans - although Oxford took consolation in winning the inaugural spin-off Stoat Race event. There are numerous other goat-related activities on offer as well as food and market stalls, live music, beer and cocktail bars, arts & crafts stands and a bookie and sweepstake tent. Kids (naturally) most welcome.

Unconfirmed dates:

Alien Revolution
March - August 2013
Royal Observatory Greenwich, Greenwich, London SE10 9NF
Since Copernicus' displacement of Earth as the centre of the universe, many people, from scientists to clergymen, have considered an infinite universe and the possible inhabitants of other planets. 'Alien Revolution' will explore the development of our opinion on aliens, in both science and culture, and how it has influenced religion, literature, philosophy, art and film. The exhibition is part of the Royal Observatory's 'Alien Season', which includes planetarium shows, public talks, workshops, sci-fi movie screenings and courses.

Children of the Sun
Opening date in March TBC
National Theatre: Lyttelton, South Bank, London SE1
Maxim Gorky's 1905 play is staged at the National Theatre with Howard Davies directing. Controversial at the time, 'Children of the Sun' refers to the privileged elite of Russia and how they are unaware of the cholera epidemic that is currently developing. The message is epitomised by the main character Protassoff who, despite being noble and idealistic, is completely unaware of the events that unfold around him. He doesn't see the love Melanya holds for him, is ignorant of the confused affection that his wife has for his best friend and is dangerously oblivious to the armed mob that are on their way to attack him.

The Great Map
Opening date in March TBC
National Maritime Museum, Greenwich, London SE10
A huge interactive world map, especially suitable for families, goes on permanent display at the National Maritime Museum in March 2013, an installation which allows visitors to use a touch-screen tablet to find out more about some of the most famous and exciting events in Britain's maritime history. Walk across the surface of The Great Map, housed in the museum's largest open space, and you'll discover seafaring stories based on the museum's collections.

Tiger Territory
Opening date in March TBC
ZSL London Zoo, Regent's Park, London NW1 4RY
In March the Sumatran tigers at London Zoo will get a five star £3.6 million home, five times the size of their previous enclosure. Their new space has been designed with the tigers needs in mind so that means they get trees to scratch on and climb up, a custom-built pool (tigers, unlike most cats, love water), and feeding poles which recreate their feeding habits in the wild. Visitors can observe the impressive felines up close through floor-to-ceiling glass windows while finding out about the important efforts being made to conserve and protect these beautiful big cats.

LONDON'S BEST

LONDON'S COMEDY CLUBS

If you're on the hunt for giggles then you're in the right place for London boasts a rip-roaring array of comedy clubs and meccas for mirth

TOP SECRET COMEDY CLUB
38 King Street, WC2E
This new Covent Garden alternative to the West End tourist traps has welcomed the likes of Scott Capurro and Andi Osho

THE FUNNY SIDE OF COVENT GARDEN
213 The Strand, WC2R
Andy Parsons, Shazia Mirza and Paul Sinha have graced the stage of the most central Funny Side venue above The George Pub

RISE OF THE IDIOTS
12 Balham Station Road, SW12
Fans have watched both Doc Brown and Dara O'Briain for just a fiver at this popular club based at The Exhibit pub in Balham

THE COMEDY STORE
Oxendon Street, SW1
The spiritual home of London stand-up helped kick-start the careers of comedy heavyweights Paul Merton and Eddie Izzard

CLAPHAM COMEDY CLUB
68 Clapham Manor St, SW4
This friendly and intimate club puts on weekly Thursday shows at The Bread & Roses pub with the likes of Danny Bhoy and Nick Helm

HOOTING BROADWAY
60 Selkirk Road, SW17
Brand new stand-up comedy nights make the Tooting massive laugh on the last Wednesday of the month in The Selkirk pub

OUTSIDE THE BOX
56 Old London Road, KT2
Bill Bailey, Jimmy Carr and Robin Williams have all performed at this Kingston club, voted fourth best in London by the Guardian

CRIKEY IT'S COMEDY
265 Camden High St, NW1
Monthly comedy shindig at the Etcetera Theatre, the famous pub theatre that is the beating heart of the Camden Fringe festival

THE COMEDY TREE
4 Fulham High Street, SW6 3LQ
Putney Bridge club set up by comics Pete Jonas and Erich McElroy in 2002 and renowned for its quality line-ups and intimate atmosphere

---

LONDON COMEDY NEWSLETTER

→ To receive the London Comedy Newsletter from LondonTown.com send a blank email now to: **comedy@londontown.com**
PRIVACY PROMISE: We will never (and that means never) give your email address to anyone else. You mean too much to us.

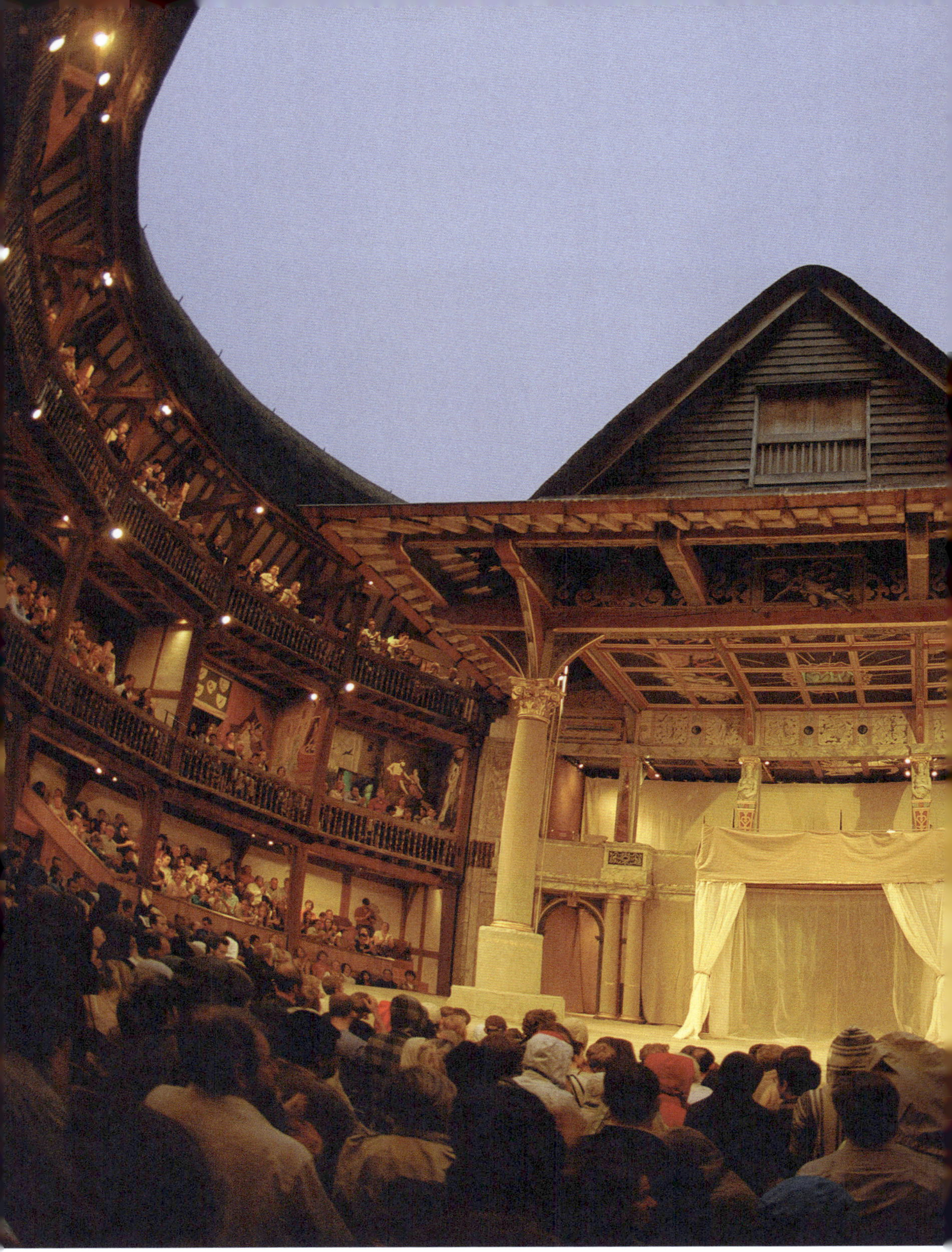

From Sundance to Stravinski, via Vogue, Bach and Ibsen, April's cultural landscape is staggering even before the Globe's season kicks off...

PAGE 123

APRIL

WHAT'S ON WHERE IN APRIL

LondonTown.com

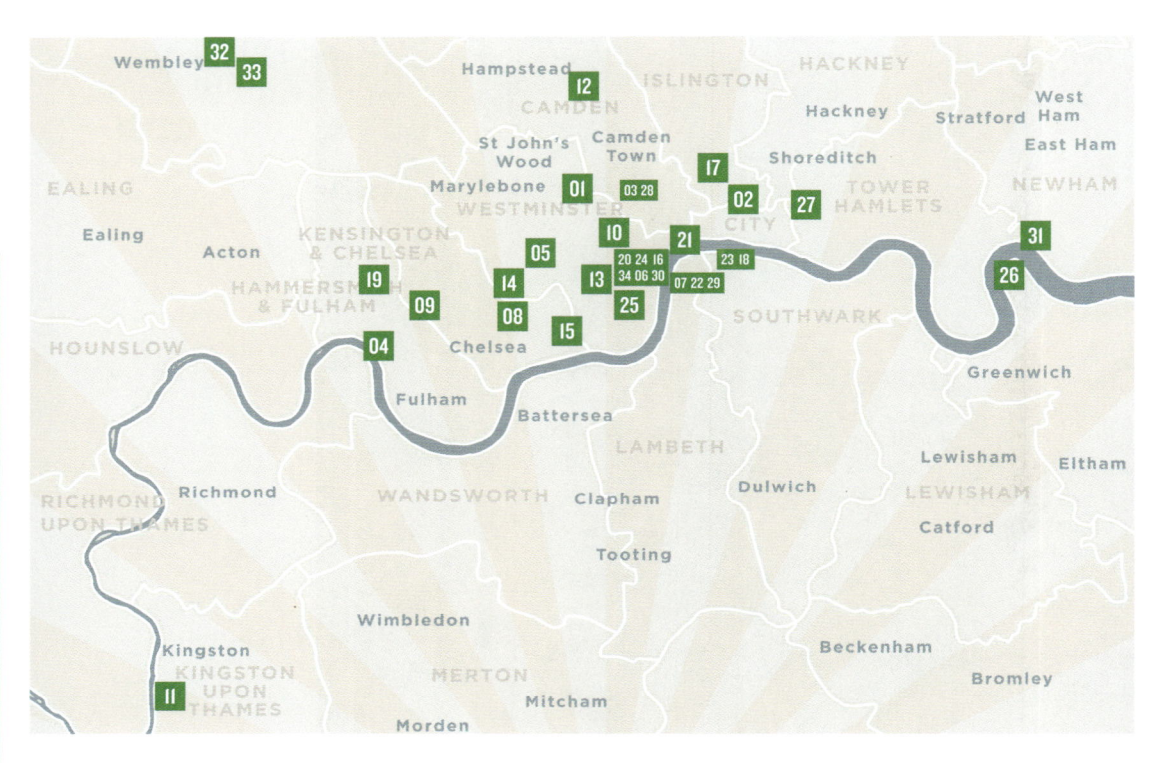

01 Ambika P3
Page 120
02 Barbican Centre
Pages 118, 119 & 123
03 Bloomsbury Theatre
Page 119
04 Hammersmith Apollo
Pages 117, 121 & 125
05 Hyde Park
Page 122
06 London Coliseum (ENO)
Page 126
07 Olivier Theatre
Page 126
08 Natural History Museum
Page 119
09 Olympia
Page 125

10 Photographers' Gallery
Page 121
11 Rose Theatre Kingston
Page 123
12 Roundhouse
Page 117
13 Royal Academy of Arts
Page 118
14 Royal Albert Hall
Pages 115, 117, 124 & 126
15 Royal Court Theatre
Page 117
16 Royal Opera House
Pages 117, 120 & 122
17 Sadler's Wells Theatre
Page 118
18 Shakespeare's Globe
Page 126

19 Shepherd's Bush Empire
Page 124
20 Soho Theatre
Pages 115 & 123
21 Somerset House
Pages 115 & 125
22 Southbank Centre
Pages 118, 119, 121 & 122
23 Tate Modern
Page 120
24 The Donmar Warehouse
Page 121
25 The Mall
Page 122
26 The O2 Arena
Pages 92, 116, 121 & 124
27 The Old Truman Brewery
Page 124

28 The Place
Page 120
29 The Young Vic
Page 116
30 Trafalgar Square
Pages 119 & 123
31 Trinity Buoy Wharf
Page 116
32 Wembley Arena
Page 125
33 Wembley Stadium
Pages 117 & 119
34 Wyndhams Theatre
Page 120

APRIL 2013

PICK

ART

Pick Me Up Contemporary Graphic Art Fair

1st - 11th April 2013 – TBC
Somerset House, Strand, London WC2R 1LA

THIS PAGE

1st - 20th
Pappy's: Last Show Ever
1st - 20th April 2013
Soho Theatre, 21 Dean Street, Soho, London W1D 3NE
"One of the finest sketch troupes of the last decade" (The Guardian) perform their smash hit show of the 2012 Edinburgh Festival for a three-week run at the relentlessly brilliant Soho Theatre. Full of five-star sketches, songs and silliness, 'Pappy's: Last Show Ever' showcases a trio at the height of their powers - and well worth their shortlisting for Best Show at last year's Fringe. Let's hope they're good liars too, for it would be an abomination if this really was Pappy's swansong gig.

1st
Bach Marathon
Monday 1st April 2013
Royal Albert Hall, Kensington Gore, London SW7 2AP
Sir John Eliot Gardiner's ambitious Easter Monday Bach bonanza features twelve inspiring and elevating hours of back to back (Bach to Bach?) music celebrating the baroque composer. Join Sir John's Monteverdi Choir, the English Baroque Soloists and an array of distinguished guests for a day paying homage to the man Mozart described as the "original father of harmony".

1st - 11th
Pick Me Up Contemporary Graphic Art Fair
1st - 11th April 2013
Somerset House, Strand, London WC2R 1LA
This is the fourth year for the UK's first contemporary graphic arts fair after a successful launch in April 2010. The

most innovative graphic artists, collectives and galleries in the country and from across the world will be on display at 'Pick Me Up' offering an exuberant mix of artworks for sale to the public. A lively series of events and activities accompanies the eleven day fair, including a Portfolio Surgery and workshops given by the artist in residence - Rob Ryan in 2010, Anthony Burrill in 2011, and the Peepshow Collective in 2012. The spectacular Somerset House once again hosts this excellent opportunity to discover the latest talents in the graphic art scene and purchase prints from as little as £10.

2nd – 20th
A Doll's House
2nd – 20th April 2013
Young Vic, Waterloo, London SE1 8LZ
The well received 'A Doll's House' returns for another run at the Young Vic. The sell-out success was widely praised, "warmly recommended" (The Telegraph) and nominated for three Evening Standard Awards in 2012. Now, the "sexy, passionate interpretation" (The Evening Standard) of Henrik Ibsen's 1879 play returns for 2013. Controversial at the time, 'A Doll's House' is acutely critical of 19th century marriage norms but, despite beliefs to the contrary, Ibsen insisted the play was not a fight for women's rights. This revival will see Hattie Morahan and Dominic Rowan return in the title roles as Nora and Torvald.

2nd – 27th
Project Colony
2nd - 27th April 2013
Trinity Buoy Wharf, Docklands, London E14 0JY
The audience becomes part of the action, playing colony inspectors in 'Project Colony', an immersive, site-specific piece at Trinity Buoy Wharf which is based on existentialist author Franz Kafka's short story, 'In the Penal Colony'. Meeting at a designated pick-up point the audience is transported to the colony on a double-decker bus in this unusual production presented by the Fourth Monkey theatre company. Once on the island, they experience the true life of the colony from both sides of the coin before being returned safely to whence they came. Conceived and directed by James Yeatman and Hamish MacDougall, two young directors who last collaborated on the Complicite 'Master and Margarita' at the Barbican, 'Project Colony' promises a unique theatrical experience delivered by a large ensemble cast.

3rd
Biffy Clyro
Wednesday 3rd April 2013
The O2 Arena, Greenwich, London SE10 0DX
Scottish rockers Biffy Clyro perform at the O2 on the back of their sixth studio album 'Opposites'. Renowned for their energetic live performances, the three-piece from Kilmarnock hit the big time with their fifth album 'Only Revolutions', which gained platinum status and was nominated for the 2010 Mercury Prize. Laying claim to possibly the worst name in rock, the band has previously linked their name to an Ayr United footballer and as a tribute to a biro belonging to Cliff Richard. There's also a school of thought that their moniker is an acronym for Big Imagination For Feeling Young 'Cos Life Yearns Real Optimism. Whatever the case, 'Only Revolutions' led to the rise of Biffy Clyro and the album of "irresistible tunes" was described as "Biffy's finest hour" by The Guardian. Not bad for a band that was started as a tribute to Nirvana.

3rd – 6th
Sutra
3rd – 6th April 2013
Sadler's Wells, Rosebery Avenue, London EC1R 4TN
Flemish and Moroccan choreographer Sidi Larbi Cherkaoui called upon the expertise of Turner Prize-winning artist Antony Gormley, Polish composer Szymon Brzoska, and 17 Shaolin Monks to create 'Sutra', a spiritually inspired dance at Sadler's Wells. The work includes aspects of kung fu and tai chi, set against an original score and striking staging from Gormley.

3rd – 20th
My Perfect Mind
3rd – 20th April 2013
Young Vic, Waterloo, London SE1 8LZ
Directed by Kathryn Hunter and performed by Edward Petherbridge and Paul Hunter, 'My Perfect Mind' is a Told

Prick up your ears: Michael Keegan-Dolan's 'The Rite of Spring' is revived at Sadler's Wells → 118

by an Idiot production that makes a moving yet comical exploration of the resilience of the human spirit. Once cast as King Lear, acclaimed actor Edward Petherbridge got to work on his rehearsals. However, on the second day he suffered a stroke that left him barely able to move. As he struggled to make a recovery, he made a fascinating discovery: the entire role of Lear still existed word for word in his mind. To go from being cast as one of Shakespeare's most revered roles to being helpless in a hospital bed, Petherbridge could never have foreseen the tragedies and comedies that lay in store for him.

From 5th
A New Play
5th April – 4th May 2013
Upstairs, Royal Court Theatre, Sloane Square, London SW1W 8AS
Anthony Neilson's latest play currently has no name, no narrative and no cast. 'A New Play' will conclude the Royal Court Theatre's season and is to be created from scratch in the rehearsal room. Known for his ground-breaking and imaginative work, Neilson's previous productions at the Royal Court include 'Get Santa!', 'The Wonderful World of Dissocia' (winner of Best Production in both the TMA and Critics' Award for Theatre in Scotland), 'The Lying Kind' and 'The Censor'. His reasoning behind the lack of title is the amount of creative control that it provides him: "Because I want to write from passion, not obligation. Because I want to write for the actors I've cast, not cast for the parts I've written. Because I want to surprise you".

From 5th
La Bayadere
5th April – 22nd May
Royal Opera House, Covent Garden, London WC2E 9DD
Romantic India provides the setting for one of The Royal Ballet's favourite full-length works: 'La Bayadere', a tale of love, murder and vengeful judgement by the gods. A principal piece in the repertoire of the Mariinsky Ballet, 'La Bayadere' is performed to music composed by Ludwig Minkus and is choreographed by Natalia Makarova. At the centre of this showcase of classical dancing are the warrior Solor and his love Nikiya, the beautiful temple dancer of the title. Threatening their love is the jealous High Brahmin, who is also in love with Nikiya; enraged at being rejected, he becomes furious with Solor and is determined to have him killed.

6th – 27th
Nofit State Circus: Bianco
6th – 27th April 2013
Roundhouse, Camden Town, London NW1 8EH
This April, the Roundhouse will be engrossed by a mesmerising and enthralling promenade performance from Nofit State Circus. Last seen at the Camden venue in 2009 with their sell-out show 'Tabu', the company are now returning to this ideal venue for their latest venture 'Bianco'. Taking place above, behind and all around a standing audience, the show is an all-consuming, spellbinding concoction of contemporary and traditional circus, dance, beautiful stage design, and music from a live band. "Gymnastic feats that make you gasp...a saucy melange of tightrope walks and acrobatics" (The Telegraph).

The Globe's 2013 Shakespeare season kicks off in April → 123

7th
Johnstone's Paint Trophy Final
Sunday 7th April 2013
Wembley Stadium, Wembley, London HA9 0WS
The third most important club cup competition is open to the 48 clubs in Football League One and League Two - the bottom two in the four fully professional top divisions in English football. To further complicate things, the final is always between the Northern and Southern area winners: last year, the north prevailed with Chesterfield beating southern softies Swindon Town 2-0.

8th & 9th
Alfie Boe
8th & 9th April 2013
Royal Albert Hall, Kensington Gore, London SW7 2AP
English tenor Alfie Boe returns to the Royal Albert Hall as part of his biggest UK tour to date. Dubbed 'The Nation's Tenor', Blackpool-born Boe is now a household name after becoming one of the huge success stories of 2011: his breakthrough year saw him sell almost 700,000 copies of his hit albums 'Bring Him Home' and 'Alfie'. He also starred as Jean Valjean in the blockbuster West End run of 'Les Misérables', as well as performing in the Last Night of the Proms on the back of a 23-date UK tour. Last year Alfie hit new heights as the 39-year-old performed in the Queen's Diamond Jubilee Concert in front of a global audience of millions, singing 'Somewhere' from 'West Side Story' on the balcony of Buckingham Palace with the American soprano Renee Fleming. With a book and a DVD out ahead of Christmas, it's all go for the king of classical crossover and operatic pop.

8th & 9th
Emeli Sandé
8th & 9th April 2013
Hammersmith Apollo, London W6 9QH
Aberdeenshire-born Emeli Sandé has risen to success in the past year. Having collaborated on 'Diamond Rings' with UK rapper Chipmunk, Sandé first entered the UK music charts in 2009. She has since gone on to write several successful

songs for other artists, win the Critics' Choice Award at the 2012 BRIT Awards, release a double platinum album and perform at both the London 2012 Opening and Closing Olympic Ceremonies; viewed by more than 20 million people, these performances boosted Sandé's album sales and saw her become the best-selling artist of 2012. Now, promoting the release of a special edition of 'Our Version of Events', the singer-songwriter will be performing at the Hammersmith Apollo for two nights as part of her 2013 UK tour.

10th – 20th
Ubu Roi
10th – 20th April 2013
Barbican Centre, Silk Street, London EC2Y 8DS
Cheek By Jowl performs Alfred Jarry's brutal French language satire about greed and the abuse of power at the Barbican. Drawing heavily from Shakespearean drama and boasting a bigger body count than a Quentin Tarantino film, 'Ubu Roi' tells the story of the anarchic Pere Ubu, egged on by his monstrous wife to murder the royal family of Poland and usurp the crown. There follows a reign of terror, the perversely evil yet comically absurd nature of which inspired riots upon the play's Paris première in 1896. Subsequently outlawed for its scandalous language (Ubu's first two words are 'Merde' - the French for shit), violence and disrespect for authority, Jarry's curious work inspired future absurdist playwrights such as Beckett and Ionesco, and is celebrated for its quality and impact despite its often nonsensical phrasing.

11th - 13th
The Rite of Spring/ Petrushka
11th - 13th April 2013
Sadler's Wells, Rosebery Avenue, London EC1R 4TN
Celebrating the 100th anniversary of one of the 20th century's great masterpieces, Sadler's Wells associate artist Michael Keegan-Dolan brings his Olivier-nominated version of 'The Rite of Spring' for a very limited run. Keegan-Dolan's version of Stravinsky's ground-breaking ballet premièred at the London Coliseum in 2009 to great critical acclaim, being described as one of the few accounts that truly realise the Russian composer's vision. The evening is completed by Keegan-Dolan's new interpretation of 'Petrushka', composed by Stravinsky in 1911, to be performed by the exceptional dancers of Fabulous Beast Dance Theatre. This is the first of three events in 'A String of Rites', a series dedicated to Stravinsky's masterpiece.

From 11th
Udderbelly Festival
11th April - 14th July
South Bank, by Golden Jubilee Bridge, London SE1
Look out for an upside-down purple cow as you're crossing over the Golden Jubilee footbridge to the Southbank Centre from mid-April - failing that, just listen out for the belly laughs - and you'll find your way to London's funniest summer event. The colourful, comic, curvaceous cow marks the spot of the Udderbelly - a two-month festival of comedy, cabaret and theatre from around the globe. There's a huge variety of entertainment taking place both in and outside the bulbous bovine - which also appears at

25th - 28th
The London Original Print Fair **PICK**
25th – 28th April 2013
Royal Academy of Arts, London W1J 0BD

THE LONDON ORIGINAL PRINT FAIR, London's premier print fair, offers the chance to see specialist dealers displaying their etchings, engravings, linocuts and lithographs in the grand setting of the Royal Academy of Arts. Over the past 20 years it has become a firm favourite with dealers and print fans alike. Prices start from £100 and rise to £1,000,000 covering old Masters (including Rembrandt and Durer), 18th and 19th century painters (Hogarth, Goya, Sickert) and top names from the contemporary scene (Hockney and Hirst). Whether you're looking for an investment or something pretty to put on your walls, limited edition prints offer a more affordable alternative to one-off, original art works - and it's great fun to browse.

APRIL 2013

the Edinburgh Festival - with something going on almost every night. Confirmed acts for 2013 include Festival of the Spoken Nerd, Susan Calman, Doc Brown, Tony Law and Nick Helm.

From 11th
Salgado's Genesis
11th April - 8th September 2013
Natural History Museum, Cromwell Road, SW7 5BD
The culmination of eight years' work exploring 32 countries, the world première of Sebastião Salgado's 'Genesis' unveils 250 extraordinary images of landscapes, wildlife and remote communities by the world-renowned Brazilian photographer. Depicting the majesty of nature and the balance of human relationships with our fragile planet, the striking pictures provide unique glimpses into ancestral traditions and cultures.

12th & 13th
Richard Herring: Talking Cock
12th & 13th April 2013
Bloomsbury Theatre, 15 Gordon Street, London WC1H 0AH
It's an object of shame and pride; it inspires laughter, awe and fear; it's a symbol or power and lust, yet it's both fragile and ugly; it can be a sound pound of flesh or a spam gram of wrinkles; often used to express love, it's more frequently shrouded in guilt (and a pair of ghastly Y-fronts). Most of the time, it just wees. Richard Herring's 'Talking Cock' is "man's answer to the 'Vagina Monologues'" (The Guardian), a study of masculinity, cultural identity and sexual anthropology - as well as a chance to joke about flutes of love, flesh canoes, porridge guns and schlongs. First performed in 2002, Herring's tenth anniversary update of his critically acclaimed show comes to the Bloomsbury for back-to-back nights of what The Metro describes as a "constantly pleasurable hour" despite its "stiff proposition". We only wish it could be a little longer...

12th – 20th
Sunken Garden
12th – 20th April 2013
Barbican Theatre, Silk Street, London EC2Y 8DS
The English National Opera and the Barbican are coming together to collaborate for this unique multi-platform world première. Telling the story of a missing person and those who are searching for him, this film-opera explores what connects the disappearance of a software engineer with a neurotic film maker and a gullible patroness of the arts. It delves into hoax and dark truth, the virtual and the real. Best-selling author David Mitchell will be providing a libretto and Michel van der Aa, the Dutch composer, film and stage director, will make an ENO debut with one of opera's first uses of 3D film. Using his internationally acclaimed technique, Van der Aa will mix live and recorded images and sounds to create this multimedia occult mystery opera.

12th – 21st
Alchemy Festival
12th – 21st April 2013
Southbank Centre, London SE1 8XX
Returning for a fourth year, the Alchemy festival brings a mix of dance, music, talks and debates exploring the rich cultural connections between India, South Asia and the UK to the Southbank Centre. A celebration of music, dance, debate, literature, film, craft and fashion, Alchemy also explores the culture of India, Bangladesh, India, Pakistan and Sri Lanka and takes a close look at their relationships with and influence on the UK and vice versa. Festival-goers can expect cutting-edge music, a huge range of free workshops, classes and even a Bollywood film.

13th & 14th
FA Cup Semi-Finals
13th & 14th April 2013
Wembley Stadium, Wembley, London HA9 0WS
Despite an outcry from the traditionalists, both FA Cup semi-finals have been played at Wembley Stadium over one weekend since its reopening in 2008. Last year's draw threw together two local derbies with Liverpool beating Everton 2-1 in Saturday's game before eventual winners Chelsea hammered sorry Spurs 5-1 on Sunday.

14th
Vaisakhi on the Square
Sunday 14th April 2013
Trafalgar Square, London WC2N 5DS
Every spring sees Trafalgar Square transformed into a colourful celebration to welcome in the Sikh New Year. The Vaisakhi Festival is truly a sight to behold with traditional and modern Asian music and dancing and an array of exotic culinary delights on offer. The official date for Vaisakhi is usually April 14th, but the festival in Trafalgar Square is often

The ubiquitous Emeli Sandé sings at the Apollo → 117

APRIL 2013

'The Magic Flute' plays the right tune at Royal Opera House

held on a different day – last year it was held on May 6th – so it's a good idea to check for a confirmed date nearer the time. Commemorating 300 years of the consecration of Sri Guru Granth Sahib as the eternal Guru, the Vaisakhi festival includes performances of music such as Shabad Kirtin (religious hymns), as well as modern dance music and DJs. In previous years crowds of 30,000 have attended the celebrations, which end with a final prayer for the good and well-being of the whole of humanity. Vegetarian food prepared by the Sikh community is usually on sale during the afternoon. This year's date has not yet been confirmed.

15th – 28th
The Other Art Fair
15th – 28th April 2013
Ambika P3, London NW1
Snap up some original art from some of London's most promising emerging artists, before they get signed and the prices soar. All the artists showing at The Other Art Fair have been carefully selected by an eagle-eyed committee of art experts, so even if you're not buying, this show is a great day out for art-lovers looking to discover new talent.

From 16th
Die Zauberflöte
16th April – 9th May 2013
Royal Opera House, Covent Garden, London WC2E 9DD
Sir Colin Davis and David Syrus conduct a revival of David McVicar's beautiful staging of Mozart's 'Die Zauberflöte', with Joseph Kaiser and Kate Royal singing the roles of Tamino and Pamina opposite Christopher Maltman as Papageno. Drawing on the magical spectacle and earthy comedy that was popular in Viennese theatre in the late 18th century, 'The Magic Flute' tells the tale of Prince Tamino and his mission to save the Queen of the Night's daughter, Pamina, from the enchanter Sarastro. The fairytale story transports the audience into a fantasy world of dancing animals, flying machines and glittering starry skies, and is often seen as an expression of Mozart's spiritual beliefs and his search for wisdom and virtue.

From 16th
Doktor Glas
16th April – 11th May 2013
Wyndham's Theatre, Charing Cross Road, London WC2H 0DA
After an acclaimed run in Sweden, 'Doktor Glas' is now transferring to London's Wyndham Theatre to be performed in its original Swedish with English surtitles. Krister Henriksson, star of Sweden's hit television series 'Wallander', will make his West End debut as he takes on the role of Doktor Glas. The story follows a 19th century physician who falls for a beautiful young wife and soon becomes her confidante as she despairs of her failing marriage. Agreeing to help in whatever way he can, Doktor Glas is forced into a situation where he has to choose between his passion and his morality which, ultimately, leads to a dramatic climax.

17th – 27th
The Place Prize Dance Finals
17th – 27th April 2013
The Place, Euston, London WC1H 9PY
The dance equivalent of the Turner or a Man Booker, the Place Prize is a prestigious accolade in the dance world. It is awarded annually and is worth £25,000 for the winning choreographer. Having been selected from video entries, 16 acts are commissioned £5,000 and given three weeks to perfect their piece, after which they battle it out in the semi-finals. Four acts make it through to the final stages – three of which are chosen by the judges while the fourth is voted for by the audience. During the finals in April the audience vote for nightly awards of £1,000 but it is the judging panel who decide on the overall winner. The 2013 finals will see h2dance, Riccardo Buscarini, Rick Nodine and Eva Recacha compete for the prize. The judging panel includes The Daily Telegraph's Sarah Crompton and Jonzi D of Breakin' Convention.

From 17th
Saloua Raouda Choucair
17th April – 20th October 2013
Tate Modern, 25 Sumner Street, London SE1 9TG
Tate Modern presents the UK debut of pioneering Lebanese abstract artist Saloua Raouda Choucair in an exhibition which brings together paintings, sculptures and other objects made by the artist over five decades. Born in Beirut in 1916, Choucair, now in her 90s, was an early innovator of abstract art in the Middle East and her passions for both Sufic and scientific principles

can be translated through her experimental and geometric sculptures.

18th
Gaucho International Polo
Wednesday 18th April 2013
The O2 Arena, Greenwich, London SE10 0DX

This evening celebration of Argentina's sporting and cultural heritage returns to the O2 Arena for a third year. Arena Polo is to polo what Twenty20 cricket is to cricket: smaller teams of three and a smaller sand pitch makes for a faster and more exciting game that is spectator friendly and far less exclusive than the traditional game. Last year, Scotland beat Ireland in a warm-up game before England took on Argentina in the night's showpiece fixture, pitching the UK's finest player Jamie Morrison against the global polo superstar that is Nacho Figueras. A thrilling encounter saw England win 1-0 on penalties after a nail-biting 15-15 draw, while extra entertainment came from Grammy award-winning 'electrotango' band, Bajofondo.

From 18th
The Weir
18th April – 8th June 2013
Donmar Warehouse, Seven Dials, London WC2H 9LX

Returning to the stage this year, Conor McPherson's 'The Weir' first premièred in 1997 and won the Evening Standard, Critics' Circle and Olivier Award for Best New Play, establishing McPherson as one of the greatest living playwrights. Opening with a gathering of three men in a rural Irish pub, a routine daily pint is soon interrupted by the arrival of a further friend and a female companion. The presence of the woman encourages the men to embark on telling stories that have a supernatural theme. Delving into tales of Irish folklore, ghosts, fairies and mysterious happenings, one story is eventually told that is so realistic and chilling that it surpasses anything the men could have envisaged. Directed by Josie Rourke, the return of this modern classic will be its first major London revival since the première.

19th
Milton Jones: On The Road
Friday 19th April 2013
Hammersmith Apollo, London W6 9QH

The crazy-haired king of one-liners is back on the road with a selection of garish shirts and this new live show, the imaginatively entitled 'On The Road'. Star of TV's 'Mock The Week' and Radio 4, Milton Jones is the comedic genius behind wonderfully simplistic jokes such as: "My wife, it's difficult to say what she does… she sells seashells on the seashore" and "To the man on crutches, dressed in camouflage, who stole my wallet… you can hide but you can't run" and "Here's a picture of me with REM. That's me in the corner". You get the picture. This night at the Hammersmith Apollo brings Jones's 'On The Road' tour to a no-doubt raucous conclusion.

From 19th
Deutsche Borse Photography Prize 2013
19th April - 30th June 2013
The Photographers' Gallery, Soho, London W1F 7LW

The renowned annual £30,000 prize rewards the living

27th & 28th
Vogue Festival
Saturday 27th & Sunday 28th April 2013
Southbank Centre, London SW1

PICK

THE FIRST VOGUE FESTIVAL was such a success that they're bringing it back in 2013 but this time it'll be at the Southbank Centre's Queen Elizabeth Hall. Like last year, it will be a two day event that brings together fashion's top designers, models, photographers and writers to showcase their work and interact with visitors. Fashion followers will be able to immerse themselves into the industry by posing questions to some of the industry's most influential names, as well as take part in workshops, makeovers and watch fashion films. With Vogue being the doyenne of fashion publications, they promise only the best in the creative industry will be present, so expect a programme packed with fashion heavyweights - Tom Ford, Domenico Dolce and Stefano Gabbana and Diane von Furstenberg all appeared last year. Tickets are on sale from February 2013.

APRIL 2013

photographer, of any nationality, who has made the most significant contribution to the medium of photography during the past year. The four shortlisted artists for the 2013 prize are South African duo Adam Broomberg & Oliver Chanarin, whose 'War Primer 2' book pays homage to the great Bertolt Brecht through a contemporary prism of internet and mobile phone images; Mishka Henner for his exhibition 'No Man's Land', which re-appropriates urban and rural images used by Google Street View; Chris Killip for his black and white study of industrial Britain's decline in 'What Happened Great Britain 1970-90'; and Christina De Middel for her publication on Zambia's short-lived space programme, 'The Afronauts'.

From 19th
Cheese and Wine Festival
26th – 28th April 2013
& 11th – 13th October 2013
Southbank Centre, London SE1

Now in its fifth year, the Cheese and Wine Festival is an event dedicated to promoting high quality and ethical produce. Previous years have had plenty of highlights on display, including a cooking demonstration from stage host Valentina Harris and a wine tasting session with the BBC's Tim Atkin MW. Companies will be selling a variety of cheeses and wines from around the world and there will also be cheese making kits, cheesecakes, accessories and more. Visitors can plan the event around lunch or dinner and enjoy some delicious hot savoury foods made with cheese or wine.

From 19th
Mayerling
19th April – 15th June 2013
Royal Opera House, Covent Garden, London WC2E 9DD

Kenneth Macmillan's harrowing tale of Crown Prince Rudolf's passage from a lonely youth, through a series of affairs, and finally to suicidal erotomania, returns to the Royal Opera House with all its edginess intact. Based on the true story of the mysterious, violent deaths of the Austrian heir and his lover in 1889 and set to music by Franz Liszt, the two leads' descent into their frenzied madness is played with wonderful skill. The lucid poise of the role of the doomed Prince perfectly complements the fervid obsession of his young mistress. This is a demanding and ambitious ballet, performed with pulsating eroticism by a superb cast.

21st
Virgin London Marathon
Sunday 21st April 2013
Starts at Greenwich Park and Blackheath | Finishes at The Mall

Every spring, around 30,000 runners flood the streets of the capital to take part in the London Marathon - one of the top five international marathons and the largest annual fund-raising event in the world. Serious competitors mingle with charity fun-runners in the April sunshine as the 26.2 mile route comes alive to the sounds of bands, cheering crowds and pounding feet. The race kicks off at Greenwich Park and Blackheath with a loop around Charlton and Woolwich, continues through Rotherhithe and Bermondsey, crosses the Thames on Tower Bridge before circling Canary Wharf and the City ahead of the showpiece finish along the Embankment, past Parliament Square and onto The Mall in the shadow of Buckingham Palace. Last year it was Kenya who stole the show: Wilson Kipsang led a Kenyan one-two in the men's elite race while Mary Keitany recorded a second successive win in the women's race.

21st
The Queen's Birthday Gun Salutes
Sunday 21st April 2013
Hyde Park, London W2 2UH | Tower Hill, City, London EC3N 4AB

The Queen usually celebrates her actual birthday, 21st April, privately, but the occasion is marked publicly by gun salutes in central London: there's a 41 gun salute in Hyde Park, a 21 gun salute in Windsor Great Park and a 62 gun salute at the Tower of London, all taking place at midday. The Queen's Birthday Gun Salutes take place on her actual birthday, ahead of her official birthday in June which is marked by Trooping the Colour. At Hyde Park the Queen's Birthday Gun Salute is carried out by the King's Troop Royal Horse Artillery who ride into the park from the north

Gaucho International Polo returns to the O2 Arena for a night of three-on-three action → 121

by Marble Arch along North Carriage Drive, line up abreast and gallop down the parade ground to roughly opposite the Dorchester Hotel. The Troop itself arrives at around 11.45am ready to fire the first round at midday. The guns are then unhooked and the salute is fired off. Duty performed, the horses gallop back up towards North Carriage Drive. The band arrives separately and can usually be seen from about 11.30am. It is a spectacular show of pomp and ceremony and it's also the only time when you will see horses legally at a full gallop in Hyde Park - with a ton and a half of cannon in tow! Happy Birthday Lizzy!

22nd & 23rd
Ludovico Einaudi
22nd & 23rd April 2013
Barbican Hall, Silk Street, London EC2Y 8DS
Italian pianist Ludovico Einaudi, the supreme talent behind the wonderful soothing scores for the British TV drama 'This Is England' and the French film 'Untouchable', plays two nights at the Barbican Hall with his band this spring. Blending minimalism, pop, classical, jazz, chillout and world music, the bespectacled Einaudi performed his chillingly affecting music on the Europe stage at the BT River of Music ahead of last summer's Olympics. The 57-year-old from Turin has a definite ear for a poignant melody and his emotional, moving, simple, sad yet uplifting cinematic strains have seen Einaudi compared to the great Michael Nyman. Einaudi's music transports and mesmerises in equal measure and having amassed a silent legion of fans, the Italian should sell-out the Barbican for these concerts, which come on the back of his latest album.

23rd
St George's Day
Tuesday 23rd April 2013
Trafalgar Square, London WC2N 5DS
St George's Day is on 23rd April and in 2013 it falls on a Tuesday. Although it hasn't been confirmed as yet, London usually holds an official event in Trafalgar Square in recognition of England's dragon-slaying patron saint on the Saturday before or after the saint's day. Flag waving is encouraged at this free event where live bands play on the main stage while food stalls and street actors put on a very English display. William Shakespeare's birthday falls on the same date, and Shakespeare's Globe often hosts its own set of celebratory activities at the theatre to tie in with St George's Day. Workshops and interactive fun and games bring the Bard to life for all-comers, young and old. Sadly, despite tireless campaigning to make St George's Day a national bank holiday, celebrations on the actual day itself will have to fit in with working hours.

23rd – 27th
Twelfth Night
23rd – 27th April 2013
Rose Theatre, Kingston KT1
Running concurrently with 'The Taming of the Shrew', 'Twelfth Night' is brought to the Rose Theatre by the all-male Shakespeare company Propeller. Seeking to find a more engaging way to present Shakespeare, they take influences from classic and modern film, animation, and music from all ages to ensure their productions appeal to a greater audience. Another one of Shakespeare's most loved comedies, 'Twelfth Night' is a tale of disguise, mistaken identity, love and heartbreak. When one of the characters disguises herself as a boy, it causes confusion, love triangles and a fine line between reality and illusion. Overall, it examines what happens when you fall in love with the wrong person.

From 23rd
Frank Skinner, Work in Progress
23rd April – 4th May 2013
Soho Theatre, 21 Dean Street, London W1D 3NE
British presenter, writer, actor and all-round funny guy, Frank Skinner takes to the stage without his television side kick, David Baddiel, at the Soho Theatre. For fans, this is a chance to enjoy some of the comedian's new material and a rare opportunity to see him perform in such an intimate venue.

From 23rd
The Tempest
23rd April - 18th August 2013
Shakespeare's Globe, Bankside, London SE1 9DT
Shakespeare's late great masterpiece, 'The Tempest', starts Shakespeare's Globe's 2013 season on 23rd April with a play which uses Renaissance costumes and music composed by Stephen Warbeck, who won an Academy Award for his

Carlos Acosta stars in 'La Bayadère' at the Royal Opera House → 117

APRIL 2013

The spellbinding Nofit State Circus returns to the Roundhouse → 117

score for Shakespeare in Love. 'The Tempest', along with 'A Midsummer Night's Dream' (from 24th May) and 'Macbeth' (from 22nd June) will sit at the heart of the Globe's 2013 season, while three new plays will receive world premieres - 'Gabriel' by Samuel Adamson, 'Blue Stockings' by Jessica Swale, and 'The Lightning Child' by Ché Walker. One sure to be a highlight will be Footsbarn's 'Indian Tempest' which runs from 29th July to 3rd August.

24th – 27th
The Taming of the Shrew
24th – 27th April 2013
Rose Theatre, Kingston KT1
The all-male Shakespeare company Propeller will be bringing two simultaneous plays to the Rose Theatre this year: 'The Taming of the Shrew' and 'Twelfth Night'. A controversial comedy from Shakespeare, 'The Taming of the Shrew' is viewed by some as derogatory to women due to their submissive tendencies throughout. Two competing suitors are striving to gain the hand of the beautiful Bianca. However, Bianca's father will not allow her to date until Kate, her older, vicious-tempered sister (the shrew), also starts dating. The suitors therefore take on disguises while they attempt to win her affection. Meanwhile, gold-digging Petruchio agrees to wed Kate and so the taming of the shrew begins.

24th
Chris de Burgh
Wednesday 24th April
Royal Albert Hall, Kensington Gore, London SW7 2AP
Ladies in red will no doubt flock to the Royal Albert Hall as pop maestro Chris de Burgh promotes his latest album, 'Home' - an acoustic selection of his favourite songs from previous albums. The leather blouson-clad balladeer, who has sold 45 million records, will also treat the audience to some of his greatest hits as well as songs from his 2011 album 'Footsteps 2', which includes his interpretations of ABBA, Mike & The Mechanics and Roy Orbison.

24th – 28th
Pink – The Truth About Love Tour
24th, 25th, 27th & 28th April 2013
The O2 Arena, Greenwich, London SE10 0DX
Known for her autobiographical songs and spectacular live concerts, Pink will be touring Europe for the first time in two years in 2013. Concluding with four nights at the O2 Arena, the tour will support the release of her sixth studio album and, if previous tours are anything to go by, is anticipated to be yet another extravagant affair. The Grammy Award-winning singer-songwriter has previously captivated fans with tours such as 'Funhouse' and 'Summer Carnival', which saw her pour in every drop of physical and emotional strength as she sung about her much publicised love life and performed impressive acrobatic stunts. Now, following the storytelling of her ups and downs in love, the feisty songstress is returning and promises to tell her fans 'The Truth About Love'.

25th – 28th
Sundance London
25th – 28th April 2013
The O2 Arena, Greenwich, London SE10 0BB
Following the success of the first ever Sundance London film and music festival last year, the event returns to the O2 for four days in April 2013. The spin-off of America's indie film festival founded by Robert Redford in 1987 will showcase films screened at the Utah-based film festival in January. Last year the film festival included 27 film screenings, including many European premieres, and performances by 17 musical acts. Prince Charles attended one of the premieres, and Rufus and Martha Wainwright performed live following the world première of Lian Lunson's film about the music of their mother. If last year's format is repeated, audiences will be treated to thought-provoking panel discussions featuring industry experts, live music performances, screenings and panel discussions.

25th – 28th
London Coffee Festival
25th – 28th April 2013
The Old Truman Brewery, Brick Lane, London E1 6QR
The London Coffee Festival returns once again and embraces the fact that the capital is gaining respect as a great place to uncover, experience and indulge in artisan coffee. The festival launched in 2011 and enticed 7,500 coffee enthusiasts, food lovers and professional baristas to enjoy three days of coffee-fuelled activities. The festival is divided into themed zones - London landmarks Hyde Park, Soho

and Shoreditch among them - where visitors can interweave between a number of tastings, demonstrations and entertainment. Features include a Tea Garden, Chocolate Factory, Street Food, Artisan Markets and the Roastery.

26th
The Feeling
Friday 26th April 2013
O2 Shepherd's Bush Empire, London W12 8TT
With the finishing touches being made to The Feeling's fourth album, we can expect a few new tunes to be played at this Shepherd's Bush Empire gig, the final night of a 10-date UK tour in April 2013 - the band's first since 2011. Announcing the tour, The Feeling frontman Dan Gillespie Sells said, "We had such a great summer, playing festival shows and working on the new album. Now that it's almost ready, we can't wait to get back out on the road to play some new songs and all the old favourites. It's going to be a blast." And the Friday night hometown show at London's Shepherd's Bush Empire will be the last blast.

26th & 27th
Jimmy Carr: Gagging Order
26th & 27th April 2013
Hammersmith Apollo, London W6 9QH
Crude comedian Jimmy Carr takes time out from filing his offshore tax returns to continue his 'Gagging Order' UK tour. Renowned for his acerbic scattergun one-liners and vile, brutally honest anecdotes, Carr is deliciously rude for some and downright unacceptable for others. Audiences should really leave their moral compass at home before settling in for an evening of Carr's "guilty-pleasure, playground humour" and "laser-guided tongue-lashings" (Evening Standard). The gagging order in question refers to the reaction that followed Carr's infamous quip a few years back about amputee soldiers doing well in the Paralympics. Presumably his next show is to be called 'Tax Avoidance'. One of the hardest-working men in comedy, Carr also performs at Brixton Academy on 18th May 2013.

From 26th
World Photography Awards Exhibition
26th April - 12th May 2013
Somerset House, The Strand, London WC2R 1LA
The very best professional and amateur contemporary photography from around the world goes on display at Somerset House for the 2013 Sony World Photography Awards Exhibition. Showcasing the winning and shortlisted photographers from the awards, the exhibition spans photo-journalism, fine art and commercial photography. The overall winners will be announced at an Awards Ceremony Gala at the Hilton Hotel on 25th April. This year, the event coincides with the World Photo London festival, a collection of events, seminars, talks and workshops which runs for three days (26th - 28th April) in Somerset House and another as yet unidentified venue.

27th – 28th
The Great British Tattoo Show
27th – 28th April 2013
Olympia, London W14 8UX
Offering newly introduced fashion catwalks, burlesque dancing and body painting, The Great British Tattoo Show returns for the second time in 2013. Held at Olympia, the unique event brings together world class artists, vendors and traders for a truly spectacular show. As the one and only tattoo convention in the country, it is a great excuse for tattoo enthusiasts to head down for a few hours with mates.

28th
British Basketball League Play-off Final
Sunday 28th April 2013
Wembley Arena, Empire Way, London HA9 0AA
Wembley Arena will have a distinctively trans-Atlantic feel to it with the showpiece showdown of the British basketball calendar. The BBL Play-off Final features the two best sides in the UK's professional basketball league and last season saw Newcastle Eagles defeat Leicester Riders 71-62 to complete a clean sweep of the domestic titles. The final is preceded by the UK Slam Dunk Contest trophy - featuring top slam dunkers from all over the country - while the whole event will be spiced up by acrobatic dunking ensembles, FOXY the dunking mascot and - most importantly - the glorious 'BBL Babes Cheerleaders'.

The showpiece fixture of the British basketball season is played at Wembley

28th
Mick Hucknall
Sunday 28th April 2013
Hammersmith Apollo, London W6 9QH
Flame-haired soul singer Mick Hucknall swings by the Apollo to conclude a mini UK tour showcasing his new solo album 'American Soul', which features the former Simply Red frontman's own take on classic songs that have inspired him throughout his heavily documented life. With the curtain falling on Simply Red at their triumphant sell-out 'Farewell' tour in 2010, 'American Soul' marks a new beginning for the smooth Mancunian, who begins a new chapter in his life as a solo performer. Renowned for his sweet mature vocals, love-torn lyrics and curly copper-red locks, Hucknall interprets classics from the American soul genre, including 'I Only Have Eyes For You',

APRIL 2013

Edward Petherbridge and Paul Hunter in 'My Perfect Mind' → 116

'I'd Rather Go Bling' and 'That's How Strong My Love Is'. Lock up your daughters (or mothers).

28th & 29th
Bonhams Classic Car Auction
Sunday 28th & Monday 29th April 2013
RAF Museum, Grahame Park Way, London NW9 5L
On Monday 29th April auction house Bonhams will be holding its annual classic car auction in the Dermot Boyle Wing of the Royal Air Force Museum in Hendon, northwest London. Even if you're not in a position to buy, you can see the wide variety of vehicles that will form part of the auction the day before the sale, on Sunday 28th April. One of the highlights of last year's sale was an unrestored 1959 Austin Mini Se7en, a remarkable time-warp survivor and the eighth of its type produced.

29th
Pink Martini
Monday 29th April 2013
Royal Albert Hall, Kensington Gore, London SW7 2AP
The Oregon-based 'little orchestra' Pink Martini bring their "swiftly intoxicating and elegantly chilled" (The Telegraph) blend of multilingual lounge pop back to the Royal Albert Hall for a night of easy-listening world music. Founded in 1994 by bandleader and pianist Thomas Lauderdale and his fellow Harvard student China Forbes - the "Diva next door" with an uncanny ability to sing in an extraordinary number of languages - Pink Martini have been described as the United Nations of music, blending '30s Cuban dance, classical chamber music, Brazilian marching street band, speakeasy cocktail jazz and Japanese film noir. The mesmerising Forbes was absent for the ensemble's debut visit to the Royal Albert Hall in 2011, making this return all the more appealing for Pink Martini's cosmopolitan hordes of fans.

From 29th
La Bohème
29th April – 29th June 2013
English National Opera, London Coliseum, London WC2N 4ES
As Rodolfo the poet and Mimi the seamstress fall for each other by moonlight when their candles are blown out, the beginning of this production promises all the fragile romance of a great love story and Puccini's indulgent score does not disappoint. Some lovely touches bring to life the spirited world of 19th century bohemian Paris, peppered with colourful characters, including a warmly funny rent-dodging interlude and the merry chorus of a street market. Isabella Bywater's period designs evoke the grimy streets, adding a faded glamour to the story. John Copley's 1974 production has been revived countless times but its classic, evocative sets and beautiful, soaring music have earned it a place as one of the all-time greats.

Unconfirmed dates

Othello
Opening date TBC
National Theatre: Olivier, South Bank, London SE1
Adrian Lester, known for starring in the BBC's 'Hustle', will take on one of Shakespeare's more demanding roles when 'Othello' comes to the National Theatre this spring. The jealous and conniving Iago will be played by Rory Kinnear – winner of best actor in the Evening Standard's drama awards after his 2010 portrayal of Hamlet. Directed by Nicholas Hytner, this production of Shakespeare's drama will take to the stage as part of the National Theatre's 50th anniversary season.

The Shed
Opening date TBC
National Theatre, South Bank, London SE1 9PX
From April 2013, the National Theatre will open The Shed, a temporary performance space at the front of the South Bank building which will be used to stage plays during the Cottesloe's closure. The distinctive red wooden box, designed by architects Haworth Tompkins who are also responsible for the refurbishment of the Cottesloe, will hold 225 seats and tickets will cost £20. The programme promises to be a celebration of new theatre, a mix of emerging and established artists, with performances by visitors from around the world and a range of unexpected collaborations.

LONDON'S WEEKLY MARKETS

Vintage clothes, unusual antiques, sweet-smelling flowers and yummy street food - London's markets tick all the boxes, says *Vicki Forde*

CAMDEN MARKETS
Camden Town,
London NW1 8AF
Several contrasting markets wrapped into one canal-side shopping experience

SPITALFIELDS MARKET
Spitalfields,
London E1 6DW
This City favourite is the perfect antidote to out-of-town shopping malls

LEADENHALL MARKET
Whittington Avenue,
London EC3V 1LR
Victorian covered market that sells traditional game, fish and meat

BOROUGH MARKET
Southwark Street,
Bankside, London SE1 1TJ
Renowned food market boasting a delectable range of fresh produce and snacks

COLUMBIA ROAD MARKET
Columbia Road, Tower Hamlets, London E2 7RG
The capital's most colourful market with flowers, shrubs and bedding plants

BERWICK STREET MARKET
Soho,
London W1F 8TW
Prime eating area that offers quality street food, fresh fruit & veg, and clothing

GREENWICH MARKET
College Approach,
London SE10 9HZ
A number of markets offering a variety of hand-crafted goods, antiques and food

BRICK LANE MARKET
Spitalfields,
London E1 6RL
Bustling market with second-hand furniture, unusual clothes and curry houses

PORTOBELLO ROAD MARKET
Notting Hill,
London W11 1LU
Antiques and flea market that sells everything from vintage books to bric-a-brac

CAMDEN PASSAGE MARKET
Islington,
London N1 8EE
Offbeat selection of market stalls intermingled with antique shops and restaurants

PETTICOAT LANE MARKET
Spitalfields,
London E1 7HT
World-famous Sunday market that has clothes for men, women and children

MALTBY STREET MARKET
Bermondsey,
London SE1 3PA
Some of London's best food and drink producers gather under the railway arches

---

LONDON MARKETS NEWSLETTER

→ To receive the London Markets Newsletter from LondonTown.com send a blank email now to: **markets@londontown.com**

PRIVACY PROMISE: We will never (and that means never) give your email address to anyone else. You mean too much to us.

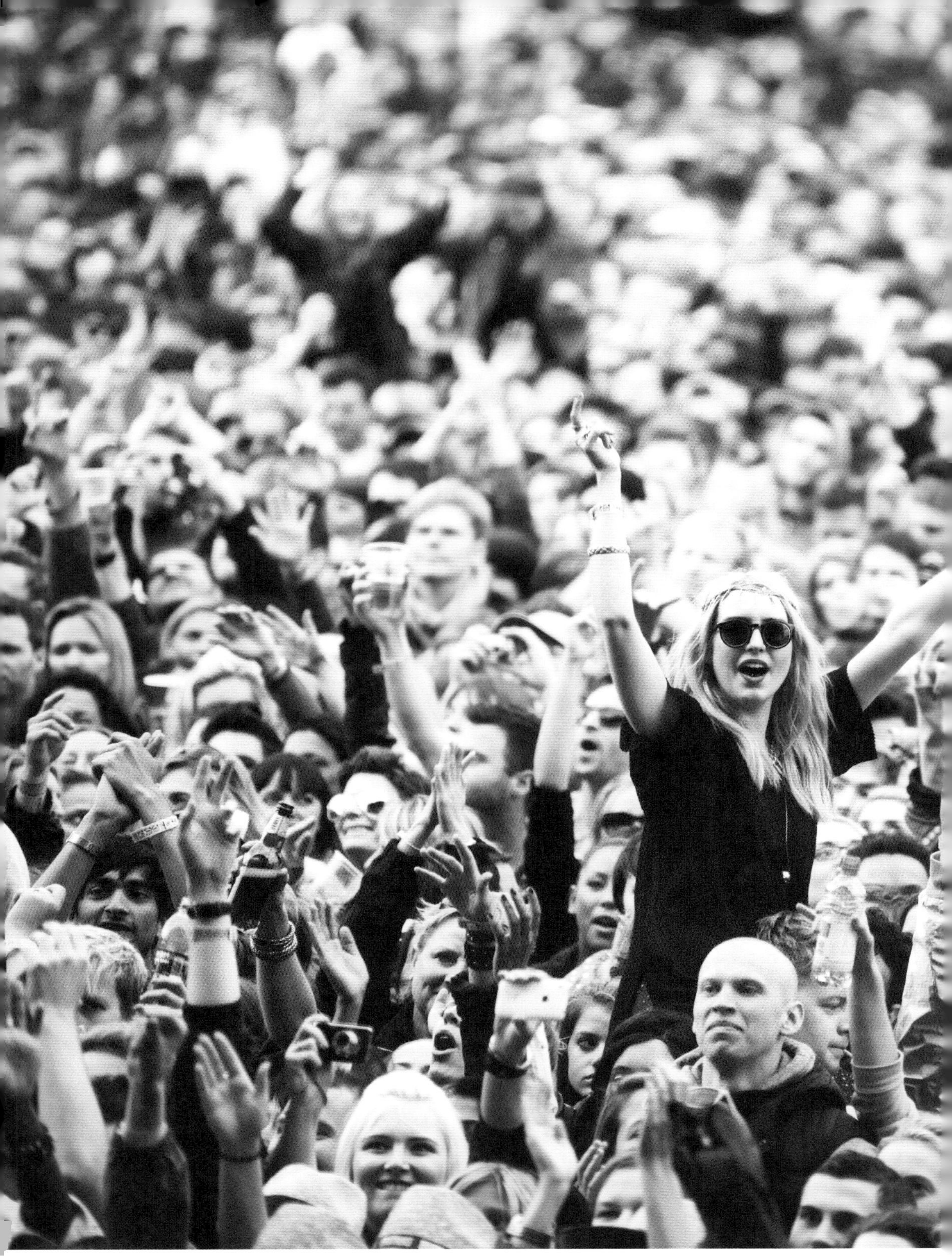

129

Summer is upon us with a flurry of football finals, fairs, flowers, Philharmonic film frenzies and festivals...

PAGES 38-39

MAY

WHAT'S ON WHERE IN MAY

LondonTown.com

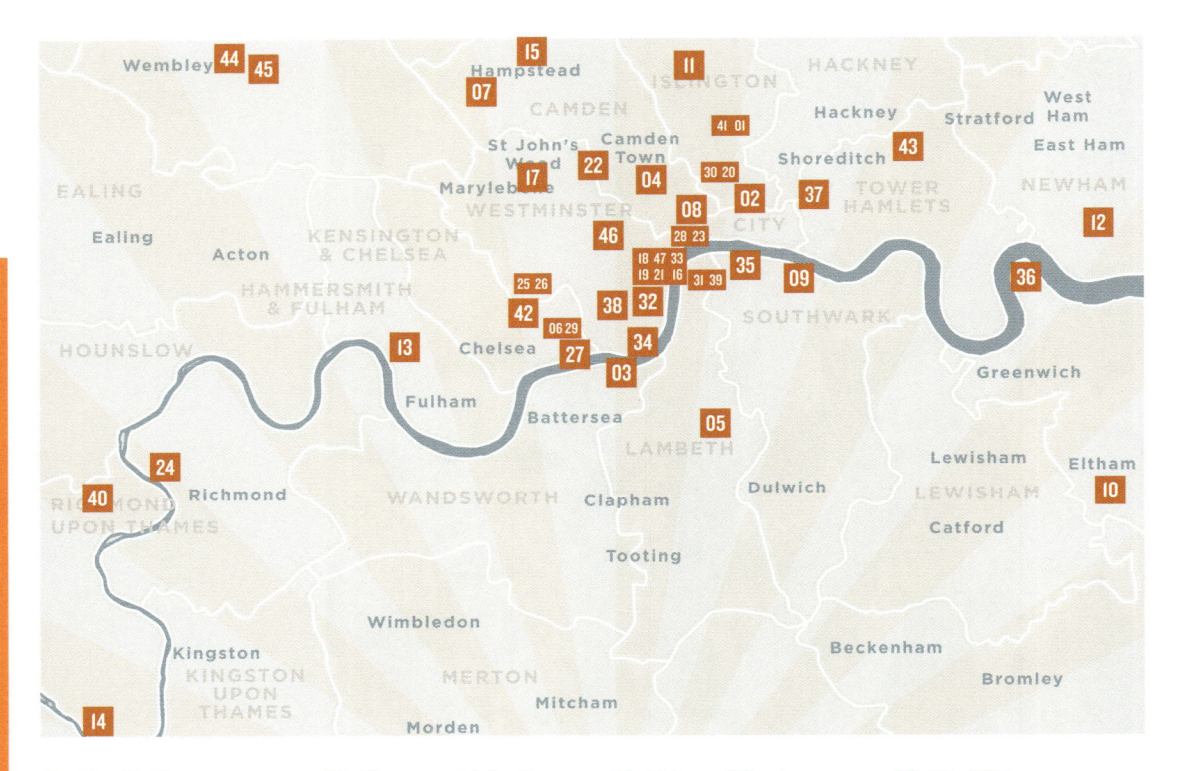

01	**Almeida Theatre** Page 137
02	**Barbican Centre** Page 133
03	**Battersea Power Station** Page 134
04	**British Library** Page 137
05	**Brixton Academy** Pages 73 & 142
06	**Cadogan Hall** Page 134
07	**Camden Arts Centre** Page 137
08	**Conway Hall** Page 137
09	**Design Museum** Page 133
10	**Eltham Palace** Page 134
11	**Emirates Stadium** Page 140
12	**ExCeL** Page 132
13	**Hammersmith Apollo** Pages 137 & 139
14	**Hampton Court Palace** Page 140
15	**Keats House** Page 140
16	**London Coliseum (ENO)** Page 135
17	**Lord's Cricket Ground** Pages 136 & 142
18	**Madame Jojo's** Page 134
19	**Mall Galleries** Page 133
20	**Museum and Library of the Order of St John** Page 141
21	**National Gallery** Page 139
22	**Open Air Theatre, Regent's Park** Page 136
23	**Peacock Theatre** Page 132
24	**Richmond Theatre** Pages 75 & 142
25	**Royal Albert Hall** Pages 133, 136, 138, 140 & 141
26	**Royal College of Art** Page 133
27	**Royal Hospital Chelsea** Page 138
28	**Royal Opera House** Pages 132, 137 & 139
29	**Saatchi Gallery** Page 133
30	**Sadler's Wells Theatre** Pages 132, 135 & 142
31	**Southbank Centre** Pages 132, 133, 135 & 139
32	**St James's Park** Page 141
33	**St Paul's Covent Garden** Page 135
34	**Tate Britain** Page 131
35	**Tate Modern** Page 131
36	**The O2 Arena** Pages 131, 136 & 142
37	**The Old Truman Brewery** Page 142
38	**The Queen's Gallery** Page 138
39	**The Young Vic** Page 133
40	**Twickenham Stadium** Pages 134 & 140
41	**Union Chapel** Page 135
42	**V&A Museum** Page 136
43	**Victoria Park** Page 140
44	**Wembley Arena** Page 134
45	**Wembley Stadium** Pages 132, 134, 137, 140, 141 & 142
46	**Wigmore Hall** Page 132
47	**Wyndhams Theatre** Page 136

LondonTown.com **MAY 2013**

PICK

EXHIBITIONS

RHS Chelsea Flower Show

21st – 25th May 2013
Royal Hospital Chelsea, Royal Hospital Road, London SW3 4SR

PAGE 138

May 2013
A Walk Through British Art – BP British Art Displays

Tate Britain, Millbank, London SW1P 4RG

The BP British Art Displays get a spring makeover with a dramatic revamp of the collection and a shift in the chronological ordering of the artworks, dating from 1540 to the present. In addition, there will be focus rooms exhibiting highlights from particular artists and periods. Henry Moore, William Blake and J.M.W Turner all receive a space dedicated to their work, and for the first time, there will be a gallery dedicated entirely to photography.

From 1st
Ellen Gallagher

1st May – 1st September 2013
Tate Modern, 25 Sumner Street, London SE1 9TG

The Tate Modern presents an exhibition of the North American artist Ellen Gallagher and her diverse body of work from the past 20 years. Her eclectic style is inspired by literature, myth, science fiction and advertising and she works in a vast quantity of materials ranging from plasticine to watercolours.

2nd
The Vaccines

Thursday 2nd May 2013
The O2 Arena, Greenwich, London SE10 0DX

With two albums released within 18 months, The Vaccines haven't paused for a breath since they first stepped onto the music scene in 2010. Described by The Independent as "the Shoreditch Strokes", they have received mixed reviews of their indie rock music. However, their latest studio album 'Coming of Age' was praised by the BBC: "Their writing and delivery is more creative and the four-piece sound more invigorated and inspired than ever." They have now added an extra date to their tour to perform at the O2 this May.

From 3rd
ZooNation Dance Company: Some Like it Hip Hop
3rd May – 30th June 2013
Peacock Theatre, Holborn, London WC2A 2HT
Kate Prince directs 'Some Like It Hip Hop', a dance-theatre fusion of the Billy Wilder film 'Some Like It Hot' and Shakespeare's 'Twelfth Night'. One of the West End's biggest success stories of last year, the show has received widespread critical acclaim for its "wit, heart and energy" (The Independent). Uniting a riveting storyline with some show-stopping dance routines, Prince, also the co-writer, presents a comical tale of romance, mistaken identity, cross-dressing and revolution - all set to original music from Josh Cohen and DJ Walde. If you're a fan of hip hop, comedy and physical theatre, then this is most definitely the one for you.

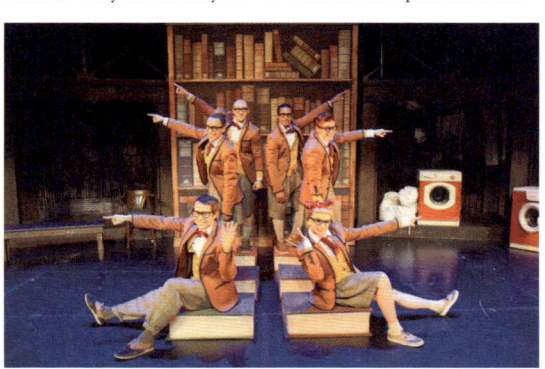

Some like it Hip Hop at the Peacock Theatre

4th
The FA Vase
Saturday 4th May 2013
Wembley Stadium, Wembley, London HA9 0WS
So lowly are the teams involved in this knock-out competition that the winners do not receive a cup or a trophy - just a meagre vase. Open to amateur teams in the eighth and lower tiers of the Football League system (including outfits from the Channel Islands and the Isle of Man), the FA Vase was won last year by Dunston UTS, who beat West Auckland Town 2-0 in front of a crowd of 5,126. But what a day out for everyone involved!

4th - 6th
Breakin' Convention
4th - 6th May 2013
Sadler's Wells, Rosebery Avenue, London EC1R 4TN
This annual three-day international festival of hip hop and dance theatre, curated by Sadler's Wells associate artist Jonzi D, celebrates its 10th anniversary in 2013. 'Breakin' Convention' features performances from some of the world's greatest poppers, lockers, B-boys and B-girls, and includes a whole evening dedicated to world premieres from UK companies. It's a frenzy of cutting-edge moves with one head-spinning act after another taking to the stage to wow audiences. Alongside world class performances the weekend is packed with live aerosol jams, workshop programmes, DJ demos, freestyle circles and a world record attempt for the longest continuous popping wave.

4th – 6th
Chorus
4th – 6th May 2013
Southbank Centre, London SE1 8XX
Back at the Southbank Centre for its sixth year, 'Chorus' is a celebration of the voice and the power of singing. The festival embraces all genres of music and welcomes gospel, indie, world music, a capella and classical to the line-up. Many of the events are free and audiences are encouraged to join in for the sing-along events. Further highlights of the programme include the chance to become part of a mass improvised choir, special guest performances and a number of workshops.

4th – 12th
Grand Designs Live
4th – 12th May 2013
ExCeL Centre, London E16
Based on the hugely popular Channel 4 TV series, in which the general public aim to build their dream homes, the multi-award-winning 'Grand Designs Live' returns to the ExCeL Centre this spring. Presented by design guru Kevin McCloud, the show is the perfect place to come for ideas and inspiration for the home with over 500 exhibitors, top TV celebrities, shopping and fabulous show features. Whether you're building a conservatory, renovating a new home or just trying to sort out your hideous living room, there will be something for you at this ultimate exhibition for people passionate about home and garden design.

4th & 22nd
Schumann: Under the Influence
4th & 22nd May 2013
Wigmore Hall, London W1U
Young American pianist Jonathan Biss produces this series of concerts at Wigmore Hall that will pay homage to the legacy of Robert Schumann and his music. Regarded by some as a happy accident of history, Schumann's music is seen as uniquely original and yet a crucial link in a chain of composers across centuries. This series will look into that progression and will feature the work of four composers who could not have existed without the influence of Schumann.

4th – 25th
Don Carlo
4th May – 25th May 2013
Royal Opera House, Covent Garden, London WC2E 9DD
This grand opera was cut and re-cut for over 20 years after its Paris debut in 1867 but 'Don Carlo' - returning to the Royal Opera House in Nicholas Hytner's production - remains Verdi's longest work. It gives new meaning to the word 'epic', taking in a broad sweep of 16th century history and playing out the usual collection of operatic storylines involving lost love, jealous revenge and political ambition. The main action focuses on Don Carlo falling for Elisabetta di Valois, who despite loving him in return has

to marry Don Carlo's father King Philip II as part of the peace treaty between Spain and France. Nicholas Hytner's wealth of experience across all three genres of theatre, opera and film promises a dramatic frisson not usually associated with this monumental work.

From 4th
Public Enemy
4th May – 8th June 2013
Young Vic, Waterloo, London SE1 8LZ
Another Henrik Ibsen revival to take to the Young Vic stage this year, 'Public Enemy' – originally titled 'Enemy of the People' - is a story of corruption, pollution and courage. When he discovers that the waters of a new public spa are toxic, Dr Stockmann expects gratitude and glory. Instead, he becomes the most hated man in town. With the townspeople desperate to keep the dirty secret of their most lucrative tourist attraction, how far will one man go to stand up for the truth? Ibsen wrote the play to address the irrational tendencies of the masses and point out the hypocrisy in the political system of the time.

Monday 6th May
May Day (Bank Holiday)

8th & 9th
Leona Lewis
8th & 9th May 2013
Royal Albert Hall, Kensington, London SW7 2AP
Plucked from obscurity on her way to winning series three of the 'X Factor' in 2006, the shy, unassuming but unquestionably stunning girl from Hackney went on to become a multi-platinum selling artist and three-time Grammy Award nominee, conquer America and prove to be one of Simon Cowell's biggest successes to date. Leona embarked on her debut tour 'The Labyrinth' in 2010 to promote her first two albums. Now, on the back of her third album 'Glassheart', Leona Lewis will perform at the Royal Albert Hall for two nights as part of a 16-date UK tour.

From 8th
Edward Barber and Jay Osgerby
8th May – 25th August 2013
Design Museum, 28 Shad Thames, London SE1 2YD
After winning the Design Museum's Design of the Year award in 2012 for their London 2012 Olympic Torch, designers Edward Barber and Jay Osgerby return to the museum for a show which presents their unique view on the production of everyday objects. The pair were chosen to design the torch from submissions made by over 600 design agencies. In this Design Museum exhibition, visitors can explore the designers' multidisciplinary practice - they design everything from furniture and lighting to watering cans - and the way in which it challenges the boundaries of industrial design, architecture and art. Their work with manufacturers, engineers and factories is also examined as an integral part of their studio's award-winning projects.

9th – 12th
20/21 International Art Fair
9th – 12th May 2013
Royal College of Art, Kensington Gore, London SW7 2EU
This is the fifth year this major commercial art fair, specialising in art from the 20th and 21st centuries, comes to the Royal College of Art in Kensington Gore. The 20/21 International Art Fair - run by the same organisers as the 20/21 British Art Fair, held here in September - offers a similar focus on affordable art by big names but on an international scale. Modern and contemporary art comes from China, Japan, Russia, Australia, the Ukraine, Poland, France and Ireland as well as Britain. Pieces are on sale from artists including Modigliani, Matisse, Chagall, David Hockney, Bridget Riley, and Damien Hirst.

9th – 24th
Royal Society of Portrait Painters Exhibition
9th – 24th May 2013
Mall Galleries, St James's, London SW1Y 5BD
The country's leading portrait exhibition displays painted and drawn portrait submissions by both national and international artists, including high profile commissions and works by artists never-before-seen. This year the exhibition will be drawn from three sources: work by members, the best work chosen from open submission and a gallery of shortlisted works for the new SELF portrait prize, worth £20,000. Further prizes include the Prince of Wales's Award for Portrait Drawing, the Changing Faces Commission Prize, the de Lazlo Prize for the most outstanding portrait by an artist aged 35 years or under, and the £10,000 Ondaatje Prize for the most distinguished painting, one of the most prestigious prizes in the world of portraiture, which also earns the winner the Society's Gold Medal.

10th – 12th
Spring Real Bread Festival
10th – 12th May 2013
Southbank Centre, London SE1 8XX
Britain is a country raised on bread: sliced, toasted, cut into triangles, we just can't get enough of the stuff. But if you want to know exactly where your bread comes from, what goes in to it and who is making it, head to the Spring Real Bread Festival to taste some real artisan bread baked by Britain's most passionate bread makers.

10th – 12th
A Scream and an Outrage
10th - 12th May 2013
Barbican Centre, Silk Street, London EC2Y 8DS
In May the Barbican hosts 'A Scream and an Outrage', a marathon weekend of new music curated by composer Nico Muhly, featuring premieres and specially commissioned work from Muhly's mentor Philip Glass. It's "all about composers writing for their friends, and creating environments for great performances", says Muhly. This translates into a piece created by David Lang and played by the innovative Brooklyn-based quartet So Percussion, Paola Prestini's multimedia extravaganza, and music from the 16th century composer Thomas Tallis, among others.

10th – 13th
Collect
10th – 13th May 2013
Saatchi Gallery, Chelsea, London SW3 4SQ
Launched by the British Crafts Council in 2004, the 'Collect' craft show returns to the

Saatchi Gallery this May for its 10th anniversary. 'Collect' is the one of the largest art fairs for contemporary craft in Europe with over 300 artists representing 36 galleries from Britain and around the world. Desirable design objects include ceramics, glass, jewellery, textiles, wood, furniture and work in precious metals. With galleries from across the world coming together - from the UK, Belgium, Denmark, Germany, Japan, Sweden, Switzerland and the Netherlands - it's an impressive collection of talent.

10th – 19th
London Burlesque Festival

10th – 19th May 2013
Various venues around London

Prudes avert your eyes, for the London Burlesque Festival returns for the seventh year at a number of venues across the capital. Brought to you by the infamous King of Burlesque, Chaz Royal, the man behind 'Pavabotti - The Naked Tenor', this year's event is bigger and more glamorous than ever. What was initially a weekend of glitz, vaudeville and sizzling striptease is now a whole ten nights of raucous exotic entertainment showcasing the very best in British burlesque and beyond. Venues across London take part and the festival typically concludes with a glittering Saturday night finale, in which burlesque beauties battle insatiably for the British and World Female Crown.

10th - 20th
Moscow State Symphony Orchestra: Tchaikovsky Cycle

10th - 20th May 2013
Cadogan Hall, Belgravia, London SW1X 9DQ

Described by the L.A. Times as "the world's least-heralded great orchestra", the Moscow State Symphony Orchestra performs three concerts celebrating the key works of Tchaikovsky this May. The first concert features the 'March Slave', 'Piano Concerto No.1', and 'Fourth Symphony'; the second concert includes the Russian composer's 'Francesca da Rimini', 'Rococo Variations' and dramatic 'Fifth Symphony'; the final concert of the cycle features Tchaikovsky's 'Violin Concerto' and 'Sixth Symphony', the 'Pathétique', and the 'Polonaise' and 'Waltz' from 'Eugene Onegin'. Voted one of the 10 greatest conductors of the 20th century, Pavel Kogan conducts a line-up of virtuoso young soloists for this tantalising treat.

11th
The FA Cup Final

Saturday 11th May 2013
Wembley Stadium, Wembley, London HA9 0WS

After months of knock-out matches, the last two teams standing come head to head at Wembley Stadium for the final of the FA Cup - the world's oldest domestic football cup competition. Last year, Chelsea beat Liverpool 2-1 to claim their fourth FA Cup title in six years: a second half Andy Carroll goal was not enough after Chelsea went two-up either side of the break thanks to Brazilian midfielder Ramirez and talismanic striker Didier Drogba. Spanish schemer Juan Mata was man of the match - but Drogba took the accolades by becoming the first player in history to score in four different FA Cup finals. Time will tell which teams will line up for this clash - but with Drogba now gone, perhaps Chelsea's aura of invincibility will be lifted.

11th
Eddie Izzard: Force Majeure

Saturday 11th May 2013
Wembley Arena, Empire Way, London HA9 0DH
Saturday 8th June 2013
The O2 Arena, Greenwich, London SE10 0DX

Not content with running seven weeks of back-to-back marathons (thankfully in trainers, not stilettos), Eddie Izzard embarks on his most extensive comedy tour ever - visiting 25 countries throughout Europe, the USA, Africa, Russia, Australia, New Zealand, India, Nepal and the Far East. 'Force Majeure' is Izzard's first tour since 2009's 'Stripped', which ran for two years and saw the inimitable comic take on a three-month residency in Paris performing entirely in French. No one does rambling, whimsical, intelligent, surreal and seemingly unscripted stream-of-consciousness quite as well as Izzard, a veritable master of self-referential pantomime.

11th
The MoonWalk

Saturday 11th May 2013
Battersea Power Station, Battersea, London SW8 5BP

The world's only Power Walking Marathon returns for its 16th birthday. 'The MoonWalk' attracts 15,000 participants and raises money for Walk the Walk, a breast cancer charity that makes grants available to support medical research and also funds emotional and physical care for those who already have cancer. This year's theme has yet to be announced but you can expect the walkers to stride out in some outrageous outfits; wearing a colourful decorated bra has become de rigueur on the walk, so look out for the most flamboyant.

11th & 12th
HSBC Sevens World Series: Marriott London Sevens

Saturday 11th & Sunday 12th May 2013
Twickenham Stadium, London TW1 1DZ

With Rugby Sevens being drafted in for the Rio 2016 Olympics, there should be extra interest in the Marriott London Sevens tournament this year. Held at Twickenham over one weekend, the event is the last of 10 rounds in the HSBC Sevens World Series, which features the 16 best international teams in this high-octane, fast-moving format of the game. There are four competitions in total, with the top two teams of each group advancing to the Cup and Plate competitions, and the two losers battling it out for the Bowl and Shield categories. Last year, Fiji took the main Cup competition after brushing aside New Zealand in the semis before thrashing Samoa 38-15 in the final. Hosts England narrowly lost 14-12 to great rivals Australia in the Plate final, Wales beat Scotland in the Bowl and France prevailed over the USA in the Shield.

11th & 12th
Eltham Palace Art Deco Fair

11th & 12th May 2013
7th & 8th September 2013
Eltham Palace, Court Yard, London SE9 5QE

If there's one place in London that merits an Art Deco Fair, it's Eltham Palace, one of London's secret wonders, a captivating blend of 1930s art deco decadence and classic medievalism. The much-loved weekend fair is held twice over the summer and gives visitors the chance to buy original 1930s objects - from furniture and collectables to hats, handbags and jewellery.

11th – 25th
Wozzeck
11th – 25th May 2013
English National Opera, London Coliseum, London WC2N 4ES

The latest offering from promising Young Vic director Carrie Cracknell is a vivid retelling of the Berg operatic masterpiece, 'Wozzeck', based on the tragic tale of a troubled soldier who murders his unfaithful wife, before accidentally drowning and leaving behind an orphaned child. The production will be conducted by award-winning ENO Music Director Edward Gardner.

12th
Aled Jones
Sunday 12th May 2013
Union Chapel, Islington, London N1 2UN

Welsh treble singer, BBC Radio presenter and 'Songs of Praise' presenter Aled Jones concludes his tour of British cathedrals with this rescheduled show at Union Chapel. Initially known for his 1982 cover of 'Walking in the Air' from 'The Snowman', Jones has gone on to release 29 albums and sell more than six million records. He now presents 'Daybreak' on ITV.

12th
Covent Garden May Fayre and Puppet Festival
Sunday 12th May 2013
St Paul's Church, Covent Garden, London WC2E 9ED

The annual Covent Garden May Fayre and Puppet Festival celebrates the red-nosed, stick-wielding puppet, bringing together dozens of puppeteers in a colourful and highly entertaining afternoon. In 2013 it's Mr Punch's 351st birthday and celebrations in Covent Garden draw puppeteers from all over the country as well as folk musicians, dancers, clowns, jugglers and stalls. The location is appropriately close to the spot where Samuel Pepys first sighted Mr Punch on 9th May 1662 and recorded the fact in his diary - which is why the birthday celebrations fall on or near to 9th May. The day's events start with a toast to Mr Punch and a brass band-led Grand Procession starting at St Paul's Church garden. There follows a special service with a sermon administered by Rev Mark Oakley and Mr Punch himself.

14th – 18th
Northern Ballet - The Great Gatsby
14th – 18th May 2013
Sadler's Wells, Rosebery Avenue, London EC1R 4TN

Days after the UK release of Baz Luhrmann's cinematic adaptation, Northern Ballet's interpretation of the 'Great American Novel' takes to the stage at Sadler's Wells. Set in America's roaring 1920s, 'The Great Gatsby' tells the compelling story of young Nick Carraway and his infamous neighbour Jay Gatsby – an aloof character with a secret

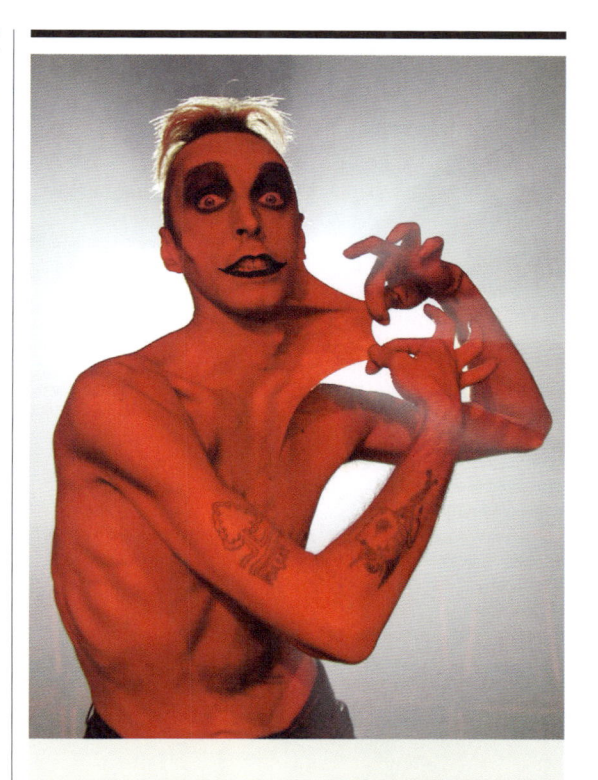

From 6th
London Wonderground
6th May – 29th September 2013
Southbank Centre, London SE1 8XX

PICK

HAVING MADE ITS FIRST APPEARANCE last year, bringing Coney Island-style attractions and cabaret performed in a Speigeltent in the shadow of the Southbank Centre, the London Wonderground makes a welcome return in May. Transforming the riverside site into an amusement ground, it entices visitors in with fairground rides, circus shows and a programme of international cabaret, music and fringe theatre. In its inaugural year the festival drew over 800,000 visitors (including Madonna and 15 members of her entourage), and presented 277 different performances from 46 different acts, including the Australian circus hit Cantina, Hercules & Love Affair, British comedy trio Fascinating Aida, and Gary Stretch, the man with the stretchiest skin in the world. Expect similar freaks and misfits to form this year's line-up.

past. As he is invited further into the world of lavish parties and extravagant glamour, Carraway starts to unravel the truth that's hidden behind the sparkling façade of his neighbour's world.

From 14th
Relatively Speaking
14th May – 31st August 2013
Wyndhams Theatre, Charing Cross Road, London WC2H
Felicity Kendal stars in Alan Ayckbourn's classic comedy 'Relatively Speaking' at the Wyndham's Theatre, its first West End revival since its original London run in 1967. Lindsay Posner directs the cast of four which also includes Kara Tointon, Max Bennett and Jonathan Coy. There are many laugh-out-loud moments in this tale of mistaken identity as Greg, who only met Ginny a month ago, decides she's the woman for him. Finding a scribbled address, Greg follows Ginny to her parents' house to ask her father's permission to marry. The only trouble is, the couple he finds in the garden are not Ginny's parents, so who are they?

15th
Royal Philharmonic Orchestra: Film Music Gala
Wednesday 15th May 2013
Royal Albert Hall, Kensington Gore, London SW7 2AP
Paying homage to the spectacular world of film music, the Royal Albert Hall invites the Royal Philharmonic Orchestra to play some favourite pieces from both recent Hollywood blockbusters and timeless classics. Highlights of the evening include music from 'Gladiator', 'The Lord of the Rings', 'Jurassic Park', 'Pirates of the Caribbean' and 'Harry Potter'.

16th
McCoy's Premier League Darts
Thursday 16th May 2013
The O2 Arena, Greenwich, London SE10 0DX
The world's four leading darts players descend upon the O2 Arena for the play-offs of the McCoy's Premier League Darts to mark the culmination of the event's three-month tour of the UK and Ireland. The likes of reigning champion Phil "The Power" Taylor and current world champion Adrian Lewis will take part in the tournament, which is played over 14 consecutive Thursday evenings starting on 7th February in Belfast. With each of the eight players facing each other twice, the top four stars in the table will qualify for this showpiece event at the O2.

16th - 18th
Museums at Night
16th - 18th May 2013
Museums across London
This annual campaign treats visitors to after-hours fun in some of London's finest museums, galleries and heritage sights. The London Transport Museum, Victoria and Albert Museum, Old Operating Theatre and London's Royal Observatory have all participated in previous years along with around 70 other venues. If you think the idea of spending the night in a dusty old museum sounds a bit dull then think again: previous participants have enjoyed sunset hovercraft rides, live action 'Cluedo', toy sleepovers and tunnel tours by lantern-light. One venue hosted a 'Thunderbirds' themed night to exhibit rare models, complete with 1960s music, screenings of the TV show and an interview with a voice artist.

16th – 20th
1st Investec Test: England v New Zealand
16th – 20th May 2013
Lord's Cricket Ground, St John's Wood, London NW8
By the end of 2013, England's cricketers should be so familiar with all things New Zealand that they'll be filling their burgers with pickled beetroot and fried eggs. If a winter tour Down Under featuring three Tests, three ODIs and three T20s in February and March wasn't enough, New Zealand in turn travel across the world for a summer tour of England boasting two Tests, three ODIs and two T20s. The First Investec Test takes place at Lord's and you can expect it to be a rather one-sided affair: at the time of writing, England are the second best ranked side in test cricket while visitors New Zealand are the second bottom outfit, tailed only by minnows Bangladesh.

From 16th
Regent's Park Open Air Theatre Summer Season
16th May – 7th September 2013
Open Air Theatre, Regent's Park, London NW1 4NU
This is the 81st season for the Regent's Park Open Air Theatre and seeing a play here is an essential part of summer in London. After last year's showing of only two productions, this season will revert to its usual arrangement of a sombre opening, large scale musical production and a kids' adaptation of Shakespeare. It kicks off with Harper Lee's American classic 'To Kill a Mockingbird', adapted for the stage by Christopher Sergel. Following this, Jane Austen's ultimate romantic comedy 'Pride and Prejudice', which celebrates its 200th anniversary this year, will play, and 'The Winter's Tale', reimagined for everyone aged six and over, will run from late June. The finale of the season will be 'The Sound of Music' - an open air theatre debut for Richard Rodgers and Oscar Hammerstein II.

From 16th
To Kill a Mockingbird
16th May -15th June 2013
Open Air Theatre, Regent's Park, London NW1 4NU
This year, the Regent's Park Open Air Theatre season commences with Harper Lee's Pulitzer Prize-winning 'To Kill a Mockingbird'. When a small town is engulfed by racial injustice, it takes the courage of one man to disregard what's expected of him and stand up for what's right. Atticus Finch is a lawyer who seeks the truth and is determined to prove the innocence of a black man wrongly accused. His daughter fights for his honour and faces terrible circumstances as a result, but the determination of the pair gives hope to other locals in the town. The story's strong themes of compassion and bravery have lent it enduring popularity and it will now be revived in the idyllic setting of the open air theatre.

17th - 26th
Eric Clapton
17th - 26th May 2013
Royal Albert Hall, Kensington Gore, London SW7 2AP

Legendary guitarist Eric Clapton returns to his favourite London venue to celebrate his 50th year as a professional musician. Over the last half-century Clapton has established himself as one of the most influential guitarists of all time - and he's the only three-time inductee to the Rock and Roll Hall of Fame. "This is like walking into my front room," old Slowhand Clapton joked ahead of a previous Royal Albert Hall residency in 2011. Supported by his impressive long-time touring partners - Doyle Bramhall II (guitar), Steve Jordan (drums), Chris Stainton (piano and keyboards), and Willie Weeks (bass) - Clapton will focus on a back catalogue from The Yardbirds and Cream as well as his popular solo material, including some of his recent blues and honky-tonk offerings. There's no reason to cry about this journeyman.

From 17th
Chimerica
17th May – 29th June 2013
Almeida Theatre, Islington, London N1 1TA
Twenty three years after the event, Joe, a young American photojournalist, is driven to discover the truth behind the unknown hero he captured on film in Tiananmen Square, 1989. 'Chimerica', a new co-production presented by the Almeida theatre and Rupert Goold's acclaimed Headlong theatre company, and written by Lucy Kirkwood ('NSFW', Royal Court) gets its world première at the Islington theatre. This provocative piece which examines the changing fortunes of the two countries is directed by Lyndsey Turner ('Posh', at the Royal Court and the West End) who makes her Almeida theatre debut. The play will be the final production at the Almeida Theatre under Michael Attenborough who steps down as its artistic director after 11 years in the role.

From 17th
Dieter Roth: Diaries and other works
17th May – 14th July 2013
Camden Arts Centre, London NW3 6DG
Influential German-Swiss artist Dieter Roth was known as a sculptor, painter and conceptualist explorer. Back in the sixties he made 'literature sausages' by mashing books to a pulp and created paintings using melted cheese and yoghurt. His final project records the last year of his life, in a slow evolving self-portrait. He was an avid diarist, and filled countless journals with pages of colourful doodles and notes. The Camden Arts Centre now hosts an exhibition of these diaries and other highlights from his bold and unedited career.

From 17th
La Donna Del Lago
17th May – 11th June 2013
Royal Opera House, Covent Garden, London WC2E 9DD
John Fulljames directs Rossini's famous love story set against the turbulent background of the 16th century Scottish Highlands. King James V falls for Elena, a beautiful and mysterious woman (the "lady of the lake") who is not only the daughter of the enemy but also desperately in love. But the object of her affection is neither the king nor her own fiancé...

From 17th
Propaganda: Power and Persuasion
17th May – 17th September 2013
The British Library, Bloomsbury, London NW1 2DB
From the iconic depictions of Margaret Thatcher as Napoleon, to the representation of the Olympics, propaganda comes in many forms and affects us all on a daily basis. The British Library presents an exhibition exploring and uncovering the methods used to persuade and influence citizens, and reveals the powerful messages behind the cartoons, the films and the posters.

18th & 19th
Football League Play-off Finals
18th & 19th May 2013
Wembley Stadium, Wembley, London HA9 0WS
The League One and Two play-offs - contested by the teams finishing from third to sixth in their respective leagues - come to a head with this Wembley weekend of back-to-back finals. First up is Saturday's League Two play-off final which last year saw Crewe Alexandria beat Cheltenham Town 2-0 to rise to League One. Sunday's League One play-off final will struggle to beat the drama of last year's game: although goalless, a nail-biting penalty shootout saw all 22 players (including goalkeepers) take spot-kicks with Huddersfield Town emerging 8-7 winners over Sheffield United to reach the Championship.

19th
The School of Life Sunday Sermon: Jon Ronson
Sunday 19th May 2013
Conway Hall, Bloomsbury, London WC1R 4RL
Jon Ronson, the journalist and author of 'The Psychopath Test', will deliver a secular sermon as part of the thought provoking 'School of Life Sunday Sermon' series. His book, 'The Men Who Stare at Goats', "an inspired study of America's war on terror" (The Guardian), was made into a major motion picture in 2009 and his most recent novel, 'Lost at Sea: The Jon Ronson Mysteries', was published in October 2012. On reading 'The Psychopath Test' Will Self said of Ronson, "he does indeed force us to think more deeply about the subject at hand".

Covent Garden's May Puppet Festival packs a punch → 135

19th & 20th
Lana Del Rey
Sunday 19th & Monday 20th May 2013
Hammersmith Apollo, London W6 9QH
When her 'Video Games' single became a hit on YouTube, American singer-songwriter Lana Del Rey became an overnight success and suddenly she was one of the most talked about acts of 2012. Can she actually sing? Or write songs? After a shaky start on Jay Leno's US TV show she triumphed with some spellbinding live performances at the summer festivals - "her charisma was off the scale" said The Guardian of her performance at 'Latitude' 2012. Now the award-winning singer returns to the UK in 2013 for two live shows as part of a European tour. If further proof of her popularity were needed you need only look at her album sales - over 2.5 million copies of 'Born To Die' have been bought worldwide.

21st - 25th
RHS Chelsea Flower Show
21st – 25th May 2013
Royal Hospital Chelsea, Royal Hospital Road, London SW3 4SR
The RHS Chelsea Flower Show celebrates its centenary in 2013, and it promises to be an extraordinary event with a nostalgic look back at the past 100 years. Held in the grounds of the Chelsea Royal Hospital since 1913, most of London society, including the Queen, regards the Chelsea Flower Show as a highpoint of the London summer season, so if you get bored of the blooms you can have a great time celeb-spotting. Particularly spectacular are the gardens created by eight hundred of the greatest exponents of imaginative garden design, who spend nearly a month creating a horticultural wonderland over the 11-acre site. This beautiful and inspiring show is a real treat, even for non-gardeners.

22nd
Zucchero
Wednesday 22nd May 2013
Royal Albert Hall, Kensington Gore, SW7 2AP
Italian singing sensation Zucchero performs his greatest hits along with tracks from his latest album, 'La Sesión Cubana', which was recorded in Havana and features collaborations with some of Cuba's most important musicians. Once described by Ray Charles (no less) as "probably one of the best blues musicians I've ever worked with", Zucchero burst onto the international scene with his 1987 album 'Blue's', which became the highest-selling album in Italian history and featured the original version of his hit 'Senza Una Donna' (later to be recorded as a duet with Paul Young). Blending gospel, blues and rock, Zucchero jumps from boogie to ballads, rubbing shoulders with world famous artists such as Eric Clapton, Elton John, Sting and Pavarotti.

22nd
The Man Booker International Prize
Wednesday 22nd May 2013
Victoria and Albert Museum, London SW7 2RL
Following the finalist announcements at the Jaipur Literary Festival in January, the Man Booker International Prize returns to London to announce the 2013 winner. The £60,000 prize is awarded to a

From 10th
In Fine Style: The Art of Tudor and Stuart Fashion
PICK

10th May – 6th October 2013
The Queen's Gallery, Buckingham Palace, London SW1A 1AA

THE FASCINATION WITH royal fashion began long before Kate Middleton stepped onto the scene. Back in the 16th and 17th centuries social status was highly dependent on dressing in the best possible taste. Satin gowns, fur trims, sumptuous velvet and bejeweled necks were the epitome of style in daily court life, and that was just for men. The Tudor and Stuart fashions were captured in all their intricate detail by many great artists including Van Dyck and Nicholas Hilliard. The Queen's Gallery presents a collection of more than 60 paintings alongside jewellery, garments, armour and other artefacts from the period.

fiction novelist every two years. This year the winner is being determined by a panel of five judges including Aminatta Forna and Sir Christopher Ricks.

22nd
Wagner Anniversary Concert
Wednesday 22nd May 2013
Royal Festival Hall, Southbank Centre, SE1 8XX
Sir Andrew Davis conducts a concert commemorating the exact 200th anniversary of Richard Wagner's birth with music from 'Die Meistersinger', 'Tristan und Isolde' and 'Die Walküre' with soloists Giselle Allen, Susan Bullock and James Rutherford. 'The Valkyries' is one of Wagner's finest artistic achievements - and the prelude to Act III, 'The Ride of the Valkyries', has become rooted in popular culture since the 1979 film 'Apocalypse Now', where an American air regiment bellows out Wagner's powerful piece on helicopter-mounted loudspeakers during an assault on a Vietnamese village. This Philharmonia Orchestra concert kicks off 'Wagner 200' - a wide-ranging, London-based festival celebrating the bicentenary of the German composer's birth.

From 22nd
Birth of a Collection: The Barber Institute of Fine Arts and the National Gallery
22nd May – 1st September 2013
National Gallery, Trafalgar Square, London WC2N 5DN
The Barber Institute of Fine Arts celebrates its 80th anniversary, marking the occasion with a display of 19th century and Old Master paintings. The artworks were first displayed and stored together in the National Gallery during the early days of the Barber Institute back in the 1930s. This exhibition will reunite the collection, which includes masterpieces by Nicolas Poussin, Joseph Mallord William Turner and Claude Monet.

From 23rd
Michael Landy: Saints Alive
23rd May – 24th November 2013
National Gallery, Trafalgar Square, London WC2N 5DN
The 2013 Associate Artist in residence at the National Gallery, Michael Landy, is the subject of a free exhibition in the gallery's Sunley Room where seven kinetic sculptures go on display from May. In 'Saints Alive' Landy's large-scale works, consisting of fragments of National Gallery paintings cast in three dimensions, represent a contemporary view of the lives of the saints. Landy scours car boot sales and flea markets to create his works, recycling rubbish to create something new. One of the YBAs (Young British Artists) of the 1990s, he is best known for his 2001 installation, 'Break Down', where he catalogued and then destroyed all of his possessions.

From 24th
London Literature Festival
24th May - 5th June 2013
Southbank Centre, Belvedere Road, London SE1 8XX
The Southbank serves up its annual dose of world class literature with a delectable array of spoken word performances, exciting new collaborations, workshops and talks from major writers and thinkers from around the world. Now in its seventh year, the festival has jumped forward a couple of months to May. Programme highlights include a strand on Alternative Lifestyles; artistic and scientific perspectives on the world's bees; a celebration of the history, neighbourhoods and creative tensions of London; as well as a line-up of the world's best writers, poets, performers and thinkers, not to forget the ever-popular Women's Prize for Fiction Readings. Previous speakers at the popular two-week event have included literary greats such as Philip Pullman, Bret Easton Ellis, Andrea Levy, Barbara Kingsolver and Jeanette Winterson.

24th & 25th
Micky Flanagan: Back In The Game
24th & 25th May 2013
Hammersmith Apollo, London W6 9QH
3rd October 2013
Wembley Arena
16th and 17th October 2013
The O2 Arena
Cockney comic and man-of-the-moment Micky Flanagan travels the length and breadth of the UK and Ireland for one of the most anticipated comedy tours of 2013. Following on from his sell-out 'Out Out' tour of last year, 'Back In The Game' has three major stops in London. The 49-year-old funnyman came to comedy late, his debut show telling of his rise from working class East End lad to arty-farty East Dulwich resident - and earning him a best newcomer nomination at the 2007 Edinburgh Fringe. Comedy glory beckoned, with Frank Skinner claiming Flanagan was "arguably the funniest comedian in the world". He's now a regular on TV panel shows and a household name - a far cry from his first job as a fish porter at Billingsgate Fish Market.

24th – 26th
Tea and Coffee Festival
24th – 26th May 2013
Southbank Centre, London SE1 8XX
Unsurprisingly, the organisers of the Tea and Coffee Festival at London's Southbank Centre are extremely keen on their tea and coffee and Londoners are invited to get out of Starbucks or Costa and head down to the festival where these drinks will be properly celebrated and showcased. The festival will be a celebration of all things tea and coffee - enjoy the drinks in their pure form, tea and coffee based cocktails, macaroons, churros with mocha sauce, coffee flavoured cheesecakes and plenty more. There'll be tastings, masterclasses, talks, demonstrations and much more and with three days to choose from, you can be sure you'll find plenty to keep you enthused.

From 24th
Raven Girl / Symphony in C
24th, 28th, 29th May, 3rd & 8th June 2013
Royal Opera House, Covent Garden, London WC2E 9DD
Multi award-winning British choreographer Wayne McGregor returns to the Royal Opera House main stage with 'Raven Girl', an exciting collaboration with novelist Audrey Niffenegger, author of 'The Time Traveler's Wife'. The pairing of the choreographer in residence at the Royal Ballet and the American author, who is also a visual artist, is an exciting prospect which promises to be a highlight of the year at the

Ooh la la! The London Burlesque Festival returns to the capital → 134

Covent Garden opera house. 'Raven Girl' will be performed as a double bill with Balanchine's 'Symphony in C'.

25th
Field Day
Saturday 25th May 2013
Victoria Park, Tower Hamlets, London E3 5SN
East London's Field Day offers a more diverse, fresh selection of acts than some of the more mainstream pop festivals in London. Think subdued electro, melancholic folk, bold dance acts and a dreamy summer vibe to match. Last year had a corker of a line-up with the likes of Franz Ferdinand, Metronomy and DJ SBTRKT taking to the stage, so 2013 is sure not to disappoint. Following the main event, neighbouring clubs put on some cracking after-parties to carry those dancing feet through till dawn. Just keep your fingers crossed that the sun shines over leafy Victoria Park.

25th
UEFA Champions League Final 2013
Saturday 25th May 2013
Wembley Stadium, Wembley, London HA9 0WS
History is made as Wembley becomes the first stadium to host the Champions League final twice in three years - as UEFA doffs its cap in celebration of 150 years of the Football Association's existence. While Wembley may be the spiritual home of English football, it's not as if the 'home' advantage did much good back in 2011 when Barcelona coasted past Manchester United 3-1 to win the first European Cup final to be held at the stadium since its reopening in 2007. Last year, Chelsea became champions of Europe for the first time with a penalty shoot-out win over Bayern Munich in Munich's Allianz Arena. Perhaps it will be third-time lucky for the home nation, and maybe this May we'll see another London club take the spoils at Wembley.

25th
Aviva Premiership Rugby Final 2013
Saturday 25th May 2013
Twickenham Stadium, London TW1 1DZ
Rugby union's biggest domestic club final sells out Twickenham Stadium and sees the two best sides in the country go head to head in a bruising winner-takes-all encounter. Nine months of fiercely contested rugby - that's 135 games between the top 12 teams, plus two playoffs between the top four - all boil down to one 80-minute match in the battle for the Premiership crown. The final takes place following play-off matches between the table toppers and the 4th ranked team, and the 2nd and 3rd ranked teams, with the highest-placed team having home advantage. Last year, Harlequins, first place in the table, beat Leicester Tigers 30-23 in the final despite a late rally in front of 81,779 fans.

25th
Roger Hodgson
Saturday 25th May 2013
Royal Albert Hall, Kensington Gore, London SW7
The legendary songwriter and vocalist Roger Hodgson - the former frontman of '80s progressive rock outfit Supertramp - performs both solo work and some classic Supertramp hits such as 'Dreamer', 'Breakfast in America', 'The Logical Song' and 'It's Raining Again'.

25th & 26th
Muse
25th & 26th May 2013
Emirates Stadium, London N5
Musical heavyweights Muse are known for their ambitious fusion of rock, opera, classical and electronica, and their latest work has proved no exception. Released in 2012, 'Survival' was quite possibly the most ridiculous song that could have been chosen as an anthem for the London Olympic Games. Yet, with its over-dramatic chorus and corny lyrics, it blared from speakers across London to gee on the athletes. '2nd Law', the album from which the single was taken, is the band's sixth studio album and offers a "mad sci-fi mix of prog rock, cinematic strings, pop melodies and dubstep-inflected electronica" (The Telegraph). This tour will no doubt offer plenty of the trio's famed energetic and extravagant stage displays to accompany the outlandish songs.

25th - 27th
Hampton Court Foodies Festival
25th - 27th May 2013
Hampton Court Palace, Surrey KT8 9AU
Meet Michelin-starred chefs, see live demonstrations and sample food from London's top restaurants at the Foodies Festival. Cooking is made to look easy thanks to demos from top chefs and if the mere thought of all that makes you hungry then you can head to the restaurant tents where you can sample signature dishes from well-known restaurants. Wash it all down with posh fizz from Veuve Clicquot and you can guarantee an atmosphere of bon viveur. Around 25,000 people are expected to attend which just goes to show the popularity of London's restaurants. Much like the 'Taste of London', these 'Foodies' offer a winning combination of sampling, slurping and learning, all in the open air. A foodie's treat. The festival will also take place in Battersea Park from 27th - 29th July.

From 25th
Keats House Summer Festival
25th May – 2nd June 2013
Keats House, Hampstead, London NW3 2RR
The fourth annual summer

celebration of the English Romantic poet John Keats gives literary lovers a chance to enjoy the great poet's work through readings, performances, music and creative workshops. The nine day festival is held in his restored home, and the garden in which he wrote 'Ode to a Nightingale'.

Monday 27th May
Spring Bank Holiday

27th
BUPA London 10,000
27th May 2013
St James's Park and various London venues
Presented by the London Marathon, BUPA London 10,000 is run on the same course as the 2012 Olympic Marathons. Starting and finishing in The Mall, the route goes clockwise around the City of Westminster and the City of London, passing famous sights such as Nelson's Column, St Paul's Cathedral, the London Eye and Big Ben. Having won the race for the past four years, it's likely that Olympic champion Mo Farah will return in an attempt to defend his title and no doubt strike a pose at the finish line. Aside from the serious competitors, the streets will also be flooded with thousands of charity fun-runners and humorous costumes.

27th
Football League Championship Play-off Final
Monday 27th May 2013
Wembley Stadium, Wembley, London HA9 0WS
There is no single sporting event in the world more valuable to the winners than the Championship play-off final, which decides the third and final team to rise to the riches of the Premier League. Last year, West Ham United (who finished third in the Championship) beat fifth-place Blackpool 2-1 thanks to a late goal by Ricardo Vaz Te to ensure an immediate return to the top flight after the east London club's shock relegation in 2011. The 87th-minute goal was worth an estimated £85m factoring in TV revenue. The loser traditionally keeps all gate receipts from the final - not that this is much consolation for the fans (especially if they've travelled all the way from Blackpool). At the end of the day, there will be tears of joy or pain either way.

From 27th
Mark Knopfler
27th May - 1st June 2013
Royal Albert Hall, Kensington Gore, London SW7
One of Britain's biggest exports returns to the prestigious venue for six special nights to promote his latest album 'Privateering', "a warm, authentic and durable record" (The Telegraph). The former Dire Straits frontman is hailed as one of the greatest guitarists of all time and has sold in excess of 120 million albums. At these eagerly anticipated concerts Knopfler's full eight-piece band will choose material from his eight solo albums, as well as the major Dire Straits hits including 'Money For Nothing', 'Sultans of Swing', 'Romeo and Juliet' and 'Walk of Life'. Since leaving Dire Straights, Knopfler has matured into a master of low-key country blues, eclipsing even Bob Dylan with his thoughtful musicianship and genuine soul when the pair toured together in 2011. This should be quite special.

21st - 23rd
Clerkenwell Design Week *PICK*
21st – 23rd May 2013
Various venues in Clerkenwell

A THREE DAY FESTIVAL of installations, workshops, presentations, product launches and debates celebrating contemporary design. Taking place at various venues in Clerkenwell - including The Farmiloe Building, a former Victorian glassworks on St John Street - Clerkenwell Design Week celebrates the creativity, social relevance and advancements in technology behind design. It's a typical festival-type occasion, with exhibitions, street entertainment, music, food and receptions, all centred on the design theme. Last year's design week saw 30,000 people attend and this year is billed to be even bigger.

28th
The Specials
Tuesday 28th May 2013
O2 Academy Brixton, London SW9 9SL
Expect a sea of pork pie hats and mod-style suits as the legendary ska band The Specials reform for a 10-date tour around the UK. The band, who are best known for their hits 'Too Much Too Young' and 'Ghost Town', have been stacking up hits for over 30 years and they land in London for one night at the O2 Brixton Academy.

28th & 29th
Depeche Mode
28th & 29th May 2013
The O2 Arena, Greenwich, London SE10 0DX
The '80s cool-definers Depeche Mode continue a career that has seen them sell over 100 million records and become heroes to two very different generations. The name means 'Fashion Update', and it was their ability to stay on the cutting edge of both music and fashion that allowed them to make the transition from Euro-synth stars to world-conquering electronic pioneers. Now, on the back of their 13th studio album, the band are back to perform their new material and much loved early work.

From 28th
iTMOi
28th May - 1st June 2013
Sadler's Wells, Rosebery Avenue, London EC1R 4TN
One hundred years after its first performance took Paris by storm, Igor Stravinsky's masterpiece 'The Rite of Spring' is celebrated at Sadler's Wells with a radical reinterpretation by leading choreographer Akram Khan - one of the stars of the Olympic Opening Ceremony. Boasting an international cast of 12 dancers, 'iTMOi' ('in The Mind Of igor') explores the human condition and the way in which Russian composer Stravinsky transformed his work by evoking emotions through pattern, rooted in the concept of a woman dancing herself to death. Featuring an original score by Nitin Sawhney, Jocelyn Pook and Ben Frost, 'iTMOi' is part of the Sadler's Wells 'A String of Rites' series and blends Khan's brilliance with a talented artistic team including costume designer Kimie Nakano.

From 28th
Free Range 2013
28th May – 22nd July 2013
The Old Truman Brewery, Brick Lane, London E1 6QL
Since its inception in 2001, 'Free Range' has been showcasing art, fashion, design, graphics, illustrations, textiles and photography from creative graduates from all over London and the UK. The annual event returns to the Old Truman Brewery in May, providing college students with the opportunity to showcase their work on an international level. For the public it's a (free) chance to spot the latest trends and newest talents. Shows change every Friday so if you visit every weekend you'll be rewarded with a new artistic barrage each time. What's more, as it's a stone's throw from Brick Lane and its popular markets, 'Free Range' can be part of a wider day out in one of the East End's hippest neighbourhoods. All the exhibitions and displays are free but take note that the fashion catwalk shows are by invite only, while Thursday nights are private viewings.

From 29th
The Seagull
29th May – 1st June 2013
Richmond Theatre, Surrey TW9 1QJ
The popularity of Chekov adaptations continues as Rupert Goold's Headlong Theatre troupe takes on 'The Seagull'. The original play drew upon themes of desire and aspiration, whilst introducing subtext and realism to the stage. This new production - more than 100 years later - is reinterpreted by John Donnelly, with promising young director Blanche McIntyre taking the reins.

31st
England v New Zealand: First NatWest Series ODI
Friday 31st May 2013
Lord's Cricket Ground, St John's Wood Road, London NW8 8QN
The first of three NatWest Series one-day internationals between England and New Zealand takes place on the last Friday of May at Lord's. The last ODI series between the two sides took place back in 2008 with New Zealand prevailing in the five-game series 3-1, culminating with a 51-run win at Lord's. The hosts will hope history doesn't repeat itself. After this match at Lord's there will be games at The Ageas Bowl in Hampshire and Trent Bridge.

From 31st
Investec Derby Festival
31st May - 1st June 2013
Epsom Downs Racecourse, Epsom KT18 5LQ
This famous race meeting is one of the oldest and greatest horse races in the world, established by the Earl of Derby in 1779. Today the main race - the Investec Derby - attracts prize money of over a million pounds and crowds approaching 100,000. Held at the Grade I listed Epsom Racecourse, the Investec Derby Festival is one of the most glamorous events in the international racing calendar, with the Queen arriving by carriage followed by thousands of spectators in their best togs. The famous Investec Derby itself takes place on the Saturday, while Friday features a prestigious race called The Investec Oaks, and, more importantly, Investec Ladies' Day, which is as much a fashion show as a horse race. Last year, the Derby was won by 'Camelot', the 8/13 favourite ridden by 19-year-old jockey Joseph O'Brien and trained by his father Aidan.

From 31st
International Stadium Poker Tour
31st May – 6th June 2013
Wembley Stadium, Wembley, London HA9 0WS
The inaugural International Stadium Poker Tour comes to Wembley Stadium for a week-long tournament with a guaranteed prize fund of more than £16 million. 30,000 players are expected to compete on the opening day in an online competition using laptops in the stadium's stands. This will decide the 3,000 players who will go on to take a seat at the poker tables on the pitch for live play over the remaining six days. Of course, entry comes at a price: there's a 600 (£488) buy-in for all those wishing to take part. The ISPT aims to create the world's largest poker event each year, each time using a prestigious stadium in a different country. It remains to be seen if the event will attract enough players (or backers) to ensure the cards are in the air.

LONDON'S GOLDEN OLDIES

They say life begins at 40 - but try mentioning that to these singing stars of yesteryear still plying their trade on London's big stage

DONNY AND MARIE
The O2
Sunday 20th January
Perma-tanned singing siblings bring their Las Vegas show to town for a single night

THE STRANGLERS
Roundhouse
Friday 15th March
Progressive punk outlaws continue their renaissance with the 'Feel It Live' tour

ERIC CLAPTON
Royal Albert Hall
17th to 26th May
There's no reason to cry as the guitar god celebrates 50 years in the business

CHRIS DE BURGH
Royal Albert Hall
Wednesday 24th April
There will be ladies in red aplenty for the leather-clad balladeer

ELVIS COSTELLO
Royal Albert Hall
4th & 5th June
Genre-bending maestro returns with The Imposters for '13 Revolvers' tour

MARK KNOPFLER
Royal Albert Hall
27th May to 1st June
Former Dire Straits frontman and sultan of swing plays low-key country blues

BRUCE SPRINGSTEEN
Wembley
Saturday 15th June
The Boss dons double denim for a night of heartland rock with his E Street Band

CLIFF RICHARD
Hampton Court
Saturday 22nd June
Sir Cliff headlines the Palace's annual summer festival - bring your umbrellas

MICK HUCKNALL
Apollo
Sunday 28th June
Simply Red's flame-haired soul singer goes solo on a mini UK tour

LONDON CONCERTS NEWSLETTER

→ To receive the London Concerts Newsletter from LondonTown.com send a blank email now to: **concerts@londontown.com**
   PRIVACY PROMISE: We will never (and that means never) give your email address to anyone else. You mean too much to us.

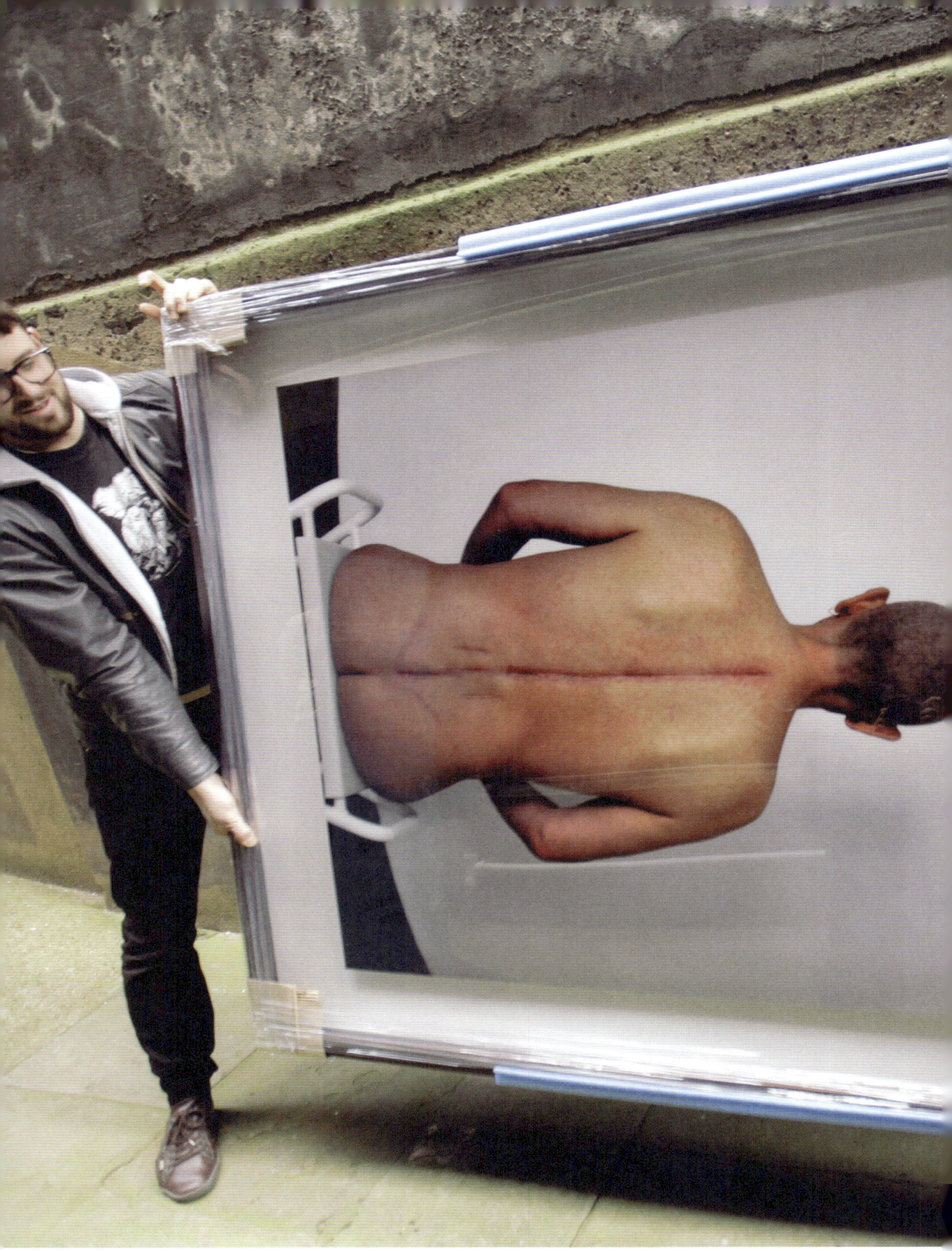

145

Andy Murray targets Wimbledon and Daniel Radcliffe hits the stage, while The Royal Academy Summer Exhibition gets going...

PAGE 150

JUNE

WHAT'S ON WHERE IN JUNE

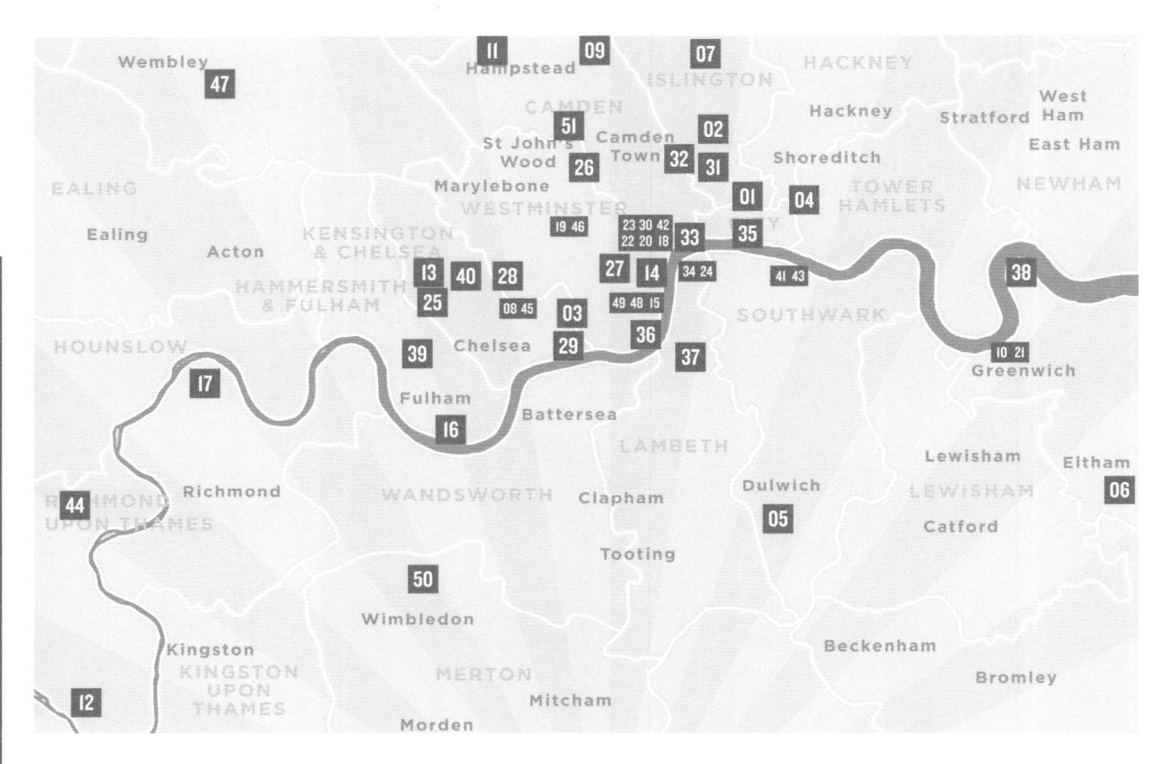

01	Barbican Centre	14	Horse Guards Parade	27	Royal Academy of Arts	40	The Roof Gardens
	Page 157		Page 153		Page 150		Page 149
02	Business Design Centre	15	Houses of Parliament	28	Royal Albert Hall	41	The Scoop
	Page 156		Page 153		Pages 148 & 151		Page 158
03	Cadogan Hall	16	Hurlingham Park	29	Royal Hospital Chelsea	42	Theatre Royal
	Page 151		Page 149		Page 157		Page 156
04	Christ Church Spitalfields	17	Kew Green	30	Royal Opera House	43	Tower Bridge
	Page 155		Page 155		Pages 154 & 157		Page 147
05	Dulwich Picture Gallery	18	London Coliseum (ENO)	31	Sadler's Wells Theatre	44	Twickenham Stadium
	Page 151		Pages 148 & 152		Pages 149, 153 & 155		Page 153
06	Eltham Palace	19	Midori House Courtyard	32	Scala	45	V&A Museum
	Page 152		Page 153		Page 154		Page 158
07	Emirates Stadium	20	National Gallery	33	Somerset House	46	Wallace Collection
	Page 147		Page 156		Pages 149, 151 & 154		Page 154
08	Exhibition Road	21	National Maritime Msm	34	Southbank Centre	47	Wembley Stadium
	Page 158		Page 158		Page 152		Pages 152 & 158
09	Finsbury Park	22	National Portrait Gallery	35	St Paul's Cathedral	48	Westminster Abbey
	Page 148		Page 155		Page 156		Page 151
10	Greenwich	23	Noel Coward Theatre	36	Tate Britain	49	Westminster College Gdn
	Page 154		Page 150		Pages 148 & 156		Page 150
11	Hampstead Heath	24	Old Vic Theatre	37	The Oval	50	Wimbledon
	Page 151		Page 149		Pages 148, 150, 151, 153, 154 & 156		Page 157
12	Hampton Court Palace	25	Olympia	38	The O2 Arena	51	ZSL London Zoo
	Page 152		Pages 148 & 151		Pages 134, 151, 155 & 158		Page 158
13	Holland Park Theatre	26	Open Air Thtr Regent's Prk	39	The Queen's Club		
	Page 148		Pages 154 & 157		Page 150		

PICK

ART

Yoko Ono's Meltdown

14th - 23rd June 2013
Southbank Centre, London SE1 8XX

PAGE 152

1st
GB Row 2013
Saturday 1st June 2013
Tower Bridge, London SE1
More people have walked on the moon than have successfully rowed around Great Britain's coastline – and this, the world's richest rowing race, looks to overturn that striking anomaly. As many as 15 boats are expected to take part in the gruelling 2,000-mile race, which is organised by the Anglo American Boat Club and starts at Tower Bridge on 1st June. Chasing a bounty of £100,000, crews of two, four or eight oarsmen and women will brave treacherous tides and some of the most dangerous shipping lanes on the planet as they row non-stop and unassisted from London, around Land's End, up to John o' Groats and back to the capital.

1st
Green Day
Saturday 1st June 2013
Emirates Stadium, London N5
Punk trio Green Day are due to play a major live gig at Arsenal's Emirates Stadium - provided frontman Billie Joe Armstrong recovers from a drugs-related public meltdown late last year. This major gig was the first UK date confirmed by the band for 2013 and is expected to be followed by a number of summer stadium gigs. Expect a mixture of Green Day's energetic back-catalogue and songs from their three most recent albums - '¡Uno!', ¡Dos!' and '¡Tré!' - which were released between September and January.

1st - 28th
The Perfect American
1st – 28th June 2013
English National Opera,

London Coliseum, London WC2N 4ES
Making its London debut, Philip Glass's 2011 opera is a fictionalised vision of Walt Disney's last few years, seen from the perspective of a disgruntled former employee. The opera opens with a scene around Disney's death bed and progresses into a flashback that includes surreal imaginings of Abraham Lincoln and Andy Warhol – representing the unimaginable and, at times, disturbing aspects of Disney's life and American culture. For spurious legal reasons, the theatre company has created sinister interpretations of Mickey, Minnie and friends - recognisable, but "in a nightmarish sort of way".

4th & 5th
Elvis Costello & The Imposters
4th & 5th June 2013
Royal Albert Hall, Kensington Gore, SW7 2AP
Fresh from the success of last year's 'Revolver' tour, legendary genre-bending musician Elvis Costello returns to the Royal Albert Hall with his band The Imposters for a fresh whirl of his gigantic vaudevillian 'Spectacular Spinning Songbook'. Part of the prolific Costello's new '13 Revolvers' tour, the concept is deliciously simple: after each performed number, the band members or members of the audience spin a wheel packed with different songs from throughout Costello's career; whichever song comes up next, The Imposters perform.

From 4th
Opera Holland Park
4th June – 2nd August 2013
Holland Park Theatre, Holland Park, London W8
This annual summer highlight sees a temporary theatre erected in West London's Holland Park and operatic arias soar over the tree tops. The magical atmosphere of these productions owes a lot to their surroundings but it's also a tribute to a remarkable opera company that has defied expectations and budgets to put on productions of the very highest standard. The 2013 season includes 'Madama Butterfly', Puccini's much-loved tragic opera, and the relatively unknown 'I gioielli della Madonna' by Ermanno Wolf-Ferrari. Welsh soprano Natalya Romaniw is among the talented young cast for what promises to be one of the season's most exciting highlights. Also on the bill: 'Pagliacci', part of a double bill with 'Cavalleria rusticana'; 'Les pecheurs de perles' by Bizet; and 'Donizetti's L'elisir d'amore'.

From 4th
Patrick Caulfield
4th June – 8th September 2013
Tate Britain, Millbank, London SW1P 4RG
The celebrated British painter Patrick Caulfield, who came to prominence in the 1960s, is the subject of this Tate survey exhibition. Caulfield trained at the Royal College of Art, where he was a year behind Hockney, and despite appearing in the defining 'New Generation' exhibition at the Whitechapel Art Gallery in 1964, he preferred not to be labelled a pop artist, preferring instead the label of "a 'formal' artist". Known for his vibrant paintings of modern life, around 30 of which are shown in this exhibition, Caulfield was a master of colour and graphic elegance.

From 4th
Gary Hume
4th June – 8th September 2013
Tate Britain, Millbank, London SW1P 4RG
English painter, draughtsman and printmaker Gary Hume emerged as one of the leading figures of the group of young artists labelled the YBAs (Young British Artists) in the 1990s. He graduated from Goldsmiths College in 1988 and his work appeared in the seminal 'Freeze' show that same year. Tate Britain stages a show on the artist who represented Britain at the 48th Venice Biennale in 1999 and more recently filled the White Cube, Mason's Yard and Hoxton Square, with his 'Paradise Paintings' and limestone sculptures. Visitors can double up with the Patrick Caulfield exhibition (see above) and take in the works of two influential contemporary British artists in one day.

6th - 16th
Olympia International Fine Arts and Antiques
6th-16th June 2013
Olympia Exhibition Centre, London W14 8UX
Over 150 dealers from Britain and abroad showcase their often startling collections of antiques, jewellery, paintings, ceramics and contemporary designs. The fair, which comes to the Olympia every June and November, attracts over 30,000 people and includes items as varied as pre-Raphaelite paintings, collectable canes, vintage toys, contemporary art and furniture. Among the highest prices achieved at last year's June fair was a toilet service set which sold for a staggering £1.5 million.

7th
ICC Champions Trophy: West Indies v Pakistan
Friday 7th June 2013
The Kia Oval, Kennington, London SE11 5SS
The top eight one-day international sides gather in England and Wales this June for the seventh ICC Champions Trophy, with four round-robin games and a semi-final all played at the Oval. Second in importance only to the Cricket World Cup, the competition features Australia, England, New Zealand, Sri Lanka, India, Pakistan, South Africa and the West Indies. This is the first Champions Trophy since 2009, which was held in Pakistan and saw Australia take the spoils for a second consecutive tournament. The opening Group B clash sees 2004 winners West Indies take on Pakistan, who have yet to reach the final of the tournament.

7th & 8th
The Stone Roses
7th & 8th June 2013
Finsbury Park, London N4 1EE
Ian Brown's alt rockers The Stone Roses, renowned for their seminal indie and psychedelic pop classics, play their first official London concerts since the band reunited following a split in 1996. Their comeback gig in Manchester's Heaton Park saw all 220,000 tickets snapped up within 68 minutes, entering the Guinness Book of Records in the process. Remarkably for a band so legendary, the Roses have only released two albums - although there is talk of a third in the pipeline, with Brown saying the band are "ready to take the world by storm".

7th – 9th
Polo in the Park
7th – 9th June 2013
The Hurlingham Park, London SW6 3NG
Now in its fifth year, Polo in the Park is quickly becoming one of London's great summer outdoors events. Aimed at bringing polo to the people, the three-day World Series event showcases a more accessible version of the sport, mirroring the effect Twenty20 has had on cricket. Teams of three from cities around the world take part; this year sees London, Delhi, Buenos Aires and Sydney all competing. There's usually also a steady flow of celebrities (Jodie Kidd) and royalty (Princess Beatrice), medieval jousting and an array of bars, shops and food stalls, not to mention red trousers galore.

7th – 16th
London Jewellery Week
7th – 16th June 2013
Somerset House, Strand, London WC2R 1LA
There can be precious few people who aren't partial to a sparkling bit of bling and the UK's biggest jewellery festival - which takes place at Somerset House and various other venues around town - will provide Londoners with the chance to celebrate the city's unique heritage of high quality jewellery design. Whether you're looking for the latest and most glamorous piece to add to your collection or you're a novice buyer, desperately seeking expert advice, this is the place to be.

8th
Open Garden Squares Weekend
Saturday 8th June 2013
Hidden gardens throughout London
From the iron-fenced residential parks of west London to the landscaped churchyards of the City, hundreds of garden squares play a vital part in maintaining London's status as one of Europe's greenest cities. This wonderful weekend is the one time of the year when these gardens open their gates to everyone - many of these private spaces are not accessible to the public for the rest of the year. Over 200 gardens typically take part - and last year, even the garden at 10 Downing Street got involved (albeit to twenty-five lucky ticket holders only). If you have youngsters in tow, many of the gardens stage activities for families too.

8th
RIOT Offspring
Saturday 8th June 2013
Sadler's Wells, Rosebery Avenue, London EC1R 4TN
In 1913, the avant-garde nature of the music and choreography of Stravinsky's 'The Rite of Spring' nearly incited a riot at its opening night in Paris. 100 years later, and prompted by the recent London riots, 'RIOT Offspring' explores perceptions of rites, rituals and riots to create a powerful piece of dance theatre in the culmination of Sadler's Wells' 'The Rite of Spring' centenary celebrations. Featuring a large cast of around 80 non-professional participants of all ages and abilities - including some over 60s - 'RIOT Offspring' is performed in a double bill alongside the debut performance of the new National Youth Dance Company in a specially commissioned work from guest artistic director Jasmin Vardimon.

From 1st
Sweet Bird of Youth   (PICK)
1st June – 31st August 2013
Old Vic Theatre, The Cut, London SE1 8NB

'SEX AND THE CITY' STAR KIM CATTRALL takes on the role of fading Hollywood legend Alexandra Del Lago in Tennessee Williams's 'Sweet Bird of Youth', directed by Marianne Elliott, co-director of 'War Horse'. Appearing at The Old Vic for the first time, Cattrall has already proved her mettle on stage, last appearing in the West End in 2010 in Noel Coward's 'Private Lives', a production that subsequently transferred to Broadway. Reviewing the play, Charles Spencer, writing in The Telegraph, was reminded of "the kind of woman Marilyn Monroe might have become had she lived a little longer..." - just the kind of woman well suited to playing a fading Hollywood legend.

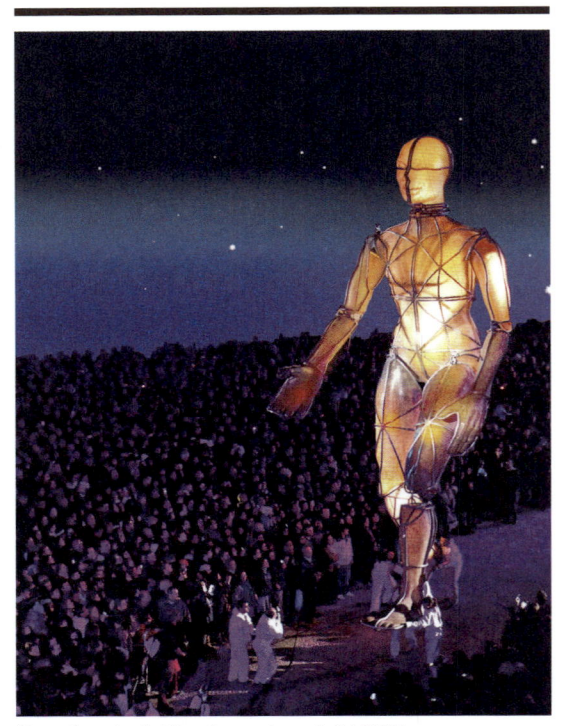

'Prometheus Awakes' from last year's wonderful GDIF → *154*

8th
Nightrider
Saturday 8th June 2013
Crystal Palace, SE19 2AZ or Alexandra Palace, Wood Green, London N22 7AY
Take to the streets of London by bike on a moonlit night, riding past some of the city's iconic landmarks in a bid to raise £2m for charity. The 100km route begins at Crystal Palace or Alexandra Place - you can choose which starting point suits you. It's not for beginners but anyone with a reasonable level of fitness and confidence on the road can take part. Cycling past sights like Tower Bridge, St Paul's Cathedral and the London Eye while the city sleeps is one way of putting the 'fun' in fundraising.

From 8th
The Cripple of Inishmaan
8th June – 31st August 2013
Noel Coward Theatre, St Martin's Lane, London WC2N 4AU
Martin McDonagh's 'The Cripple of Inishmaan' is coming to the Noel Coward Theatre for its first major London revival since its première in 1996. Part of Michael Grandage's Noel Coward season – featuring five plays with over 100,000 tickets at £10 – the revival of this dark comedy will see Daniel Radcliffe take the lead role. 'Cripple' Billy Claven is eager to broaden his horizons and escape the gossip, poverty and boredom of the small isle of Inishmaan. After learning that a Hollywood film crew will be setting up camp on the neighbouring isle to create a documentary about life on the islands, Billy takes a chance and tries out for a part in the film. Surprisingly, he succeeds and sets out to prove to everyone how much he wants to realise his dream.

10th – 16th
AEGON Championships
10th – 16th June 2013
The Queen's Club, Barons Court, London W14 9EQ
Controversy reigned at last year's Queen's Club Championships when Argentinian David Nalbandian was disqualified in the second set of the final for kicking a court-side advertising board, resulting in a nasty cut leg for a line judge. In rather anti-climactic scenes the towering Croatian Marin Cilic, who lost the opening set, was awarded the win. The Championships attract most of the world's top grass-court players to the prestigious Queen's Club, whose courts have been described by four-time former winner Andy Roddick as "arguably the best in the world".

From 10th
Royal Academy Summer Exhibition
10th June – 18th August 2013
Royal Academy of Arts, Burlington House, London W1J 0BD
Anyone can submit to the Royal Academy's Summer Exhibition which gives it a wonderful element of surprise. Over 11,000 pieces are sifted through from relative unknowns to famous artists and members of the RA. The fun part for visitors is choosing a favourite and, with the majority of works on sale at varying price ranges, you can even buy one if you really fall in love with it. First held in 1769, the Royal Academy Summer Exhibition is the largest regular contemporary art exhibition in the world. It's an impressive show that gives an excellent cross-section of contemporary art every summer. Each year, a prominent sculpture greets visitors to the exhibition as they walk through the Royal Academy's great courtyard; last year Chris Wilkinson's 'From Landscape to Portrait', a twisting series of wooden frames, offered weary visitors a welcome seat.

11th
ICC Champions Trophy: India v West Indies
Tuesday 11th June 2013
The Kia Oval, Kennington, London SE11 5SS
West Indies play their second successive game at the Oval in this ICC Champions Trophy Group B clash against India. Neither team progressed to the semi-finals in the last tournament in Pakistan in 2009, with India finishing third in their table ahead of rock-bottom and win-less West Indies.

11th
House of Lords v House of Commons Tug of War
11th June 2013
Westminster College Garden, London SW1P 3PA
They managed to raise over £10,000 for Macmillan Cancer Support last year and this summer they're going at it again - the annual Lords v Commons Tug of War is back for a 26th year. The typically English setting of Westminster College Gardens plays host to this light-hearted skirmish between the two houses of Parliament. Last year it was the Commons who came out on

top, retaining their victory from previous years. BBC2's Jeremy Vine often plays the role of commentator and brings a witty repartee to the occasion.

11th
Royal Philharmonic Orchestra: Leonard Bernstein Evening
Tuesday 11th June 2013
Cadogan Hall, Sloane Terrace, London SW1X 9DQ
America's most famous conductor of all time is celebrated in a special evening of Broadway and Bernstein. Best known for his hit musical 'West Side Story', Leonard Bernstein was also the man behind classics such as 'Candide', 'On The Town', 'Wonderful Town' and 'Trouble in Tahiti'. Featuring some of the composer's orchestral gems, including the irresistible love theme from 'On the Waterfront', this is a must for anyone easily swept away by the glamour of Broadway show-tunes.

From 11th
A Crisis of Brilliance
11th June – 22nd September 2013
Dulwich Picture Gallery, London SE21 7AD
Some of the most well-known British artists of twentieth century feature in 'A Crisis of Brilliance', the Dulwich Picture Gallery's survey which includes works by contemporaries such as CRW Nevinson, Stanley Spencer, Mark Gertler and Dora Carrington. Students together at the Slade School of Art in London between 1908 and 1912, they formed part of what their esteemed drawing teacher Henry Tonks described as the school's last 'crisis of brilliance'. This exhibition which features over 70 original works by the group includes images which document their responses to the First World War.

12th & 13th
Kings of Leon
12th & 13th June 2013
The O2 Arena, Greenwich, London SE10 0DX
Southern US rockers Kings of Leon play their first London gig in two years. On the back of 2008's breakthrough album 'Only By The Night', the popularity of the Tennessee four-piece snowballed to such an extent that you could hardly enter a bar or turn on the radio without hearing 'Sex on Fire' for the umpteenth time. But the band had to abruptly cut short their 2011 tour due to lead singer Caleb Followill drunkenly leaving the stage mid-performance. Now, following a much needed break, Kings of Leon are returning with their sixth studio album and will play at the O2 for two nights as part of a full European tour.

12th - 14th
London International Antiquarian Book Fair
12th - 14th June 2013
Olympia, Hammersmith Road, London W14 8UX
At 57 years of age, the annual LIABF is almost as old as some of the classic tomes on display. Certainly, it's the oldest such book fair in the world, attracting exhibitors from all over the globe. The fair will be brimming with printed works dating from the 15th to the 21st centuries including manuscripts, prints, ephemera, photographs, maps and atlases from all ages and from all corners of the earth. But you don't have to be a collector to enjoy all that's on offer; the LIABF is ideal for any book lover with a curious eye and an interest in history. Tickets are free if you register in advance, if not you'll have to pay a tenner on the door.

12th - 23rd
English National Ballet: Swan Lake
12th – 23rd June 2013
Royal Albert Hall, Kensington Gore, London SW7
Derek Deane's critically acclaimed in-the-round production of 'Swan Lake' is revived at London's most magical venue after a successful run at the Coliseum last summer. The English National Ballet will join with international guest artists to share the lead roles of Odette/Odile and Prince Siegfried, and the stage will be flooded with 120 performers and 60 swans to create a large-scale "ravishing and sumptuous spectacle" (The Sunday Times).

13th
ICC Champions Trophy: England v Sri Lanka
Thursday 13th June 2013
The Kia Oval, Kennington, London SE11 5SS
England's first London game in the ICC Champions Trophy is this appetising Group A evening clash at the Oval against Sri Lanka. In the previous tournament's round-robin stage, England beat Sri Lanka by six wickets before crashing out in the semis to eventual winners Australia.

13th
Coronation Jubilee Concert
Thursday 13th June 2013
Westminster Abbey, London SW1P 3PA
A special concert celebrating the Diamond Jubilee of the Coronation of Her Majesty Queen Elizabeth II will be held at Westminster Abbey on Thursday 13th June 2013. While the full programme, ticket prices, and booking details are going to be announced in February 2013, we can confirm that the concert will begin at 7pm and, being held in the magnificent Abbey where she was crowned on this day in 1953, it's sure to be a special occasion.

13th - 16th
Affordable Art Fair Hampstead
13th - 16th June 2013
Hampstead Heath, Highgate Road, London NW3 7JR
The second Affordable Art Fair of the year in Hampstead is the little sister of the Battersea Park original, which takes place earlier in the year in March. Originally held in a winter marquee on the Heath in November, the fair switches to a June weekend in 2013 for what should be a perfect summer's day out in north London. There are over 100 galleries under one roof, exhibiting paintings, original prints, sculpture and photography - all priced from £40 to £4,000.

13th - 16th
Treasure
13th – 16th June 2013
Somerset House, Strand, London WC2R 1LA
Returning for its sixth year, 'Treasure' will be the largest event at this year's London Jewellery Week. Showcasing designs from over 150 jewellers, there will be an assortment of contemporary pieces that display innovative design and cutting-edge technology. With designers from across the UK and around the world displaying their work, they will be able to

sell directly to the consumer. Exhibitors include Alice Mentor, known for her luxurious and bold designs with an industrial edge; Paul Spurgeon, who designs elegant and timeless jewellery with the clever use of diamonds and minimal lines; and Gina Stewart Cox, who combines colourful durable cord with precious metals and gemstones to create quirky everyday pieces.

13th - 22nd
Hampton Court Palace Festival
13th – 22nd June 2013
Hampton Court Palace, Surrey KT8 9AU
Returning for its 21st year with over 10 nights of concerts, the Hampton Court Palace Festival is one for the older generation. British icon Sir Cliff Richard will headline the concert, which takes place in the open-air court of King Henry VIII's Palace. The line-up also boasts the likes of Russell Watson, the UK's bestselling classical artist, and Jools Holland, now a veteran of this annual festival. Guests can bring their own hampers with champers or take advantage of the pre-ordered picnic options on offer. Drinks and more basic meal options are also available from stalls, while those who want to go the whole hog can opt for the hospitality package in the Hampton Court State Apartments which includes VIP seating, a champagne reception with canapés, and a dinner with fine wines.

14th & 15th
Grand Medieval Joust
14th & 15th June 2013
Eltham Palace, Court Yard, London SE9 5QE
Experience the pageantry of a medieval joust in one of London's most captivating settings, where armoured knights will enter a thrilling horseback contest of strength, skill and bravery. Other entertainment includes japes from the jester Peterkin the Fool, musical medieval minstrels, costumed re-enactors, falconry displays, interactive games and a hearty banquet.

14th - 23rd
Meltdown Festival
14th – 23rd June 2013
Southbank Centre, London SE1 8XX
Each year the iconic Meltdown festival produces a wildly eclectic line-up of acts curated by one of pop music's great innovators - including David Bowie, John Peel, Morrissey, Jarvis Cocker and Lee 'Scratch' Perry. This year, the festival will be directed by worldwide cultural icon Yoko Ono. Celebrating her 80th birthday in 2013, she will be bringing a lifetime of achievement in music, visual art and peace activism to the Southbank Centre. Having performed at Ornette Coleman's 2009 Meltdown, Ono is no stranger to the festival and is now ready to take the reins. Her Meltdown will be no doubt be tinged with her strong affiliation to environmentalism, feminism and space.

14th - 26th
Death in Venice
14th – 26th June 2013
London Coliseum, St Martin's Lane, London WC2N 4ES
In the year of Benjamin Britten's centenary, the ENO will be staging his much admired final opera 'Death in Venice'. Two unspoken themes run throughout the opera: the unrequited love that Aschenbach, an old guest at a Venice hotel, has for the young and athletic Tadzio, and the cholera epidemic that the authorities are desperately trying to keep quiet. The physical decay of the city and the mysterious, sinister characters that Ashenbach meets on his daily travels add up to a haunting theatrical narrative that explores what moral and ethical repercussions can be caused by unarticulated love.

15th
Bruce Springsteen
Saturday 15th June 2013
Wembley Stadium, Wembley, London HA9 0WS
The Boss dons his famous double denim combo and heads to Wembley for a night of heartland rock with his E Street Band. Following unforgettable performances in Hyde Park in

'The Discovery of Paris' at The Wallace Collection includes this watercolour by J.M.W. Turner → 154

2009 and 2012, bandana-boasting Bruce will play material from his latest chart-topping five-star album, 'Wrecking Ball', as well as pounding out some of his iconic hits, which include 'Born in the USA', 'Dancing in the Dark' and 'Born to Run'. Let's hope the promoters don't pull the plug on Springsteen like they did last summer, cutting short his pre-Olympic jam with Sir Paul McCartney.

15th & 16th
Rihanna
15th & 16th June 2013
Twickenham Stadium, Twickenham, London TW1 1DZ
Rihanna has had us hook line and sinker ever since that frustratingly catchy single 'Umbrella' back in 2007, and with her feisty attitude and chameleon appearance we've remained a nation obsessed. Not one to shy away from controversy, her latest studio album is aptly titled 'Unapologetic' – perhaps also the response given to the 150 journalists, bloggers and competition winners involved in the revolt of 2012's ambitious '777' tour. Returning to our shores once again, the sexy Barbadian will be performing at Twickenham Stadium this June as part of her 'Diamonds' world tour.

15th
Trooping the Colour
Saturday 15th June 2013
Horse Guards Parade, Whitehall, SW1A 2AX
A vibrant display of ceremony and military history, Trooping the Colour marks the second of the Queen's two birthdays (this is the official one, her actual birthday is on 21st April). It's a spectacular piece of pageantry as hundreds of well-disciplined soldiers in full dress uniform march past at the Horse Guards Parade. A different Battalion gives the Royal Salute each year, all accompanied by stirring military music from the massed bands. On the same day, a 41 gun Royal Salute takes place in Green Park at 12.52pm and there's a 62 gun salute at the Tower of London at 1pm. But if you want to avoid the crush at the Mall, you can see the Horse Guards practising for the grand parade at two smaller rehearsals in the days leading up to the grand event - namely the Major General's Review on Saturday 1st June 2013 and the Colonel's Review on Saturday 8th June.

15th & 16th
The Monocle Country Fayre
Saturday 15th & Sunday 16th June 2013
Midori House Courtyard, Marylebone, W1U 4EG
In the courtyard outside Monocle's Marylebone HQ, the global affairs magazine hosts its annual Country Fayre, a free weekend of entertainment which celebrates the most English of traditions from a global perspective. Much like the magazine - which reports on matters as diverse as the doggy pampering industry in Japan, and Brazil's command of the UN peace-keeping mission in Haiti - the Monocle Country Fayre is both entertaining and informative. Market stalls hosted by local shopkeepers, cooking demonstrations, face painting for the kids, live music and DJs attract around 2,000 people to Midori House during the course of the weekend.

From 15th
Bike Week
15th – 23rd June 2013
Various venues nationwide
Running since 1923, Bike Week is the UK's biggest mass participation cycling event, promoting everyday cycling for everyone. While details of the specific events, which take place nationwide, are not confirmed at the time of writing, 2012 saw almost half a million people taking part in the celebrations of cycling across the country. In London last year, the annual All Party Parliamentary Bike Ride, in which MPs and key figures in the cycling world rode the three miles from the London Transport Museum to the House of Commons, marked the official launch of Bike Week.

Sunday 16th June
Father's Day

17th
ICC Champions Trophy: Sri Lanka v Australia
Monday 17th June 2013
The Kia Oval, Kennington, London SE11 5SS
The final round-robin game of the 2013 ICC Champions Trophy sees Sri Lanka take on defending champions Australia in Group A. Australia will probably enter the evening game as favourites given their position as concurrent reigning champions. The winner of Group A will return to the Oval for their semi-final clash two days later.

18th – 20th
The Forsythe Company
18th – 20th June 2013
Sadler's Wells, Rosebery Avenue, London EC1R 4TN
Arriving at Sadler's Wells for three nights only, The Forsythe Company is one of the unmissable foreign guest companies visiting the east London dance house in the first half of 2013. The 14-strong company named after the contemporary choreographer who founded it in 2004 after the closure of the Ballet Frankfurt, present 'Study #3', a piece which includes movement sequences, compositional methods, music, text, props, costumes, lighting, scenery and technical effects from 30 works spanning the last 30 years.

18th - 22nd
Royal Ascot
18th – 22nd June 2013
Ascot Racecourse, Ascot, Berkshire SL5 7JX
The Royal Ascot returns to the Berkshire racecourse where it has pretty much been an annual fixture since 1711. With nearly £4 million in prize money at stake, this meeting attracts all the biggest names in the racing fraternity, and, of course, more than 300,000 visitors, all dressed in their finest attire. Ascot is as famous for its hats as it is for the racing, especially on Ladies' Day. Every year the ladies try to outdo each other with tremendous towering creations and outlandish designs. The gents usually go for a more understated look - with morning suits and top hats the norm. It's as much a giant outdoor party as a race meet: punters at the track will drink over 150,000 bottles of champagne, 14,000 bottles of Pimm's and, of course, will place untold millions in bets.

19th
Lanterns on the Lake
Wednesday 19th June 2013
Scala, Kings Cross, London N1 9NL
Folk band Lanterns on the

Lake blend together graceful folk with aspects of rock on their debut album 'Gracious Tide, Take Me Home'. Using a smorgasbord of instruments - from the familiar guitar, violin and piano to the quirkier synth, glockenspiel and mandolin, as well as a combination of breathy female and silky male vocals - the sextet from Newcastle have embraced familiar wistful folk music while still offering a little more depth and originality.

19th
ICC Champions Trophy: Semi-Final
Wednesday 19th June 2013
The Kia Oval, Kennington, London SE11 5SS
The winners of Group A (Australia, England, New Zealand and Sri Lanka) take on the runners-up of Group B (India, Pakistan, South Africa and West Indies) in this opening semi-final of the 2013 ICC Champions Trophy. The second semi-final takes place one day later in Cardiff before the final of the tournament in Edgbaston on Sunday 23rd June.

20th - 23rd
Taste of London
20th – 23rd June 2013
Regent's Park, London NW1 4NR
Direct your rumbling stomach to Regent's Park for four days of al fresco gluttony as over forty of London's best restaurants, including a flurry of Michelin-starred eateries, show off their culinary handiwork. Work your way through a range of miniature speciality dishes - bought with the event's currency, 'crowns' - hot off the plates from upmarket places like Scott's, L'Anima, Petrus, Launceston Place, Benares, Bocca Di Lupo and Barbecoa - to name but a bunch. Top chefs such as Michel Roux Jr, Jamie Oliver, Nuno Mendes, Raymond Blanc and Gary Rhodes will also be doing the rounds, while the civilised sounds of live jazz and opera will fill the air and aid digestion at this gourmet grazing picnic extraordinaire.

20th - 29th
Greenwich and Docklands International Festival
20th – 29th June 2013
Various venues in Greenwich and Docklands, SE10
The whole of Greenwich comes alive for this 10-day festival of street performances, art and dancing. The festival offers a free and inclusive programme of world class theatre and dance, family entertainment, two extraordinary spectacles and a Greenwich Fair. The GDIF is especially good at putting on outdoor dance spectaculars and last year was a particularly special event with the festival's Artistic Director, Bradley Hemmings, appointed Co-Artistic Director of the London 2012 Paralympic Opening Ceremony. The line-up for 2013 is still to be announced, but with events taking place across Greenwich, the Isle of Dogs, Canary Wharf, Stratford and Woolwich, there's bound to be plenty to keep the expected crowds of 50,000 entertained.

From 20th
Gloriana
20th June – 6th July 2013
Royal Opera House, Covent Garden, London WC2E 9DD
In Benjamin Britten's centenary year, Richard Jones directs a deliciously wistful production of the composer's 'Gloriana'. Commissioned by the Royal Opera House to mark the coronation of Elizabeth II in 1953, 'Gloriana' is an opera for our time, exploring tensions between affairs of state and affairs of the heart. The action takes place in Tudor England as Queen Elizabeth I is approaching the last years of her reign and has to balance her amorous feelings towards the Earl of Essex with his own mounting ambitions.

From 20th
Pride and Prejudice
20th June – 20th July 2013
Open Air Theatre, Regent's Park, London NW1 4NU
Jane Austen's much loved romantic comedy comes to the Regent's Park Open Air Theatre this summer season. Following the Bennet sisters as they unsuccessfully search for love, it focuses mainly on Elizabeth as she comes to terms with the manners, upbringing, morality, education and marriages that are expected in the society of the landed gentry of early 19th- century England. However, it is when the eligible Mr Darcy enters her life that the real story begins to unfold. Despite being set in the 19th century, this loveable romantic tale still gains much admiration today and the beautiful setting of the Regent's Park Open Air Theatre is sure to add to its charm.

From 20th
The Discovery of Paris: Watercolours by Early Nineteenth-Century British Artists
20th June – 15th September 2013
The Wallace Collection, Marylebone, London W1
Although the Wallace Collection is rightly considered a great British institution, at least part of its roots lie in Paris, where both the 4th Marquess of Hertford and Sir Richard Wallace, who founded the collection, spent much of their lives. In 'The Discovery of Paris', a free, temporary exhibition at the grand Manchester Square house in Marylebone, the French capital is shown as an important site for British painters, including J.M.W. Turner, in the early 19th century.

From 20th
Collecting Gaugin: Samuel Courtauld in the 20s
20th June – 8th September 2013
The Courtauld Gallery, Strand, London WC2R 1LA
Between 1923 and 1929 Samuel Courtauld bought a series of paintings by French post-Impressionist artist Paul Gauguin and in June 2013 the Courtauld Gallery showcases these important art works from its impressive permanent collection. The exhibition includes major paintings and works on paper as well as one of only two marble sculptures ever created by the artist. Other significant works include 'Martinique Landscape', an important work dating from 1887, and 'Te Rerioa', the last Gauguin painting Courtauld acquired and one of the highlights of the gallery's collection.

From 20th
BP Portrait Award
20th June – 15th September 2013
National Portrait Gallery, St Martin's Place, London WC2H 0HE
The annual BP Portrait

Award returns to the National Portrait Gallery for three months this summer. Open to anyone, it's the world's most prestigious open competition for portrait painting. The prize typically attracts over 2,000 international entries of which around 55 selected works feature in the exhibition. The amount going to the winner has been increased to £30,000 this year, but this competition is not just about the money, it's also about prestige; many previous winners have gone on to gain important commissions. Craig Wylie, who won the award in 2008, is one example – he was commissioned by the National Portrait Gallery to create a portrait of Dame Kelly Holmes.

22nd
Kew Fete
Saturday 22nd June 2013
Kew Green, TW9 3AA
When the sun's out, there are few more idyllic village settings in London than Kew, which hosts its annual midsummer fete on Saturday 22nd June. Kew Green is a sight to behold even on a regular weekend, when local cricket teams leisurely battle it out on the square as people watch from the sidelines, pints in hand. But for the Kew Fete, the whole place comes to life as around 7,000 people flock to the green to take in the vintage fairground, live music, dog show and 100 stalls selling everything from cards to chutney. There are some delicious offerings from Spanish paella to English hog roast, cream teas to crepes as well as a beer tent, and a wine and Pimm's bar. Throw in some jazz, funk and blues from local bands, and a charity raffle, and you get one big village fete a stone's throw from central London.

From 22nd
Sadler's Sampled
22nd June – 27th July 2013
Sadler's Wells, Rosebery Avenue, London EC1R 4TN
Sadler's Wells popular 'Sadler's Sampled' event has been expanded into a two week festival in 2013, the year the venerable dance house celebrates its 15th anniversary. As the name suggests, you get a taster of a huge variety of dance - from ballet to contemporary to hip hop to flamenco - with short dance pieces from each, all performed in one night at the world class dance venue. Tickets start at just £8. In addition to Hofesh Shechter's 'Political Mother: The Choreographer's Cut', audiences will be able to see Anne Teresa De Keersmaeker's 'Drumming' and work from Russell Maliphant, Sidi Larbi Cherkaoui and Wayne McGregor in 'Made at Sadler's Wells'.

23rd & 24th
Maroon 5
23rd & 24th June 2013
The O2 Arena, Greenwich, London SE10 0DX
If you think you've got 'Moves like Jagger' you might want to get yourself down to the O2 this June to dance the night away to Maroon 5. Following their fourth studio album, 'Overexposed', the LA five-piece will be gracing London with their presence for back-to-back gigs. Other than a couple of band member adjustments, Maroon 5 has been a consistent unit since 1994, working hard to gain recognition. Achieving this sought after success in 2002,

7th - 22nd
Spitalfields Summer Music Festival
PICK
7th - 22nd June 2013
Spitalfields and around, London E1 6DW

THE COMMUNITY-MINDED SUMMER FESTIVAL returns with small-scale classical, folk and contemporary music held in a splendid variety of performance spaces. The best thing about the Spitalfields festivals (a winter festival is held either side of Christmas) is the array of contrasting venues: Old Spitalfields Market comes alive with what seems like impromptu musical performances, while the stunning 18th century Hawksmoor-designed Christ Church hosts a cluster of classical concerts. Shoreditch's hip Village Underground holds some of the more contemporary offerings, and there could not be a more apt setting for city-based bucolic folk than the Spitalfields City Farm. The eclectic programme includes lashings of baroque, jazz and world music, while there is a series of talks and debates, walks and visits, and interactive workshops.

with their debut album 'Songs About Jane', the band have since reaped the rewards of the music industry with numerous awards – including three Grammys – four successful studio albums and a number of sell out tours.

From 23rd
City of London Festival
23rd June – 26th July 2013
St Paul's Cathedral, London EC4M 8AD & various venues
Founded in 1962, the City of London Festival is a summer programme of music, visual arts, film, walks and talks. It takes place across several venues (including St Paul's Cathedral) and outdoor spaces, and events and activities are frequently free (particularly if outdoors). Last year the festival celebrated its golden jubilee: 50 years of animating the city with world-class arts. With over 100 free festival events, the line-up included the Sydney Dance Company, and English National Ballet at St Paul's Cathedral. There was also the return of a favourite feature with Londoners and visitors alike - the Golden Street Pianos, which saw 50 golden pianos left out in random spots in the capital for anyone to play. This year is sure to offer another exciting programme along with more themed pianos dotted throughout the city.

25th & 27th
1st & 2nd NatWest International T20s: England v New Zealand
25th & 27th June 2013
The Kia Oval, Kennington, London SE11 5SS
England's fourth and fifth Twenty20 clashes of the year against New Zealand take place at the Kia Oval on Tuesday and Thursday evenings in the last week of June. Following three T20 games in New Zealand in the winter, the tables will turn this summer with the Kiwis' tour of England coming to a conclusion with these two T20 fixtures. The two sides last met in the Super Eights phase of the 2012 ICC World Twenty20, with England winning by six wickets thanks to Luke Wright's smash-and-grab 76 off 43 balls. The victory was not enough as both teams were eliminated from the competition after finishing outside the top two of their group.

From 25th
Charlie and the Chocolate Factory
From Tuesday 25th June 2013
Theatre Royal Drury Lane, London WC2B 5JF
Who could forget the heart-warming tale of forlorn little Charlie Bucket and his poverty stricken family, his four grandparents huddled together for warmth in one double bed and his parents struggling to feed the family? The tale takes a dramatic turn when Charlie pulls back the wrapper of his favourite chocolate bar to reveal a life-changing golden ticket. This much loved Roald Dahl story was recently revived in a Tim Burton movie starring Johnny Depp, and now makes the bold move from screen to stage in a new production directed by Sam Mendes, with original music from Marc Shaiman and Scott Wittman. Theatre Royal Drury Lane will be filled with an utterly surreal mix of giant lollipops, dancing dwarfs and human blueberries. After the successful transition Dahl's 'Matilda The Musical' made to the West End stage, this equally joyous and bizarre tale promises to be a much anticipated addition to Theatreland.

From 25th
Lowry and the Painting of Modern Life
25th June – 20th October 2013
Tate Britain, Millbank, London SW1P 4RG
Criticised in the past for neglecting his work (most vocally by Sir Ian McKellen), Tate Britain dedicates a solo show to LS Lowry, the Lancashire painter who documented life in Britain in the industrial age. 'Lowry and the Painting of Modern Life', one of the highlights of Tate Britain's 2013 season, will run from June to October bringing around 80 works to London in an exhibition which "aims to re-assess Lowry's contribution as part of a wider art history". It will also show how Lowry was influenced by 19th-century French painters such as Camille Pissarro and Maurice Utrillo.

26th - 29th
The Global Party
26th – 29th June 2013
Secret location to be revealed to guests 12 hours before the party begins
Three hundred and sixty secret locations in 120 cities across the world take part in The Global Party, four nights of partying for a worthy cause. Following the success of The Global Party 2011, a second world event is scheduled for June 2013; this time inspired by 360˚. Billed as "an awe-inspiring global gathering", the organisers are inviting more than 360,000 of the world's VIPs to party while raising awareness and money for more than 360 local charities as well as The Global Charity Trust. Clubbing with a conscience.

26th - 29th
New Designers Exhibition Part One
26th – 29th June 2013
Business Design Centre, Islington, London N1 0QH
Young designers gather in their thousands to showcase their fresh and innovative creations for two weeks this summer. Acting as a springboard for young graduates exiting the safety of higher education the exhibition brings together designers from all ends of the spectrum. Everything from fashion to graphic design, interiors to architecture is displayed as over 3,500 students represent over 200 top United Kingdom design courses. Shining a spotlight on the hottest trends to come and a glimpse into the future of great British design, whether you work in the industry, love discovering new talent, or just enjoy a good browse New Designers is sure to have something that will catch your eye. The New Designers Exhibition Part Two takes place a few days later between Wednesday 3rd and Saturday 6th July 2013.

From 26th
Vermeer and Music: The Art of Love and Leisure
26th June – 8th September 2013
National Gallery, Trafalgar Square, London WC2N 5DN
Two musical Vermeer paintings owned by the National Gallery, 'Young Woman Standing at a Virginal' and 'Young Woman Seated at a Virginal', are brought together

with Vermeer's 'Guitar Player' for the first time in a free exhibition displayed in the gallery's Sainsbury Wing. By juxtaposing paintings by Vermeer and his contemporaries with musical instruments and songbooks of the period 'Vermeer and Music: The Art of Love and Leisure' gives visitors an insight into music as a pastime of the elite in the northern Netherlands during the 17th century. We also discover how music was often a metaphor, used for symbolic purposes, to indicate harmony, transience or to show the sitter's position in society.

From 27th
Masterpiece London
27th June – 3rd July 2013
Royal Hospital Chelsea, Royal Hospital Rd, SW3 4SR
Dedicated to finding the best in art and design, Masterpiece London, held on the South Grounds of the Royal Hospital Chelsea, is a high-end exhibition for serious art collectors. It showcases the best fine and decorative arts with premium collectors' items such as classic cars, fine wines and exquisite jewellery for sale. Last year highlights included a curated exhibition by Vogue's Jewellery Editor, a 'Room to Remember' curated by New York-based designer Jamie Drake, and Afternoon Insights - free to attend talks which took place on the exhibitor's stand, giving visitors an opportunity to learn about important exhibits, their makers and influences. What's more, weary art buyers can dine at the custom-built Le Caprice restaurant or at the upmarket Mount Street Deli from Mayfair.

From 27th
Simon Boccanegra
27th June – 16th July 2013
Royal Opera House, Covent Garden, London WC2E 9DD
The happy rise and tragic fall of Simon Boccanegra is depicted in Elijah Moshinsky's powerful production of Giuseppe Verdi's opera, which comes to the Royal Opera House in the composer's bicentenary year. Having been reunited with his long-lost daughter, Boccanegra finds his position as Doge of Genoa threatened by political enemies. Blending moments of intimacy with the story drama of state politics, this is the acclaimed 1881 revised version of Verdi's compelling work.

28th
Laurie Anderson & Kronos Quartet
Friday 28th June 2013
Barbican Centre, Silk Street, London EC2Y 8DS
The European première of a new, evening-length work from two legendary forces working in new music since the 1980s. Artist and composer Laurie Anderson collaborates with the string ensemble Kronos Quartet for the first time, in the year the Seattle-based string quartet mark their 40th anniversary.

From 29th
The Winter's Tale
29th June – 20th July 2013
Open Air Theatre, Regent's Park, London NW1 4NU
Continuing with their Shakespeare productions aimed at younger audiences, the Regent's Park Open Air Theatre will be staging a reimagining of 'The Winter's Tale' this summer. Sticking with the play's original narrative, the charming story

From 24th
Wimbledon Championships
24th June – 7th July 2013
The All England Club, Wimbledon, London SW19 5AE

NOW THAT ANDY MURRAY is both a Grand Slam winner and Olympic gold medallist, surely it's merely a matter of the Scot turning up at The All England Club to finally end Britain's 77-year wait for a Wimbledon winner? Murray has often carried the weight of history into the Wimbledon fortnight, and last July he looked well on track after taking a masterful first set against Roger Federer in the final. But the Swiss maestro rallied to take the match 3-1 and tie Pete Sampras's record seven Wimbledon wins. A month later, Murray's tears turned to jubilation when the 25-year-old gained revenge over Federer in the Olympic final on Centre Court, following it up with victory over Novak Djokovic in the US Open final. On such a roll, Murray could well enter the tournament as favourite - while in the women's competition, reigning champion Serena Williams will eye a sixth SW19 title.

JUNE 2013

has been re-imagined to make it suitable for anyone aged six and over. 'The Winter's Tale' tells the tale of a lost princess who has been raised by a shepherd and of her secret romance with a prince. Following her adventure, the audience will encounter a bear chase, a statue that comes to life, a sheep shearing contest and an unexpected family reunion.

29th & 30th
Robbie Williams
29th & 30th June 2013
Wembley Stadium, Wembley, London HA9 0WS
Having played three sold-out gigs at the O2 in November 2012, Robbie Williams announced his return to London in 2013 as part of his 'Take the Crown' stadium tour. The Take That singer will be joined by 'X Factor' star Olly Murs as a special guest on the 17-date jaunt. Expect old favourites and new material from his latest solo album 'Take the Crown', including No.1 single 'Candy'.

From 30th
Michael Bublé
30th June – 7th July 2013
The O2 Arena, Greenwich, London SE10 0DX
The Grammy Award-winning and chart-topping Canadian singer-songwriter performs pop and smooth jazz hits for six nights at the O2 in Greenwich. The series of shows will be the third longest run of dates ever performed at the O2 by a male solo artist - only exceeded by Prince and Pink Floyd's Roger Waters who, incidentally, will also play a big London gig in 2013, on 14th September at Wembley Stadium.

Unconfirmed dates
Revelations: Experiments in Photography
June – September 2013
Science Museum, South Kensington, London SW7 2DD
For the first exhibition at their brand new Media Space gallery the Science Museum invited a selection of contemporary artists to respond to scientific photography from the last two centuries. The result is an exhibition of nearly 80 works which draw upon important historical photographs from the collections of the National Media Museum and the Science Museum. Scientific photographs can have psychological and emotional power, revealing the world in new and surprising ways. The creation of these images and their dissemination among different audiences has changed over time as have their uses, impact and status.

More London Free Festival
June – September 2013
The Scoop, More London, The Queen's Walk, London SE1 2AA
The Scoop at More London, in the shadow of City Hall, is a sunken open air amphitheatre next to the Thames, making it an ideal al fresco venue for a Free Festival of music, theatre, film and fringe performances. Running throughout the summer, the festival includes open-air theatre, musical interludes and free films. Last year the festival offered special Olympic walking routes, a screening of 'The Best Exotic Marigold Hotel', 'Senna' - the award-winning documentary by Asif Kapadia, and the 1961 musical 'West Side Story'. This is what al fresco summer entertainment should be about: no tickets necessary - so you can just turn up and enjoy the show, and it's all for free.

V&A Illustration Awards
June - December 2013
Victoria and Albert Museum, London SW7 2RL
The annual V&A Illustration Awards are given to the best book and editorial illustration published in the UK each year and the prize money – £2,000 to each category winner plus an additional £2,000 for the overall winner – makes it one of the most substantial financial prizes for illustration in the industry. The winning works, announced on Monday 3rd June, make up a small, free display in the V&A.

Visions of the Universe
June – September 2013
National Maritime Museum, Greenwich, London
Telling the story of astronomical imaging, this summer exhibition will bring together some of the best astronomical photographs ever made. From the earliest hand drawings to the latest pictures from Hubble and the Mars Curiosity rover, it will showcase more than a hundred images of stars, planets, galaxies and celestial highlights. 'Visions of the Universe' will also showcase images from NASA, the Russian space programme and some of the best telescopes across the world. This exhibition, along with 'Turner and the Sea' which begins in November, is one of two major exhibitions staged at the National Maritime Museum in 2013.

Zoo Lates
Every Friday night in June & July
ZSL London Zoo, Regent's Park, London MW1 4RY
If you're a party 'animal' head to the London Zoo for its after-hours entertainment which is laid on every Friday night in June and July. Details of the night's entertainment depends on which night you go so you might get improvised comedy in the aquarium, Twisted Cabaret in the amphitheatre, a Silent Disco or a street food festival. They also encourage you to bring out your inner-animal with the facepainting, animal masks and silly outfits provided. But the real stars of the show are the animals who you can get to know through talks, demonstrations and feeding time. Zoo Lates is an adults-only event, not suitable for under 18s.

Exhibition Road Music Day
Saturday 21st June 2013
Exhibition Road, Kensington, London SW7
This free event on 'museum mile' is London's contribution to European Music Day as the leading arts, scientific, academic and cultural organisations gather to present a day of exciting sounds from around the world. A large range of indoor and outdoor stages will play host to a variety of musical performances, covering as many genres as one can think of. From urban to jazz and folk to rock, there'll be plenty of different types of performances taking place and plenty of new music to enjoy. First celebrated in 1982, on the 21st of June - the day of the summer solstice - European Music Day was set up with the aim of "bringing out onto the streets all musicians".

LONDON'S BEST

KIDS THEATRES

Keep your little ones entertained with a trip to my favourite family friendly theatres, many of which are dedicated entirely to children. *By Crinan Potter*

LITTLE ANGEL THEATRE
14 Dagmar Passage, Islington, London N1 2DN

This tiny treat of a theatre is a veritable hub of passionate puppeteering activity and provides regular workshops

UNICORN
147 Tooley Street, Southwark, London SE1 2HZ

With productions for children of all ages, this theatre has a multicultural focus inside its award-winning home

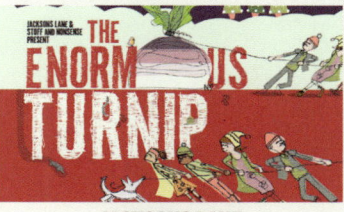

JACKSONS LANE
269a Archway Road, Highgate, London N6 5AA

A diverse programme of plays, circus acts and cabaret ensures Jacksons Lane has something for everyone

ARTS DEPOT
5 Nether Street, Tally Ho Corner, North Finchley, London N12 0GA

Boasting a glorious assortment of events, the Arts Depot regularly stages family-friendly performances

SOUTHBANK CENTRE
Belvedere Road, South Bank, London SE1 8XX

Families are spoilt for choice at the Southbank's numerous riverside studios and theatres

POLKA
240 The Broadway, Wimbledon, London SW19 1SB

This community-driven Wimbledon hub is one of the few venues in the UK that produces and directs works only for kids

CHICKENSHED
Chase Side, Southgate, London N14 4PE

One of the nation's most vibrant theatre companies encourages child participation with its unique methods

LYRIC HAMMERSMITH
Lyric Square, 2 King Street, London W6 0QL

Embracing work by emerging artists, the Lyric provides reasonably priced beautiful theatre

BAC
Old Town Hall, Lavender Hill, Battersea, London SW11 5TN

Carrying many of the capital's best fringe productions, the BAC regularly stages child-friendly productions

---

LONDON WITH KIDS NEWSLETTER

➜ To receive the 'London with kids' Newsletter from LondonTown.com send a blank email now to: **kids@londontown.com**

PRIVACY PROMISE: We will never (and that means never) give your email address to anyone else. You mean too much to us.

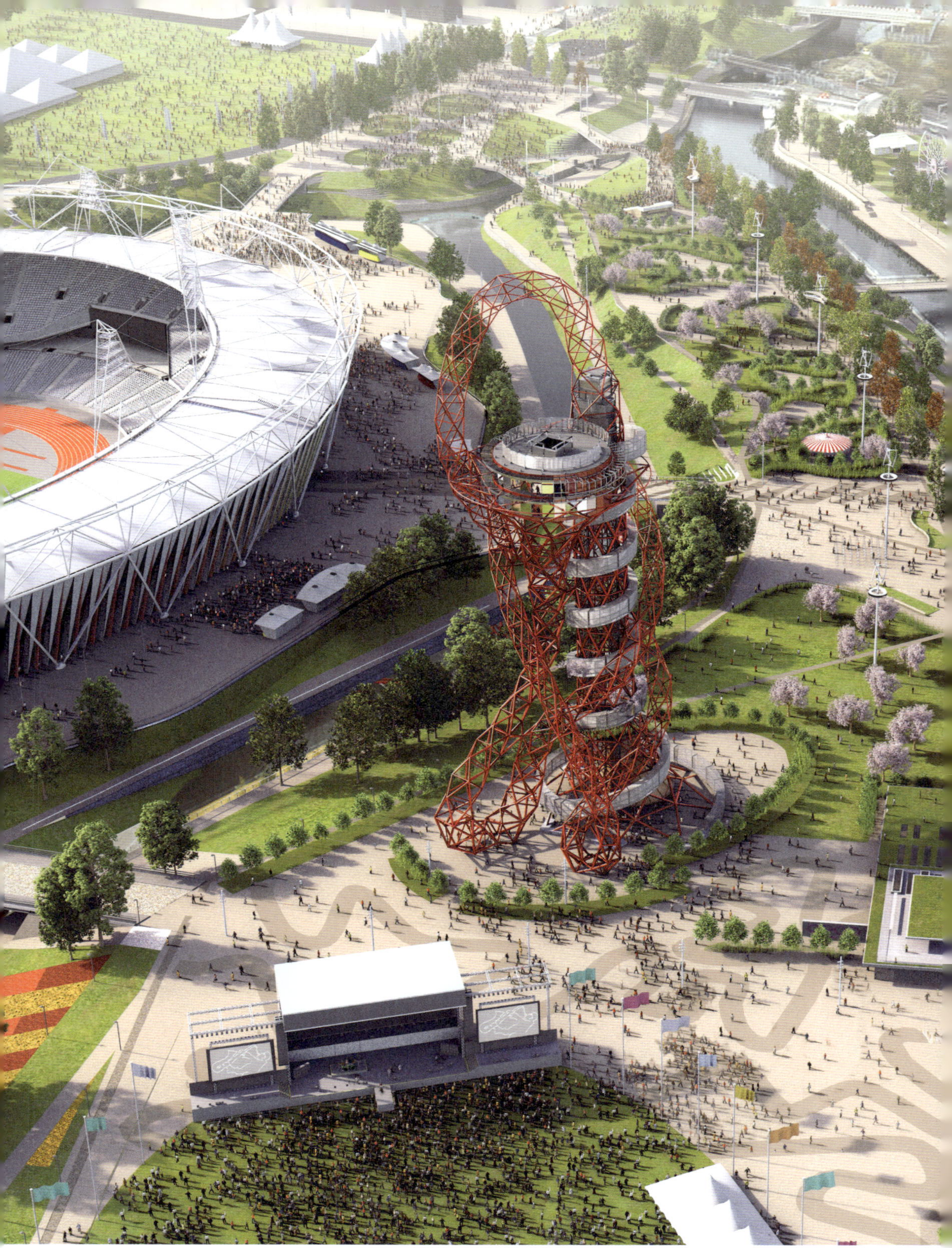

161

Summer hots up with the arrival of the Ashes and Proms, festivals galore, and the reopening of the Olympic Park...

`PAGE 173`

JULY

WHAT'S ON WHERE IN JULY

LondonTown.com

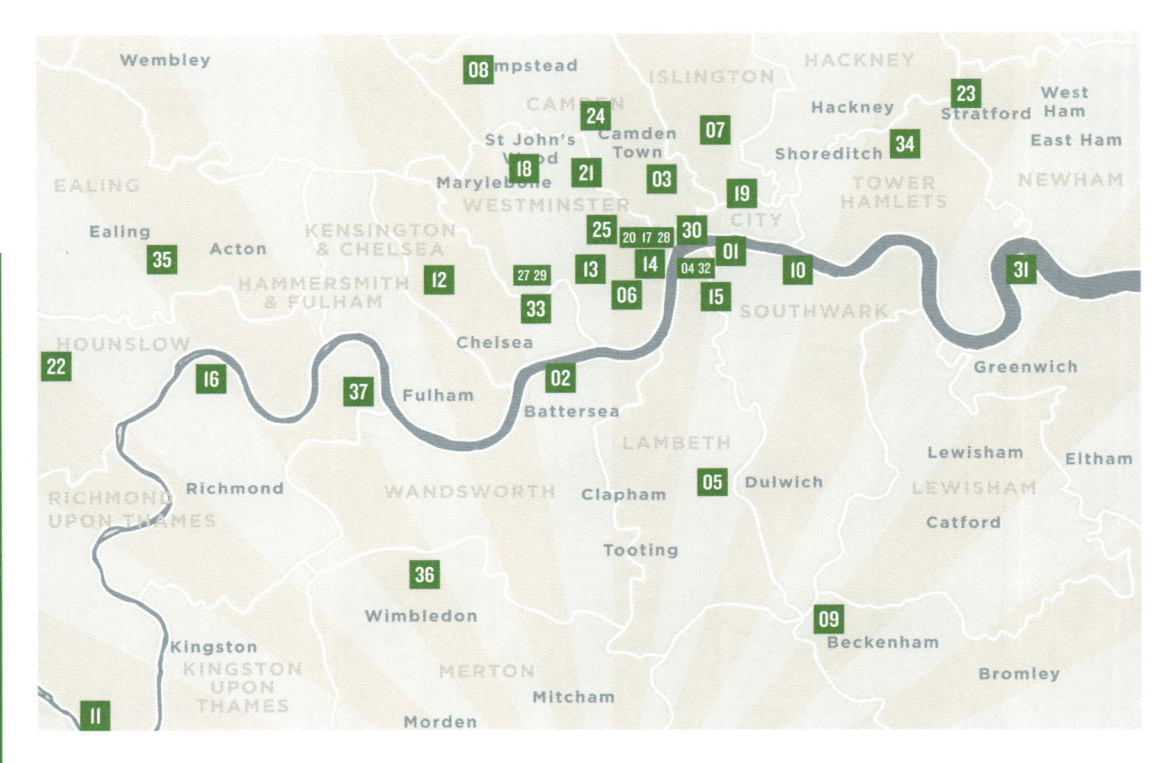

01	**Bankside Gallery** Page 165
02	**Battersea Park** Page 171
03	**Bedford Square Gardens** Page 169
04	**BFI Southbank** Page 168
05	**Brockwell Park** Page 169
06	**Buckingham Palace** Page 165
07	**Business Design Centre** Page 163
08	**Camden Arts Centre** Page 171
09	**Crystal Palace Sports Centre** Page 170
10	**Design Museum** Page 169
11	**Hampton Court Palace** Page 165
12	**Holland Park Theatre** Pages 167 & 169
13	**Hyde Park Corner Tube** Page 167
14	**ICA Cinema 1** Page 167
15	**Imperial War Museum** Page 168
16	**Kew Gardens** Page 165
17	**London Coliseum (ENO)** Pages 163 & 172
18	**Lord's Cricket Ground** Page 167
19	**Museum of London** Page 166
20	**National Portrait Gallery** Page 165
21	**Open Air Thtr Regent's Pk** Pages 170 & 172
22	**Osterley Park and House** Page 166
23	**Queen Elizabeth Olympic Pk** Page 171
24	**Roundhouse** Page 163
25	**Royal Academy of Arts** Page 165
27	**Royal Albert Hall** Page 166
28	**Royal Opera House** Page 164
29	**Serpentine Gallery** Page 172
30	**Somerset House** Page 164
31	**The O2 Arena** Page 167
32	**The Young Vic** Page 164
33	**V&A Museum** Page 164
34	**Victoria Park** Page 168
35	**Walpole Park** Page 172
36	**Wimbledon** Page 164
37	**Wetland Centre** Page 169

LondonTown.com | **JULY 2013** | 163

PICK

ART

Coronation Festival

11th - 14th July 2013
Buckingham Palace, London SW1A 1AA

PAGE 166

1st - 31st
iTunes Festival
1st – 31st July 2013
Roundhouse, Camden Town, London NW1 8EH
The line-up for this month-long series of free gigs is always kept under wraps until the last minute – but last year saw the festival's biggest line-up to date with 65 acts performing over 30 days in the iconic Camden venue. In the past the festival has featured some stellar acts, including Coldplay, Foo Fighters, Adele, One Direction, Ed Sheeran and Calvin Harris – to name but a few. Tickets for these intimate gigs are free but to apply you must enter a competition by going to the festival's official website, Facebook page or downloading the app for up to date additions to the line-up.

3rd – 6th
New Designers Exhibition Part 2, Business Design Centre
(see New Designers Exhibition Part 1, Page 156)

From 3rd
Boston Ballet: 50th Anniversary Season
Programme 1 3rd, 4th, 6th, & 7th July 2013 – Programme 2 5th & 6th July 2013
London Coliseum, St Martin's Lane, London WC2N 4ES
The Boston Ballet returns to London for the first time in 30 years, appearing for a six performance debut at the Coliseum as part of a tour celebrating the ballet's 50th anniversary season. The American dance company, led by artistic director Mikko Nissinen, presents two programmes between 3rd and 7th July with a mix of

JULY 2013

classical ballet, neo-classical dance and cutting edge contemporary dance representing the company's diverse range. Programme 1 features Vaslav Nijinsky's 'Afternoon of a Faun', George Balanchine's 'Serenade' and 'Symphony in Three Movements' and resident choreographer Jorma Elo's 'Plan to B'. Programme 2, available for two nights only, includes 'Bella Figura', one of Jiri Kylian's most famous ballets which sets contemporary dance to a slow, hypnotic score of Baroque music.

The Boston Ballet returns to London to celebrate its 50th anniversary at the London Coliseum → 163

3rd - 7th
Henley Royal Regatta
3rd – 7th July 2013
Henley-on-Thames, Oxfordshire RG9 2AQ
The Henley Regatta is an historic occasion, set in a riverside village that has hardly changed in the last two centuries and bringing some serious competition to the water in one of Britain's most famous summer sporting events. It has been running since 1839, and has grown from a local event into one of the biggest meetings in rowing, attracting crews of international quality to an array of Challenge Trophies. The draw is still conducted on a knock-out basis with only two boats racing in each heat. Nineteen events take place over the five days including six classes of races for Eights and aces for Coxless Pairs and Double Sculls. But this is just as much a social event, with thousands gathering to eat picnics on the grass and drink Pimm's aplenty along the riverbank. Expect lots of Tim-Nice-But-Dims as the English upper class and middle classes descend in their hordes.

5th – 21st
La Rondine
5th – 21st July 2013
Royal Opera House, Covent Garden, London WC2E 9DD
Puccini's passionate story of Magda, who falls in love with handsome newcomer Ruggero, is set in 1920s Paris in Nicolas Joël's production of Puccini's tender opera at the Royal Opera House. There's a quiet sadness to the opera's exquisite melodies as our heroine knows she can never be with her younger, naive lover because she is indebted to her elderly romancer Rambaldo.

6th
Wimbledon Ladies' Singles Final
Saturday 6th July 2013
The All England Club, Wimbledon, London SW19 5AE
Serena Williams still has a long way to go if she wants to equal Martina Navratilova's nine Wimbledon wins – but it will be six for the American defending champion if she prevails today.

6th - 18th
Summer Series
6th – 18th July 2013
Somerset House, Strand, London WC2R 1LA
Some of the best current live acts drop into the central courtyard of Somerset House for this year's Summer Series. It's an idyllic, intimate, calming, escapist location for a concert on a summer's evening and as a breeze drifts in off the Thames you'll forget the city bustle outside and tune into some great music, surrounded by one of eighteenth century London's most spectacular buildings. Last year's line-up offered quirky Australian comedian Tim Minchin, Peckham born dubstep singer Katy B, soul diva Jill Scott, four-piece indie band Temper Trap, Mercury Prize nominated Anna Calvi, British rockers The Enemy and stylish songstress Paloma Faith. For detailed information on this year's festival, keep checking the Somerset House official website.

From 6th
A Season in the Congo
6th July – 13th August 2013
Young Vic, Waterloo, London SE1 8LZ
Not one to do things by halves, British director Joe Wright is following his theatre directing debut in February – 'Trelawny of the Wells' at the Donmar Warehouse – with yet another theatre project this July. Best known for 'Anna Karenina', 'Atonement', 'Pride and Prejudice' and the Brad Pitt 'Chanel No. 5' adverts, Wright admits that these new projects are about as far away from his usual works as you can get: "I'm terrified. And that is another very good reason to do it". 'A Season in the Congo' tells the true story of the 1960 rebellion against Belgian rule and the fall of legendary leader Patrice Lumumba. With the play featuring about 50 characters, it is an ambitious project that Wright intends to portray with the use of only eight actors, three dancers and some musicians.

From 6th
Mexico: A Revolution in Art, 1910-1940
6th July – 29th September 2013
Royal Academy of Arts, Burlington House, W1J 0BD
In Mexico, the years between 1910 and 1920 ushered in a period of profound political change in which the arts were placed centre stage. That's the premise behind 'Mexico: A Revolution in Art, 1910-1940', an exhibition in the Sackler Wing of the Royal Academy of Arts which examines the thirty year period. The exhibition places works by national artists, such as the 'three greats' of Mexican art, Diego Rivera, Jose Clemente Orozco and David Alfaro Siqueiros, alongside those of international artists affected by their experiences in Mexico. German-born artist Josef Albers is one such who, with his wife, wrote to Wassily Kandinsky in 1936 saying, "Mexico is truly the promised land for abstract art".

7th
Wimbledon Men's Singles Final
Sunday 7th July 2013
The All England Club, Wimbledon, London SW19
Could this be the year that Andy Murray finally wins Wimbledon? The Scot came agonisingly close last year but lost to the record-equalling Roger Federer. But with his Grand Slam luck now broken, Murray could well shine on Centre Court this July.

8th - 13th
International Garden Photographer of the Year
8th – 13th July 2013
Bankside Gallery, SE1 9JH
October 2013
Nash Conservatory, Kew Gardens, London TW9 3AB
Hosted at a central London location, the Bankside Gallery, for the first time, this exhibition gives visitors the chance to see the winning and finalists' images from the International Garden Photographer of the Year competition. Displaying the best garden, nature and outdoor photography from around the world, the images will offer an insight into the world of plants, gardens, landscapes, nature and the photographer's perception of this beautiful world. The exhibition will also take place in its usual home at Kew Gardens in the Nash Conservatory later in the year, in October 2013.

9th - 14th
RHS Hampton Court Palace Flower Show
9th – 14th July 2013
Hampton Court Palace, Surrey KT8 9AU
Henry VIII built one of the finest gardens in the world at Hampton Court Palace, so it is only fitting that the world's largest horticultural show should take place there. The Hampton Court Palace Flower Show includes displays from over 150 specialist nurseries. Some are beautiful, complex works of living art, filled with rare blooms and water features. However, many are on a smaller scale, and should give you ideas for improving your own garden. While show gardens compete for the RHS medals, the rose marquee is Britain's largest annual display of roses in full bloom; the sweet scent is overwhelming. The event opens with a special preview evening complete with fireworks and at the end of the show, on the final afternoon, many of the exhibitors sell off their plants at bargain prices - you can bet the gardening gloves come off for this free-for-all.

9th - 14th
Kew the Music
9th – 14th July 2013
Kew Gardens, London TW9 3AB
Blondie, Paul Weller and Jools Holland and his Rhythm and Blues Orchestra are on the Kew the Music line-up when it returns in July 2013. The six-day festival offers a series of outdoor picnic concerts set against the backdrop of the Victorian Temperate House at Kew Gardens. In previous years these concerts have proved to be a great success with the likes of Status Quo, James Morrison and Gipsy Kings playing. For the ultimate package there is also the option to become a VIP for the evening with picnic hampers, a BBQ at the Pavilion Restaurant and reserved seating.

Carlos Acosta's new show presents the highlights of his career → 172

11th – 14th
Coronation Festival 2013
11th - 14th July 2013
Buckingham Palace, London SW1A 1AA
The main Diamond Jubilee celebrations may have taken place last year but in 2013 we have the Coronation Festival, a four day celebratory event marking the 60th anniversary of the Queen's Coronation. Over 200 companies who hold the Royal Warrant will be showcasing their crafts, industries, designs, innovations and more. Over the festival period, there will also be evening Gala performances showcasing British performing art talent. The unique event which takes place in the gardens of Buckingham Palace, the Queen's London home, is open to members of the public who can buy a ticket for the daytime event (£30), or the evening Gala (£90), when

the entertainment will be a celebration of music and dance over the past 60 years.

From 11th
Laura Knight Portraits
11th July – 20th October 2013
National Portrait Gallery, St Martin's Place, London WC2H 0HE
English impressionist Dame Laura Knight, known for her paintings of the London ballet and theatre scene, was the first woman to be given a retrospective at the Royal Academy with her 1965 exhibition. The artist, who was an Official War Artist in the Second World War, and who recorded the Nuremberg Trials, is the subject of a temporary exhibition at the National Portrait Gallery which draws on Knight's own writing in two autobiographies to give an insight into her life and art.

From 12th
The BBC Proms
12th July – 7th September 2013
Royal Albert Hall, Kensington Gore, London SW7 2AP
The centenary of the birth of Benjamin Britten, one of the greatest British composers, will be the focal point of the 2013 BBC Proms. Held yearly at the Royal Albert Hall (with Saturday matinees in nearby Cadogan Hall), the Proms is arguably the most popular season of classical music the world over, featuring a varied but accessible programme that regularly draws huge audiences, concluding on the fabled last night when seas of Union Jack waving Brits belt out 'Jerusalem' and the national anthem. Most Proms blend the popular and familiar with the surprising and innovative, encouraging spectators to discover new composers as well as hearing their favourite pieces. More than 500 standing tickets are available for each Prom on the door for just £5 - half the price of a central London cinema ticket. Full details will be announced in April 2013.

13th & 14th
Osterley Weekend
13th & 14th July 2013
Osterley House & Park, Jersey Road, Isleworth, London TW7 4RB
Billed as a 21st century village fete in the city, the annual Osterley Weekend brings the grounds of the magnificent redbrick Tudor masterpiece Osterley House to life with a range of activities including a fun fair, mini farm, archery, dance and music workshops, family fun and a range of food and drink stalls.

13th - 28th
Festival of British Archaeology
13th – 28th July 2013
Various venues across London
Get to grips with London's local heritage and see archaeology in action at the Festival of British Archaeology, a nationwide festival which includes special events taking place all over London. With excavation open days, behind-the-scenes tours, workshops, guided walks, talks and family fun days, there will be something for everyone. Previous years have seen the Museum of London offer a curator-led tour around the remains of part of Roman London's fort dating back to around 200 AD and the chance to be an osteologist for the day, discovering how human skeletons are analysed.

From 18th
Richard Rogers RA: Ideas in Progress
(PICK)
18th July – 13th October 2013
Royal Academy of Arts at 6 Burlington Gardens, London W1S 3ES
INTERNATIONALLY RENOWNED PRITZKER PRIZE-WINNING British architect, Richard Rogers, is the subject of a summer exhibition at the Royal Academy's Burlington Gardens exhibition space, timed to coincide with his 80th birthday on 23rd July 2013. 'Richard Rogers RA: Ideas in Progress' will include previously unseen material, drawings and personal items from one of the most influential figures in contemporary architecture. Best known for his designs for the Pompidou Centre, the Lloyd's of London building, and the Millennium Dome (now the O2), he will add 3 World Trade Centre to the list when it is completed in 2013. The exhibition gives visitors an insight into Rogers' pioneering ideas about architecture, his influence on the way we think about cities and how we live in them.

Further London venues that frequently take part are the Tower of London, the Cuming Museum the Rose Theatre and the Petrie Museum of Egyptian Archaeology. Digging up the past, the Festival of British Archaeology promises to reveal there's more under your feet than mere concrete and soil.

14th
The British 10K London Run

Sunday 14th July 2013
Hyde Park, London SW1X
Now in its thirteenth year, this huge annual fundraiser – which is expected to attract 30,000 runners - has made the second Sunday in July all its own. Starting at Hyde Park Corner the course heads down Piccadilly and Pall Mall to Trafalgar Square, along the Embankment to the City, taking in St Paul's and Tower Bridge, and finally back to Whitehall, looping past the London Eye on the way. The runners are joined by a bunch of celebrities and athletics champions; a number of Olympic Ambassadors took part in the 2012 race while Paula Radcliffe and Mo Farah helped bring the cheers with inspirational film footage.

From 16th
Opera Holland Park: L'Elisir d'Amore

16th July – 3rd August 2013
Holland Park Theatre, London W8 6LU
'L'Elisir d'Amore' (The Elixir of Love) by the Italian composer Gaetano Donizetti is part of the 2013 Opera Holland Park season which includes a double bill of 'Cavalleria Rusticana' and 'Pagliacci,' Puccini's 'Madama Butterfly', 'Les Pecheurs de Perles' by Bizet, and 'I Gioielli della Madonna', Wolf-Ferrari's relatively unknown tale of passion, sacrilege and madness.

18th – 22nd
2nd Investec Ashes Test: England v Australia

18th – 22nd July 2013
Lord's Cricket Ground, St John's Wood, London NW8
Since 2009, England have generally bettered their old foe Australia in Test cricket - and Alastair Cook's side will enter the 2013 Ashes series on the back of two consecutive series victories in cricket's oldest rivalry. The 2010-11 series Down Under was manna from the cricketing heavens for England fans: the 3-1 series win was the only one in which a team had won three Tests by innings margins and the first time England has scored 500 or more four times in a single series. This second Ashes Test at Lord's comes just four days after the series opener at Trent Bridge and will therefore be crucial. In the last Ashes Test at Lord's, in 2009, England won by 115 runs thanks to a five-wicket haul by Andy Flintoff just days after he had announced his impending retirement. Can Cook's new-look side continue the domination ushered in by Flintoff and co?

18th – 21st
Cirque du Soleil: Alegria

18th – 21st July 2013
The O2 Arena, Greenwich, London SE10 0BB
Entertainment company Cirque du Soleil provide Londoners with a second spellbinding show for 2013 – the first being 'Kooza' in January. One of the company's most popular productions, 'Alegria' focuses on power, the handing down of power over time and the evolution from ancient monarchies to modern democracies. Against the backdrop of these themes and through the use of contortion, synchronised trapeze, fire-knife dance and hand balancing – to name just a few – an array of characters play out the story: the Clowns, witnesses to the passing of the centuries, provide an endearing and child-like aura that turns the world into a circus; Nymphs, youthful and ethereal, exude beauty as they glide across the stage; and the White Singer – whose alter ego the Black Singer also features – is the storyteller who echoes what she sees in the form of song.

18th - 25th
Rushes Soho Shorts Festival

18th – 25th July 2013
Various Soho venues
Proving that great things come in small packages, the

Fans gather in Victoria Park for the Lovebox weekender → *168*

Over 150 specialist nurseries come to Hampton Court for the annual RHS Flower Show → 165

Rushes Soho Shorts festival celebrates UK and International film making with 10 days of exciting visual treats throughout Soho and beyond. London's screens will be graced by a variety of contemporary delights ranging from live action to animation, fiction to factual, and a whole lot of experimental action to boot. The festival awards new and established film makers for their work and also offers a range of discussions and debates. Many familiar faces and recognisable names feature in the programme.

18th - 25th
London Indian Film Festival
18th - 25th July 2013
BFI Southbank and various venues all over London
There's cause for celebration at this year's London Indian Film Festival, which commemorates 100 years of Indian cinema. A century ago, on 3rd May 1913, the silent film 'Raja Harishchandra' was released, considered to be the first Indian feature film produced. 100 years on and India is now the world's largest democracy, second largest population and also the world's most prolific film producing nation (releasing around 1,000 pictures a year - that's twice as many as Hollywood). LIFF aims to dispel the myth that this is an industry confined to the Bollywood stereotype by putting on a far-reaching programme of events that includes thrillers, dramas, comedies, short films, documentaries and, of course, - its fair share of song-and-dance blockbusters. Also expect seminars, Q&As and live music events throughout the eight-day bonanza.

From 18th
Horrible Histories: Spies and Secret War, Imperial War Museum
From 18th July 2013
Imperial War Museum London, Lambeth Road, London SE1 6HZ
The Imperial War Museum in London reopens in July 2013, having closed its doors for redevelopment on 2nd January 2013, with a new family exhibition, 'Horrible Histories: Spies'. Based on the popular children's book series by Terry Deary, the display will immerse visitors into the world of World War Two espionage, including codes and ciphers, disguises, camouflage, forgeries and gadgets. The spy theme will continue in 'Secret War', an on-going IWM London exhibition exploring the clandestine world of espionage, covert operations and the work of Britain's Special Forces. Over the next decade the Imperial War Museum's flagship branch will be transformed by a £35 million project. The first phase will be launched in summer 2014 with the opening of new First World War Galleries to mark the 100 year anniversary of the start of the First World War.

19th – 21st
Lovebox
19th – 21st July 2013
Victoria Park, Tower Hamlets, London E3 5SN
London's answer to Glastonbury is back for 2013 with three days of unadulterated partying. The Lovebox Weekender is the park party that comes closest to capturing the vibe of a proper festival, with a huge range of musical styles across multiple stages, and a friendly, music-loving crowd. Vicky Park

is a great festival venue, with loads of space and a sympathetic council who let them turn the music up really loud. Running from Friday afternoon through until Sunday evening, each day will have its own distinct musical identity. Friday kicks off with bone shaking beats and a big injection of carnival spirit. Saturday welcomes pop superstars and rock icons before Sunday sees an out and out explosion of flamboyant and fierce hedonism.

20th & 21st
Traditional Crafts Weekend
20th & 21st July 2013
WWT London Wetland Centre, Barnes, London SW13 9WT
Shire horses and Morris dancers join a range of skilled craftspeople demonstrating ancient crafts at the award-winning London Wetland Centre. Many of the craft demonstrations and talks over the weekend focus on wetlands and how they provide people with food, building materials and tools. Watch an unusual coracle boat being constructed and check out the fascinating eel display.

20th & 21st
Lambeth Country Show
20th & 21st July 2013
Brockwell Park, London SE24 0PA
The countryside comes to south London for a weekend, cows and all, as the leafy expanse of Brockwell Park welcomes herds of hairy visitors, accompanied by brilliant live music. The annual Lambeth Country Show is a weird and very entertaining mixture: city kids get to soak up a taste of rural England - falconry shows, jousting, sheep dog displays, a fruit and veg competition, steam engines and the like - then restore their urban cool with two days of top ska, soul and reggae with music from some of Brixton's finest sound systems. Local acts feature on the main stage while over on the Village Green stage you'll find acoustic and folk music followed by some jazz and classical groups. A fantastic free family festival and a tribute to the enduring spirit of London's liveliest borough.

From 23rd
Opera Holland Park: I Gioielli della Madonna
23rd July – 2nd August 2013
Holland Park Theatre, London W8 6LU
Opera Holland Park concludes its 2013 season with 'I Gioielli della Madonna' ('The Jewels of the Madonna'), a relatively unknown tale of tumultuous passion, sacrilege and madness. This opera in three acts by Ermanno Wolf-Ferrari will feature young, talented singers including Welsh soprano Natalya Romaniw. It's the final offering from Opera Holland Park which in 2013 includes a double bill of 'Cavalleria Rusticana' and 'Pagliacci', Puccini's 'Madama Butterfly', 'Les Pecheurs de Perles' by Bizet, and 'L'Elisir d'Amore' by Donizetti.

From 24th
Making the Future: A New Industrial Revolution
24th July – 3rd November 2013
Design Museum, Southwark, London SE1 2YD
In recent years technology has developed at an alarming rate, new products are constantly being released and our desire for the latest, fastest and most

20th
The Chap Olympiad [PICK]
20th July 2013
Bedford Square Gardens, Bloomsbury, London WC1B 5BL

NOT SO MUCH A SPORTING OCCASION as a celebration of buffoonery and sporting ineptitude, orchestrated by The Chap magazine, for gentlemen (and gentlewomen) of good taste, 'The Chap Olympiad' is a spiffing non-sporting event. Bedford Square Gardens, centred on one of the best preserved set pieces of Georgian architecture in London, is a fitting backdrop for such a distinguished gathering. All events can be entered by members of the public - as long as they're not sporting sportswear. Zany showdowns include 'Umbrella Jousting', using bicycles and brollies instead of horses and lances, and the 'Tug of Hair' in which the rope is substituted with a lengthy handlebar moustache. Yikes! Good old fashioned fun for tweed loving chaps and chapettes - and if a second day like last year's is confirmed, the Olympiad will run over a full weekend with banjos, boaters and Pimm's by the bucket load.

JULY 2013

The Ashes return to Lord's Cricket Ground with the 2nd Investec Test between England and the visitors Australia → 167

innovative devices is relentlessly increasing. Partnering with the Technology Strategy Board, the Design Museum is hosting 'Making the Future: A New Industrial Revolution'. This exhibition will explore our changing relationship with the design world and will delve into what drives innovation and new manufacturing techniques that can increase growth and productivity. There will also be the chance to view emerging technologies that are set to become the growth sectors of tomorrow.

From 25th
The Sound of Music
25th July – 7th September 2013
Open Air Theatre, Regent's Park, Marylebone, London NW1 4NU
Rodger and Hammerstein's classic production 'The Sound of Music' will provide the conclusion to this year's open air season – a Regent's Park Open Air Theatre debut for the masterful musical-writing duo. Based on the memoirs of Maria von Trapp, the heart-warming show was an instant hit when it took to the stage in 1959 and has since become one of the world's favourite musicals. Directed by Rachel Kavanaugh and choreographed by Alistair David, audiences can expect all the timeless scores such as 'Do-Re-Mi', 'Climb Ev'ry Mountain, 'My Favourite Things', 'Sixteen Going on Seventeen' and 'Edelweiss'.

26th & 27th
British Athletics London Grand Prix
26th & 27th July 2013
Crystal Palace National Sports Centre, Upper Norwood, London SE19 2BB
After the biggest year of athletics the country has ever seen, world-class athletics returns to London in 2013 with the British Athletics London Grand Prix at Crystal Palace. A host of Olympic stars will no doubt be in action at what is considered one of the best Samsung Diamond League meets in the world. Last year saw a host of British and international champions put in show-stopping performances, with Mo Farah sowing the seeds of glory for his Olympic double with a commanding performance in the 5,000m to the delight of the capacity crowd. Not only is this the only two-day Diamond League event on the circuit, it's also the final athletics event of the season - with Saturday's closing day marking exactly one year since the start of London 2012. Let the memories come flooding back...

From 26th
Jockum Nordström
26th July – 29th September 2013
Camden Arts Centre, London NW3 6DG
A major survey of work by artist Jockum Nordström arrives at the Camden Arts Centre in July. The work of the Swedish artist, in the words of New York Times critic

Roberta Smith, "is a more or less truculent crazy quilt of images, styles and events". Delicately and elegantly constructed works include collages, watercolors, graphite drawings, and architectural sculptures which feel improvisational and spontaneous, yet are rich in detail. Nordström was born in 1963 in Stockholm, where he continues to live and work. In 2010, his fifth gallery show, titled 'Who is sleeping on my pillow', marked the first time he exhibited alongside his artist-wife Karin Mamma Andersson in concurrent solo exhibitions.

From 26th
Emma Hart: Dirty Looks
26th July – 29th September 2013
Camden Arts Centre, London NW3 6DG
London-based British artist Emma Hart, already part of a group exhibition at Camden Arts Centre earlier in the year, returns with solo show 'Dirty Looks' in July. The artist, praised for her "gleeful inventiveness and refreshingly daft sense of humour" by The Guardian when reviewing her critically acclaimed 2010 solo show at Matt's Gallery, works with ceramics, photography, video and carving, creating products from her imagination.

27th
Queen Elizabeth Olympic Park First Phase Opening
Saturday 27th July 2013
Queen Elizabeth Olympic Park, Stratford, London E20 2ST
The first phase of the Queen Elizabeth Olympic Park, the opening of the North Park, launches on Saturday 27th July 2013 as a site of over 250 acres of beautifully landscaped open space and 6.5 km of waterways becomes available for public use.

27th - 29th
Battersea Park Foodies Festival
27th – 29th July 2013
Battersea Park, Albert Bridge Road, London SW11 4NJ
Meet Michelin-starred chefs, see live demonstrations and sample food from London's top restaurants at the Foodies Festival, taking place at Battersea Park in July following an earlier outing at Hampton Court Palace in May. Cooking is made to look easy thanks to demos from top chefs and if the mere thought of all that makes you hungry then you can head to the restaurant tents where you can sample signature dishes from well known restaurants. Wash it all down with posh fizz from Veuve Clicquot and you can guarantee an atmosphere of bon viveur. Around 25,000 people are expected to attend which just goes to show the popularity of London's restaurants. Much like the 'Taste of London', these 'Foodies' events - which also take place in Bristol, Oxford and Edinburgh (coinciding with the Festival) - offer a winning combination of sampling, slurping and learning, all in the open air. A foodie's treat.

From 30th
Glorious Goodwood
30th July - 3rd August 2013
Goodwood Racecourse, Chichester PO18 0PS
Edward VII famously described Glorious Goodwood as a "garden party with racing tacked on" and the former King

From 9th
Club to Catwalk: London Fashion in the '80s
From 9th July 2013
Victoria and Albert Museum, London SW7

STONE WASHED JEANS, BAT WINGS, PUFFBALL SKIRTS: if you're old enough to remember these 'fashions' then 'From Club to Catwalk: London Fashion in the '80s' is for you. The Victoria & Albert Museum takes a step back in time to Thatcher's England when designers like Betty Jackson, John Galliano and Vivienne Westwood ruled the catwalks. In those days it was a short hop from couture to club wear as fashion magazines like i-D and Blitz promoted the trend for theatrical dressing.

of England certainly knew a few things about horses and socialising. A chain-smoking, fashionable dandy renowned for his genial bonhomie more than his political nous, Edward's steed Ambush II once won the Grand National but this five-day meeting at one of the world's most beautiful racecourses was dearest to his heart. The Glorious Goodwood Festival remains to this day one of the highlights of the British summer sporting and social calendars, bringing together some of the finest thoroughbreds (both horses and humans) to the picturesque Sussex Downs.

From 30th
Carlos Acosta
30th July – 4th August 2013
English National Opera, London Coliseum, London WC2N 4ES
The era-defining Cuban-born dancer Carlos Acosta, currently Principal Guest Artist with the Royal Ballet, is a phenomenon in the world of modern ballet; he's fresh, contemporary and captivating whilst maintaining the exquisite beauty of classical lines. In July he returns to the London Coliseum for five performances only, with a new show, 'Classical Selection', presenting highlights of his glorious career. He is joined by a supporting cast of world-class dance partners with whom he has performed in the past to celebrate the year of his 40th birthday.

Unconfirmed dates
Serpentine Gallery Pavilion
July – October 2013
Serpentine Gallery, Kensington Gardens, London W2
While the exact details of the thirteenth commission in the Serpentine Gallery's annual Serpentine Gallery Pavilion series have yet to be revealed, the project is always an interesting prospect. The brief tasks a world-renowned architect who has never completed a project in England, to design a temporary pavilion for its lawn in Kensington Gardens. The design should be a covered space that can be used as a café by day and a forum for learning, debate and entertainment at night. Last year's project was carried out by the pairing of Herzog & de Meuron and Chinese artist Ai Weiwei, the team behind the highly acclaimed Beijing National Stadium. Whoever is chosen for the 2013 commission will join past alumni including the Olympic Aquatics Centre architect Zaha Hadid who was the first to create such a pavilion in 2000.

Dance Al Fresco
One weekend in July and August 2013
The Broadwalk, Outer Circle, Regent's Park, London NW1
Dancers leave behind the safety of the ballroom and take their moves outdoors as Dance Al Fresco returns to London's Regent's Park. Since making its debut back in 1998 with an emotionally charged open-air Argentine tango, 'Dance Al Fresco' has become a much loved summer highlight, capturing the minds of picnickers and dog-walkers alike with a great line-up of professional dancers, including, in the past, 'Strictly Come Dancing''s Vincent Simone and Flavia Cacace. The shows are free for spectators, but if you're after a bit more excitement then get your dancing shoes on and join in with one of the ticketed dances classes: all proceeds go towards tree planting in the park. If you wish to be sure if an event is taking place, you may call the organiser on 07970 599445.

Ealing Blues Festival
Saturday 20th July 2013 TBC
Walpole Park, Ealing, London W5 5EQ
Since 1987 Walpole Park in Ealing has played host to a one-day festival of blues which returns to the west London park each summer. The location is an appropriate one to host such a festival, being the birthplace of British Rhythm and Blues, a scene that started in Ealing in 1962. They often have a high calibre of performers and listening to the blues & rock and boogie woogie musicians perform in the beautiful surroundings of Walpole Park is an appealing prospect on a lazy summer's day. The festival is organised by The Ealing Club (or Ealing Jazz Club), one of Ealing's legendary venues where the British Rhythm and Blues boom of the 1960s kicked off.

The annual Serpentine Gallery Pavilion returns for three months this summer

ARCHITECTURE

TRANSFORMING THE OLYMPIC PARK

London's newest urban park will be a lasting legacy of the Summer Games.
By Francesca Young

On saturday 27th july 2013, exactly one year after the Opening Ceremony marked the beginning of the 2012 Olympic Games, the former Olympic Park reopens as the Queen Elizabeth Olympic Park – adding a new public park the size of Hyde Park to London's existing 17,000 acres of green space.

From this date onwards there will be phased openings of the park, revealing the results of a £292 million project which will transform the Olympic Park into a lasting legacy for London. It's not just the iconic venues which will be available: new family homes, artists' workshops, pop-up restaurants, micro-breweries and street markets are all part of the Olympic legacy.

The significantly extended North Park, greener with new trees, shrubs and bulbs planted, will be the first to open, offering visitors over 250 acres of beautifully landscaped open space and 6.5 km of waterways. South Plaza and Park Hub, a 28 acre area which has been designed by James Corner Field Operations, the same firm that designed New York's High Line, will be centred on a 12 metre wide tree-lined boulevard leading to outdoor 'rooms' containing fountains, climbable walls, giant swings and a revitalised traditional lock. By spring 2014 the whole 560 acre park will be open.

In summer 2013 the Copper Box, which hosted handball during the Olympics and goalball during the Paralympics, will be one of the first venues to reopen. With the capacity to seat 7,500 people it will be the third largest arena in London, used for concerts, sports and community projects as well as cultural and business events. It will also be the home of British Basketball League team MK Lions, who will be rebranded as the London Lions. Both the Zaha Hadid-designed Aquatics Centre and Anish Kapoor's giant 114 metre ArcelorMittal Orbit – which will become a visitor attraction with views across London from the two glass enclosed platforms – will reopen from spring 2014. But the area surrounding them will be open from mid-2013 creating an urban entertainment plaza where a programme of events will run.

In 2013 cyclists will also be able to use parts of the cycling venues used in the Olympics including the Velodrome – the scene of so many Team GB and ParalympicsGB successes at London 2012 – BMX course, outdoor road circuits and off-road mountain bike trails at the Velopark. Both the Velopark and the neighbouring Eton Manor sports complex, managed by the Lea Valley Regional Park Authority, will be open to the public.

On sunday 4th august 2013, a new event, RideLondon, will be the first to embrace the cycling legacy created by the London 2012 Olympics. An opportunity for amateurs then professionals to compete in a one-day race, the two events will encourage participants to take to the roads of London on a modified version of the course made famous in last summer's Games. The 100-mile route will start at the new Queen Elizabeth Olympic Park and follow the closed roads through the capital, Richmond Park and into the Surrey countryside, before finishing on The Mall.

Eton Manor, which hosted the Paralympic wheelchair tennis competition and warm-up swimming pools during the Games, is to become a new sports facility called Lee Valley Hockey and Tennis Centre. The Hockey Centre will host the 2015 European Hockey Championships. A neighbourhood of about 850 new homes, 70 per cent of which are due to be family homes of three bedrooms or more, to be known as Chobham Manor, is to be built where the Basketball Arena once stood, due to open in autumn.

The Press and Broadcast Centre is expected to become a new commercial and employment site. Although a buyer hadn't been found at the time of writing, the centre was built with flexibility in mind to be adapted for a wide range of uses and it's anticipated that more than 3,500 jobs will be based in the building.

The reopening of the £429 million Olympic Stadium which still has to find a tenant, although Premier League West Ham United remain the favourites, has been delayed from its original 2014 date and may not reopen until August 2016, or August 2015 at the earliest. Whoever ends up taking it on, the stadium will host the World Athletics Championships in 2017.

The transformation project, at a cost of £292 million, will bring affordable housing, parkland, sports and entertainment facilities to a once deprived area and from 2016, the London Legacy Development Corporation estimates the area will attract more than 9 million visitors a year. The E20 area now has good transport links connecting it to central London - you can get from Stratford International to King's Cross in just seven minutes - and you can get there by bike on the improved cycle paths.

Can't wait until 27th July? If you want to see what's happening while work is in progress there's a viewing gallery on the third floor of the John Lewis store within the Westfield Shopping Centre at Stratford, or you can book a free bus tour on Wednesdays, Thursdays and some weekends until the park begins to open in July.

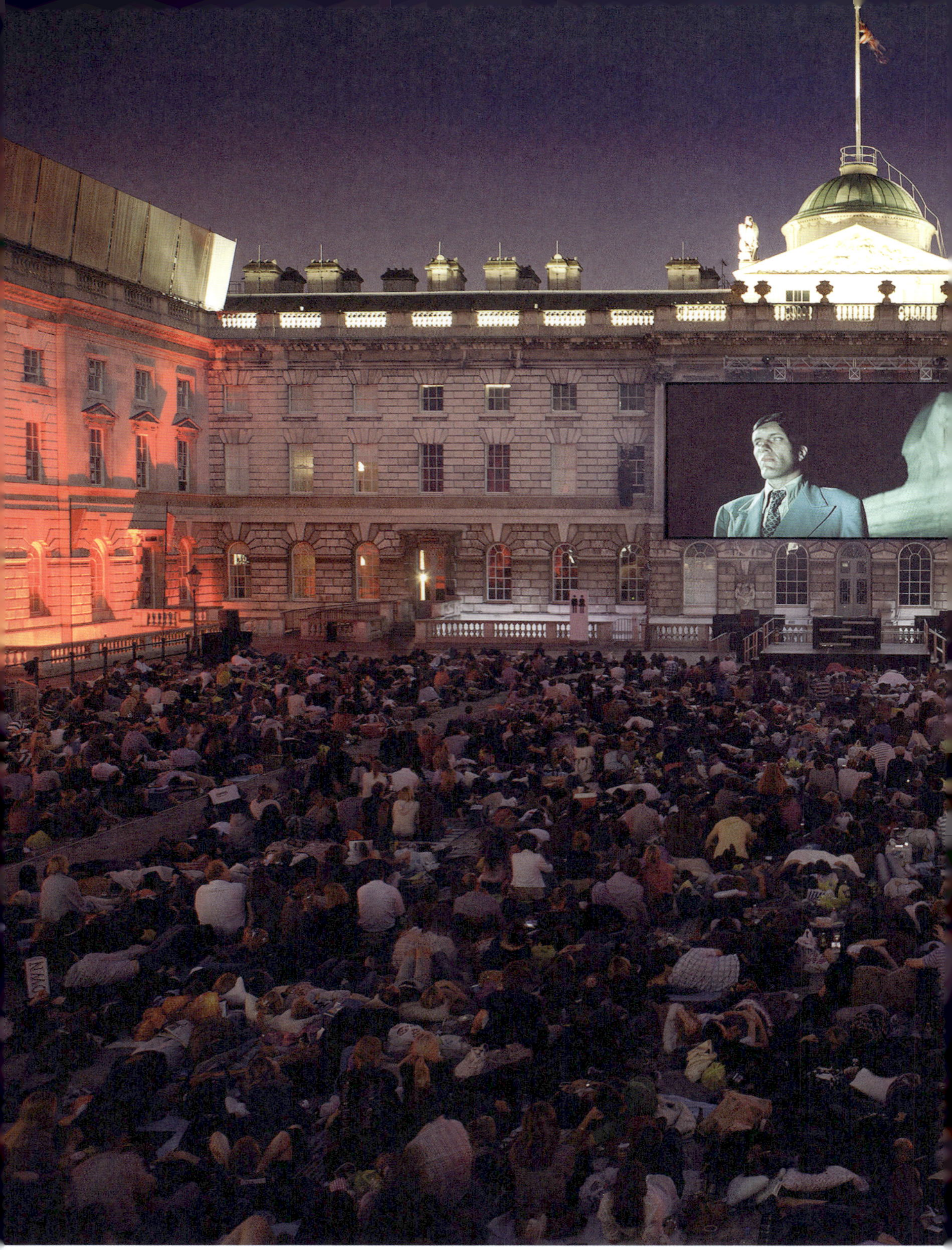

175

Get your jaws into a month filled with Bank Holiday festivals, major sporting showdowns and summer screenings…

PAGE 179

AUGUST

WHAT'S ON WHERE IN AUGUST

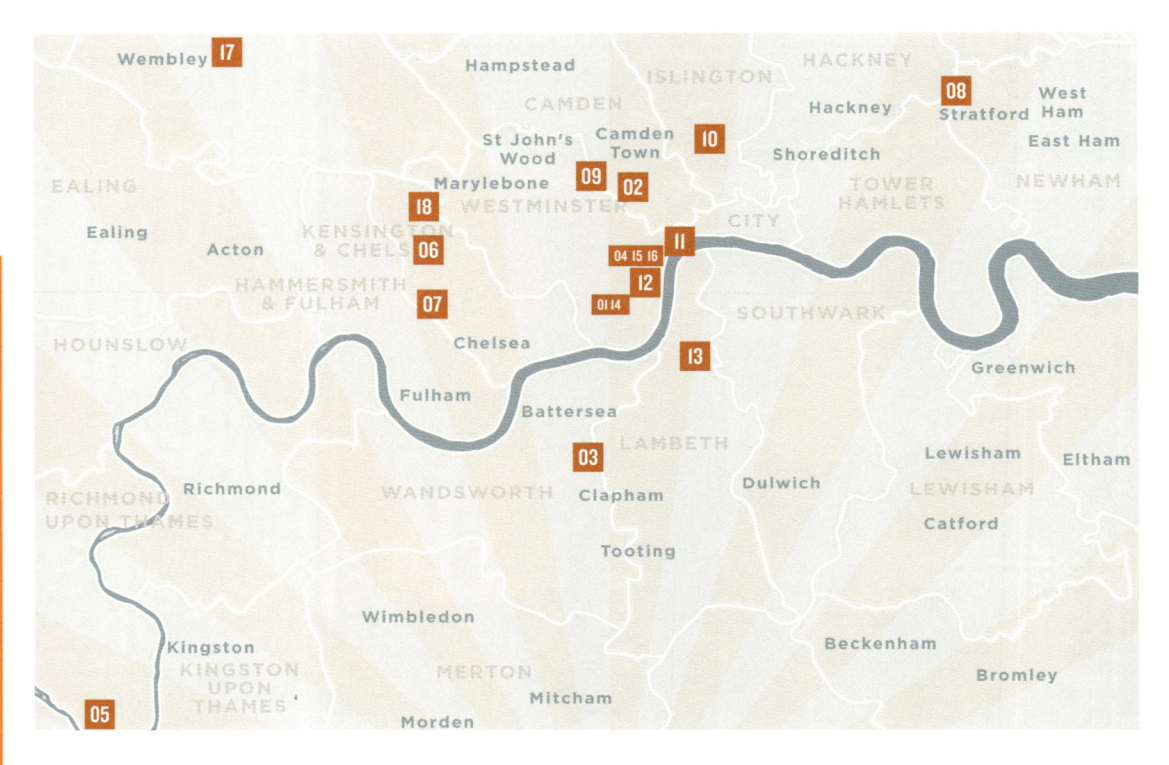

LondonTown.com

01 Buckingham Palace
Page 177
02 Camden People's Theatre
Page 181
03 Clapham Common
Page 180
04 Empire Leicester Square
Page 180
05 Hampton Court Green
Page 181
06 Notting Hill
Page 180
07 Olympia
Page 178
08 Queen Elizabeth Olympic Pk
Page 177
09 Regent's Park
Page 180
10 Sadler's Wells Theatre
Page 178
11 Somerset House
Page 179
12 St James's Park
Page 177
13 The Oval
Page 179
14 The Mall
Page 177
15 The West End
Page 182
16 Trafalgar Square
Page 178
17 Wembley Stadium
Pages 178 & 180
18 Westbourne Studios: Under the Westway
Page 181

PICK

HISTORIC PALACES

Buckingham Palace Summer Opening

3rd August - 29th September 2013
Buckingham Palace, London SW1A 1AA

THIS PAGE

From 3rd
Buckingham Palace Summer Opening

3rd August – 29th September 2013
Buckingham Palace, London SW1A 1AA
Every summer inquisitive visitors get the chance to look around Buckingham Palace and admire the interiors of the principal royal residence. Visitors for the Summer Opening tour are permitted access to the nineteen State Rooms which are still used by the Royal Family to receive and entertain guests on state and ceremonial occasions. Decorated in lavish fashion, they include paintings by Rembrandt, Rubens and Canaletto, Sevres porcelain and some of the finest English and French furniture in the world. There are also some exquisite royal gifts, including Fabergé eggs, on display. This is a fascinating opportunity to admire the taste - often wonderful, sometimes comically bad - of Britain's monarchy.

3rd & 4th
RideLondon

Saturday 3rd & Sunday 4th August
Olympic Park, Stratford
This two-day festival of cycling is the first large-scale event to use the new Queen Elizabeth Olympic Park following its summer 2013 reopening. First up, Saturday's FreeCycle welcomes 70,000 cyclists to ride along an eight-mile, traffic-free loop in central London. Britain's biggest bike festival culminates with Sunday's RideLondon 100 - a 100-mile race for amateurs that organisers have described as the London Marathon on wheels. Other Sunday events include the RideLondon Grand

The RideLondon festival culminates with a new pro race → 177

Prix - a series of criterium-style races through central London for professional women, junior riders and hand-cyclists - and the RideLondon Classic - the biggest ever men's professional one-day race in Britain. Both the Classic and 100 races will start at the Olympic Park and cover a similar route to that used in the London 2012 Olympics - taking in all eight London boroughs, Richmond Park and the Surrey countryside, before finishing on The Mall. Ride on!

From 7th
West Side Story
7th August – 22nd September 2013
Sadler's Wells, Rosebery Avenue, London EC1R 4TN
The original Broadway classic returns to Sadler's Wells after its sell-out 50th anniversary season back in 2008. Set in hot and restless downtown New York in the 1950s, Tony and Maria are our American Romeo and Juliet who find themselves torn between warring families and rival gangs until the situation inevitably ends in tragedy. The film won ten Academy Awards and featured a remarkable performance from Natalie Wood, whose tragic drowning continues to cause mystery and controversy in the press. Joey McKneely's revival will feature the original choreography from Jerome Robbins and will see Donald Chan lead the live orchestra to play Leonard Bernstein's iconic score.

11th
Eid in the Square
Saturday 11th August
Trafalgar Square, London WC2N 5DC
Eid al-Fitr is the global Muslim celebration which marks the end of the holy fasting month of Ramadan. 'Eid' is the Arabic word meaning 'festivity', while 'al-Fitr' means 'conclusion of the fast'. As Christians have Christmas, Muslims have Eid - which gives you an idea of how big the celebrations are. It's certainly a major event in London - and since 2006 there has been a mass gathering in Trafalgar Square organised by the Mayor of London and Muslim groups in the capital (although last year's event was cancelled because of the Olympics). The event features live music - past performers have included Polish-Egyptian hip-hop artists Quest-Rah, French-based rappers Akeem and North African Rai band Cheb Nacim among others - as well as food stalls, exhibitions and displays about Islam. There will also be other local events happening across London in what should prove to be a vibrant and uplifting occasion for everyone involved.

11th
FA Community Shield
Sunday 11th August
Wembley Stadium, Wembley, London HA9 0WS
The winners of the FA Cup take on the Premier League champions in the annual season curtain-raiser at Wembley Stadium. Last season's clash saw Manchester City come from behind to beat Chelsea 3-2. The match was played at Villa Park in Birmingham because the usual venue, Wembley Stadium, was being used to host the final of the Olympic football tournament. Held one week before the start of the Premier League campaign, this gives fans a first taste of who will shine over the rest of the season.

13th - 17th
The Great British Beer Festival
13th – 17th August 2013
Olympia Exhibition Centre, London W14 8UX
Over 66,000 people flock to this massive celebration of our national drink, which features over 700 real ales, ciders, perries and beers from around the world. Although the Great British Beer Festival sounds like a fun event, don't be surprised to see a lot of very serious faces and concentration; some real ale experts are genuinely obsessive - and for them this isn't merely an occasion to get sozzled. Tutored tastings are on offer for anyone who wants to learn the subtleties of what makes a great beer. For the rest of us, though, this is a jolly day out with some delicious brewed drinks. Besides the amber nectar, there's a load of activities to keep you interested, including traditional pub games, live music and, to soak it all up, some hearty traditional pub snacks.

14th
England v Scotland
Wednesday 14th August 2013
Wembley Stadium, Wembley, London HA9 0WS
One of international football's oldest rivalries is rekindled as England take on Scotland at Wembley Stadium in a friendly match in celebration

AUGUST 2013

Clapham Common comes alive over the August bank holiday weekend with the annual South West Four dance music festival →181

of the FA's 150th anniversary. The two sides met in the first official international football match ever played back in 1872 at Partick, near Glasgow. England playing Scotland is now, according to England manager Roy Hodgson, "one of the finest fixtures in international football", and a game which means the world to both sets of supporters. The sides have not met since 1999 when Scotland won 1-0 in the second leg of a Euro 2000 qualifying play-off at Wembley (England had won the first leg 2-0 at Hampden Park and so secured passage to the knock-out phases). This mid-week match should be a classic.

15th - 26th
Film4 Summer Screen
15th – 26th August 2013 TBC
Somerset House, Strand, London WC2R 1LA
Possibly the most famous of all the open air film events to take place in London, 'Summer Screen' returns to Somerset House in association with Film4 to bring cinema lovers a truly eclectic mix of movies. The 2012 season had an impressive line-up that included the UK première of 'On the Road', Brazilian director Walter Salles' adaptation of Jack Kerouac's autobiographical novel. The programme also saw a series of genre defining flicks grace the giant screen including Alfred Hitchcock's 'The Birds' and the finale was the UK première of action-drama 'Lawless', which stars an impressive cast including Tom Hardy, Gary Oldman and Guy Pearce. If this offering is anything to go by, 2013 is set to be another blockbuster year.

17th
Carnaval del Pueblo
Saturday 17th August 2013
London Pleasure Gardens, Royal Victoria Docks, London E16 2BS
This loud and colourful fiesta is the biggest outdoor celebration of Latin America in Europe, with over 100,000 people traditionally turning up for a summer Saturday of salsa and samba. The event has been cancelled for the past two years – in 2011 due to works at the festival's former venue of Burgess Park, and in 2012 owing to the Olympics – and so 2013 should prove to be quite a spectacle. Yet to be confirmed, the Carnaval will take place in the London Pleasure Gardens with a programme of live acts from Cuba, Paraguay, Brazil and other Latin American countries. There promises to be a three-mile procession of over 15 floats and four large bars, with 200 stalls offering a variety of food and drinks. Dancing usually goes on late into the night, with the Coronet Theatre in Elephant and Castle a

16th - 18th
LolliBop Festival
PICK

16th – 18th August 2013 TBC
Regent's Park, London NW1 4NR

GLASTONBURY FOR THE UNDER-10S, the LolliBop Festival- "the big bash for little people" - returns to Regent's Park this summer with live music on the bandstand, circus fun in the Big Top and appearances from some of your children's favourite characters. As well as the live acts on stage there are plenty of activities where you can get involved whether it's a workshop on hula hooping or creating a carnival costume, and the arts and crafts tent always proves popular with little ones who like to create. There's something for all the family including fairground rides for the kids and a dedicated baby change tent for parents. If you've had enough you can always run away to the LolliBop circus and be entertained by the talented troupe of performers.

traditional after-party venue for reggae, Latin hip-hop and much Brazilian samba dancing.

21st – 25th
5th Investec Ashes Test: England v Australia
21st – 25th August 2013
The Kia Oval, Kennington, London SE11 5SS

The fifth, final and potentially most crucial Ashes Test takes place at the Kia Oval more than a month after the opening Test at Trent Bridge. England have, of course, beaten fierce rivals Australia in the past two Ashes series and only time will tell if Alastair Cook's side can make it a triumphant treble. There were scenes of jubilation four years ago when a man-of-the-match performance by pace bowler Stuart Broad (not to mention a game-changing direct hit from Andy Flintoff to run out Ricky Ponting when the game was in the balance) helped England regain the Ashes with a 197-run win over Australia in the Fifth Test at the Oval in 2009. The victory gave England a 2-1 series win and started this current mini era of domination that the visitors will be only too keen to overturn.

22nd - 26th
Film4 Frightfest
22nd – 26th August 2013
Empire Cinema, Leicester Square, London WC2H 7NA

The Empire Cinema will once again host the Film4 'FrightFest' this August. The home of horror, the festival has been running since 2009 and has rapidly grown in popularity. With four days of screenings, audiences can expect to be scared witless with a devilishly delightful line-up of premieres, previews and special screenings of fantasy and horror films. Last year saw the festival's most ambitious line-up to date with a whole host of films that included: 'Sinister', 'Chained', 'Maniac', 'The Possession' and the humorously titled 'Cockneys vs Zombies'. With previous years' events welcoming a number of esteemed visitors, including Danny Boyle, 2013 is set to see even more cushion grabbing movies and an array of celebrity guests and talks.

24th
RFL Challenge Cup Final
Saturday 24th August 2013
Wembley Stadium, Wembley, London HA9 0WS

Believe it or not (and most southerners will not), rugby league is the second most popular team sport in Britain and this, the Challenge Cup Final at Wembley, is one of the most prestigious matches in world rugby league. While the game's roots are firmly in the north of England, this knock-out cup competition is now open to a few teams from France and Russia, as well as teams from the Army, Navy and RAF, and some amateur and university sides. Last year saw Super League giants Warrington Wolves beat Leeds Rhinos 35-18 to net their third win in four years.

From 24th
Blue Stockings
24th August - 11th October 2013
Shakespeare's Globe Theatre, Bankside, London SE1 9DT

'Blue Stockings' is one of three new plays receiving their world premieres at Shakespeare's Globe this summer. Written by Jessica Swale, Artistic Director of Red Handed, the London based theatre company which she set up seven years ago, the play is set in 1896 in Girton College, Cambridge, England's first residential college for women. The story of four young women and the hardships they face, from economic difficulty to the distractions of men and radical politics, is set against the backdrop of women's suffrage, a fitting subject in the year that marks the centenary of the death of Emily Wilding Davison who famously ran in front of the King's horse during the Epsom Derby.

24th & 25th
South West Four Weekender
24th & 25th August 2013
Clapham Common, London SW4 9DE
The South West Four Weekender celebrates its 10th anniversary and welcomes festival-goers to Clapham Common over the August bank holiday for two days of dance-music mayhem. The UK's premier inner city dance festival has previously attracted big names Chase and Status, Carl Cox, Foreign Beggars and Skrillex to the bill. Taking place on Saturday and Sunday (leaving you the bank holiday Monday to recover), "SW4" has proved a great success over its first nine years, filling Clapham Common with revellers united in the knowledge that they don't have to slum it in a tent and that there's no work the next day - so the party can go on and on. The music may finish around 9pm both nights but there are after-parties for those keen on all-night revelry.

25th & 26th
Notting Hill Carnival
25th & 26th August 2013
Notting Hill, London W11
Held since 1966, the Notting Hill Carnival was originally a local affair for west London's homesick Caribbean community, and has evolved into Europe's biggest street party. Carnival sets London on fire in a blaze of Caribbean spirit as extravagantly costumed dancers, calypso and soca musicians, giant sound-systems and steel bands are joined by over a million revellers of all ages. Sunday is officially Children's Day, but there are loads of kids on both days enjoying the bright colours of the floats and the dancers' feathered costumes. Adults can shake their booty at dozens of stages: our favourites are Channel 1's booming dub, and the jazz-reggae at Gaz's Rockin' Blues, but there are tunes for all tastes, from house to hip-hop. It's a huge area, and can get very crowded, so be prepared for an exhausting day out, but for anyone who loves a party, Carnival remains the absolute highlight of the London summer.

Raise your glass to the Great British Beer Festival at the Olympia → 178

Monday 26th August
Summer Bank Holiday

From 29th
Portobello Film Festival
29th August – 15th September 2013
Westbourne Studios, Ladbroke Grove, London W10 & The Tabernacle, London W11
Created in 1996 as a reaction to the state of the British film industry, the Portobello Film Festival aims to provide a platform for exciting new film makers and to give daring and ground-breaking directors a chance to get their films seen. The festival hasn't had an easy ride and has even found itself without a cinema screen at times – but screenings in parks, theatres, clubs and bars have all added to the diverse nature of the event. With annual premieres of shorts, documentaries and animations, plus lots of talks and workshops with top film directors, the Portobello Film Festival is an exciting event in any film fanatic's diary. The theme of this year's festival is 'Rock and Roll Cinema and Art'.

Three new plays receive their premieres at the Globe this summer → 180

AUGUST 2013

Unconfirmed dates

Camden Fringe
August
Various Camden venues
Bringing together comedy, theatre, poetry, dance and much more, the Camden Fringe boasts 400 performances of 100-odd (and some very odd) shows across various venues in north London throughout August. Whether you want to catch some of the edgiest stand-up around or witness a new twist on Shakespeare or watch a group of OAPs rap, the Camden Fringe has become the metaphorical David, ready "to challenge the Edinburgh Goliath" (The Guardian). Now in its eighth year, this rapidly growing four-week festival is offering fresh opportunity for both new and established acts to get themselves noticed in a creative environment outside Edinburgh.

Jolly Day Out
August
Hampton Court Green, Surrey KT8 9AT
Enjoy a 'Jolly Day Out' at this family festival on Hampton Court Green. You can see pig racing, dancing sheep and welly wanging, as well as enjoying the kids' shows, live music and fun fair rides. For younger members of the family there are live shows in the theatre tent and demonstrations, circus skills, arts and crafts, and animal farms. There's a summer market so you can indulge in some retail relaxation and food stalls offering an array of delectable treats. Add a Pimm's or a pint of real ale and you've got all the ingredients for a splendid summer family day out.

The macabre 'American Mary' from the 2012 Film4 'Frightfest' → 180

Kids Week
Throughout August 2013
Various venues in the West End
It's now over a decade since the excellent idea of Kids Week was first conjured up. A truly inspired summer treat for families, Theatreland is available for free to excitable tots and teens for the whole month of August. Children aged 5 to 16 can see an awesome selection of dazzling West End hits gratis - as long as an adult pays full price - and another two children can go half price. Tickets for the most popular shows go fast, so it's best not to make any promises until you've booked. Aside from the shows themselves, there's a whole raft of free children's activities. Kids can peek backstage, participate in workshops, dabble with make-up, learn to dance, scribble a few lines in writing classes and even sing with the cast. It's a fantastic initiative and one which can only inspire kids' enthusiasm for the stage in later life.

Old Spitalfields Market Paw Pageant
Monday 26th August 2013
Spitalfields Market, Horner Square, London E1 6EW
For the past two years, cool canines, perfect pooches, hip hounds and masterly mutts have come together on the August bank holiday Monday to strut their stuff on the dog catwalk at Old Spitalfields Market. The 'Paw Pageant' sees London's best-dressed, 'fugliest' and smartest dogs competing to win prizes across eight categories – from 'Dressed Up to the K-Nines' to the 'Shoreditch Show Off'. Sponsored by the Battersea Dogs & Cats Home, the 'Paw Pageant' also includes puppy training displays and a specialist bowwow market selling a variety of great gear and tasty grub for man's best friend.

LONDON LIDOS

Plunge into one of London's historic lidos on a warm summer's day – or join the hardy souls who take a dip even in the depths of winter. *By Vicki Forde*

PARLIAMENT HILL LIDO
Hampstead, NW5
Following an extravagant revamp, this is one of London's more spacious outdoor pools and has a stainless steel lining to retain heat

SERPENTINE LIDO
Hyde Park, W2
The Serpentine boating lake offers year-round swimming; and in summer the lido's paddling pool, sandpit and swings are ideal for families

TOOTING BEC LIDO 01
London, SW16
At 90m long, this is the largest open-air fresh water swimming pool in the UK. After some upgrades it now even features saunas and Jacuzzis

HAMPSTEAD HEATH PONDS
Hampstead, NW5
Once a reservoir, the ponds have been frequented by swimmers for centuries. With ponds for men and women as well as a mixed pond

HILLINGDON OUTDOOR POOL
Uxbridge, UB8
Previously called 'Uxbridge Lido' the outdoor pool has been restored to maintain the Grade II listed features of the original 1935 pool

HAMPTON OPEN AIR POOL
Hampton, TW12
On the edge of Bushy Park, the heated waters at Hampton are inviting all year round. In July, summer picnic concerts are staged by the pool

LONDON FIELDS LIDO
London Fields, E8
If you want lido luxury complete with a hipster crowd, then this is your best bet. Olympic sized and heated to a temperate 25c year round. Bliss

OASIS SPORTS CENTRE
Covent Garden WC2
An unexpected haven within the high-rise blocks of Holborn and Covent Garden, this pool – the most central in London – is heated all year round

BROCKWELL LIDO
Brockwell Park, SE24
Nicknamed 'Brixton Beach', the lido – built in 1937 – is an urban oasis adjacent to an extensive park with a very good cafe

---

LONDON SUMMER NEWSLETTER

→ To receive the Summer in London Newsletter send a blank email now to: **summer@londontown.com**
PRIVACY PROMISE: We will never (and that means never) give your email address to anyone else. You mean too much to us.

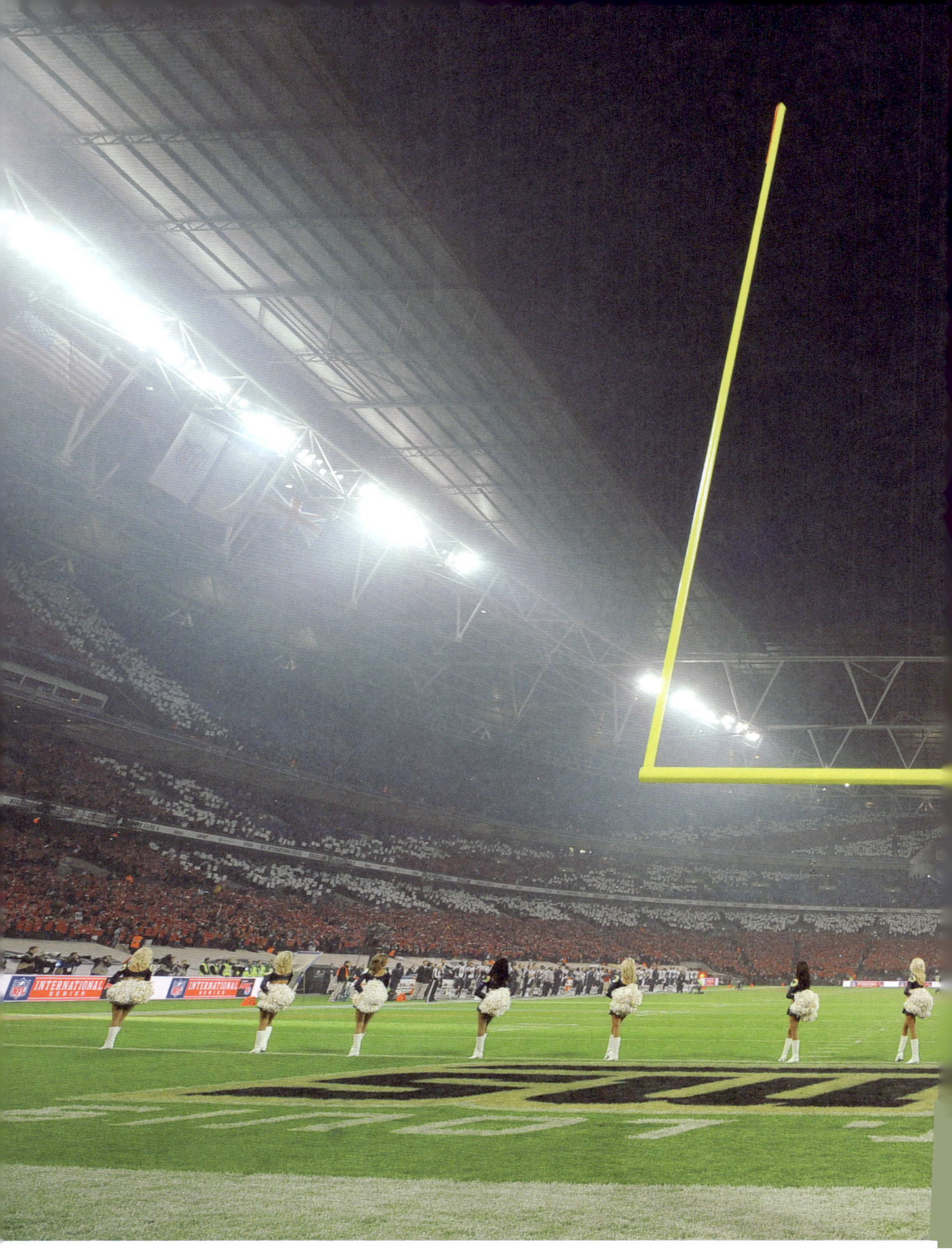
INTERNATIONAL SERIES

Proms in the Park, London fashion weekend and Scotch egg challenges and American football, all touch down in town...

PAGE 194

SEPTEMBER

WHAT'S ON WHERE IN SEPTEMBER

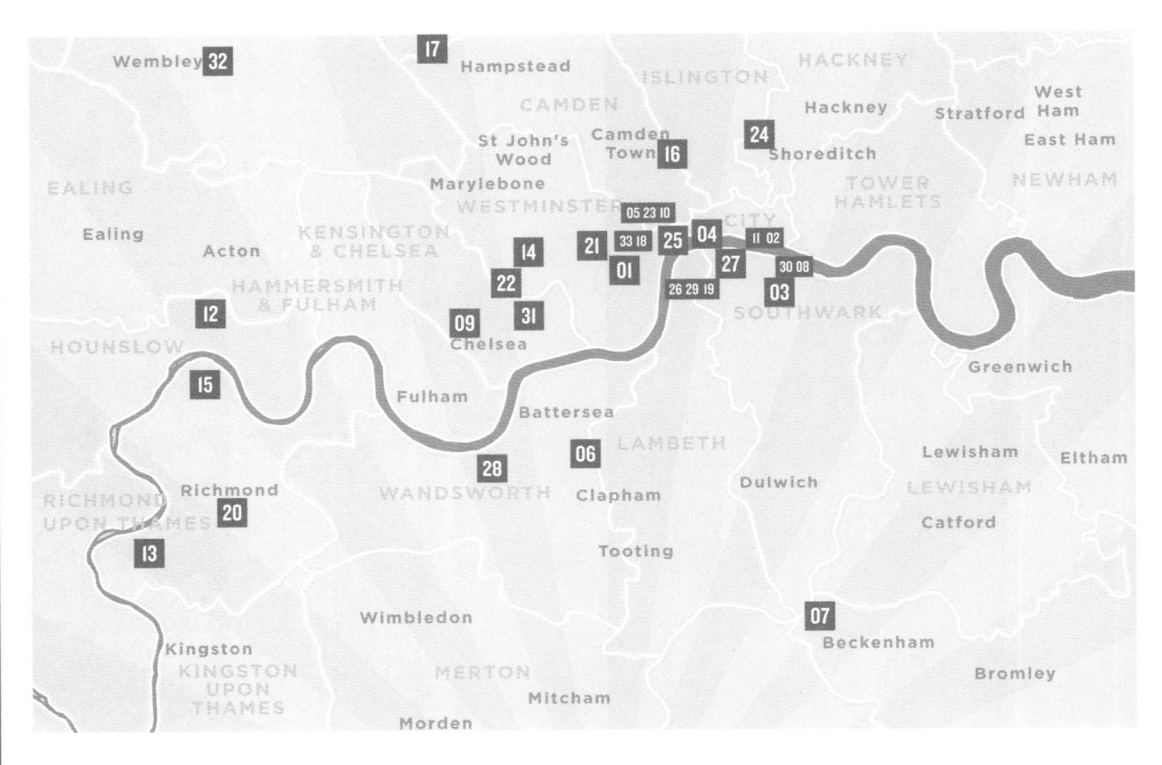

01	**Apollo Piccadilly** Page 193
02	**Bank of England Museum** Page 192
03	**Bermondsey Square** Page 191
04	**Blackfriars Bridge** Page 190
05	**British Museum** Page 189
06	**Clapham Common** Page 191
07	**Crystal Palace Sports Ctr** Page 187
08	**Design Museum** Page 189
09	**Earls Court** Page 191
10	**Freemason's Hall** Page 190
11	**Guildhall** Page 194
12	**Gunnersbury Park** Page 187
13	**Ham** Page 188
14	**Hyde Park** Pages 188 & 194
15	**Kew Gardens** Page 189
16	**Kings Place** Page 189
17	**Jewish Cultural Centre** Page 191
18	**Noel Coward Theatre** Page 188
19	**Old Vic Theatre** Page 188
20	**Richmond Park** Page 194
21	**Royal Academy of Arts** Page 192
22	**Royal Albert Hall** Pages 192 & 193
23	**Shaftesbury Theatre** Page 194
24	**Shoreditch Park** Page 194
25	**Somerset House** Pages 189, 190 & 191
26	**Southbank Centre** Page 193
27	**Tate Modern** Page 193
28	**The Ship** Page 193
29	**The Young Vic** Page 190
30	**Tower Bridge** Page 191
31	**V&A Museum** Pages 190 & 192
32	**Wembley Stadium** Pages 187, 190 & 194
33	**Wyndhams Theatre** Page 188

BEHIND THE SCENES

Open House Weekend

21st & 22nd September 2013
Hundreds of venues all over London

PAGE 192

1st
London Mela
Sunday 1st September 2013
Gunnersbury Park, London W3 8LQ
The London Mela in Gunnersbury Park is a wonderful celebration of Asian music and culture which always draws a big crowd with its line-up of British Asian music, Bollywood figures and traditional and classical performances. Entertainment is spread over nine different zones, all showcasing different types of music with urban, classical and experimental music, DJs, circus and comedy as well as dance, arts and a children's play area. There will also be a fun fair and hundreds of stalls selling food and handicrafts, all of which makes the London Mela a magnet for a multitude of Londoners out for a good time.

1st
Tri Together
Sunday 1st September 2013
Crystal Palace National Sports Centre, London SE19
The award-winning series of triathlons for people of all ages and abilities returns to London in September, raising money to support Leonard Cheshire Disability. All 'Tri Together' events are open to disabled and non-disabled people, from complete beginners to the seasoned swimmer, biker and runner. There are junior and senior races, while competitors may take part on their own, or in relay teams of twos or threes.

6th
World Cup Qualifier: England v Moldova
Friday 6th September 2013
Wembley Stadium, Wembley, London HA9 0WS

Anything less than a firm Friday night thrashing would be disappointing for Roy Hodgson's England, who beat lowly Moldova 5-0 in their away fixture back in September 2012. In fact, the only thing which should keep the goal tally down is the fact that England play main Group H rivals Ukraine four days later in Kiev.

From 6th
Barking in Essex
6th September 2013 – 4th January 2014
Wyndham's Theatre, Charing Cross Road, London WC2H 0DA
Rubber-faced comedian Lee Evans and well known actress Sheila Hancock star in 'Barking in Essex', Clive Exton's black comedy which tells the story of notorious gangster Algie Packer who is finally coming home after seven years in the clink. The quality cast and crew behind the production, with Evans playing the hapless, dim-witted Darnley and Sheila Hancock as Emmie, his fearsome mother, means there will be high demand for tickets for the show which previews from the 6th September 2013 at Wyndham's Theatre.

7th
Proms in the Park
Saturday 7th September 2013
Hyde Park, London W2 2UH
Now in its 18th year, the BBC Proms in the Park is Britain's largest classical music event and a rousing alternative finale to two months of the BBC Proms for those unable to snare tickets to the Last Night of the Proms. While the whole Last Night shebang is broadcast live on the BBC, nothing quite beats experiencing the biggest night in the classical music calendar under the stars in Hyde Park. Families and friends gather with picnic hampers and rugs for five hours of evening entertainment hosted by Radio 2 DJ Tony Blackburn and the inimitable Sir Terry Wogan. With a sensational firework finale above the stage to cap things off, the only thing you'll have to worry about is the weather.

7th
The Great River Race
Saturday 7th September 2013
London Docklands to Ham
Regarded as the rowing equivalent of the London Marathon, the Great River Race is bursting with colour, spectacle, intense competition and casual fun. The race is run upstream, starting at Millwall Slipway in London's Docklands and finishing with a spectacular riverside party at Ham. The extensive 21-mile course takes crews from the industrial cityscape of the Docklands all the way along the Thames to the idyllic semi-rural Richmond shores. Since launching in 1987, entries have snowballed from a mere 72 to a massive 300 boats carrying over 2,000 competitors, racing for 35 trophies. Festivities along the river at Richmond will begin at noon with live music, a children's beach, donkey rides and food and drink stalls.

From 7th
A Midsummer Night's Dream
7th September – 16th November 2013
Noel Coward Theatre, St Martin's Lane, London WC2N 4AU
Taking to the stage at the Noel Coward Theatre, this revival of Shakespeare's popular comedy is one of five plays in the Michael Grandage season – for which 100,000 £10 tickets are available. The penultimate play in the season, 'A Midsummer Night's Dream', has an impressive cast. Sheridan Smith, quite the regular on the theatre circuit, will play Titania, and David Walliams takes on the role of Bottom. The comedy has three intertwining plots, connected by the wedding of Duke Theseus of Athens and the Amazon queen, Hippolyta. It tells the story of four young Athenian lovers, Lysander, Demetrius, Helena and Hermia, and a group of amateur actors, who are manipulated by the fairies who inhabit the forest in which the play is set.

From 7th
Much Ado About Nothing
7th September – 16th November 2013
Old Vic Theatre, The Cut, London SE1 8NB
'Jerusalem' actor and former artistic director of Shakespeare's Globe Mark Rylance directs Vanessa Redgrave and James Earl Jones (the voice of Darth Vader) in The Old Vic's staging of Shakespeare's comedy 'Much Ado About Nothing'. Last seen in the West End together in 2011, in 'Driving Miss Daisy' at Wyndham's Theatre, the two lead actors play reluctant lovers Beatrice and Benedick in this A-list production which begins in the month that marks Kevin Spacey's 10th anniversary as artistic director of the Old Vic.

11th – 15th
ITU World Triathlon Finals
11th – 15th September 2013
Serpentine Boating Lake, Hyde Park, London W2 2UH
Following the overwhelming success of last summer's Olympics, London's Hyde Park has been selected to host the eighth and final leg of the 2013 ITU World Triathlon Series. Bronze medallist in London 2012, home hope Jonathan Brownlee is the current defending champion; his older brother, Olympic Gold medallist Alistair, took the title in 2011 but missed most of last season prior to the Olympics through injury. The course is identical to the one used during London 2012, setting the scene perfectly for a dramatic showdown

Australian art is showcased at the Royal Academy → 192

between the Brownlees, who will be joined by 5,000 of the world's top triathletes (from varying age-groups) over six days of action in and around the Serpentine Boating Lake, culminating in the elite women's and men's races.

From 11th
Designers in Residence
11th September 2013 – 5th January 2014
Design Museum, 28 Shad Thames, London SE1 2YD
Each year, the Design Museum holds its Designers in Residence exhibition giving visitors the chance to see the work of young designers at the beginning of their careers. The annual show is the culmination of a year-long programme which supports and nurtures up-and-coming designers. The show includes specially created new work from the year's finalists and is backed by a series of events and talks, offering visitors the chance to meet the designers while giving them a test-bed for new ideas.

12th - 14th
Kew the Movies
Thursday 12th - Saturday 14th September 2013
Kew Gardens
Returning after a successful debut last year, 'Kew the Movies' sees the beautiful botanical gardens of southwest London host a pleasant pop-up cinema beneath the stars over three consecutive nights. Screenings in 2012 included the previous two Academy Award-winning films, 'The Artist' and 'The King's Speech', as well as celebrated classics 'Grease', 'Breakfast at Tiffany's' and 'Mamma Mia'. The iconic Kew Palace acts as a grand backdrop to the giant screen while guests are invited to bring picnics to spread out on the lawns. Just cross your fingers the rain keeps away - and the Kew queues aren't too long.

From 12th
Colombian Gold
12th September 2013 – 12th January 2014
British Museum, Bloomsbury, London WC1
Featuring up to 150 masterworks from the Gold Museum in Bogota, Colombia, alongside pieces from the British Museum's own collection, this exhibition will examine the ritual that lies behind the myth of El Dorado and the 'Lost City of Gold' that kept European explorers fascinated for more than two centuries.

13th - 15th
Kings Place Festival
Friday 13th - Sunday 15th September 2013
Kings Place, 90 York Way, King's Cross, London N1 9AG
The sixth annual Kings Place Festival takes place in mid-September with a unique formula of 100 events and concerts squeezed into just three days. Audience numbers have risen with every year and are expected to be at an all-time high this year. A jam-packed schedule in the halls, galleries and foyers of the King's Cross arts hub blends musicians, artists and cultural figures over one balmy long weekend. The festival presents an extraordinary line-up of classical, contemporary, experimental, folk, jazz and blues music, alongside the finest spoken word, visual art, comedy and food. If you book more than three events, you can benefit from the 'click'n'mix' discount offers.

13th - 20th
London Fashion Week
13th – 20th September 2013
Somerset House, Strand, London WC2R 1LA

This September London Fashion Week will once again inject a burst of style into Somerset House; the iconic building with its famous courtyard is a magical setting for this high profile fashion industry event. The week features 200 of the industry's most creative designers and businesses, in the UK and internationally, with catwalk shows, exhibitions and award ceremonies. It's all wildly exclusive, of course, and if you don't have any connections with the fashion industry there's no chance of acquiring tickets to the main event, however the whole capital will no doubt be bustling with fashion fever and the streets could become your very own catwalk.

13th - 17th
Vauxhall Fashion Scout

13th – 17th September 2013
Freemason's Hall, Camden, London WC2B 5AZ
London Fashion Week has spawned a whole off-schedule show in 'Vauxhall Fashion Scout', which gives up and coming designers the chance to show their latest work to the trend making fashion editors and buyers in town. The event has been responsible for showcasing some of the most innovative names in the industry including David Koma, Peter Pilotto, Felder Felder and Phoebe English. Previous years have also boasted the likes of Emma Watson, Jade Parfitt and Jasmine Guinness filling the front row.

13th - 17th
London Fashion Week Exhibition

13th – 17th September 2013
Somerset House, Strand, London WC2R 1LA
Running concurrently to the main event, the London Fashion Week Exhibition is open to all UK and international media and buyers. The exhibition houses work from more than 100 designers and offers a presentation of London's ready-to-wear and accessories brands. The stands include the Estethica stand which highlights the best in fair-trade and ethical design, the NEWGEN stand (sponsored by TOPSHOP) which picks out the finest up-and-coming designers, and Headonism which showcases new British milliners. While the exhibition at Somerset House is for industry insiders only, London Fashion Weekend which follows offers the general public the chance to get a heads up on next season's trends.

The sun sets over last year's inaugural Kew the Movies event → 189

13th - 24th
American Lulu

13th – 24th September 2013
Young Vic, Waterloo, London SE1 8LZ
Olga Neuwirth presents this radical reworking of Alban Berg's opera 'LuLu'. Set in 1950s New Orleans, 'American Lulu' transports audiences into a world of smoky jazz clubs set against the backdrop of the civil rights movement. The story follows a young dancer as her world is torn apart by the jealous and overpowering men and women who long to be her lover. Taking a look back at her past, the seductive yet scarred Lulu is confronted by a sordid history of sex, murder and suicide.

14th
Roger Waters: The Wall

Saturday 14th September 2013
Wembley Stadium, London HA9
The revival of 'The Wall', 30 years after Pink Floyd first toured their most famous concept album, has already played 192 shows to over three million fans. Now, Roger Waters brings the show to London's Wembley Stadium as part of a 24-date European stadium tour. 'The Wall' is not simply a gig, but a spectacle of a show, featuring a 36ft wall, animations by Gerald Scarfe, a bunch of school children, fireworks and plenty of giant inflatables. If the politicised story at the centre of the show is a little oblique (young man Pink turns his back on his family and society in general), bassist Roger Waters's singing more than makes up for it, as does the brilliance of his six piece band and male backing singers.

14th & 15th
Mayor's Thames Festival

Saturday 14th & Sunday 15th September 2013
The Thames between Westminster Brdg & Tower Brdg
The Mayor's Thames Festival takes place in September each year, celebrating the main waterway which winds its way through the heart of the city. There's a carnival ambience to the two-day festival with street entertainment, art installations, music and dancing all performed at various riverside locations. All this fun entertainment is free and, for the grand finale, there's a colourful night procession featuring costumed performers with tambourines and whistles travelling along Victoria Embankment and via Blackfriars Bridge, culminating in a mammoth free fireworks display. More than a ton of pyrotechnics explode over the River Thames in just ten minutes and large crowds line up along the river to see it.

14th - 22nd
The London Design Festival

14th – 22nd September 2013
Various venues
The London Design Festival is an ambitious project. Hundreds of events, locations, shops, universities and design agencies are involved in the nine days of talks, exhibitions, competitions and activities. It's a true celebration of the capital's all-encompassing design industry, taking in sectors as diverse as fashion, architecture, retail, typography, photography, textiles, interior decoration and manufacturing. Events come in all shapes and sizes from product launches in tiny boutiques to massive trade shows including '100% Design' at Earls Court, the UK's largest contemporary design trade event.

14th - 22nd
Colourscape Music Festival
14th – 22nd September 2013 TBC
Clapham Common, London SW4 9DE
Colourscape is one of the UK's most unusual music festivals, combining colourful visual art with contemporary music. The festival runs for a whole week, with concerts on the weekends and colour and music workshops throughout the week. The Colourscape installation, a centrepiece of the festival, is described as 'a labyrinth of intense colour that expands the appreciation of some of the finest performances of contemporary music and dance'.

15th - 17th
Hampstead & Highgate Literary Festival
15th – 17th September 2013
Ivy House, Golders Green, London NW11 7SX
Organised and hosted by the London Jewish Cultural Centre, the Hampstead and Highgate Literary Festival has quickly become a much loved event in London's literary calendar. This will be the fifth time the three day book festival returns since launching back in 2009, putting well known authors in the spotlight. Last year Michael Palin, Kathy Lette, Peter Hain MP, and Rachel Joyce - who was on the long list for the Man Booker Prize in 2012 - were among the speakers. There are close to 60 festival events to choose from, hosted in the former home of prima ballerina Anna Pavlova in a picturesque part of town, with book sales and signings at nearby Daunt Books after each event.

18th - 21st
100% Design
18th – 21st September 2013
Earls Court Exhibition Centre, London SW5 9TA
Devoted to the latest product launches, ideas, designs and technology, '100% Design' boasts more than 400 exhibitors, hundreds of interior design and architectural product launches. Attracting talent from all over the world, the event is the best place to marvel at the newest and most innovative designs. If that's not enough, the event also encompasses '100% Design'; an interactive feature with suppliers and manufacturers showcasing their products through samples and workshops and '100% Futures'; a section of the show dedicated to the design superstars of the future. There are also a number of seminars running throughout the four day programme with all sessions free to attend.

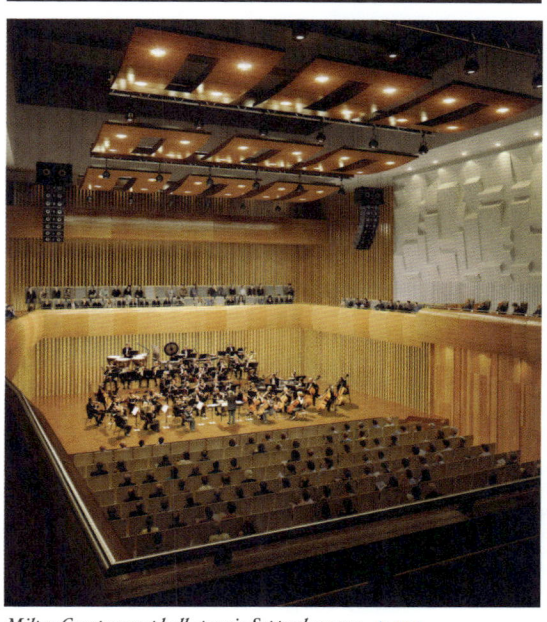

Milton Court concert hall opens in September 2013 → 201

19th - 22nd
London Fashion Weekend
19th – 22nd September 2013
Somerset House, Strand, London WC2R 1LA
Along with the main London Fashion Week event, the open-to-all London Fashion Weekend is returning this September. This fashion-focused weekend is an opportunity for everyone to get access to the latest designer trends - even if they don't have a stylist's little black book. The frenzied London Fashion Week is all about work for models, buyers and fashion editors who run around at breakneck speed. This consumer show, which takes place the weekend after the main event, offers savvy shoppers the opportunity to check out the latest fashions at a far more leisurely pace. But it's not just about the latest clothes; you can also get makeovers and styling tips while sipping on a champagne cocktail - very stylish.

21st
Bermondsey Street Festival
Saturday 21st September 2013 TBC
Bermondsey Square, Southwark, London SE1 3UN
Bermondsey Street Festival returns to South London, bringing street fashion shows, al fresco films and live bands to the area. The brainchild of Rob Wray, local DJ, filmmaker and the man behind Bermondsey Square's independent Shortwave Cinema, the festival has been successfully bringing a party vibe to the area each September for the past six years. Popular festival favourites are back including the dog show and screenings at the outdoor cinema. Make your way from Delfina cafe, up Bermondsey Street towards the Square and

you'll see all the attractions extending into nearby Tanner Street Park including maypole dancers, an acoustic music tent, arts and crafts and food stalls.

21st
Great Gorilla Run
Saturday 21st September 2013
Tower Bridge, London SE1 2UP

There's some serious monkey business going on in London this September; back for its 11th year, the Great Gorilla Run will be bounding through the streets of the capital. Raising money to save the world's remaining gorillas, hundreds of people will be pulling on their gorilla costumes and running, jogging or walking the 7km City and Bankside route. Expect to see many humorously adapted costumes, including cheerleading gorillas prancing across Tower Bridge and ballerina gorillas perfecting their poise by the Tate Modern. Runners hoping to participate need to pay a registration fee which can be done through the Gorilla Organisation website (a gorilla costume is included!).

21st & 22nd
London Open House Weekend
Saturday 21st & Sunday 22nd September 2013
Various venues in London

For one weekend a year many of London's architectural landmarks open their doors offering us a glimpse behind doors which are, for the rest of the year, closed to the public. There's a wealth of architectural gems to choose from including some of the most beautiful buildings - old and new - in the city. You can also get inside some of the grandest private homes in your own neighbourhood - it's a voyeur's dream come true. For the more serious student of contemporary design, this is a chance to visit spaces by famous modern architects, some of whom give talks and tours of the buildings they've designed. An inspired idea and a real treat whether you're a lover of architecture or just plain nosy.

From 21st
Australia
21st September – 8th December 2013
Royal Academy of Arts, Burlington House, London W1J 0BD

The Royal Academy of Arts presents a 'long overdue' survey of Australian art, the first major exhibition on the country in the UK in over 50 years. Indeed, "the last time the RA looked meaningfully at Australian art was 1923", notes The Guardian. Australia, put together in partnership with the National Gallery of Australia, will reveal the development of Australian art through over 180 paintings, prints and drawings, watercolours, photographs and multimedia works. These will include works by Aboriginal artists, 19th century European immigrants as well as the Australian Impressionists and early Modernists. The presence and influence of Australia's land and landscape will be an underlying theme throughout the exhibition.

From 21st
Pearls
21st September 2013 – 19th January 2014
Victoria and Albert Museum, London SW7 2RL

From humble beginnings,

7th
Last Night of the Proms (PICK)
Saturday 7th September 2013
Royal Albert Hall, Kensington Gore, London SW7 2AP

The world famous Last Night of the Proms at the Royal Albert Hall brings the terrific summer season of the Proms to a fitting finale. Described by conductor Jiri Belohlavek as "the world's largest and most democratic musical festival", the much loved classical celebration now encompasses more than 100 concerts each year. The Last Night traditionally follows a lighter, 'winding-down' vein than the previous eight weeks, often pandering to popular classics and patriotic anthems (Rule, Britannia!, anyone?). Tickets are almost as hard to come by as Centre Court passes for the Wimbledon finals, but like the tennis, the whole thing is broadcast live on the BBC.

starting with a grain of sand, pearls become beautiful jewels, treasured for their beauty and you can see some of the best examples in the world at the Victoria & Albert Museum's autumn exhibition. A pair of drop pearl earrings owned by Elizabeth Taylor, a 16th-century salamander pendant, and a group of tiaras worn by European royalty are among the highlights. But as well as displaying robes dripping in pearls worn by Far Eastern rulers, this exhibition will explore the history of pearls beginning with the early Roman Empire - when an entire military campaign could be financed by selling just one pearl earring.

25th
Nicola Benedetti
Wednesday 25th September 2013
Royal Albert Hall, Kensington Gore, London SW7 2AP
Just weeks after the Proms 2013 season concludes, Scottish classical violinist Nicola Benedetti performs a one-off recital at the Royal Albert Hall. The former BBC Young Musician of the Year and last year's Classic BRIT Award winner may upset the musical snobs with her risky avant garde interpretations and her absence of historic assertion - but there's no denying Benedetti is hot property having played an extraordinary three Proms at the tender age of 25 in 2012.

From 25th
Raindance Film Festival
25th September – 6th October 2013
Apollo Piccadilly, Lower Regent Street, London SW1Y
The Raindance Film Festival is the UK's largest independent film festival and has been running for over 20 years. The festival, which also played a role in founding the British Independent Film Awards in 1998, mixes famous names and rising stars appearing in films made with small budgets. The full line-up has yet to be announced but you can expect a wide choice of feature films and cutting-edge documentaries. All films are screened at the Apollo Cinema in Piccadilly Circus, except for the Opening Night which is usually a première followed by an after-party with live music.

From 25th
Mira Schendel
25th September 2013 – 19th January 2014
Tate Modern, 25 Sumner Street, London SE1 9TG
One of Latin America's most important post-war artists, Mira Schendel and her contemporaries reinvented the language of European Modernism in Brazil. Bringing together 250 paintings, prints and sculptures, this exhibition will represent works from across her entire career, including some works which have never before been exhibited.

27th – 29th
Real Food Festival
27th – 29th September 2013
Southbank Centre, London SE1 8XX
This is your chance to meet and sample food from specialist producers, chosen for their high standard of quality goods, produced ethically without cutting corners. As well as street food to sample, there are demos by top chefs, the Sheep Show featuring live animals, and plenty of live music. This three-day festival champions

17th
Scotch Egg Challenge 2013
Tuesday 17th September
The Ship, 41 Jew's Road, London SW18 1TB

PICK

Some of London's leading chefs take to their kitchens with the aim of elevating the humble bar snack to new heights in a cook-off and blind tasting to find the nation's best scotch egg. The challenge is a must-see (and taste) event for any posh foodie fan - with the competitors cooking enough eggs for the audience to feed their faces for free. Eggs are judged on three categories - taste, texture and appearance - and last year's zany combinations included chorizo with fennel, curried smoked haddock and wild boar, heart and liver, black pudding and also - gasp - vegetarian. The gold medal went to the Bladebone Inn in Berkshire for a genre-bending "ham, egg and chips" offering made with duck egg, truffles, and a potato 'n' Parma ham breadcrumb coating.

small producers, the kind who are often too small or niche to set up a rent paying shop. So it's down to events like this to give them a platform. It's a great way of networking and building a little black book of trusted suppliers - and most likely ones that the top London restaurants are using too.

28th
Beethoven's Ninth
Saturday 28th September 2013
Royal Albert Hall, Kensington, London SW7 2AP
This all-Beethoven evening will see David Hill conduct the Royal Philharmonic Orchestra and members of London Philharmonic Choir for Beethoven's Piano Concerto No. 5 'Emperor' and Symphony No. 9 'Choral', which climaxes with the 'Ode To Joy'. Taking place in the majestic setting of the Royal Albert Hall, this is set to be a spectacular evening of music.

29th
NFL International Series: Minnesota Vikings v Pittsburgh Steelers
Sunday 29th September 2013
Wembley Stadium, Wembley, London HA9 0WS
For the first time in history, not one but two NFL regular-season games touch down in London in 2013. The first clash sees the Minnesota Vikings play their first game in the UK since a 1983 pre-season clash at the old Wembley. The Vikings host record six-time Super Bowl winners Pittsburgh Steelers, who are making their first ever London appearance. The Steelers' President is called Art Rooney II - and with a name like that, he'll look for inspiration in a stadium where his namesake footballer often gets on the scoresheet. American football at Wembley is seen as something of a curious novelty in the UK, with crowds topping the 80,000-mark every year since the New York Giants and the Miami Dolphins played the first NFL game back in 2007. In the second 2013 NFL International Series game, the Jacksonville Jaguars take on the San Francisco 49ers in October.

29th
Pearly Kings & Queens Harvest Festival
Sunday 29th September 2013
Guildhall Yard, Gresham Street, London EC2V 5AE
Each year London's Pearly Kings and Queens come together to welcome the new season in style - and boy what a style they have, with extravagant Smother Suits covered top to toe in sparkly buttons, badges and glitter. The free festival starts in the afternoon at 1pm at Guildhall Yard before a parade to St Mary-le-Bow church for a harvest festival service. No doubt the celebrations will then continue with some pints of ale and plates of jellied eel at an East End boozer - perhaps interspersed with a spot of Morris dancing. Offerings are donated to the Whitechapel Mission, a charity aiming to help those caught in poverty. A second Pearly Kings and Queens Harvest Festival is held on Sunday 20th October in Covent Garden, starting at 10am in St Paul's Church.

From 30th
From Here To Eternity
30th September 2013 - 31st Jan 2014
Shaftesbury Theatre, Covent Garden, London WC2H 8DP
Following a ten-year absence from the London theatre scene, the much loved lyricist Tim Rice returns with 'From Here to Eternity', a musical version of James Jones's classic 1951 novel. In a career spanning five decades, Rice has written lyrics for 'Evita', 'Jesus Christ Superstar' and 'The Lion King', earning him three Oscars and an Olivier Award for his 'outstanding contribution to musical theatre'. For his latest project he teams up with young composer Stuart Brayson, author Bill Oakes and director Tamara Harvey to bring the tale about the trials and tribulations of American soldiers in the run up to Pearl Harbor to the stage. Priscilla Queen of the Desert star Ben Richards plays Sergeant Warden, the part played by Burt Lancaster in the 1953 movie.

Unconfirmed dates

London Duathlon
September 2013
Richmond Park, London TW10 5HS
The world's biggest duathlon returns to Richmond Park, which sees athletes prime themselves to run, bike and run a little bit more on closed roads in south west London's area of outstanding natural beauty. This double-discipline endurance test is ideal for sporty types who fancy doing a triathlon but are put off by the cold water of the Thames. There are three main categories: fun (5km run/10km ride/5km run), challenge (10km run/20km ride/5km run) or challenge team relay (10km run/20km ride/5km run). While 50 per cent of the 3,500 entrants are competing for the very first time, top athletes will also be able to take part in separate elite and junior elite sprint races. The London Duathlon is sponsored by Chelsea and Westminster Health Charity and encourages participants to raise money for charity.

1-2-3-4 Shoreditch
September 2013
Shoreditch Park, Hoxton, London N1 6TA
The 1-2-3-4 Shoreditch music festival returns for a sixth outing. Given the fashionable east London location, it's no surprise that this whippersnapper of a festival is branded as one for 'stylish bands, stylish fans and stylish sounds'. Perhaps the least corporate music festival you'll get all year, the 1-2-3-4 will no doubt throw up a bevy of 'heard-them-here-first' bands alongside many 'will-never-hear-of-again' offerings.

Radio 2 Live in Hyde Park
September 2013
Hyde Park, London SW1X
Radio 2 broadcasts from one of London's favourite parks for the BBC Radio 2 Live in Hyde Park concert. The one-day event sees the radio station's regular presenters joined by bands and singers that the broadcaster is associated with. Last year's line-up boasted the likes of Tom Jones, 'The Voice UK''s judge Jessie J, British rockers Status Quo, Simply Red's Mick Hucknall, London songstress Paloma Faith, Scottish funksters Average White Band and hot new talent Emeli Sande. To find out up-to-date information on this year's artists, keep an eye on the BBC's official website.

CABARET & BURLESQUE

Tassels and corsets galore, Londoners have acquired a taste for a glamorous show and cheeky striptease. Prim and proper we may be, but even we Brits have to let our hair down.

PROUD CABARET
City EC3 & Camden NW1
Providing dinner and a show, these 1920s themed restaurants treat Londoners to a sumptuous three-course dinner with a side serving of sultry songstresses and glamour

VOLUPTE LOUNGE
Holborn, London EC4A 1EJ
This decadent supper club provides weekly Burlesque-themed events including Afternoon Tease, their saucy take on the British tradition

CAFÉ DE PARIS
Soho, London W1D 6BL
With extravagant chandeliers, lavish décor and velvet galore, this opulent bar invites risqué entertainers to perform at their cabaret evenings

MADAME JOJO'S
Soho, London W1F 0SE
This former sleazy strip club is now notorious for its burlesque and cabaret club nights and plays host to Chaz Royal's annual Burlesque Festival

CELLAR DOOR
Aldwych, London WC2E 7DN
Decorated to reflect a futuristic take on Weimar Germany, this intimate bar is enlivened with nightly jazz, cabaret and burlesque performances

ROYAL VAUXHALL TAVERN
Lambeth, London SE11 5HY
Crowned as the Best London Cabaret Venue 2012, this pub-cum-performance venue offers an intriguing weekly programme of events

LONDON CABARET NEWSLETTER
→ To receive the London Cararet Newsletter from LondonTown.com send a blank email now to: **cabaret@londontown.com**
PRIVACY PROMISE: We will never (and that means never) give your email address to anyone else. You mean too much to us.

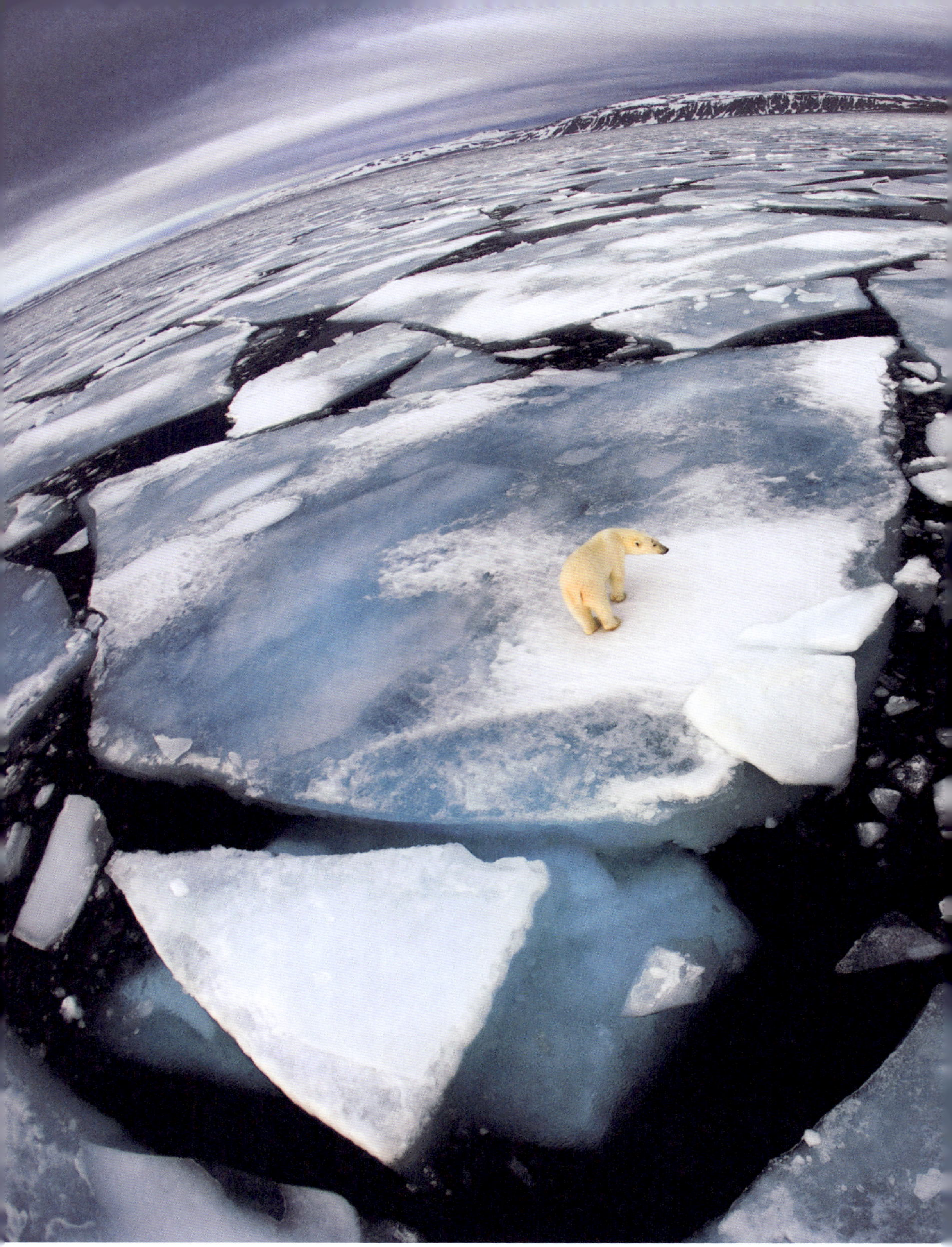

197

It's art month in London as the Frieze funfair comes to town alongside an array of spin off events – including Wildlife Photographer of the Year...

PAGE 206

OCTOBER

WHAT'S ON WHERE IN OCTOBER

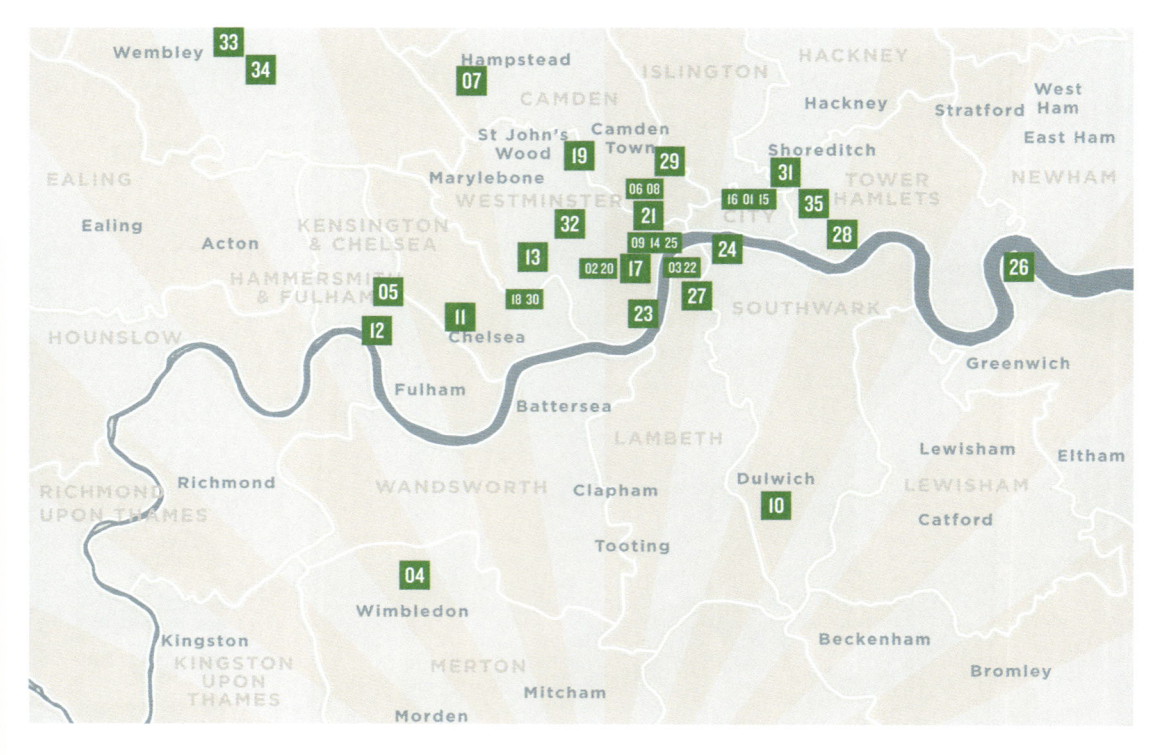

01 Barbican Centre Pages 200, 201 & 205	**10 Dulwich Picture Gallery** Page 204	**19 Regent's Park** Page 204	**28 Tobacco Dock** Page 203
02 Berkeley Square Page 204	**11 Earls Court** Page 206	**20 Royal Academy of Arts** Page 206	**29 Bloomsbury Festival** Page 205
03 BFI Southbank Page 202	**12 Hammersmith Apollo** Page 206	**21 Seven Dials** Page 202	**30 V&A Museum** Pages 199, 200 & 205
04 Wimbledon Common Page 202	**13 Hyde Park** Page 202	**22 Southbank Centre** Pages 202 & 205	**31 Village Underground** Page 205
05 Blythe House Page 201	**14 London Film Museum** Page 203	**23 Tate Britain** Page 200	**32 Wallace Collection** Page 204
06 British Museum Page 201	**15 Milton Court** Pages 201 & 205	**24 Tate Modern** Page 203	**33 Wembley Arena** Page 139
07 Camden Arts Centre Page 203	**16 Museum of London** Page 205	**25 The Courtauld Gallery** Page 205	**34 Wembley Stadium** Pages 202, 203 & 206
08 Central Saint Martins Page 201	**17 National Gallery** Page 202	**26 The O2 Arena** Pages 139 & 206	**35 Whitechapel Gallery** Page 200
09 Covent Garden Piazza Page 194	**18 Natural History Museum** Page 203	**27 The Old Vic Tunnels** Page 199	

OCTOBER 2013

PICK

DINING

London Restaurant Festival

First two weeks of October
Over 800 London venues

THIS PAGE

1st - 15th
London Restaurant Festival

1st – 15th October 2013 – TBC
Various venues
The London Restaurant Festival is a celebratory and all-encompassing food affair, showcasing a huge variety of events at venues across the capital. The annual event takes place during October and incorporates over 800 restaurants from around the capital. The Gourmet Odyssey is a hugely popular feature so we can only hope it's returning for 2013, taking diners to three top restaurants to sample a different course at each. Other highlights included a Gastropub Quiz, which took place in five pubs across London simultaneously, a Tapas Tour of Fernandez and Wells, Brindisa Soho, Iberica, Pix and Copita, and a mix of street food, music and poetry with Street ThEATre at The Old Vic Tunnels, sushi and sake masterclasses and a three-course menu inspired by Tom Parker-Bowles's favourite film.

1st - 31st
The Big Draw

1st – 31st October 2013 – TBC
Various venues
The Big Draw takes place nationwide throughout the month of October and museums, galleries, heritage sites, libraries, schools and parks all play host to a variety of events encouraging people of all ages to discover how drawing can connect them with their surroundings and communities. Put together by the Campaign for Drawing, a charity which aims to eradicate the words, "I can't draw", this is one of the world's largest drawing festivals and more than 1,000 venues typically take part

- last year 22 countries joined the UK in organising events. London institutions like the V&A, the Wellcome Collection and the British Library all usually host events.

From 1st
Photomonth
1st October – 30th November 2013
Whitechapel Gallery, London S1 7QX and various venues
Misleadingly, this international photography festival in east London straddles both October and November, with the aim of demonstrating the diversity of contemporary photography while reaching the widest audience. Now in its 13th year, Photomonth traditionally includes more than 200 exhibitions (both free and ticketed) in more than 60 galleries showcasing inventive, thought-provoking, strange and dazzling images. The whole thing is extremely interactive - with a number of classes, lectures and guerrilla events thrown in as the organisers search for new and challenging ways to exhibit work from both established and emerging talents.

From 1st
'Tomorrow', Elmgreen & Dragset at the V&A
1st October – 2nd January 2014
Victoria and Albert Museum, London SW7 2RL
Best known in the UK for their 'Powerless Structures, Fig 101' sculpture - the boy on the rocking horse in Trafalgar Square - Scandinavian contemporary artists Michael Elmgreen and Ingar Dragset have been commissioned by the V&A to create a major site-specific installation in the museum's former Textile Galleries. The domestic interior of a fictional architect will be the setting for a new film drama, played out alongside objects from the museum's collection. The duo are known for their witty satirical approach, often staging paradoxical scenarios that challenge and sometimes shock. We'll have to wait until 'Tomorrow' to see if that's the case with their latest work.

From 2nd
Sarah Lucas
2nd October – 2nd December 2013
Whitechapel Gallery, London E1 7QX
Sarah Lucas, the Young British Artist who famously set up a shop on Bethnal Green Road with Tracey Emin, is the subject of a major solo exhibition at the Whitechapel Gallery in the autumn of 2013. A participant in the landmark YBA exhibitions, 'Freeze' in 1988, and 'Sensation' in 1997, Lucas is widely regarded as one of Britain's leading sculptors, using inanimate objects to create her artworks. In this display iconic works including 'Unknown Soldier' (2003), 'Two Fried Eggs and a Kebab' (1992), 'Au Naturel' (1994), and the more recent 'Bunny' series are presented alongside new works including a tailor-made commission created especially for the Whitechapel Gallery.

From 2nd
Art Under Attack: Histories of Iconoclasm in Britain
2nd October 2013 – 5th January 2014
Tate Britain, Millbank, London SW1P 4RG
Exploring the history of attacks on art in Britain, Art Under Attack will demonstrate how religious, political, moral and aesthetic controversy can become platforms for assaulting art. It will examine how over the centuries this desire to break art has been accompanied by the need to make it and how some modern and contemporary artists use destruction as a driving creative force.

3rd - 6th
London Bicycle Film Festival
3rd - 6th October 2013
Barbican Screen, Barbican Centre, London EC2Y 8DS

Works by Gustav Klimt appear in 'The Portrait of Vienna' → 202

Originating in New York City in 2000, the Bicycle Film Festival has become a firm fixture in the London calendar and returns for its tenth season in 2013. As well as a programme of short films and documentaries, screened at the Barbican Centre, the festival celebrates the bicycle through a series of quirky events including Roller Racing, the annual Bike Polo tournament, BMX jams, bike rides and interactive activities. With Bradley Wiggins' Tour de

France win and last summer's excitement in the Velodrome still fresh in the mind, visitors to the 2013 Bicycle Film Festival could well reach record numbers.

From 3rd
Shunga: Sex and Humour in Japanese Art
3rd October 2013 – 5th January 2014
British Museum, Bloomsbury, London WC1B 3DG
Shunga refers to a group of sexually explicit paintings, prints and illustrations that were produced in Japan between 1600 and 1900. The images are often funny, tender or beautiful and have become increasingly thought of as taboo. Displaying a number of these images, this British Museum exhibition will aim to answer what shunga actually is and how it has influenced Japanese art and culture.

From 4th
The Clothworkers' Centre for Textile and Fashion Study and Conservation
Opens Friday 4th October 2013
Blythe House, Kensington Olympia, London
The V&A holds one of the most important collections of textiles and fashion in the world, with around 104,000 items ranging from archaeological textiles to contemporary haute couture. The new Clothworkers' Centre based at Blythe House, will provide world-class facilities for the care, study and enjoyment of this outstanding collection and will bring the V&A's extensive textiles and fashion collection together under one roof for the first time. Designed by Haworth Tompkins Architects, it will provide a spacious new public study room, a seminar room, upgraded conservation studios and modern, custom-built storage offering visitors and researchers increased access and improved facilities to study and enjoy this important collection.

4th
Guildhall Symphony Orchestra
Friday 4th October 2013
Milton Court, Silk Street, Barbican, London EC2Y 8DT
This performance by the Guildhall Symphony Orchestra will be the first at Milton Court, the Guildhall School's brand new state-of-the-art performance venue which includes a 608-seat concert hall, a 227-seat theatre, and a flexible studio theatre. Following this Friday night performance of Beethoven's Symphony No. 9 in D minor played by alumni of the school, Milton Court's theatres will open with a Chekhov season with two of the Russian dramatist's major plays featuring actors in their final year.

4th - 13th
Dance Umbrella
4th – 13th October 2013
Central Saint Martins College of Art and Design, Granary Building, London N1
'Dance Umbrella' has been bringing new dance experience to London since 1978 and this year's edition is no different. One of the world's leading dance festivals, 'Dance Umbrella' presents a range of affordable and free-to-view events taking place in unique places and showcasing exciting new and established talent. The ten-day programme of contemporary dance at the purpose built performing arts centre at Central Saint Martins' College is curated by choreographer

From 25th
London International Animation Festival
PICK

25th October – 3rd November 2013
Barbican Screen, Silk Street, London EC2Y 8DS

THE LONDON INTERNATIONAL ANIMATION FESTIVAL is a showcase of creative animation taking place throughout the city with gala premieres, Q&As, workshops and the Best of the Festival screening. The Festival aims to dispel the myth that animation is little more than cartoons for children by screening a broad range of entertaining and provocative films from across the planet. LIAF features a comprehensive ten-day programme featuring the best of the international indie animation scene, encapsulating every style, genre and technique possible.

Jonathan Burrows and Betsy Gregory, who steps down as Artistic Director of 'Dance Umbrella' following the 2013 festival having completed 16 years in the role.

4th - 19th
Ether Festival
4th – 19th October 2013 TBC
Southbank Centre, London SE1 8XX
The Southbank Centre's eccentric Ether Festival is an annual celebration of electronic music, innovation in music, art and cross-arts experimentation. The festival has evolved over the years, blending mainstream acts such as Brian Eno, David Byrne, Peaches and Royksopp, alongside little-known acts, oddball movements and even some classical artists. Technological pioneers and musical innovators past and present come together for a series of concerts, talks and strange collaborations that often baffle as much as they astound. Last year's schedule included the Mercury-prize nominated Ghostpoet, the Velvet Underground's John Cale, and a handful of events celebrating the 100th anniversary of experimental composer John Cage – not least, a dance performance with a cat.

5th - 13th
Wimbledon BookFest
5th - 13th October 2013
Big Tent on Wimbledon Common
The nine-day literary festival is now in its seventh year and has welcomed a raft of top authors since its debut in 2007, including the likes of Salman Rushdie, William Boyd, Michael Morpurgo, AS Byatt and Victoria Hislop. The BookFest is a community-driven event which aims to spread a love of reading and writing, and fire the ambition of local writers, both young and old. The heart of the festival is a special Big Tent on Wimbledon Common, but author events take place in a variety of venues in and around the local area.

6th
Royal Parks Foundation Half Marathon
Sunday 6th October 2013
Starts & finishes in Hyde Park, London W2 2UH
Now in its sixth year, this popular half marathon takes in four of central London's best loved parks, an iconic stretch of the Thames and some of the capital's most famous landmarks. What's more, at 13.1 miles, it's a manageable run for those still daunted by the colossal feat of April's full marathon. Starting and finishing in Hyde Park, runners pass Buckingham Palace, St James's Park and the Houses of Parliament before following the river to Blackfriars Bridge and back. The next leg takes them under both the Admiralty and Wellington Arches, through Green Park, all around Hyde Park and Kensington Gardens before passing the Royal Albert Hall and across the finish line. An interesting fact: Kenyan middle distance ace John Muriithi won the inaugural run - wearing a rabbit mask. Ballot opens on 28th January 2013.

7th – 13th
London Cocktail Week
7th – 13th October 2013
Seven Dials, Covent Garden, London WC2H 9DD
If you've ever seen the 1988 film 'Cocktail' and wished you had the ability to mix and pour drinks with the style and rhythm that Tom Cruise does, then you're in for a treat at London Cocktail Week. Taking place at more than 100 cocktail bars across London, Cocktail Week offers cocktail lovers tasting sessions, tours, pop-up events, parties and masterclasses in the art of pouring the perfect concoction. Cocktail lovers simply have to purchase a wristband from the official website to be treated to a number of deals and bespoke drinks.

9th - 24th
The BFI London Film Festival
9th – 24th October 2013
BFI Southbank & selected cinemas, London SE1 8XT
It's the 57th year of the London Film Festival, which attracts Hollywood players and indie film-makers from around the globe. The 2012 event was the first for new director Clare Stewart and contained several new elements: as well as 225 films (including 14 world premieres) shown over 12 days, gala films and celebrity-studded ceremonies, a commendable amount of programme time was given over to small independent films, foreign language cinema, documentary work, animation and BFI National Archive classics. The comprehensive programme is usually enhanced by a number of related events, such as informal post-screening Q&As, guest appearances, workshops and masterclasses. The 2013 programme is yet to be announced.

From 9th
The Portrait in Vienna
9th October 2013 – 12th January 2014
National Gallery, Trafalgar Square, London WC2N 4DN
Vienna during its time as the capital of Austria-Hungary, from 1867 to 1918, is the subject of a major National Gallery exhibition in autumn 2013 which looks at the works of avant-garde artists such as Gustav Klimt, Egon Schiele and painter, draughtsman and lithographer Oskar Kokoschka. The period saw a flourishing of modern art in the city and 'The Portrait in Vienna' will reveal how portraiture and the avant-garde overthrew the traditional imperialist art of the time. The exhibition is divided into six sections including one which examines the use of the portrait to declare love and commemorate the dead, and a final section where unfinished works will be displayed.

11th
World Cup Qualifier: England v Montenegro
Friday 11th October 2013
Wembley Stadium, Wembley, London HA9 0WS
This 2014 World Cup qualifying clash could well be closer than most expect when you factor in Montenegro's impressive 6-0 away thrashing of San Marino. After all, Roy Hodgson's side only managed to net five goals against the Mediterranean minnows in their old back yard... Star striker Mirko Vucinic of Juventus could be the one to watch at Wembley.

From 11th
Kara Walker
11th October 2013 – 5th January 2014
Camden Arts Centre, London NW3 6DG
American artist Kara Walker fills the Camden Arts Centre galleries with the process of her art in her first major solo

'Au Naturel' by Sarah Lucas, who exhibits at the Whitechapel Gallery this autumn → 200

exhibition in the UK. Intimate watercolours, large scale graphite drawings, printed text works and film installations are added to by a new cut paper piece which will be produced on-site. Walker's art is layered with images that reference history, literature, culture, and the darker aspects of human behaviour.

12th & 13th
The Scandinavia Show
12th & 13th October 2013
Tobacco Dock, Wapping, London E1W 2SF
Besides some top-notch TV crime thrillers, Scandinavia includes some of the most beautiful and stylish destinations in the world - and every October a slice of Nordic essence comes to London with this annual show. Tobacco Dock will be brimming with Finnish music, Danish food, Swedish dancing and much more. Scandinavia is home to many intriguing natural beauties, including Iceland's geothermal landscape, Norway's fjords and of course the Northern Lights, so head to this show for anything from Nordic tales to Swedish style.

14th - 20th
Chocolate Week
14th – 20th October 2013
Across London
The third week of October sees the nation celebrate one of womankind's (and some men's) great loves: chocolate. Chocolate Week is a nationwide celebration and London embraces this with a number of sickly sweet events across the city. Last year saw famed chocolatier Hotel Chocolat team up with The Botanist and The Chiswell Street Dining Rooms to offer 'choctails', Mexican restaurant Benito's Hat served a chocolate feast throughout the week, more chocolate cocktails were served at cabaret bar Volupte and, the finale of the week was 'Chocolate Unwrapped' - a two-day festival that invited the world's top chocolatiers to display their finest work.

15th
World Cup Qualifier: England v Poland
Tuesday 15th October 2013
Wembley Stadium, Wembley, London HA9 0WS
Given the amount of Poles in London, there should be quite a good turnout at Wembley Stadium for England's World Cup qualifying match against Poland. Let's hope it goes better for Roy Hodgson's side than the corresponding fixture in Warsaw last October: a waterlogged pitch saw the game postponed 24 hours before a jaded England were held to a limp 1-1 draw.

From 15th
Paul Klee
15th October 2013 - 9th March 2014
Tate Modern, 25 Sumner Street, London SE1 9TG
Tate Modern's major autumn exhibition is a long overdue solo exhibition dedicated to Paul Klee, the influential Swiss-born artist who taught at the Bauhaus school in Germany in the 1920s. The exhibition - the first in the UK in over a decade - reveals Klee as a unique artist whose "cold Romanticism" style - as he defined it in the catalogue of his first major solo exhibition in 1914 - drew on expressionism, cubism, and surrealism. Leaving behind his diaries and abundant correspondence, including his lectures 'Writings on Form and Design Theory', Klee's influential theories on modern art are still significant today.

From 16th
Whistler in London: Battersea Bridge and the Thames
16th October 2013 – 12th January 2014
Dulwich Picture Gallery, London SE21 7AD
Over 70 objects relating to the American artist James Whistler go on display at the Dulwich Picture Gallery when it hosts an autumn exhibition of paintings from his first sojourn in the capital which began in 1859. The first major exhibition in London dedicated to this period of Whistler's life, 'Whistler in London: Battersea Bridge and the Thames' showcases paintings, etchings and drawings produced between 1859 and 1903 and includes many of his most famous scenes of London and the Thames. Familiar London landmarks include the River Thames, Chelsea, Battersea Bridge and Wapping, the painting of which Whistler kept secret from rivals such as Courbet for fear that his ideas would be stolen.

17th-20th
Frieze Art Fair
17th – 20th October 2013
Regent's Park, London NW1
As the country's leading contemporary art fair, the Frieze Art Fair draws the world's most influential art buyers to Regent's Park each October. Specially commissioned art works are exhibited alongside curated exhibitions as well as the pieces for sale presented by 173 of the most highly respected contemporary art galleries in the world. Among the paintings and installations in Regent's Park there's an amazing jumble of the comical, the beautiful and the shocking. You can expect site-specific projects, short films, a prestigious talks programme and an artist-led education schedule all presented in a captivatingly chaotic atmosphere. It's packed into a vast temporary structure in the park with work by around 1,000 contemporary artists crammed in. Frieze Masters, a showcase of Old Masters and art up to the 20th century, is expected to return this year following its successful inaugural show last year.

From 17th
PAD London Art Fair
17th – 20th October 2013 – TBC
Berkeley Square, Mayfair, London W1J 5AX
Returning to Berkeley Square in Mayfair for a seventh year, the PAD London Art Fair, or Pavilion of Art & Design London if you prefer, brings together exceptional works of modern art, design, decorative arts, photography, jewellery and tribal art from 1860 to today. With 50 distinguished international exhibitors from Barcelona, Brussels, Cologne, Geneva, London, Milan, New York, Paris and Zurich, select galleries from around the world exhibit at this exclusive art fair each year. PAD London, which takes place at the same time as the Frieze and Moniker art fairs, helps to attract the world's most influential art buyers to London each October.

From 17th
Moniker Art Fair
17th – 20th October 2013
London location TBC
One of the three big London art fairs which take over the capital in October, the Moniker Art Fair returns in 2013 as a reminder of the international scope of street art and beyond. Putting east London on the art fair map the buying exhibition features works by international artists and challenges traditional conventions with a variety of gallery exhibits and further signature project spaces ready to whet the appetite. Moniker has established a positive reputation among art collectors, critics and lovers alike with over 10,000 people attending. As well as the main art fair, Moniker Projects commissions a series of off-site projects including public artworks, film screenings and educational workshops, offering the public plenty of opportunities to get involved.

17th - 24th
Chekhov: The Seagull
17th – 24th October 2013
Milton Court, Silk Street, Barbican, London EC2Y 8DT
One of two Chekhov dramas to christen the new Milton Court theatres, 'The Seagull' is played out at the Milton Court Studio

From 24th
The Male Nude: Eighteenth-century drawings from the Paris Academy
PICK

24th October 2013 – 19th January 2014
The Wallace Collection, London W1U 3BN

OOH LA LA! THE MALE NUDE is the subject of a free exhibition at the Wallace Collection from October 2013 for which close to forty drawings from the late seventeenth to the late eighteenth centuries have been loaned from France's equivalent of the Royal Academy, the École nationale supérieure des Beaux-Arts in Paris. Students at the Academy could only progress to drawing the nude figure after they had mastered all the other skills so this exhibition shows superior studies by artists such as Rigaud, Boucher and Jean-Baptiste Isabey, the leading painter of miniature portraits in early nineteenth-century France. The influence of the all-male Academy was far-reaching, producing alumni like Jean-Jacques Bachelier who went on to become Director of Design and Decoration at the Sevres porcelain factory, influencing many of the pieces in the Wallace Collection.

Theatre by final year actors from the Guildhall School, directed by Christian Burgess.

From 17th
The Young Durer: Drawing the Figure

17th October 2013 – 12th January 2014
The Courtauld Gallery, Strand, London WC2R 1LA
Focusing on the formative years of the young Albrecht Durer, when he completed his artistic training before being exposed to new experiences while travelling (1490-96), this exhibition examines the early figure drawings of the German artist. 'Drawing the Figure' brings together outstanding sketches by Durer from international collections as well as rare works by precursors and contemporaries who remain little known in the UK.

From 18th
The Cheapside Hoard: London's Lost Jewels

18th October 2013 – 27th April 2014
Museum of London, 150 London Wall, London EC2Y 5HN
In this major exhibition the Museum of London will use new research and state-of-the-art technology to showcase the insights that the Cheapside Hoard offers on Elizabethan and Jacobean London. Discovered in 1912, this extraordinary collection of 16th and early 17th century jewels and gemstones had been buried in a cellar on Cheapside, London. Now, displaying the collection in its entirety for the first time in over a century, the museum will explore the mysteries behind the jewels that were lost among the cataclysmic events of the mid-17th century: who did the Hoard belong to, when and why was it hidden and why didn't anyone ever reclaim it?

19th
Mozart's Requiem

Saturday 19th October 2013
Royal Festival Hall, Southbank Centre, London SE1
Mozart's choral masterpiece crowns a sublime evening of his greatest works performed by the English Chamber Orchestra at the Royal Festival Hall. Left unfinished at the time of his death, Mozart's enigmatic, seductive and deeply religious 'Requiem' is one of the most recognisable choral pieces in sacred music, with reverberations throughout modern day popular culture, from 'The Big Lebowski' to 'X-Men'. The programme also features the composer's 'Piano Concerto No.21' with its famous three-part Andante, and the lively but haunting 'Overture to Don Giovanni'.

19th & 20th
Battle of Ideas

19th & 20th October 2013
Barbican Centre, Silk Street, London EC2Y 8DS
Returning for a ninth year - and a second at the Barbican - Battle of Ideas is a weekend of high-level, thought-provoking public debate. Guest speakers exchange views on some of the biggest issues facing the world, covering a range of topical themes in a mixture of interactive talks, sessions and open discussions. Visitors are invited to do battle in a war of words in which free speech is the primary weapon.

19th & 20th
Bloomsbury Festival

19th & 20th October 2013
Various venues in Bloomsbury, London WC1
This weekend-long festival in swish Bloomsbury boasts more than 150 free cultural events taking place in garden squares, museums, shops, pubs and other venues in the area. Celebrating the longstanding culture and arts community of the area in London made famous by the Bloomsbury Set of writers of the first half of the 20th century, the Bloomsbury Festival has a bit of everything for all ages. Last year's highlights included non-stop performances on the SOAS World Music Stage, craft markets and literary groups in Russell Square, candle-lit folk music at the Perseverance pub, Handel recitals at the Foundling Museum, dancers and art installations at the Wellcome Collection and drawing workshops at the British Museum.

19th - 26th
Chekhov: The Three Sisters

19th – 26th October 2013
Milton Court, Silk Street, Barbican, London EC2Y 8DT
The first play to be performed in the main theatre of Milton Court the Guildhall School's new state-of-the-art performance venue, Chekhov's 'The Three Sisters' features final year actors from the Guildhall School and is one of two of the Russian dramatist's major plays at the theatre; 'The Seagull' is performed at the smaller Milton Court Studio Theatre from 17th to 24th October. Wyn Jones directs.

From 26th
Masterpieces of Chinese Painting 700-1900

26th October 2013 – 19th January 2014
Victoria and Albert Museum, London SW7 2RL
See some of the finest examples of Chinese painting at the V&A's autumn 2013 exhibition 'Masterpieces of Chinese Painting', the most comprehensive exhibition on the topic since 1935. Over 100 works from the beginning of the 8th to the end of the 19th century are brought together for this display which includes some of the earliest surviving Chinese paintings. Evolving themes and aesthetic preferences developed over the centuries are examined through rare works including figure paintings on silk for tombs and temples, and small-scale works by monks. A show of this scale and nature hasn't been seen in the UK since the well-received International Exhibition of Chinese Art at the Royal Academy in 1935.

From 26th
Honore Daumier (1808-1879)

26th October 2013 – 26th January 2014
Royal Academy of Arts, Burlington House, London W1J 0BD
The French printmaker, caricaturist, painter, and sculptor, Honore Daumier, described by his contemporary the poet Charles Baudelaire as, "one of the most important men, not just of caricature, but of modern art", is the subject of a solo exhibition at the Royal Academy of Arts in the autumn of 2013. The leading satirical draughtsman of the left-wing journal, La Caricature, was working during a time of great political and social change in France and the broadly chron-

ological exhibition explores themes of judgement, spectatorship and satire. Paintings, drawings, watercolours, and lithographs reveal Daumier's observations of modern life and stinging attacks on the bourgeoisie.

27th
Run to the Beat
Sunday 27th October 2013 TBC
The O2 Arena, Greenwich, London SE10 0DX
The two things that put most people off running a marathon are i) the length of the race, and ii) the habitual banning of iPods and other musical devices. Well, bypass both issues with October's Run to the Beat, London's official music half marathon. Starting at the O2 Arena and taking place around Greenwich and Woolwich, the charity race is a mere 13.1 miles and not only are iPods encouraged, there are also 12 different musical stages dotted around the course where bands play live music throughout the race in a bid to gee on the participants.

27th
NFL International Series: Jacksonville Jaguars v San Francisco 49ers
Sunday 27th October 2013
Wembley Stadium, Wembley, London HA9 0WS
The NFL International Series returns to London for a seventh consecutive year with the Jacksonville Jaguars taking on the San Francisco 49ers at Wembley Stadium. The Jaguars will play one regular season home game in London every year until 2016, with this year's game being the first. The 49ers will be making their second appearance at Wembley, having hosted the Denver Broncos in 2010 when 83,941 fans saw them take the game 24-16. American Football at Wembley is seen as a showpiece event in the UK, with fans flocking to north London in order to catch a glimpse of a sport that they are rarely able to see this side of the Atlantic. Crowds have tended to top the 80,000-mark every year since the New York Giants and the Miami Dolphins played the first NFL game at the new Wembley back in 2007.

Sunday 27th October
British Summertime ends

30th & 31st
Jason Manford
30th & 31st October 2013
Hammersmith Apollo, London W6 9QH
Cheeky northern bloke all-in-this-together comedy isn't everyone's cup of (Lancashire) tea but Jason Manford has built up quite a large following in recent years. A TV panel show regular, Manford is also a talented opera singer who has toured with Alfie Boe and performed in musicals on the West End. His last visit to the Apollo was somewhat soured, however: it was married Manford's first major appearance since quitting as co-host of the BBC's 'The One Show', amid tabloid revelations of text and Twitter flirting with female fans (his wife was pregnant at the time). Heckled mercilessly, Manford managed to hold his own - and returns to the scene of his grilling with a new show for 2013. "He's blessed with the sort of laid-back charm and sharp turn of phrase you can't manufacture," says The Telegraph (and anyone who follows him on Twitter).

From 30th
The Ski & Snowboard Show
30th October – 3rd November 2013
Earls Court Exhibition Centre, London SW5 9TA
Planning to hit the slopes next winter? Before you take off for snowier climes you'd be wise to put in some pre-ski prep work at the Ski & Snowboard Show which turns Earls Court into a giant snow dome. This snow show, which has been running for 40 years, is almost as much fun as the real thing and makes for a great day out with families and friends. As well as the chance to buy all the latest gear and clothes, there are bargain ski trips, ice skating, ice sculpting and practical advice on how to indulge your passion for skiing without giving up the day job. Centre stage is the main slope - where expert skiers perform and compete. It's a great spectator sport. Take the kids along - anyone under 11 goes free and there's a free crèche as well as ski lessons, penguins and a pop up cinema.

From mid-October
Wildlife Photographer of the Year
Mid-October 2013 - March 2014
Natural History Museum, Cromwell Road, London SW7 5BD
Some photographers wait for weeks in order to catch that one great action shot, some set up elaborate timing mechanisms; others have simply seen an opportunity, grabbed a camera and produced a unique picture of the natural world. Canadian Paul Nicklen, last year's Wildlife Photographer of the Year, snorkelled motionless in freezing water in the Antarctic while waiting for the perfect shot of an emperor penguin colony. The annual exhibition at the Natural History Museum consistently shows fresh perspectives on animals, insects, plants and landscapes - brilliantly capturing across a number of categories the most colourful and heart-warming collection of images on display in the capital.

Thursday 31st October
Halloween

Paul Klee is the focus of a major Tate Modern exhibition → *203*

BEHIND THE SCENES

Some of the UK's most intriguing and influential buildings are strictly out of bounds - *Vicki Forde* opens their doors through six backstage tours

BBC BROADCASTING HOUSE 01
Portland Place, London W1
Following their move from the Television Centre to the Broadcasting House, the BBC will provide interactive tours of the new studios from April 2013.

HOUSES OF PARLIAMENT 02
Westminster, London W1
Visitors can explore the Commons and Lords Chambers, the Queen's Robing Room, Westminster Hall and London's most famous clock tower, Big Ben.

BUCKINGHAM PALACE 03
Victoria, London SW1
While the Queen takes her annual trip to Scotland in August and September, the public are invited to explore the 19 State Rooms of Buckingham Palace.

ROYAL OPERA HOUSE 04
Covent Garden, London WC2
With three tours available, you can go backstage to see the pre-performance action, take an architectural tour of the auditorium or view an exhibition on former Music Director Georg Solti.

GLOBE THEATRE 05
Bankside, London SE1
This interactive tour uses special effects, sword fighting and costume dressing to revive the Globe into the notorious entertainment district it once was.

FULLER'S BREWERY 06
Chiswick, London W4
Discover the secret recipe of Fuller's ales, indulge in a refreshing tasting session and look back at the heritage of the brewery - home to the UK's oldest wisteria - in this intriguing tour.

LONDON TOURS NEWSLETTER

→ To receive the London Sport Newsletter from LondonTown.com send a blank email now to: **tours@londontown.com**
PRIVACY PROMISE: We will never (and that means never) give your email address to anyone else. You mean too much to us.

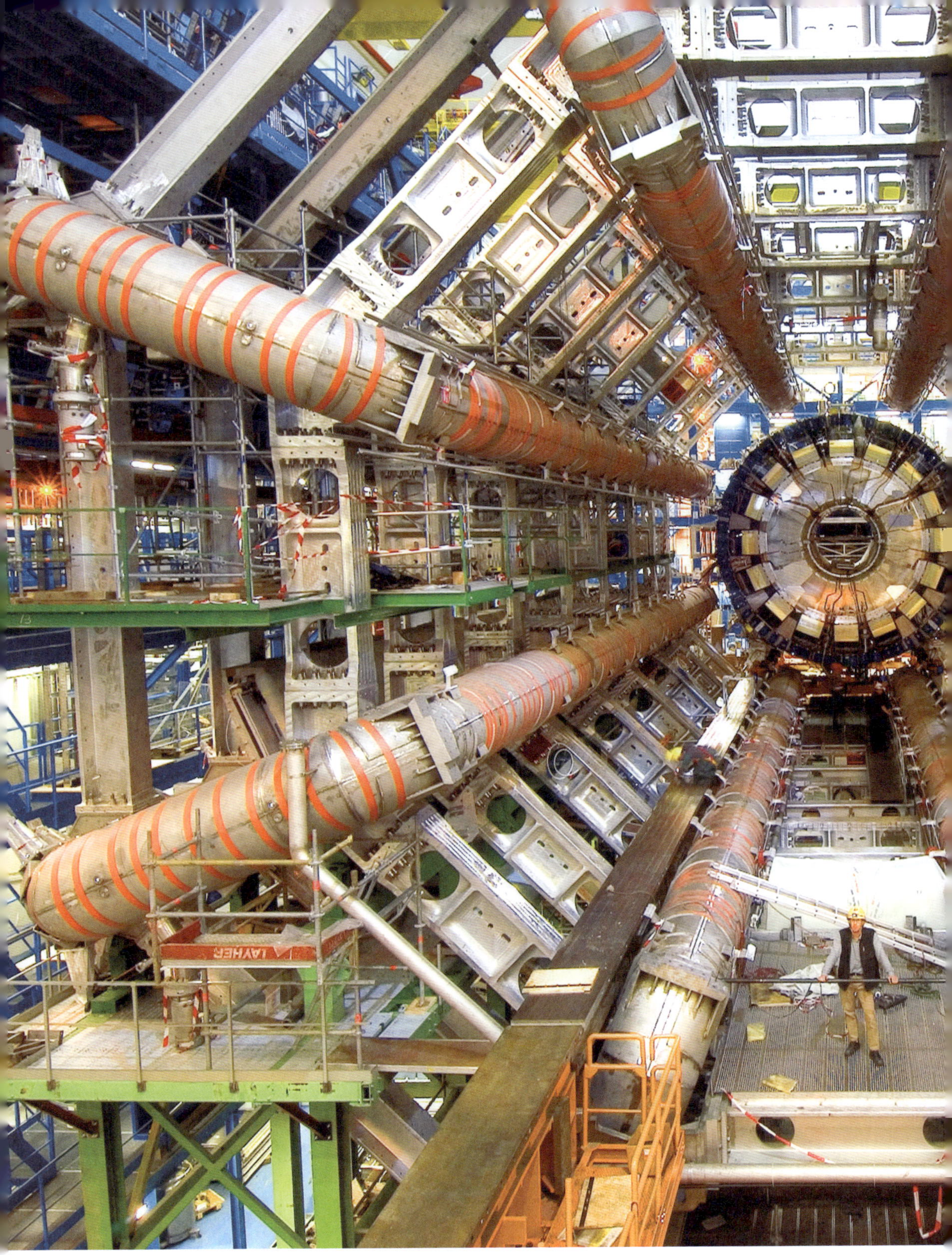

Jazz, fireworks, festivities: November has a bit of everything, - including ATP tennis, Sir Paul Smith, Turner, a bit of Britten and the Large Hadron Collider...

PAGE 215

NOVEMBER

WHAT'S ON WHERE IN NOVEMBER

LondonTown.com

01	**Barbican Centre** Page 216	10	**Hammersmith Apollo** Page 213	19	**Peacock Theatre** Page 215
02	**British Library** Page 216	11	**Hyde Park** Page 213	20	**Regent Street** Page 212
03	**Business Design Centre** Page 216	12	**Mansion House** Page 214	21	**Richmond Theatre** Page 211
04	**Cenotaph** Page 214	13	**Maritime Museum** Page 216	22	**Royal Albert Hall** Pages 214 & 215
05	**Columbia Road Market** Page 216	14	**National Portrait Gallery** Page 213	23	**Science Museum** Page 213
06	**Design Museum** Page 215	15	**Noel Coward Theatre** Page 215	24	**Southbank Centre** Pages 211 & 215
07	**Earls Court** Page 214	16	**Old Royal Naval College** Page 213	25	**Syon Park** Page 215
08	**ExCeL** Pages 212 & 216	17	**Olympia** Pages 212 & 215	26	**The O2 Arena** Page 212
09	**Geffrye Museum** Page 224	18	**Oxford Street** Page 216	27	**Queen's Gallery** Page 212

NOVEMBER 2013

PICK

LONDON DESIGN

Paul Smith

20th November 2013 - 2nd March 2014
Design Museum, 28 Shad Thames, London SE1 2YD

PAGE 215

1st – 3rd
Winter Tea and Coffee Festival
1st – 3rd November 2013
Southbank Centre, London SE1
If you can't function without your morning brew and the smell of freshly ground coffee makes you go weak at the knees, then this is the festival for you. The products will be showcased in their purest forms, as well as transformed into cocktails, hot sweet treats and delicious cakes. There will be plenty of chances to discover new beans and blends, with a packed schedule of talks, tastings and demonstrations. With tons of exhibitors showcasing everything from Chinese bubble tea to spiced tea mulled wine this is a great opportunity to pick up some Christmas gifts for those special caffeine-lovers in your life.

1st – 30th
Richmond Literature Festival
1st – 30th November 2013 TBC
Various venues in Richmond, London TW9
The Richmond Literature Festival returns to the west London borough this November for its 22nd year. The list of participants has yet to be confirmed but it always has an impressive line-up including political commentators, well known writers, broadcasters, comedians and poets. Typically, there's a huge variety of respected writers and novelists taking part so it won't be hard to pick out at least one you'd like to see. Events take place at various venues across Richmond including Richmond Theatre, Orleans House Gallery and – last year, at least – The Literary Salon, a pop-up shop where live literature

NOVEMBER 2013

events were staged for all ages. The programme often includes workshops, storytelling, poetry, and performances from renowned spoken word artists. There's also a special young people's festival which includes activities for the very young - from aged two upwards.

From 1st
The Genius of Castiglione
1st November 2013 – 16th March 2014
The Queen's Gallery, Buckingham Palace, London SW1A 1AA
The Royal Collection presents the best surviving body of work from one of the great Baroque artists, Giovanni Benedetto Castiglione. The artist led a troubled life filled with violence and excess, yet despite this he produced some of the finest Italian drawings and prints of his time, depicting rural landscapes and scenes of animals. He worked predominantly with oil and combined printmaking and drawing to create the monotype technique.

2nd
Regent Street Motor Show
Saturday 2nd November 2013 TBC
Regent Street, London W1B
The Regent Street Motor Show gives Londoners the chance to see 300 cars that span 125 years of motoring up close and personal on one of London's busiest shopping streets. Petrol-heads will be in their element as the free show, which sees Regent Street closed to regular traffic, offers a unique and interesting display of motoring from the 19th century to the present day. The street is split into zones with around 100 period vehicles, 20th and 21st century displays and a future concept display from some of today's leading manufacturers. Added to all this are stage shows, presentations and competitions making it an exciting day out for car fans.

From 2nd
Harrods Christmas Grotto
2nd November – 24th December 2013 TBC
Harrods, Knightsbridge, London SW3 1RT
A long-standing tradition at the luxury Knightsbridge store, the Santa's Grotto at Harrods gives young children a magical experience. Little ones can meet Father Christmas at his grotto and share their wish lists with him. All children, regardless of good behaviour, will be rewarded with a special memento from Santa and parents will have the chance to buy a photograph of their kids enjoying themselves in the grotto. A highlight is the annual Christmas parade which weaves through the streets of Knightsbridge led by Father Christmas. Be aware that you must be a Harrods Rewards cardholder in order to book tickets, which can be done on the Harrods website.

Saturday 3rd November
Diwali

4th – 7th
World Travel Market
4th – 7th November 2013
ExCeL Centre, London E16
Describing itself as the world's leading event for the travel industry, the World Travel Market has attracted close to 30,000 visitors in the past and its ambition shows no sign of fading. Held annually at the ExCeL Exhibition Centre, the four day business-to-business event provides its visitors with hints and tips on all sectors of the travel industry. It's a one of a kind opportunity for the whole industry to meet, network and do business and will give you a cutting edge over your competitors by keeping you up to date with all the industry's latest developments. The full four-day programme is open to all travel trade professionals and allows you to choose which days suit you best, which of the educational seminars from a list of over a hundred you feel will benefit you the most and who you want to do business with.

4th - 10th
Winter Fine Arts & Antiques Fair
4th – 10th November 2013
Olympia, Hammersmith Road, London W14 8UX
The Winter Fine Art & Antiques Fair is becoming somewhat of an antique itself, as it turns 23 this year. Taking place at London's Olympia, the annual fair should be a permanent fixture on the calendars of all art and antique aficionados. It has also become a popular social event with high-profile visitors such as Bono, Claudia Schiffer and Jools Holland helping to boost the reputation of the event. But don't worry if you don't know your art deco from your art nouveau, as the fair is equally popular with new buyers looking to decorate their homes. Each year, over 20,000 visitors are drawn to the fair with around 125 exhibitors offering everything from silver teapots and Lalique vases to Cartier earrings and letters from Queen Victoria.

4th - 11th
ATP World Tour Finals
4th - 11th November 2013
The O2 Arena, Greenwich, London SW10 0BB
The ATP World Tour Finals returns to the O2 Arena for eight days of tennis between the world's eight best men's singles players and men's doubles pairs. Last year, Serbian sensation Novak Djokovic edged Swiss maestro Roger Federer in two thrillingly tense sets to take his second World Tour title and deny his opponent a record seventh. Britain's Andy Murray made it as far as the semi-finals before being knocked out by Federer in straight sets. Watching tennis at the O2 is remarkably different than wathing at Wimbledon: it's a theatrical affair, with the audience plunged into darkness and all eyes on the bright hard court below. Expect some titanic clashes between the likes of Murray, Federer, Novak Djokovic and (injury permitting) Rafa Nadal.

Monday 5th November 2013
Bonfire Night

6th - 10th
Spirit of Christmas Fair
6th - 10th November 2013
Olympia, Hammersmith Road, London W14 8UX
Get all your Christmas shopping done under one roof at the Olympia - and get it out of the way more than a month before Santa arrives. An annual fixture in the seasonal calendar, the Spirit of Christmas Fair attracts thousands of Yuletide shoppers gearing up for the festivities. You can expect the finest seasonal products here, ranging from festive decorations and home accessories to

children's toys and seasonal eats. With over 600 companies presenting their wares, you'll find something for everyone on your Christmas list and plenty you won't find in the shops. Look out for traditional sweets, specialist cheeses, fine cuts of meat and artisan produce in the Food Hall.

7th - 9th
Greenwich International Early Music Festival & Exhibition

7th – 9th November 2013 TBC
Old Royal Navy College, Greenwich, London SE10
Jointly promoted by The Early Music Shop, the Greenwich Foundation and Trinity Laban Conservatoire of Music and Dance the Greenwich International Early Music Festival and Exhibition is the world's largest early music fair. This annual fixture showcases some of the biggest names on the early music scene at the Old Royal Naval College with an exhibition of specialist music shops as well as a programme packed with concerts, masterclasses, instrument demonstrations and free events. Trinity Laban's gifted ensembles, including their Early Music Vocal Ensemble and Junior Trinity students, typically take part.

From 7th
Taylor Wessing Photographic Portrait Prize

7th November 2013 – 16th February 2014 TBC
National Portrait Gallery, St Martin's Place, London WC2H 0HE
Showcasing the work of the most talented professional photographers, photography students and gifted amateurs from across the world, the Taylor Wessing Photographic Portrait Prize regularly attracts around 6,000 entries by over 2,500 photographers who compete for the prestigious prize, not to mention the £12,000 which goes to the winner. The exhibition, running at the National Portrait Gallery for close to twenty years, is an annual fixture and a highlight of the arts calendar in London with approximately 60 works selected from the thousands of submissions. The exhibition is recommended for its mixture of themes, styles and approaches to the contemporary photographic portrait.

8th & 9th
Sarah Millican: Home Bird

8th & 9th November 2013
Hammersmith Apollo, London W6 9QH
Charming and filthy in equal doses, Sarah Millican's star is rising - but despite a second series on TV and another live DVD breaking records for a female comic, the soft-speaking Geordie still remains faithful to her stand-up roots. In her latest live show, Millican is giving up the party scene, easing off the drinking and trying to settle down (she has a cat). Her audience learns what to take on a dirty weekend, the easiest way to blend in at posh restaurants and how to teach a pensioner to swear. And just when you thought she was going all soft - you'll be sledgehammered with some outrageous dirt.

From 8th
Large Hadron Collider

8th November 2013 - 30 April 2014
Science Museum, Exhibition Road, South Kensington, London SW7 2DD

Hyde Park Winter Wonderland

PICK

November & December 2013
Hyde Park, London SW1X 7TA

THROUGHOUT THE FESTIVE PERIOD, a corner of Hyde Park is transformed into a 'Winter Wonderland' complete with fairground rides, a giant wheel, circus, Christmas market, food and drink stalls, Santa's grotto and, of course, an ice rink. It's the seventh consecutive year that the 'Winter Wonderland' has come to Hyde Park and it's already a firm favourite for many Londoners. Doing your best Torvill and Dean impersonation is a great way to embrace the cold, and the ice rink - which surrounds the Victorian bandstand and is illuminated by over 100,000 pea-lights - is the biggest of its kind in the UK. A turn on the 53-metre-high Observational Wheel offers great views over London's most popular Christmas attraction. Zippos Circus is always a hit and the show never fails to pull crowds into its heated big top when temperatures plummet. The traditional Christmas Market, with its wooden chalets and various Bavarian-style bars and cafes, is a hoot, as is the Spiegel Saloon, a large, festive and fully covered restaurant. Don't go with an empty wallet because while the whole thing is not cheap, it's such fun you'll want to get into the spirit and spend. (Remember: advanced booking on the main attractions is advised while you'll need to buy tokens from kiosks dotted around the fair for the many rides.) Free entry to the site means you can just walk around and absorb the festive ambience - but it will take a strong will of Scrooge proportions not to dip your hands into your pockets and spend.

NOVEMBER 2013

Visitors can immerse themselves in the greatest intellectual adventure on the planet in this Science Museum exhibition dedicated to the Large Hadron Collider. Attempting to recreate conditions not seen since the Big Bang some 13.7 billion years ago, CERN's giant particle collider in Geneva is one of the largest scientific and engineering endeavours of our time, a place of wonder where scientists and engineers work at the extremes of temperature, vacuum and energy. The exhibition, which will tour museums worldwide, will provide a close-up look at remarkable examples of CERN engineering, from the bottle of hydrogen gas that feeds the great machine, to its vast dipole magnets.

9th
Lord Mayor's Show
Saturday 9th November 2013
Mansion House, The City, London EC4N 8BH
The Lord Mayor's Show has been a fixture of London calendars for nearly 800 years, making it one of the longest running and grandest pageants in the world. The procession stretches over three and a half miles and weaves through the city's historic streets. Locals and visitors turn out in their millions to watch the spectacle which involves over 6,000 people, military marching bands, Chinese acrobats, a procession of decorated floats and the Lord Mayor travelling in a gilded State Coach. The procession starts at 11am with an RAF flypast and goes on until about 2.30pm, covering the whole area between Bank and Aldwych with the mayor departing from Mansion House for the Royal Courts of Justice where he takes an oath of allegiance to the Queen. The grand finale is a spectacular fireworks display that's known to be the biggest and most dangerous that London hosts.

10th
Remembrance Sunday
Sunday 10th November 2013
Cenotaph, Whitehall, London SW1A 2BX
Members of the Royal Family join current and former members of the services to remember the dead of the UK and Commonwealth on Remembrance Sunday. Wreaths are laid at the Cenotaph followed by two minutes silence at 11am and after a short service there is a march past by thousands who served and suffered in the conflict of war.

10th
Britten's War Requiem
Sunday 10th November 2013
Royal Albert Hall, Kensington Gore, London SW7 2AP
Semyon Bychkov conducts as the BBC Symphony Orchestra performs Benjamin Britten's moving 'War Requiem' at the Royal Albert Hall on Remembrance Sunday. Interweaving the poetry of Wilfred Owen with the words of the Requiem Mass, Britten's 'War Requiem' is a deeply stirring and powerful work. Written for the consecration of Coventry Cathedral after its destruction in the Second World War, the piece remains as relevant today as ever. The concert marks a double remembrance: 22nd November is the 100th anniversary of the birth of Britten, one of Britain's greatest ever composers. His works will be celebrated all year round by the BBC while the 2013 Proms has a distinctive Britten flavour.

The London Jazz Festival turns 21 with a 10-day celebration → 215

13th - 17th
Ideal Home Show at Christmas
13th – 17th November 2013
Earls Court Exhibition Centre, London SW5 9TA
The third Ideal Home Show at Christmas will take place at Earls Court this November. Held over five days, the Ideal Home Show at Christmas will be the largest home event of the winter, full of ideas, inspiration and advice on everything you need to make your home ideal for Christmas. With over 500 exhibitors across six sections, the show will feature an Ideal Interiors and furnishings section, as well as Ideal Home Improvements, Food and Drink, Fashion and Beauty, Gifts and Decorations and Gadgets and Gizmos. There will also be celebrity guests; previous years have seen the likes of Laurence Llewelyn-Bowen, Suzi Perry and Olly Smith offering top tips and advice. And experts in the 'How to' Theatre will be on hand with ideas and inspiration on all of your home improvement and interior needs to prepare your home for that crucial Christmas deadline.

15th & 17th
Lang Lang
15th & 17th November 2013
Royal Albert Hall, Kensington Gore, London SW7 2AP
Following his sold-out Beethoven Piano Concerto cycle in 2012, Chinese piano prodigy Lang Lang returns to the Royal Albert Hall for a recital of Mozart and Chopin, performed in-the-round. While the extrovert showman is not the traditionalists' cup of tea, the technically phenomenal Lang Lang (whose name means "brilliance of the sky") has nevertheless become the world's wealthiest, busiest, and most sought-after concert pianist before turning 30. Described by *The Times* as "brilliant but superficial" and by the New Yorker as the "world's ambassador of the keyboard", Lang Lang is said to have influenced over 40 million Chinese children to take up the piano. These Friday and Sunday

night performances include three Mozart sonatas and four Chopin ballades.

15th - 17th
BBC Good Food Show
15th – 17th November 2013
Olympia, Hammersmith Road, London W14 8UX
Bringing a host of TV programmes to life including the 'Great British Bake Off', 'Saturday Kitchen' and 'MasterChef: The Professionals', the 'BBC Good Food Show' arrives at Olympia for three days this November. Plus, there's local and seasonal produce in the Producers' Village, a handpicked selection of London's best eateries in the Restaurant Experience, MasterChef Skills Pod featuring finalists from this year's TV Show and a Drinks Tasting Theatre and Fine Wine Experience.

15th - 24th
London Jazz Festival
15th – 24th November 2013
Various London venues
For jazz fans, Christmas comes a little early in London as the annual Jazz Festival returns for its 21st anniversary. LJF brings world class jazz to stages, clubs, restaurants and foyers around the capital for ten days of improv' scats, hot licks, and smooth sax solos presenting a rare chance to enjoy some iconic jazz stars and up-and-coming new musicians. There will be hundreds of acts performing in packed-out venues in all corners of the city, so expect to see fiendish jazz-fans hot-footing it around London that week. The Royal Festival Hall, the Barbican and Ronnie Scott's are always involved, plus smaller clubs like the intimate Vortex jazz club in Dalston. Highlights of previous years include a recent appearance from a sprightly Herbie Hancock, the first ever concerts from the Jools Holland and his Rhythm and Blues Orchestra and the 200-piece saxophonist troupe that opened the show.

16th
Disney Fantasia: Live in Concert
Saturday 16th November 2013
Royal Albert Hall, Kensington Gore, London SW7 2AP
Fans of Disney's surrealist musical animation 'Fantasia' can once again experience the magic live with high definition screens and the London Philharmonic Orchestra at the Royal Albert Hall. Starring the young, aspiring sorcerer, Mickey Mouse, accompanied by a classic score featuring Tchaikovsky ('The Nutcracker Suite'), Beethoven ('Pastoral' Symphony), Ponchielli ('Dance of the Hours') and Dukas ('The Sorcerer's Apprentice'), and boasting some brand new content, the sequences of 'Fantasia: Live in Concert' flit from one dreamlike scene to another with everything from fluorescent unicorns and flying horses, to dancing red mushrooms and ballerina hippos. Childish charm and humour blend with darker themes of death and evolution, eliciting an impact from even the sanest of minds.

From 20th
Paul Smith
20th Nov 2013 – 2nd March 2014
Design Museum, 28 Shad Thames, London SE1 2YD
The London Design Museum celebrates four decades of design by one of Britain's best known talents, Sir Paul Smith, a man knighted in the 2001 Birthday Honours List for services to the fashion industry. The show will include classics from his 40 years of collections and reveal something of the personality of the designer known for "Englishness combined with an unexpected twist" (GQ Magazine). But, says the Telegraph, rather than a straightforward run-through of his greatest fashion hits, the show will "explore a year in the different stages of design, production and marketing" behind the designer's catwalk collections. Not only that, the individual design of his shops - now in sixty-six countries across the world - will also be highlighted, all of which goes to show how far Sir Paul Smith has come since setting up his first shop in Nottingham in 1970.

From 22nd
Enchanted Woodland
22nd November - 8th December 2013 TBC
Syon House, London Road, London TW8 8JF
This magical event adds a significant veil of mystique to the festive season. The beautiful oak trees and gardens at Syon Park are illuminated in spectacular fashion as a guide walks visitors through the Enchanted Woodland. The trail leads you around the 18th century lake - where the shapes and textures of the ancient winter trees are reflected in the water - and past intriguing corners of the estate, all of it floodlit to maximum rainbow effect. The shadows and magic of a frosty winter's night make this an ideal opportunity for photographing the forest in a unique way. Warm clothing and stout footwear are advised and hot refreshments are available on the night.

From 23rd
Henry V
23rd November 2013 – 15th February 2014
Noel Coward Theatre, St Martin's Lane, London WC2N
Concluding his season of five plays at the Noel Coward Theatre, for which 100,000 tickets were on sale for as little as £10, Michael Grandage has collaborated once more with Jude Law on a Shakespearean piece. Having worked with him on 'Hamlet' in 2009 and on award winning production 'Anna Christie', which was part of Grandage's final season as Artistic Director at the Donmar Warehouse, Grandage has now cast Law in the lead role in 'Henry V'. The history play by Shakespeare explores the bloody horrors of war and the turmoil caused in such a crisis. Will the King of England succeed in commanding his men and leading his country to victory in France? The conclusion of the 15-month season at the Noel Coward Theatre offers theatregoers the chance to see well known actors for just £10: that's £2 less than the already affordable National theatre's Travelex tickets.

From 27th
The Snowman
27th November 2013 – 5th January 2014
Peacock Theatre, Holborn, WC2A 2HT
This staging of Raymond Briggs's 'The Snowman' by Sadler's Wells, ideal for children under 10, has become a much-loved festive tradition in London. Translating the beautifully-illustrated book to dance, the respected ballet company

creates a winter wonderland of a stage show at their West End theatre. This is the theatrical equivalent of going to see Father Christmas – except infinitely more spectacular as a young boy's snowman comes to life and the two of them fly across the sky. When Father Christmas does appear it's in a shimmering woodland, surrounded by magical reindeer, dancing penguins and a host of snowy friends. As the first notes of 'Walking in the Air' fill the theatre, the heart-melting factor will not disappoint as awe-struck children (and adults) are mesmerised by the dazzling light show of snow.

From 27th
Columbia Road Christmas Shopping Evenings
Every Wednesday from 27th November – 18th December 2013
Columbia Road Flower Market, Tower Hamlets, London E2 7RG
The independent shops along Columbia Road, the fragrant home of east London's famous flower market, open late on Wednesday evenings in the lead up to Christmas offering an endearing East End alternative to the bright lights and hefty crowds of the West End. The shops, which were originally created as a Victorian shopping arcade 150-odd years ago, are usually only open on Sundays but extend their opening hours during the Christmas period. If vintage fashion, off-beat artwork, original homewares, quirky trinkets and delicious deli goods are your cup of tea (mulled wine, even) then this is the place to be on Wednesday evenings in December.

Unconfirmed dates
The Gadget Show Live at Christmas
Dates TBC
ExCeL London Exhibition Centre, Royal Victoria Dock, London E16 1XL
The Gadget Show Live at Christmas provides the perfect opportunity to discover all the latest brand new and must-have technology from the leading industry brands. The show is held at the ExCeL and will be brimming with gadget gifts, games and toys all ready to be ticked off the Christmas wish list.

West End VIP Shopping Day
November 2013 – exact date TBC
Oxford Street and Regent Street, London W1B 5SJ
The whole of London can often feel like one big traffic jam and shopping hotspots Oxford Street and Regent Street are constantly flooded with cars and a major flow of pedestrians – especially during the festive period. The West End VIP (Very Important Pedestrian) Day offers a welcome break from this. With vehicles banned from both streets from 8am to 8pm, this one-day event allows shoppers to step away from the single file and get fully immersed in their present hunting. Major department stores will also be joining in the festive fun as they offer a number of promotions and discounts. As well as the shopping, there will be special prizes, games, live music, free entertainment and celebrity appearances. Plus, 100 trained Gift Gurus will be on hand to help pick out the perfect gifts.

The Georgians
November 2013 – March 2014
British Library, London NW1 2DB
Commemorating the 300th anniversary of the House of Hanover and the establishment of a constitutional monarchy, this major exhibition examines the extensive and cultural changes that have occurred in Britain's society since the reigns of George I, II, III and IV. Consumerism and celebrity culture are just two aspects of modern Britain that can be linked back to the Georgian period and, through the use of manuscripts, newspapers, books and printed items, the British Library's exhibition will enable visitors to understand the depths of these connections.

Turner and the Sea
November 2013–April 2014 TBC
National Maritime Museum, Greenwich, London SE10
In November 2013 the National Maritime Museum will stage the first large-scale exhibition to examine JMW Turner's lifelong pre-occupation with the sea. The 'Turner and the Sea' display in the museum's exhibition space in the Sammy Ofer wing features about sixty oil paintings, approximately half by Turner and the same number of watercolours. Described by the director of the museum as, "the most ambitious reappraisal of the subject in modern times", the exhibition is a once-in-a-lifetime opportunity to see works brought together from collections across the world, including iconic works spanning the artist's whole career.

Country Living Magazine Christmas Fair
November 2013
Business Design Centre, Islington, London N1 0QH
In preparation for Christmas, the Country Living Magazine Christmas Fair brings a taste of rural England to the Business Design Centre, with all the cosy traditionalism that goes with it. With over 400 exhibitors there's everything you need for a perfect Christmas. There are handmade toys, stocking fillers, limited edition decorations, and, of course, plenty of seasonal food - from smoked salmon and tender ham to the delights of Cornish cheese, mulled wine, sloe gin, fudge, chocolate and traditional Christmas puddings. With all that tartan and tinsel, this is the perfect place to begin getting into the Christmas mood. It also gives you the chance to deal with all those traditional seasonal nightmares long before the last minute.

Framed Film Festival
November 2013
Barbican Centre, Silk Street, London EC2Y 8DS
The Framed Film Festival serves up another unique learning experience for budding-young Scorseses and Tarantinos. Anyone aged between 4 and 18 can get involved in getting to grips with making and understanding movies. Held at a number of venues across the city it's a wonderful chance for young cinephiles to take part in workshops, learn from experts and develop new ideas. With tickets starting at £3, even those with limited pocket money have the chance to see what they like and experience cinema from different countries and cultures.

BEST CHRISTMAS MARKETS

Brightening up cold winter nights, London's Christmas markets add seasonal joy with handmade gifts, festive food and warming tipples

ANGELS CHRISTMAS MARKET AT WINTER WONDERLAND
Hyde Park, London W2 2UH
Wooden chalets and Bavarian-style bars offer an array of festive gifts and edible treats alongside fairground rides

COVENT GARDEN CHRISTMAS
London WC2H 9HW
The regular piazza market gets an injection of festivity with decorations, carols, reindeers and plenty of food

CAMDEN NIGHT MARKETS
Camden Town, London NW1 8AF
The canal-side shopping yard is transformed into a festive urban forest with twinkling lights, Christmas trees and seasonal entertainment

SOUTHBANK CENTRE CHRISTMAS MARKET
South Bank, London SE1 8XX
Riverside chalets selling gifts, decorations, food and festive tipples line pedestrian promenade beside the Thames

PETERSHAM NURSERIES CANDLELIT SHOPPING
Petersham, London TW10 7AG
Escape the hustle and bustle of the city with an enchanting evening of rustic candlelit shopping and carol singing

REAL FOOD CHRISTMAS MARKET
South Bank, London SE1 8XX
The weekly food market turns festive with a scrumptious range of seasonal produce, from wild game and ham to cheese and chutneys

CHELSEA PHYSIC GARDEN CHRISTMAS FAIR
London SW3 4HS
Heated marquees in the grounds of London's oldest Botanic Garden are full of stalls selling gifts and hot food

ST KATHARINE DOCKS WINTER WONDERLAND FRIDAYS
Tower Hamlets, London E1W 1TW
The picturesque docks host a series of Winter Wonderland Fridays with plenty of festive flair and seasonal cheer

SUTTON HOUSE CHRISTMAS FAIR
London E9 6JQ
Pop-up stalls, artisan producers and independent designers set up shop in the Tudor manor in east London - with mulled wine and a Santa's grotto

---

LONDON CHRISTMAS MARKETS NEWSLETTER

→ To receive the Christmas in London Newsletter send a blank email now to: **christmas@londontown.com**
PRIVACY PROMISE: We will never (and that means never) give your email address to anyone else. You mean too much to us.

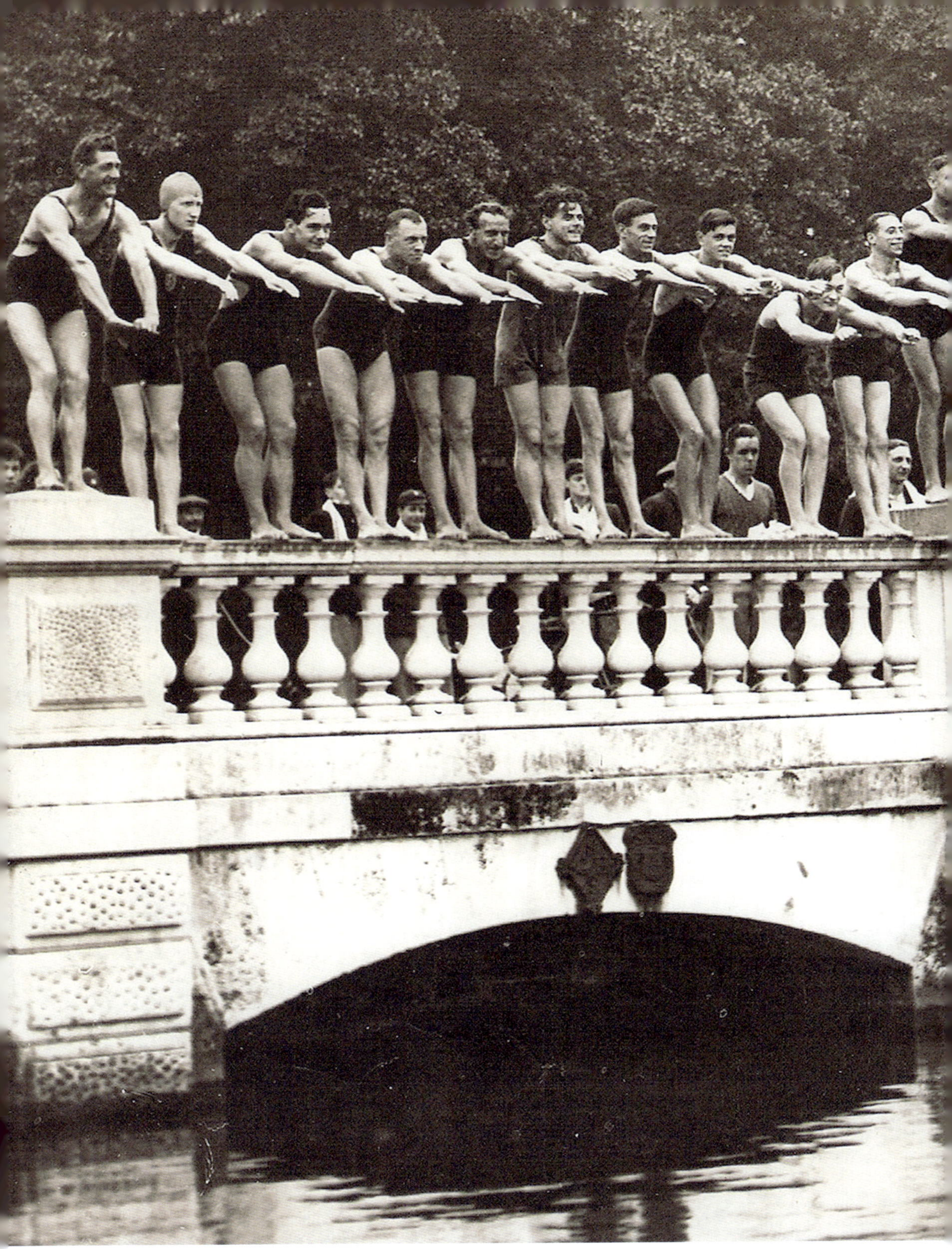

'Tis the season to be jolly – with ice skating, pantomimes, ballet, fireworks, and seasonal delights this Christmas including crazy swimming races...

PAGE 224

DECEMBER

WHAT'S ON WHERE IN DECEMBER

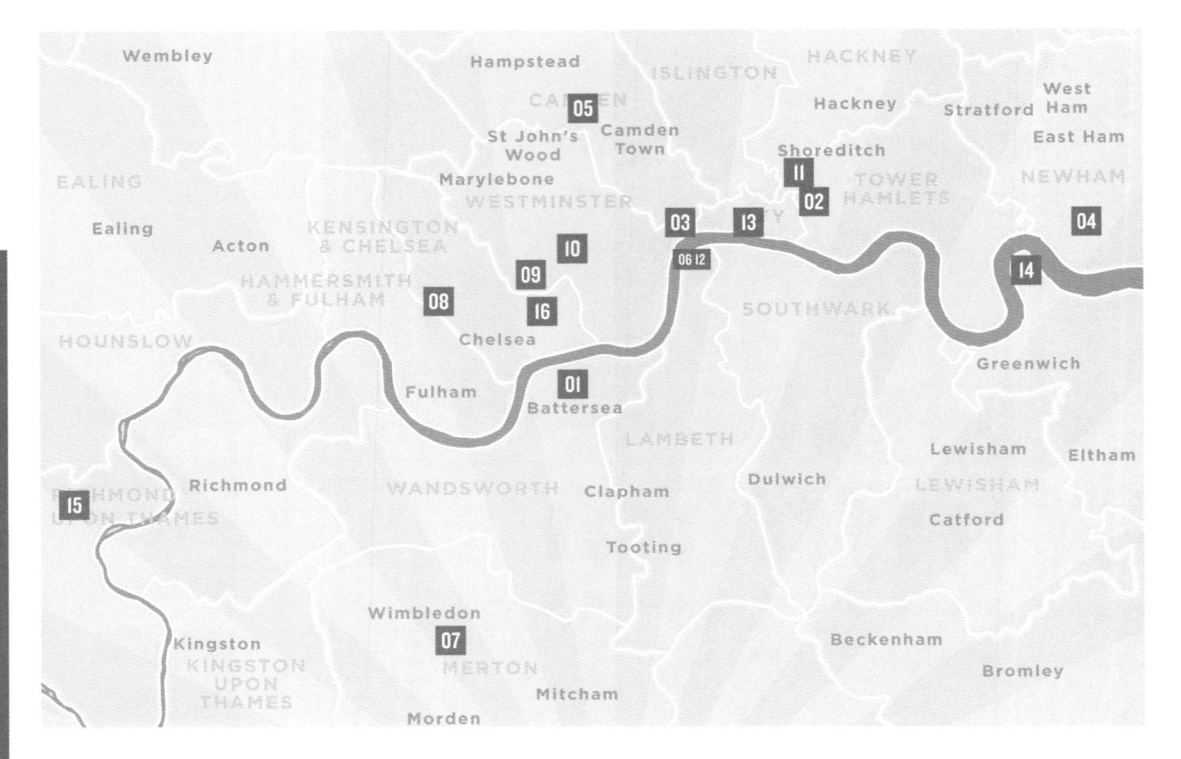

01	**Battersea Park**	09	**Royal Albert Hall**
	Page 222		Page 221
02	**Christ Church Spitalfields**	10	**Serpentine Boating Lake**
	Page 222		Page 224
03	**Covent Garden Piazza**	11	**Shoreditch Town Hall**
	Page 222		Page 221
04	**ExCeL**	12	**Southbank Centre**
	Page 222		Page 223
05	**Invisible Dot**	13	**St Paul's Cathedral**
	Page 223		Page 223
06	**London Eye**	14	**The O2 Arena**
	Page 224		Page 223
07	**New Wimbledon Theatre**	15	**Twickenham Stadium**
	Page 222		Page 224
08	**Olympia**	16	**V&A Museum**
	Page 223		Page 223

DECEMBER 2013

PICK

DANCE

The Nutcracker

9th December 2013 - 15th January 2014
Royal Opera House, Covent Garden, London WC2E 9DD

PAGE 223

4th - 8th
Masters Tennis
4th - 8th December 2013
Royal Albert Hall, Kensington Gore, London SW7 2AP

Blasts from the past battle it out in London's prettiest indoor arena in the annual Masters Tennis event at the Royal Albert Hall. Players in the ATP Champions Tour must be 35 years or older, and have been the world Number One, a Grand Slam finalist or have featured on a winning Davis Cup side - although exceptions have been made (Britain's Tim Henman, for instance). The likes of Goran Ivanisevic, Thomas Enqvist, Henman and last year's Masters and Seniors winners Fabrice Santoro and John McEnroe might have added a few pounds and lost swathes of speed and stamina over the years but they retain all the guile, poise and determination that made them champions in the first place. Expect five days of competitive singles and doubles with a healthy splash of fun as these past masters take to the court on a stage usually reserved for Brahms, Beethoven and the Beatles.

5th - 8th
East London Design Show
5th - 8th December 2013
Shoreditch Town Hall, 380 Old Street, EC1V 9LT

It may not have 'Christmas' in the title, but the East London Design Show is a stalwart in the seasonal shopping calendar. With over a hundred stalls filled with original and beautifully designed pieces all under one roof in Shoreditch, it's a great place to source a designer gift for your loved ones. Shopping is the main

DECEMBER 2013

event, but there's also a bar/cafe and workshops on sustainable gift-wrapping, hat making and toy making.

6th - 8th
Taste of Christmas
6th - 8th December 2013
ExCeL London Exhibition Centre, Royal Victoria Dock, London E16 1XL
More than 30,000 visitors typically enjoy the foodie event presented as "the perfect place for passionate foodies to get inspiration and enjoy a festive gastronomic heaven." At 'Taste of Christmas' the kings and queens of cookery share their top tips for making the festive season a culinary triumph. As well as the opportunity to take part in live cooking demonstrations you can give your Christmas a gourmet makeover and shop for top seasonal ingredients to inject some inspirational spark into your family's tried and tested festive classics. A multitude of food stalls from top London restaurants, tastings and food demonstrations add to the festive cheer.

6th
Santa Run
Battersea Park 1st weekend of December; Greenwich Park a week later
Battersea Park, Albert Bridge Road, London SW11 4NJ & Greenwich Park, London SE10 8 QY
Join hundreds of other Santas on a festive run through a London park before relaxing afterwards with mulled wine and Christmas cake. Simply register, turn up on the day, collect your free Santa outfit and tackle the 5km or 10km run. You can decide to walk, jog or run as fast or as slow as you like. Why will everyone be dressed as Santa? Well, ignoring the obvious (the time of year), proceeds from the run will be donated to charity. If you've ever fancied a fun run through London whilst dressed as Father Christmas (and let's face it, who hasn't?) then this is the one for you.

6th - 17th
Spitalfields Winter Festival
6th – 17th December 2013
Locations throughout Spitalfields
Spitalfields' end of year musical celebration returns to warm up the winter nights. Taking place at several Spitalfields locations, the festival explores the east London area's hidden corners with early and contemporary music, musical tours, opera for under 2s, and free events which bring together global and local artists. The best thing about the biannual Spitalfields festivals (a summer festival is held in June) is the array of contrasting venues: Old Spitalfields Market comes alive with what seems like impromptu musical performances, while the stunning 18th-century Hawksmoor-designed Christ Church hosts a cluster of classical concerts. Shoreditch's hip Village Underground holds some of the more contemporary offerings, and could you get a more apt setting for city-based bucolic folk than the Spitalfields City Farm?

From 6th
The New Wimbledon Theatre Panto
6th December 2013 – 12th January 2014 TBC
New Wimbledon Theatre, The Broadway, SW19 1QG
The New Wimbledon Theatre has a long and chequered history when it comes to casting the leading parts in their Christmas show. In recent years, David Hasselhoff, Pamela Anderson and a quite spectacular Dame Edna Everage have all graced the stage. But last year they pulled out all the stops and had Priscilla Presley, ex-wife of Elvis, making her London stage debut in 'Snow White and the Seven Dwarfs'. Clearly, with this sort of panto pedigree, the New Wimbledon Theatre is the place to go if you fancy a Christmas pantomime with all the trimmings.

7th
OSS December Dip
Saturday 7th December 2013 TBC
Parliament Hill Lido, London NW5 1LP
This annual freezing (not to mention crazy) dip into Parliament Hill Lido takes place on the first Saturday of December. Formerly known as the 'Plum Pudding Plunge', this is the first swim of the season organised by the Outdoor Swimming Society, who each year arrange festive swims as far away and chilly as Scotland. With mince pies to dispel the inevitable goosebumps, a hot tub, chattering teeth and general merrymaking, all swimmers, donning Christmas hats, will be encouraged to attempt two widths of the lido, with the most intrepid aiming for four or six. Swimmers must register for the event, which costs £15. Make sure you bring warm clothes, a woolly hat, swimsuits and a lot of courage. They say it's good for the circulation...

7th
Great Christmas Pudding Race
Saturday 7th December 2013 TBC
Covent Garden Piazza, London WC2E 9DD
You're familiar with the egg and spoon race. Well, how about the Christmas Pudding Race? Covent Garden Piazza swells with spectators as about 150 contestants in teams of six don fancy dress and race around a course strewn with flour-filled balloons, foam jets and other obstacles - all while trying to balance a Christmas pudding on a flimsy plate! The race has been going on every year since 1980 and it raises money for Cancer Research. At this time of year Covent Garden is a great place to be, with shops full of Christmas decorations and street entertainers putting on some diverting shows before and after the main event. The perfect way to break up a day of Christmas shopping in Covent Garden's collection of stylish stores. This year's date is yet to be announced but please see www.xmaspuddingrace.org.uk for the latest details.

7th & 8th
British Military Tournament
7th & 8th December 2013 TBC
Earls Court Exhibition Centre, Warwick Road, London SW5 9TA
The British Military Tournament comes to Earls Court in December, bringing together the best elements from the famous Royal Tournament in the largest display of military theatre in the world. This breathtaking arena show gives visitors the opportunity to marvel at and enjoy the skill and precision of the British Armed Forces with modern battle re-enactments from recently returned active troops aided by contributions, in previous years,

from celebrities like Dame Judi Dench, Joanna Lumley and Stephen Fry. It's also a great chance to show appreciation for our heroic servicemen and women.

From 9th
The Royal Ballet: The Nutcracker
9th December 2013 – 15th January 2014 TBC
Royal Opera House, Covent Garden, London WC2E 9DD
Unless your name's Ebenezer Scrooge, this glittering production of E.T.A. Hoffman's 'The Nutcracker' cannot fail to get you in the Christmas spirit. As sure as putting up fairy lights, filling Christmas stockings and having too much mulled wine at the office party, watching Clara dance in front of the Christmas tree at the Royal Opera House is a truly festive thing to do. It's hard to imagine a production more indulgently sumptuous than Peter Wright's restaging of Lev Ivanov's choreography to Tchaikovsky's famous score. From the heart-warming family party of the opening scene to the appearance of the magical kingdom, the action beckons you in, helped every ballet step of the way by Julie Trevelyan Oman's gorgeous, nostalgic designs out of the late 1800s. This is pure spectacle but The Royal Ballet pulls it off with such beauty and style that it's a Christmas cracker.

From 11th
Jameel Prize 2013
11th December 2013 – 23rd March 2014
Victoria & Albert Museum, South Kensington, London SW7 2RL
The biannual Jameel Prize, which encourages contemporary artists and designers to take their inspiration from Islamic traditions of craft and design, returns to the Victoria & Albert Museum for the third time in 2013. The work of the 10 shortlisted finalists competing for the £25,000 prize can be seen at the museum from 11th December 2013.

13th
The New Wave 2013
Friday 13th December 2013
Invisible Dot, King's Cross, London N1 9BG
Comedy producers Invisible Dot present the most promising acts emerging from the Edinburgh Fringe and the London alternative circuit. The New Wave gives comedy watchers a chance to catch "the most interesting, exciting and innovative acts" in the country at Invisible Dot's King's Cross HQ of as part of a monthly London residency ahead of a large national tour in the autumn.

13th - 15th
Christmas Chocolate Festival
13th – 15th December 2013
Southbank Centre, London SE1 8XX
The Chocolate Festival makes a welcome return this December with a special Christmassy offering. With a delectable array of artisan delights to tickle your taste buds, the festival is the ideal opportunity to indulge yourself and take home tasty Christmas presents. There will be top chocolatiers such as William Curley, Damian Allsop and Co-Couture in attendance and, as always, there will be dozens of stalls all showcasing chocolate and chocolate products, such as hot chocolate, chocolate cakes, crepes, churros, a chocolate fountain, self-making kits and much more. After all, Christmas is the time for indulgence...

13th - 23rd
Real Food Christmas Market
13th-23rd December 2013 TBC
Southbank Centre, London SE1 8XX
The Southbank Centre's weekly Real Food Market turns festive in the lead up to Christmas – an ideal chance to pick up some last-minute culinary delights. Located in the square on the Waterloo Station side of the Southbank Centre, the Christmas Real Food Market will boast a whole range of seasonal produce such as wild game, ham, charcuterie, pies, cheeses, chutneys, pickles, cakes and chocolates as well as Christmas staples like mince pies and mulled wine. This is high quality but affordable stuff – and with kind staff from carefully selected producers, plus a taste-before-you-buy policy, it's a relaxed place to make your unique Yule time food purchases.

16th - 22nd
London International Horse Show
16th – 22nd December 2013
Olympia, Hammersmith Road, London W14 8UX
London's annual equestrian fiesta graces Olympia once more for a full week of galloping, jumping and pinpoint dressage steps. There's enough to please everybody at the London International Horse Show, with the UK's only World Cup dressage qualifier, spectacular show-jumping competitions, and some fantastic equestrian shopping opportunities. As well as the elegant steeds trotting around, there are usually some dog-related competitions too, including a canine agility contest. The grand finale is an enormous festive parade with hundreds of horses, costumes and music combining to a spectacular climax.

21st & 22nd
JLS
21st & 22nd December 2013
The O2 Arena, Greenwich, London SE10 0BB
Since bursting onto the 'X Factor' scene in 2008, JLS have continued on an upward journey in their music career. Now, promoting their new studio album 'Evolution', the foursome will be taking over the O2 Arena for two nights. Working with a number of highflying American producers, this album offers a more mature sound from the band: "It's full of taut, sophisticated pop that nods to Justin Timberlake circa 2002, Timbaland circa 1999 and even some of Nicki Minaj's more experimental beats" (The Guardian). However, fans can be sure to expect the usual perfectly synchronised dance moves, cheeky winks and, of course, Aston's famed back flips on this tour.

24th
Midnight Mass at St Paul's Cathedral
Tuesday 24th December 2013 – Christmas Eve
St Paul's Cathedral, London EC4M 8AD
Sir Christopher Wren's magnificent St Paul's Cathedral, viewed by many as the spiritual home of Great Britain, is a

wonderful place to be on the night before Christmas when the Choir of St Paul's Cathedral is joined by Barbican Brass to mark the first Eucharist of Christmas. This is one of many Christmas celebrations held at the cathedral throughout December. Demand is so great that St Paul's puts on a series of special events but the high point has to be the Midnight Mass service. The cathedral's famous dome, which can be seen over the top of London's skyline from miles around, fills with the soaring sounds of the Cathedral Choir. In candlelit, majestic surroundings in the middle of the city, this is the perfect place to usher in Christmas Day before wrapping up warm and making your way home through the magically deserted streets. All you need is a fresh coating of snow to settle...

25th December
Christmas Day

25th
Peter Pan Cup Swimming Race
Wednesday 25th December 2013 – Christmas Day
Serpentine Boating Lake, Hyde Park, London W2 2UH
This lot are a hardy bunch but tradition is tradition and members of the Serpentine Swimming Club have been plunging themselves into the lake's icy waters every Christmas Day since 1864. At temperatures of below four degrees Celsius in winter, the swimmers will want to get a wiggle on so it's lucky that they are all in hot pursuit of the prestigious Peter Pan Cup. The name of the 100-yard race dates back to 1904 when J.M Barrie, the creator of the boy who refused to grow up, presented the first cup. While most of us are still tucked up in bed or delving into our stocking as the competitors line up (and pretend not to shiver) for their 9am start, a jolly crowd gathers to witness the spectacle. It's a great way to get some fresh air on Christmas morning and you'll feel like you've earned your post-lunch snooze. Behind you, Hyde Park offers a wonderful wintry landscape and, if you want to continue the Peter Pan theme, why not nip across to see the famous statue in Kensington Gardens. It was so cold and snowy in 2010 that the race had to be cancelled - although some intrepid souls still broke holes in the ice in order to have a quick dip.

26th December
Boxing Day

26th
Harrods Winter Sale Opening
Thursday 26th December 2013
Harrods, Knightsbridge, London SW3 1RT
Harrods Winter Sale has assumed iconic status among the London sales, with hopeful customers queuing early to snap up the first bargains and a celebrity to cut the ribbon. The Knightsbridge store is a national institution and the twice yearly sales create unrivalled consumer excitement. In preparation for the rush over 3,000 temporary staff are drafted in to cope with the frenetic activity on the six floors, with around 250,000 shoppers expected on the first day alone. There are some real bargains to be had and an impressive range of goods, but be prepared to struggle with the huge crowds.

26th & 27th
William Hill Winter Festival
26th & 27th December 2013
Kempton Park, Sunbury-on-Thames TW16 5AQ
The King George VI Chase is the showpiece event at the two-day post-Christmas William Hill Winter Festival at Kempton Park, the closest racecourse to central London. The King George VI is one of three Grade 1 races on Boxing Day, the best of the two days of racing. Both days are a great opportunity for racing fans to get a piece of the action so get your tickets early to avoid disappointment. With 12 races in total across the two days, the Winter Festival is the mid-season jump racing event you simply cannot afford to miss (provided you hedge your bets correctly). It's also a great opportunity to leave the parents-in-law at home and get some festive fresh air.

28th
The Big Game 6
Saturday 28th December 2013
Twickenham Stadium, Rugby Road, London TW1 1DZ
The Big Game has become a firm fixture in the Aviva Premiership calendar as Harlequins swap their smaller Stoop Stadium for the hearty home of English rugby with a festive fixture at Twickenham against one of their league rivals. This is the sixth Big Game since the inaugural fixture back in 2008 against Leicester Tigers; since then, the Quins have faced the London Wasps, Saracens and London Irish (twice). It's still a mystery who will line up in front of what has been a sell-out crowd in recent years: a capacity 82,000 fans makes the Big Game the world's best-attended rugby union regular-season game.

31st
New Year's Eve Fireworks
Tuesday 31st December 2013
London Eye, Jubilee Gardens, London SE1 7PB
The annual New Year's Eve Fireworks display, launched from the foot of the London Eye and from rafts on the Thames, is visible from most of central London: the basic rule is that if you can see the London Eye, you'll be able to see the show. They cram enough firepower for an hour-long display into ten explosive minutes, lighting up the sky for miles around. The best views are from Victoria Embankment, the South Bank, and Westminster Bridge and Waterloo Bridge. Hungerford Bridge is closed after 8pm and there's also no entry to Westminster Bridge after this time.

Unconfirmed date

Christmas Past
Throughout December
Geffrye Museum, Hackney, London E2 8EA
Each year the Geffrye Museum celebrates Christmas with a look at the way Christmas traditions have evolved over years at its annual Christmas Past exhibition, staged at the Shoreditch museum for over 20 years. It's a timely opportunity to see the museum's period rooms decorated to reflect our changing tastes at this festive time of year. There's a programme of events and family activities which tie in with the chosen theme where you can create your own Christmas decorations and enjoy the carols by candlelight.

CHRISTMAS ICE SKATING

Since the opening of the world's first artificial ice rink in Chelsea in 1876, ice skating has become a time-honoured tradition in London

HAMPTON COURT PALACE
East Molesey, KT8 9AU
Located on the west front of Henry VIII's historic home, this open air ice rink boasts a majestic backdrop

WESTFIELD SHEPHERD'S BUSH
Ariel Way, W12 7DS
Giant groundfloor rink in the atrium provides the perfect distraction from seasonal shopping

WINTER WONDERLAND
Hyde Park, W2 2UH
The UK's largest ice rink is nestled within the 'Magical Ice Kingdom' of the popular annual festive fair

SOMERSET HOUSE
The Strand, WC2R 1LA
London's most popular ice rink offers a range of events from Club Nights to children's Skate School

LONDON EYESKATE
South Bank, SE1 7PB
Combine your ice dancing with a bit of festive shopping from the German-style Christmas market on the Southbank

NATURAL HISTORY MUSEUM
South Kensington, SW7 5BD
Both adults' and kids' rinks are overlooked by a bar serving mulled wine, hot chocolate and mince pies

TOWER OF LONDON
Tower Hill, EC3N 4AB
Skaters are surrounded by history on a rink positioned in the rounded hollow of the Tower's dry moat

CANARY WHARF
Tower Hamlets, E14 5AG
Canada Square's sedate office life is given a dose of Christmas spirit with a rink lit up by thousands of dainty lights

WESTFIELD STRATFORD CITY
Olympic Park, E20 1EJ
Get a glimpse of the Olympic Park and skate with 'The Snowman' at the shopping mall's outdoor ice rink

---

CHRISTMAS IN LONDON NEWSLETTER
→ To receive the London Christmas Newsletter send a blank email now to: **christmas@londontown.com**
PRIVACY PROMISE: We will never (and that means never) give your email address to anyone else. You mean too much to us.

226 | LONDON'S BEST | LondonTown.com

HISTORIC BUILDINGS

TOWN HOUSES

London's stately homes are living history and celebrate the city's great past. *By Felix Lowe*

CENTRAL LONDON IS SURROUNDED BY a ring of elegant country estates which offer a slice of living history and a steady flow of contemporary events. While most are now run by English Heritage and the National Trust, Syon House **07** & **10** in southwest London remains the home of the Duke of Northumberland and is renowned for its Enchanted Woodland festive light show → 215. Boasting an exquisite Robert Adam interior, it was here where Henry VIII's body was stored en route to Windsor for his burial.

Syon House has many grand neighbouring properties: Ham House **04**, a 17th century treasure trove with popular walks, tours and seasonal markets; Chiswick House **02**, a neo-Palladian villa set in historic gardens with an annual Camellia Festival → 91 and open air opera, theatre and cinema in the summer; Strawberry Hill House, an eccentric Gothic castle which runs regular film screenings, bookclubs and Twilight Tours; and the Palladian Marble Hill House.

Most magnificent is Osterley House **09**, a neo-classical, redbrick Tudor masterpiece built in 1576, remodelled by Adam and once dubbed the 'palace of palaces'. Confirmed events for 2013 include the annual Osterley Weekend 21st century village fete in mid-July → 166.

North London boasts the elegant Kenwood House **01** in Hampstead Heath (under renovation until November), also remodelled by Adam, and home to a superb collection of paintings. Nearby is Fenton House **08**, a charming 17th century merchant's house with panoramic views over London.

South of the river four buildings stand out: the eccentric Southside House **03** in Wimbledon; the William Morris-designed Red House in Bexleyheath, once described as 'the beautifullest place on earth'; Queen's House, the backdrop to the Olympic equestrian events in Greenwich; and Eltham Palace **05**, one of London's secret wonders, a captivating blend of 1930s art deco decadence and classic medievalism.

Southside House will be one of the venues for the 2013 Wimbledon BookFest → 202, hosting an illustrated talk on the new updated edition of John Betjeman's 'Guide to Parish Churches'. Eltham Palace hosts two Art Deco Fairs in May and September → 134, a Grand Medieval Joust in June → 152 and the annual Great Hall Sleepover in February, where families can stay a whole night in Henry VIII's childhood home - enjoying supper, an evening tour, storytelling and a full English breakfast → 91.

Most central of them all, Apsley House **06** is perched between Hyde Park and Green Park, and owns the grandest of addresses: 'Number One London'. The Duke of Wellington's former abode houses paintings by Velazquez and Rubens as well as an unrivalled silver and porcelain collection.

London's stately homes are living history and celebrate the city's great past. A visit to these estates cannot be encouraged enough. ●

LONDON PAST

2013:
THE YEAR OF THE DEAD

Topical residents of London's 'Magnificent Seven' cemeteries by *Felix Lowe*

IN A BID TO COMBAT THE DANGEROUS OVERCROWDING in parish burial grounds in central London in the 19th century, seven private cemeteries were established on the outskirts of town. Almost two centuries on, and these 'Magnificent Seven' Victorian cemeteries have now been swallowed up by the city. Each location offers a wealth of intriguing stories from their dearly departed residents. Here are a few topical tombs to visit in each cemetery in 2013.

Kensal Green Cemetery

Inspired by Père Lachaise cemetery in Paris, Kensal Green Cemetery was the first of the seven to open, in 1832. The poet G.K. Chesterton immortalised the cemetery in his poem 'The Rolling English Road' with the lines: "For there is good news yet to hear and fine things to be seen; Before we go to Paradise by way of Kensal Green." Among the 250,000 individuals buried in 65,000 graves is the forgotten man of Victorian literature, William Makepeace Thackeray (1811-1863), who celebrates his 150th anniversary on 24th December.

West Norwood Cemetery

One of the most significant cemeteries in Europe, this Gothic Revival gem in Lambeth is the resting place of two men integral to the opening of the first London Underground train service in 1863. James Henry Greathead (1844-1896) was an engineer who invented the tunnelling shield for the deep lines, while Charles Pearson (1794-1862) was a solicitor and social reformer without whose foresight and perseverance Londoners would not be celebrating the Underground's 150th anniversary this year → 29. Pearson campaigned ferociously to improve London's decrepit transport system from 1845 and was the driving force behind the Metropolitan Underground Railway, the first underground railway in the world. An elegant, tall, Grade II-listed sarcophagus marks his grave in front of the Crematorium and in the vault of his son-in-law, Sir Thomas Gabriel (founder of Gabriel's Wharf and ancestor of the musician Peter Gabriel).

Highgate Cemetery

Arguably the most famous of the bunch, this Gothic spectacular occupies a stunning south-facing hillside perch. Not only the burial place of Karl Marx and numerous other famous interments, it's also an official nature reserve - and a huge tourist attraction to boot. 170 years ago, Nelson's Column was completed, the base of which was formed by several melted down bronze cannons salvaged from the HMS Royal George, which sunk in 1782. Timber from the same ship was also used to make the coffin for the famous menagerie owner George Wombwell (1777-1850), who requested the oak from Prince Albert after solving the confounding riddle of his frequently dying dogs. Wombwell himself died on 16th November 1850 and is buried in Highgate's West Cemetery in his Royal George coffin inside a tremendous tomb topped by a statue of his faithful docile lion, Nero.

Abney Park Cemetery

A wonderfully overgrown nature reserve with an eye-catching Egyptian revival entrance, Abney Park Cemetery in Stoke Newington is one of London's hidden gems - although it's currently at risk from neglect and decay. While its decrepit nature adds to its charm, it's fair to say that Abney Park - which was the first arboretum to be combined with a cemetery in Europe - could do with a modern day Shirley Hibberd (1825-1890), the pioneering amateur gardener who edited three gardening magazines in the Victorian era. Local resident Hibberd died on 22nd November 1890 and is buried in Abney Park under a weather-beaten headstone covered in moss and ivy. Incidentally, the graveyard scenes for the music video of the late Amy Winehouse's song Back to Black were filmed at Abney Park.

Nunhead Cemetery

The least celebrated of the 'Magnificent Seven' was originally known as All Saints' Cemetery. Also a local nature reserve, Nunhead's occupants pale in comparison to the more illustrious tenants of Highgate - the cemetery's first burial, a 101-year-old greengrocer, setting the tone for the years to come. Nunhead is, funnily enough, the resting place of a certain Captain Thomas Light (1777-1863), an old soldier and acquaintance of Thackeray, who used him as inspiration for the virtuous and upstanding leading character in his novel The Newcomes. Both Light and Thackeray died in 1863, 150 years ago.

Brompton Cemetery

In David Cronenberg's gritty 2007 thriller Eastern Promises, a young Russian Chelsea fan gets his throat slashed while peeing against a gravestone in Brompton Cemetery en route to watch the Blues at nearby Stamford Bridge. The most central of the 'Magnificent Seven' was also used in Guy Richie's first 'Sherlock Holmes' film as the location of Lord Blackwood's tomb. Beatrix Potter took the names of many of her animal characters from tombstones in the cemetery - including a certain Peter Rabbett - while the renowned suffragette Emmeline Pankhurst (who celebrates 85 years since her death) is interred in the cemetery. Brompton is the resting place of the inventor Sir Henry Cole, without whom Christmas could well be a very different preposition: in 1843, 170 years ago, Cole introduced the world's first commercial Christmas card alongside the artist John Callcott Horsley, himself buried in Kensal Green Cemetery.

Tower Hamlets Cemetery

It's 175 years since Jack the Ripper terrorised the streets of East London → 233 - and the autopsy of the Whitechapel Murderer's first victim, Mary Ann Nichols, was carried out by Dr Rees Ralph Llewellyn, who is buried in Tower Hamlets Cemetery, the last (and most working class) of the Victorian seven cemeteries to be opened, in 1841. Heavily bombed in World War II, Tower Hamlets was closed to burials in 1966 and is now - you guessed it - a nature reserve. ●

MUSEUMS

LESSER-KNOWN MUSEUMS

Circumvent the mainstream and head to one of London's hidden gems, says *Peter Watts*

ANAESTHETICS, CANALS, FANS, sewing machines and magic – London's collection of small museums devoted to the weird and wonderful is unrivalled by any city in the world. London has a museum for just about anything, and while some of these museums are only open at weekends and others by appointment only, many are open all year round and offer more interesting, thoughtful, cheaper and calmer exhibitions than the 'blockbusters' beloved by the capital's bigger institutions.

While some of these establishments are run by amateur enthusiasts – like the marvellous Museum of Brands, Packaging and Advertising **05**, which exhibits old tins, packets and boxes from the private collection of Robert Opie – others are run by academic institutions, like University College London's Petrie Museum, where there is a fine collection of Egyptian artefacts, and Grant Museum of Zoology **01**, home to real curiosities from the natural world, including a jar full of moles.

One of London's best small museums is also the best funded. The Wellcome Collection **10** on the Euston Road is a stylish modern space devoted to science and the arts. It forms a key part of the Wellcome Trust, one of the largest charitable funds in the world. In 2013, the Wellcome Collection's galleries will be refurbished but they will still hold regular exhibitions and events, including a huge display of 700 pieces of Japanese Outsider Art, featuring art made by patients at a number of Japanese mental health institutions.

Very different in nature is the sprawling Sir John Soane's Museum, located in a huge old house in Lincoln's Inn Fields that was once the home of the architect Sir John Soane and is still filled with his extraordinary collection of treasures, many of which relate to architecture (Soane designed the Bank of England and Dulwich Picture Gallery). This spring, the museum will be exhibiting architectural drawings of Paestum → 90, a Graeco-Roman city in Italy, that were made by Giovanni Piranesi, the 18th-century Italian artist.

By contrast, architecture buffs should also visit 2 Willow Road in Hampstead, where 'This Must Be The Place' explores architect Ernö Goldfinger's utopian blueprint for the modern home. Goldfinger was a Hungarian architect who worked in the UK after the Second World War, and the exhibition takes place at the modernist house he designed for himself.

If you prefer engineers to architects, check out the remarkable Brunel Museum in Rotherhithe, which celebrates the achievements of the father-and-son engineers Marc and Isambard Kingdom Brunel. It is located above their Thames Tunnel, which was built beneath the

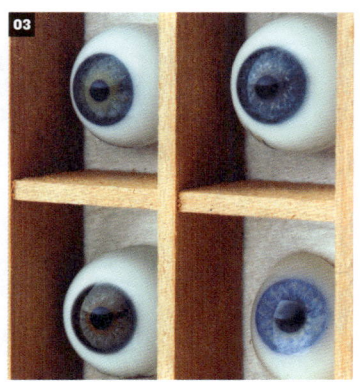

Thames between 1825 and 1843. The Brunel Museum 02 hosts a number of events throughout the year, including regular opportunities to descend into the tunnel (which now forms part of the underground network). The Brunel Museum will also be celebrating the 160th anniversary of the tunnel opening in 2013.

There are several other anniversaries to note in 2013. It is, for instance, the bicentenary of the glorious Hunterian Museum at the Royal College of Surgeons, a curious collection of medical specimens which has been based in Lincoln's Inn Fields since 1813. There will be a special exhibition to highlight the origins of the college, some of the key figures and events in its history and also look at the future of the college through the research funding and training that it provides for modern surgeons.

This year also marks 75 years since the launch of HMS Belfast, the war boat museum on the Thames at London Bridge, and the 250th anniversary of Dr Samuel Johnson meeting James Boswell, for which there will be celebratory events at Dr Johnson's House, where Johnson wrote the world's first dictionary, in the City of London. The end of the year marks the 200th anniversary of the founding of the Clockmakers' Museum collection, the oldest collection of clocks and watches in the world, which is based in Guildhall. A similar specialist is the British Optical Association Museum 03 in Charing Cross. Run by the Worshipful Company of Spectacle Makers it features historic examples of London-made spectacles and will be holding the exhibition 'Look for the Letters', to mark the 150th anniversary of the test letter chart still used today by opticians to test eyesight.

The Jubilee may be behind us, but London isn't quite done with royal celebrations. Westminster Abbey Museum will celebrate the anniversary of the coronation of Queen Elizabeth II with a special exhibition. Another British institution is the Bank of England on Threadneedle Street, and the Bank's excellent museum, located in a small corner of the huge and historic building, will be holding an exhibition called 'Cartoons and Caricatures', displaying satirical financial cartoons from the archive by artists such as James Gillray, John Tenniel and Steve Bell. Fans of cartoons should also visit the excellent Cartoon Museum close to the British Museum in Bloomsbury. They have regular, hugely entertaining, exhibitions and also organise Family Fun Days, drop-in cartooning sessions for families that are held on the second Saturday of every month.

A more unusual look at money comes from the Garden Museum in Lambeth 08, where they'll examine the story of the cut-flower trade with an exhibition entitled 'Floriculture: Flowers, Love and Money'. This museum, located in a beautiful converted church, covers the history of gardening and this exhibition in particular explores the history of flower-selling – a trade now worth £4.8m – while also looking at how cut flowers have influenced painters, and what their symbolism is in rites of passage such as marriage, funerals, and memory.

Similar themes are explored at the Foundling Museum 07 in

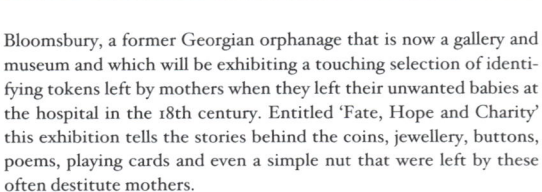

Bloomsbury, a former Georgian orphanage that is now a gallery and museum and which will be exhibiting a touching selection of identifying tokens left by mothers when they left their unwanted babies at the hospital in the 18th century. Entitled 'Fate, Hope and Charity' this exhibition tells the stories behind the coins, jewellery, buttons, poems, playing cards and even a simple nut that were left by these often destitute mothers.

Very close to the Foundling Museum is the Charles Dickens Museum, which reopens in 2013 after extensive refurbishment and will have numerous events programmed through the year. Another museum devoted to a writer is Keats' House in Hampstead, who also have events all year including a speed-dating 18th century-themed masked ball at Valentines.

If music is the food of love, Handel's House Museum in Mayfair is the place to be. Their spring exhibition focuses on the composer's close collaborator Charles Jennens – the man behind 'Messiah'. The Royal Academy of Music Museum is also worth a visit for music lovers. This Marylebone-based museum has an exhibition about enigmatic jazz trumpeter Kenny Wheeler, who has lived in London since 1952. The exhibition will feature his personal archive, instruments, awards, correspondence, scores and images, as well as a lively programme of events.

Also in Marylebone is the Anaesthesia Heritage Centre, which is devoted to the history of anaesthetics. This small space at the Association of Anaesthetists of Great Britain and Ireland hosts a temporary exhibition relating to pain relief in emergency situations such as the London tube bombings. Almost as peculiar in scope is the Fan Museum 04 across town in Greenwich. Their main exhibition for the first half of the year will be 'European Fans: 1800-1850', which is bound to be fan-tastic.

Towards the end of the year over in Islington, the Canal Museum will hold its annual costumed Halloween trip along the Regent's Canal and through the spooky Islington Tunnel. There are also regular talks and boat trips throughout the year at this museum devoted to London's canals.

As we approach Christmas, it's always worth checking out the Geffrye Museum in Hackney. The Geffrye is a museum devoted to the way the home has been decorated since 1600 and every year they have Christmas Past, an exhibition demonstrating how Christmas has been celebrated in middle-class homes in England over the past 400 years. The Brunel Museum also celebrates Christmas with special events in the tunnel and great hall.

Another great way to celebrate Christmas is with a tour of Dennis Severs House 06 in Spitalfields. This incredible house has been decorated like an 18th-century weaver's home and is open for regular tours - every Christmas it is filled with the sights and smells of Christmas past. Finally, if you fancy ending the year with a Christmas concert, you can't get much more memorable than the annual sing-along at the RAF Museum in Hendon, where carols are sung from beneath a giant Lancaster bomber. ●

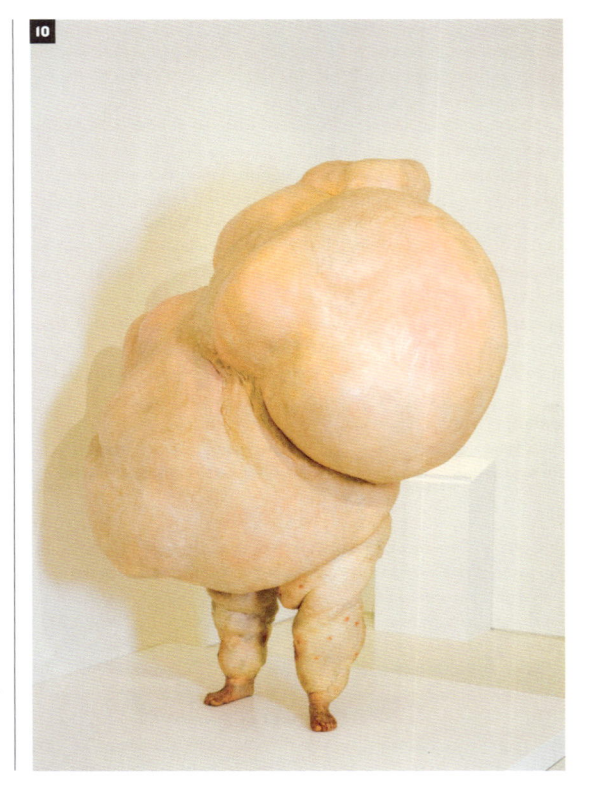

LondonTown.com   BACKPAGES   233

LONDON PAST

2013 ANNIVERSARIES

Bicentenaries for Wagner and Verdi, 100 for Britten and 80 years (and counting) for both Yoko Ono and Sir Michael Caine, *writes Felix Lowe*

01

THIS YEAR BOASTS A FLURRY OF ANNIVERSARIES commemorating cultural heavyweights past and present, dead and alive. From celebrity birthdays to King Henry V's coronation: 2013 is the year the Tube turns 150, two classical maestros complete double centuries and Jack the Ripper makes it 125 years on the loose and avoiding the noose...

Alive & Kicking

One of London's most famous sons will be blowing the bloody candles out on his 80th birthday this spring - as well as being commemorated in a special exhibition at the Museum of London. Born in Southwark on 14th March 1933 as Maurice Mickelwhite, Sir Michael Caine **03** is as much prolific actor as iconic Londoner, and the four-month exhibition focuses on key moments in both his personal life and career → 106.

Sir Michael is not the only famous face to turn 80 in 2013: Yoko Ono **04** brings a lifetime of achievement in music, visual art and peace activism to the Southbank Centre in June as she curates the annual Meltdown Festival → 152, and the award-winning British architect Richard Rogers is the subject of a summer exhibition at the Royal Academy to coincide with his own 80th birthday → 166. At the Barbican, the 'Sir Colin Davis at 85' series continues while the English conductor is at the helm of a revival of David McVicar's staging of Mozart's 'The Magic Flute' this spring → 120.

Another famous Londoner, the fabled fashion designer Sir Paul Smith, has not reached the ranks of the octogenarians just yet (he still has 14 years to go until that landmark) but his four decades in the business are celebrated in the London Design Museum from November through to spring 2014 → 215.

Dearly Departed

Two of opera's greatest pioneers - Richard Wagner and Giuseppe Verdi - celebrate their bicentenaries in 2013 with a hefty programme of commemorative events in London. Sir Andrew Davis conducts a concert on 22nd May at Royal Festival Hall commemorating the ex-

BACKPAGES

act 200th anniversary of Wagner's birth → 139. This Philharmonia Orchestra offering kicks off 'Wagner 200' - a wide-ranging festival at leading venues all over the capital. Verdi's own bicentenary begins with Peter Konwitschny's new production of 'La Traviata' at the ENO's Coliseum from February through to March → 84. 'Nabucco' - the opera to which Verdi attributed the real start of his artistic career - is performed later in the spring at the Royal Opera House → 110.

As composer Benjamin Britten reaches his centenary in 2013 there are summer productions of 'Gloriana' at the Royal Albert Hall → 154 and his much admired final opera, 'Death in Venice', at the Coliseum → 152. While the BBC Proms are taking a distinctive Britten flavour → 166, Kings Place hosts a three-day 'Britten at 100' festival in February, and the moving 'War Requiem' is performed at the Albert Hall on Remembrance Sunday → 214, 11 days before what would have been the 100th birthday of Britain's most influential composer. Meanwhile, the 175th anniversary of the French composer Georges Bizet is commemorated with a limited in-the-round run of 'Carmen' at the Albert Hall in February → 92.

Shows, Events & Pieces Of Art

Cultural landmarks of celebrating key milestones in 2013 include Igor Stravinsky's 'The Rite of Spring' (100 years), with dance companies and orchestras around the world doffing their cap to the 20th century masterpiece. From April to June, Sadler's Wells presents three separate productions that reinterpret the work for the 21st century: Akram Khan's 'iTMOi' → 142, a revival of Michael Keegan-Dolan's Olivier-nominated version of the ground-breaking ballet → 118, and 'RIOT Offspring' → 149.

Mr Darcy completes a double century as Jane Austen's 'Pride and Prejudice' is remembered with an Open Air Theatre performance of the 200-year-old romantic comedy in June → 154, while the Albert Hall commemorates the 60th birthday of the adored musical 'Singin' in the Rain' **05** with a cinematic makeover featuring a live orchestral accompaniment in March → 102. On 23rd March, the 270th anniversary of the London première of Handel's 'Messiah' is marked in a performance of the great oratorio in the Grosvenor Chapel → 107.

Bollywood was born one century ago with the release on 3rd May 1913 of the first Indian feature film. 100 years on and India is now the world's most prolific film producing nation, releasing roughly 1,000 pictures a year (twice as many as Hollywood). The annual London Indian Film Festival **06** returns in July to commemorate the industry's centenary at the BFI Southbank and other selected cinemas → 168.

Stilettos will be sharpened for the 'Rocky Horror Show' 40th Anniversary Tour featuring (bear with me) Rhydian from the 'X-Factor' → 75. Even more risqué, Richard Herring's 'Talking Cock' - "man's answer to the Vagina Monologues" - returns to the Bloomsbury Theatre for its 10th anniversary Tour in April → 119.

'Doctor Who' 01, the longest running and most successful science fiction series in the world, turns 50 on 23rd November 2013 (although we all know that the Doctor himself is around 1103 years old, don't we?). The BFI Southbank will hold a series of celebratory monthly screenings, starting with the first ever episode, 'An Unearthly Child' starring William Hartnell as the Doctor, in January → 71.

Staples & Venues
The world-famous Chelsea Flower Show celebrates 100 years at the Royal Hospital → 138 while, also in May, the 'Collect' Craft Show returns to the nearby Saatchi Gallery for its 10th anniversary → 133. Also celebrating 10 years is January's London Short Film Festival → 69, the London Bicycle Film Festival → 200 and the South West Four dance music festival → 180. Back for the 25th time, the four-day London International Ska Festival sees more than 40 acts perform across multiple venues in March → 109.

The National Theatre hits a half-century in 2013 with a 50th anniversary season that includes 'Othello' (directed by Nicolas Hytner) → 126 and 'The Captain of Kopenick' (starring Antony Sher) → 77. Sadler's Wells marks its 15th anniversary, the National Gallery celebrates 175 years on its Trafalgar Square site, while, most impressive, the Hunterian Museum turns 200 with a special exhibition.

Historical Milestones
The Tube is to London what veins and arteries are to the human body. Without the Underground, it's fair to say that the whole city comes grinding to a halt. 9th January marks 150 years since the first underground journey took place between Paddington and Farringdon on the Metropolitan Railway → 29. TfL has planned a range of events to celebrate the world's oldest underground railway, including special steam and heritage train runs across the network in January. A series of monthly talks take place at the Transport Museum's Cubic Theatre during the spring while an exhibition 07 of 150 Underground posters runs until October → 93.

It's 125 years since the streets of East London were at the mercy of Jack the Ripper, the unidentified serial killer who carried out the gruesome Whitechapel murders and whose legend is a constant source of dark fascination. The official Jack the Ripper Walking Tour will be holding several anniversary walks on 3rd April, 7th & 31st August, 8th & 30th September and 9th November that focus on the particular victims on the corresponding day in 1888.

From dying dames to the beautiful game: the Football Association, the world's oldest professional football body, celebrates its 150th anniversary with a raft of special fixtures - including two England friendlies at Wembley 08 against Samba stars Brazil in February → 84 and the old foe Scotland in August → 178. History is also made as Wembley becomes the first stadium to host the Champions League final twice in three years - as UEFA joins the big birthday party on 25th May → 140.

On 29th June it will be 400 years since the Globe Theatre burned to the ground - and although the open air Bankside venue has remained tight-lipped about its 2013 schedule, it is thought to feature 'A Midsummer Night's Dream', 'The Tempest' and 'Macbeth', as well as 'Blue Stockings' by Jessica Swale and 'The Lightning Child' by Che Walker.

Royal Anniversaries
Last year all eyes were on the Queen during her Diamond Jubilee - but the exact 60th anniversary of Her Majesty's coronation on 2nd June 1953 comes this year 02. The BBC are planning a night of live broadcasting across all major channels to tie in with the final year of BBC broadcasting from Television Centre at White City. While Buckingham Palace has yet to confirm any special events for the coronation, they have promised that the landmark event will be recognised in some way. Expect the annual Trooping the Colour on Horse Guards Parade on Saturday 15th June - which celebrates the official birthday of the Queen - to carry more sway than usual → 153.

From 60 years to 600: 9th April marks the 600th anniversary of the coronation of King Henry V. What better way to commemorate one of the most successful kings of England than watch a performance of 'Henry V' at the Noel Coward Theatre, which runs from November through to February 2014 → 215. Jude Law is cast as the title role in Michael Grandage's powerful production of Shakespeare's exploration of the horrors of war.

It's also 175 years since the ascension of Queen Victoria - although no specific events have been confirmed as yet. Perhaps a visit to the Victoria Memorial in front of Buckingham Palace - or the Victoria & Albert Museum, which marks the 400th anniversary of the Romanov dynasty from March to July with an exhibition focusing on Tudors, Stuarts and the Russian Tsars → 105. ●

Before you book your London hotel, visit the **London HotelMap**™ at LondonTown.com

Visually compare best hotel rates and availability

London's hotels all on one map

See real customer feedback on all hotels

View entertainment, including ticket prices and availability

Hotel Price Guarantee: 'We will not be beaten on price'

www.londontown.com/hotels

FREEPHONE
0800 LONDON
0800 566 366

LondonTown.com
Your Best Friend in London™

Index
Venues and Events

0-9

1-2-3-4 Shoreditch 194
100 Percent Design 191
1st & 2nd NatWest International T20s: England v New Zealand 156
1st Investec Test: England v New Zealand 136
20/21 International Art Fair 133
2nd Investec Ashes Test: England v Australia 167
5th Investec Ashes Test: England v Australia 180

A

Above Me the Wide Blue Sky 101
AEGON Tennis Championships at Queen's 150
Affordable Art Fair Battersea 101
Affordable Art Fair Hampstead 151
Alan Davies: Life Is Pain 90
Alchemy Festival 119
Aled Jones 135
Alegria Cirque du Soleil 167
Alexandra Palace 86 & 150
Alexei Sayle 75
Alfie Boe 117
Alice's Adventures In Wonderland 104
Alien Revolution 110
Almeida Theatre 73, 107 & 137
Alt-J 73
Ambika P3 120
American Lulu 190
Ansel Adams: Photography From The Mountains To The Sea 63
Antony Gormley: Model 58
Apollo Piccadilly 193
Apollo Theatre 58 & 100
Art Deco Fair 134
Art of Seeing Nature 64
Art of Seeing Nature: the oil sketches of John Constable 64
Art Under Attack: Histories of Iconoclasm in Britain 200
Ascot Racecourse 153
Aspen Magazine: 1965-1971 61
Astronomy Photographer Of The Year 59
ATP Champions Tour: Masters Tennis 221
Audience 90
Australia 192
Aviva Premiership Rugby Final 2013 140

B

Bach Marathon 115
Ballet Black 94
Ballgowns: British Glamour Since 1950 53
Banff Mountain Film Festival World Tour 92
Bank of England Museum 192
Bank of England Sports Centre 94
Bankside Gallery 165
Barber of Seville 94
Barbican Art Gallery 89
Barbican Centre 55, 61, 72, 88, 89, 100, 118, 133, 157, 205 & 216
Barbican Hall 123
Barbican Screen 200
Barbican Theatre 55 & 119
Barclays ATP World Tour Finals 2013 212
Barking In Essex 188
Barocci: Brilliance and Grace 94
Battersea Arts Centre (BAC) 69 & 90
Battersea Park 101, 171 & 222
Battersea Park Foodies Festival 171
Battersea Power Station 134
Battle of Ideas 205
BBC Good Food Show 215
BBC Proms 2013 166
BBC Proms In The Park 188
Becoming Picasso: Paris 1901 88
Bedford Square Gardens 169
Beethoven's Ninth 194
Before The Party 107
Berkeley Square 204
Bermondsey Square 191
Bermondsey Street Festival 191
BFI Future Film Festival 91
BFI Southbank 71, 76, 87, 91, 104, 168 & 202
Biffy Clyro 116
Big Draw 199
Big Game 6 224
Big Tent on Wimbledon Common 202
Bigger Splash: Painting After Performance Art 62
Bike Week 153

Birmingham Royal Ballet: Aladdin 105
Birth of a Collection: The Barber Institute of Fine arts and the National Gallery 139
Bitch Boxer 91
Blackfriars Bridge 190
Bloc Party 92
Bloomberg Commission: Giuseppe Penone 64
Bloomsbury Festival 205
Bloomsbury Theatre 72, 77, 108 & 119
Blythe House 201
BNY Mellon Boat Race: Oxford vs Cambridge 110
Bonhams Classic Car Auction 126
Book of Mormon 94
Borderline 108
Boston Ballet: Programme 1 163
Boston Ballet: Programme 2 163
BP Portrait Award 154
Breakin' Convention 132
Breaking the Ice: Moscow Art 1960s-80s 60
Brendan Cole: Licence To Thrill 88
Bride and the Bachelors: Duchamp with Cage, Cunningham, Rauschenberg and Johns 89
Brit Awards 91
British 10K London Run 167
British Athletics London Grand Prix 170
British Basketball Play-off Final 125
British Library 62, 137 & 216
British Museum 54, 56, 85, 86, 109, 189 & 201
Britten at 100 85
Britten's War Requiem 214
Brixton Academy 73, 86, 99, 101 & 142
Brockwell Park 169
Bruce Springsteen & The E Street Band 152
Buckingham Palace 165 & 177
Buckingham Palace Summer Opening 177
Bupa London 10,000 141
Bush Theatre 106
Business Design Centre 72, 106, 156, 163 & 216

C

Cabaret 55
Cadogan Hall 57, 78, 134 & 151
Cambridge Theatre 64
Camden Arts Centre 137, 171 & 202
Camden Fringe 182
Camden People's Theatre 182
Camellia Festival 91
Capital One Cup Final 93
Captain Of Kopenick 77
Carlos Acosta: Classical Selection 172
Cartier-Bresson: A Question Of Colour 56
Cartoon Museum 70 & 103
Cenotaph 214
Central Saint Martins College of Art and Design 201
Chap Olympiad 169
Charing Cross Hotel 83
Charlie and the Chocolate Factory 156
Cheapside Hoard: London's Lost Jewels 205
Cheese and Wine Festival 122
Chekhov: The Seagull 204
Chekhov: The Three Sisters 205
Chelsea Antiques Fair 104
Chelsea Old Town Hall 104
Children of the Sun 110
Chimerica 137
Chiswick House 91
Chocolate Festival 107
Chocolate Week 203
Chorus 137
Chorus Line 84
Chris Addison: The Time is Now, Again 84
Chris de Burgh 124
Christ Church Spitalfields 155 & 222
Christmas Chocolate Festival 223
Christmas Past 224
Cirque Du Soleil: Kooza 70
City of London Festival 156
Clapham Common 181 & 191
Clapham Grand 109
Clerkenwell Design Week 141
Clothworkers' Centre for Textile and Fashion Study and Conservation 201
Codebreaker: Alan Turing's Life And Legacy 64
Collect 133

Collecting Gaugin: Samuel Courtauld in the 20s 154
Colombian Gold 189
Colourscape Music Festival 191
Columbia Road Christmas Shopping Evenings 216
Columbia Road Flower Market 216
Conway Hall 87 & 137
Coronation Festival 2013 165
Coronation Jubilee Concert 151
Country Living Magazine Christmas Fair 216
Country Living Magazine Spring Fair 106
Courtauld Gallery 88, 154 & 205
Covent Garden May Fayre and Puppet Festival 135
Covent Garden Piazza 222
Cripple Of Inishmaan 150
Crisis of Brilliance 151
Crystal Palace National Sports Centre 170 & 187
Curious Incident of the Dog in the Night-time 100

D

Dance Al Fresco 172
Dance Umbrella 201
Dancing around Duchamp 89
David Bowie Is 107
Death in Venice 152
Death: A Self-Portrait 60
Depeche Mode 142
Design Museum 54, 60, 78, 109, 133, 169, 189 & 215
Designers in Residence 189
Designs Of The Year 2013 109
Deutsche Borse Photography Prize 2013 121
Di And Viv And Rose 73
Die Zauberflote 120
Dieter Roth: Diaries and other works 137
Digital Crystal: Swarovski at the Design Museum 54
Dirty Great Love Story 103
Discovery of Paris: Watercolours by Early Nineteenth-Century British Artists 154
Disney Fantasia: Live in Concert 215
Doctor Brown: Befrdfgth 108
Doctor Who: Tomb of the Cybermen 87
Doctors, Dissection And Resurrection Men 63
Doktor Glas 120
Doll's House 116
Don Carlo 132
Donmar Warehouse 57, 90 & 121
Donny And Marie 74
Duke of York's Theatre 70
Dulwich Picture Gallery 85, 151 & 205

E

E4 Udderbelly Festival 118
Ealing Blues Festival 172
Earls Court Exhibition Centre 92, 191, 206, 214 & 222
East London Design Show 221
Eddie Izzard: Force Majeure 134
Edward Barber and Jay Osgerby 133
Effect 59
Eid in the Square 178
Ellen Gallagher 131
Eltham Palace 91, 134 & 152
Elvis Costello & The Imposters 148
Emeli Sande 117
Emirates Stadium: Arsenal FC 140 & 147
Emma Hart: Dirty Looks 171
Empire Leicester Square 180
Enchanted Woodland 215
England v New Zealand: First NatWest Series ODI 142
English National Ballet 2 - My First Cinderella 109
English National Ballet: Swan Lake 151
English National Ballet: The Nutcracker 53
English National Ballet: The Sleeping Beauty 70
Epsom Downs Racecourse 142
Eric Clapton 136
Ether Festival 202
Everything Was Moving: Photography From The 60s And 70s 55
Example 92
ExCeL London Exhibition Centre 71, 73, 93, 132, 212, 216 & 222
Exhibition Road 158
Exhibition Road Music Day 158
Extinction: not the end of the world? 86
Extraordinary Stories about Ordinary Things 78

F

FA Community Shield 178
FA Cup Final 2013 134
FA Cup Semi-Finals Weekend 119
FA Trophy Final 108
FA Vase Final 132
Family Matters, The Family of British Art 60
Fashion and Textile Museum 107
Fate, Hope & Charity 76
Faulty Towers: The Dining Experience 83
Feast 76
February Fools Charity Cricket Match 94
Feeling (The) 125
Festival of British Archaeology 166
Field Day 140
Film 4 FrightFest 180
Film 4 Summer Screen at Somerset House 179
Finborough Theatre 100
Finsbury Park 148
First Doctor: An Unearthly Child 71
Fischli/Weiss: Rock on Top of Another Rock 101
Flame And Water Pots: Prehistoric Ceramic Art From Japan 56
Flamenco Festival London 10th Anniversary 104
Flook - and Humph too! 70
Floriculture: Flowers, Love and Money 88
Focus: Charles Harrison as Curator 61
Focus: Frank Bowling 63
Football League Championship Play-off Final 141
Football League Play-off Finals 137
Forsythe Company 153
Foundling Museum 76
Framed Film Festival 216
Frank Skinner, Work in Progress 123
Free Range 2013 142
Freemason's Hall 190
Frieze Art Fair 204
From Club to Catwalk: London Fashion in the 80s 171
From Here To Eternity 194
Fuerzabruta 56

G

Gadget Show Live at Christmas 216
Gaiety Is The Most Outstanding Feature Of The Soviet Union: Art From Russia 63
Garden Museum 88
Gary Hume 148
Gaucho International Polo 2013 121
GB Row 2013 147
Geffrye Museum 224
Genius of Castiglione 212
George Bellows (1882-1925) 105
George Catlin: American Indian Portraits 101
Georgians 216
Gerard Byrne: A State of Neutral Pleasure 73
Gielgud Theatre 90
Global Party 156
Glorious Goodwood 171
Goodwood Racecourse 171
Grand Designs Live 132
Grand Medieval Joust 152
Great British Beer Festival 178
Great British Tattoo Show 125
Great Christmas Pudding Race 222
Great Gatsby 91
Great Gorilla Run 192
Great Hall Sleepover 91
Great Map 110
Great River Race 188
Great Spitalfields Pancake Race 87
Green Day 147
Greenwich 154
Greenwich and Docklands International Festival 154
Greenwich International Early Music Festival and Exhibition 213
Grimaldi Clowns' Church Service 84
Grosvenor Chapel 107
Guildhall 194
Guildhall Symphony Orchestra 201
Gunnersbury Park 187

H

Halfway to Paradise: The Birth of British Rock 61
Ham 188
Hammersmith Apollo 85, 88, 90, 108, 117, 121, 125, 138, 139, 206 & 213
Hampstead & Highgate Literary Festival 191
Hampstead Heath 151
Hampstead Theatre 73 & 94
Hampton Court Foodies Festival 140
Hampton Court Green 182
Hampton Court Palace 140, 152 & 165
Hampton Court Palace Festival 152
Harold Pinter Theatre 71
Harrods 212
Harry Hill: Sausage Time 108
Hayward Gallery 78
Head of the River Race 107
Henley Royal Regatta 2013 164
Henley-on-Thames 164
Henry V 215
HMS Belfast 104
HMS Belfast: 75th anniversary 104
Holi Hindu Festival of Colour 102
Holland Park Theatre 148, 167 & 169
Hollywood Costume 56
Holy Trinity, The Clowns' Church 84
Honore Daumier 205
Horrible Histories: Spies 168
Horse Guards Parade 153
House of Lords v House of Commons Tug of War 150
Houses of Parliament 207
Howard Marks: An Audience With Mr Nice 108
HSBC Sevens World Series: Marriott London Sevens 2013 134
Hurlingham Park 149
Hyde Park 122, 188, 194, 202 & 213
Hyde Park Corner Tube 167
Hyde Park Winter Wonderland 213

I

Ian Hamilton Finlay 59
ICA Cinema 1 167
ICC Champions Trophy: England v Sri Lanka 151
ICC Champions Trophy: India v West Indies 150
ICC Champions Trophy: Semi-Final 154
ICC Champions Trophy: Sri Lanka v Australia 153
ICC Champions Trophy: West Indies v Pakistan 148
Ice Age Art: Arrival of the Modern Mind 85
Ideal Home Show at Christmas 214
Imagine 87
Imperial War Museum 168
In Fine Style: The Art of Tudor and Stuart Fashion 138
In Search of Classical Greece: Travel Drawings of Edward Dodwell and Simone Pomardi 85
In the Beginning was the End 77
Indian Tempest 126
Institute of Contemporary Arts (ICA) 69 & 76
International Friendly: England v Brazil 84
International Friendly: England v Scotland 178
International Garden Photographer of the Year 165
International Stadium Poker Tour 142
Investec Derby Festival 2013 142
Invisible Dot 223
iTMOi 142
ITU World Triathlon Grand Final London 188
iTunes Festival 163

J

Jake Bugg 94
Jameel Prize Exhibition 223
Jane Birkin sings Serge Gainsbourg via Japan 78
Jason Manford 206
Jazz Cafe 88
Jimmy Carr: Gagging Order 125
JLS 223
Jocelyn Brown 88
Jockum Nordstrom 170
Joe Bonamassa 108
Johnstone's Paint Trophy Final 117
Jolly Day Out 182
Josiah McElheny: Interactions Of The Abstract Body 54
Judas Kiss 70
Juergen Teller: Woo 76
Julius Caesar 57

K

Kaffe Fassett - A Life in Colour 107
Kaiser Chiefs 99
Kara Walker 202
Karl Ferris Psychedelic Experience 57
Keats House 140
Keats House Summer Festival 140
Kempton Park 224
Kensington Gardens 101
Kew Fete 155
Kew Gardens (Royal Botanic Gardens) 165 & 189
Kew Green 155
Kew the Movies 189
Kew the Music 165
Kia Oval Cricket Ground 148, 150, 151, 153, 154, 156 & 180
Kids Week 182
Kings of Leon 151
Kings Place 76, 85, 102 & 189
Kings Place Festival 189
Kiss Me, Kate 60
Kraftwerk 84
Kris Martin 74

L

La Bayadere 117
La Boheme 126
La donna del lago 137
La Rondine 164
La Traviata 84
Laburnum Grove 100
Lambeth Country Show 169
Lana Del Rey 138
Lang Lang 214
Lanterns On The Lake 153
Large Hadron Collider 213
Last Night of the Proms 2013 192
Laura Knight Portraits 166
Laurie Anderson & Kronos Quartet 157
Leona Lewis 133
Lesbian & Gay Film Festival 104
Lianne La Havas 103
Lichtenstein: A Retrospective 92
Life and death in Pompeii and Herculaneum 109
LIFT 77
Light From The Middle East: New Photography 63
Light Show 78
Little Mix 88
LOCO: London Comedy Film Festival 76
LolliBop Festival 180
London A Cappella Festival 76
London Art Fair 72
London Bicycle Film Festival 200
London Burlesque Festival 134
London Cocktail Week 202

London Coffee Festival 124
London Coliseum - English National Opera (ENO) 53, 57, 70, 84, 89, 94, 105, 126, 135, 147, 152, 163 & 172
London Design Festival 190
London Duathlon 194
London Eye 224
London Fashion Week 189
London Fashion Week Exhibition 190
London Fashion Weekend 191
London Film Museum Covent Garden 203
London Handel Festival 103
London Indian Film Festival 168
London International Animation Festival 201
London International Antiquarian Book Fair 151
London International Horse Show 223
London International Mime Festival 70
London International Ska Festival 109
London Jazz Festival 215
London Jewellery Week 149
London Jewish Cultural Centre, Ivy House 191
London Literature Festival 139
London Mela 187
London Open House Weekend 192
London Original Print Fair 118
London Palladium 84
London Restaurant Festival 199
London Short Film Festival 2013 69
London Super Comic Convention 93
London Transport Museum 93
London Wonderground 135
Longing 94
Looking at the View 87
Lord Mayor's Show 214
Lord's Cricket Ground 136, 142 & 167
Lovebox 168
Low Road (The) 107
Lowry and the Painting of Modern Life 156
LSO St Luke's 73
Ludovico Einaudi 123

M

Macbeth 87
Madame Jojo's 134
Magistrate (The) 58
Making the Future: A New Industrial Revolution 169
Male Nude (The) 204
Mall (The) 122 & 176
Mall Galleries 133
Man Ray Portraits 89
Manet: Portraying Life 72
Mansion House 214
Marilyn Monroe: A British Love Affair 62
Mario Testino: British Royal

Portraits 58
Mark Knopfler 141
Maroon 5 155
Master and Margarita 55
Master Drawings Uncovered: Piranesi's Paestum Drawings 90
Masterpiece London 157
Masterpieces of Chinese Painting 700-1900 205
Matilda The Musical 64
Matthew Bourne's Sleeping Beauty 56
Max Mara Art Prize for Women 106
Mayerling 122
Mayor's Thames Festival 190
McCoy's Premier League Darts 136
Medea 90
Meltdown Festival 152
Messiah Anniversary Concert 107
Mexico: A Revolution in Art, 1910-1940 165
Michael Buble 158
Michael Caine: 80th Birthday Exhibition 106
Michael Landy: Saints Alive 139
Mick Hucknall 125
Micky Flanagan: Back In The Game 139
Midnight Mass at St Paul's Cathedral 223
Midnight Tango 77
Midori House Courtyard 153
Midsummer Night's Dream 188
Mies Julie 101
Mikado (The) 57
Milton Court 201 & 205
Milton Jones: On The Road 121
MINT Polo in the Park 149
Mira Schendel 193
Modern British Childhood 1948-2012 63
Moniker Art Fair 204
Monocle Country Fayre 153
MoonWalk London 2013 134
Moscow State Symphony Orchestra: Tchaikovsky Cycle 134
Move It 102
Mozart's Requiem 205
Much Ado About Nothing 188
Mughal India: Art, Culture And Empire 62
Murillo and Justino de Neve: the Art of Friendship 85
Murillo at the Wallace Collection 85
Muse 140
Museum and Library of the Order of St John 141
Museum of London 59, 63, 106, 166 & 205
Museums at Night 136
Music Hall: Sickert and the Three Graces 105
My Perfect Mind 116

N

Nabucco 110
National Gallery 55, 94, 139, 156 & 202
National Maritime Museum 63, 110, 158 & 216
National Portrait Gallery 58, 59, 62, 89, 102, 155, 165 & 213
National Theatre 126
National Theatre: Cottesloe Theatre 59
National Theatre: Lyttelton Theatre 62, 75 & 110
National Theatre: Olivier Theatre 58, 77, 93 & 126
Natural History Museum 61, 86, & 119
NATYS 77
NBA London Live: Detroit Pistons v New York Knicks 72
New Designers Exhibition Part One 156
New Designers Exhibition Part Two 163
New Play (A) 117
New Wave (The) 223
New Wimbledon Theatre 74 & 222
New Wimbledon Theatre Panto 222
New Year's Eve Fireworks 224
NFL International Series: Jacksonville Jaguars v San Francisco 49ers 206
NFL International Series: Minnesota Vikings v Pittsburgh Steelers 194
Nicola Benedetti 193
Nightleaver 150
No Quarter 71
Noel Coward Theatre 60, 102, 150, 188 & 215
Nofit State Circus: Bianco 135
Northern Ballet - The Great Gatsby 135
Northern Renaissance: Durer to Holbein 63
Notting Hill 181
Notting Hill Carnival 181

O

O2 Arena 72, 74, 87, 91, 92, 107, 116, 121, 124, 131, 134, 136, 139, 142, 151, 155, 158, 167, 206, 212 & 223
O2 Shepherd's Bush Empire 103
Of Monsters And Men 101
Old Royal Naval College 213
Old Times 71
Old Truman Brewery 87, 124 & 242
Old Vic Theatre 60, 102, 149 & 188
Old Vic Tunnels 199
Olly Murs 102
Olympia (The) 102, 125, 148, 151, 178, 212, 215 & 223
Olympia International Fine Art & Antiques Fair 148
Once 104

One Direction 92
Onegin 74
Open Air Theatre Summer Season 136
Open Air Theatre, Regent's Park 136, 154, 157 & 170
Open Garden Squares Weekend 149
Opera Holland Park 148
Opera Holland Park: I Gioielli della Madonna 169
Opera Holland Park: L'Elisir d'Amore 167
Orleans House Gallery 102
Oskar Fischinger 63
Osterley Park and House 166
Osterley Weekend 166
Othello 126
Other Art Fair 120
Outdoors Show 73
Oxford Street 216
Oxford vs Cambridge Goat Race 110

P

PAD London Art Fair 204
Paloma Faith 85
Paper Odyssey 90
Pappy's: Last Show Ever 115
Parliament Hill Lido 222
Participatory Photography Commission: BBKP 84
Patrick Caulfield 148
Paul Klee 203
Paul Smith 215
Peacock Theatre 77, 109, 132 & 215
Pearls 192
Pearly Kings and Queens Harvest Festival 194
People 62
Perfect American (The) 147
Peter And Alice 102
Peter Pan Cup Swimming Race 224
Phoenix Theatre 78 & 104
Photographers' Gallery 121
Photomonth 200
Pick Me Up Contemporary Graphic Art Fair 115
Pink - The Truth About Love Tour 124
Pink Martini 126
Place (The) 120
Place Prize For Dance: The Finals 120
Plan B 87
Playing Cards 1: SPADES 86
Port 75
Portobello Film Festival 181
Portrait in Vienna 1867-1918 202
Poster Art 150: London Underground's Greatest Designs 93
Pre-Raphaelites: Victorian Avant-Garde 54
Pride and Prejudice 154
Prince of Wales Theatre 94

Privates On Parade 60
Project Colony 116
Project Space: Objects In Mirror Are Closer Than They Appear 59
Propaganda: Power and Persuasion 137
Proud Camden 57
Proud Chelsea 54
Public Enemy 133
Pump House Gallery 84
Putney Bridge 107 & 110

Q

Quartermaine's Terms 76
Queen Elizabeth Olympic Park 171 & 177
Queen Elizabeth Olympic Park First Phase Opening 171
Queen's Birthday Gun Salutes 122
Queen's Club 150
Queen's Gallery, Buckingham Palace 63, 138 & 212
Queen: Portraits of a Monarch 62

R

Radio 2 Live In Hyde Park 194
RAF Photographer of the Year 72
Raindance Film Festival 193
rAndom International: Rain Room 61
Raven Girl 139
Raymond Gubbay And The Royal Albert Hall Presents: Carmen 92
RBS Six Nations: England v France 93
RBS Six Nations: England v Italy 103
RBS Six Nations: England v Scotland 84
Real Food Christmas Market 223
Real Food Festival 193
Regent Street 212
Regent Street Motor Show 212
Regent's Park 154, 172, 180 & 204
Relatively Speaking 136
Remembrance Sunday 214
Renaissance To Goya: Prints And Drawings From Spain 54
Research on Paintings 64
Rest is Noise 76
Revelations: Experiments in Photography 158
RFL Challenge Cup Final 180
RHS Chelsea Flower Show 138
RHS Hampton Court Palace Flower Show 165
Richard Hamilton: The Late Works 55
Richard Herring: Talking Cock 119
Richard III 58
Richard Rogers RA: Ideas in Progress 166
Richmond Literature Festival 211
Richmond Park 194
Richmond Theatre 75, 142 & 211

RideLondon 100 177
RideLondon FreeCycle 177
RideLondon Grand Prix 177
Rihanna: Diamonds Tour 153
RIOT Offspring 149
Rite of Spring/Petrushka 118
Riverside Studios 101
Robbie Williams 158
Robin Windsor And Kristina Rihanoff: Burn The Floor 101
Rocky Horror Show 40th Anniversary Tour 75
Roger Hodgson 140
Roger Waters: The Wall 190
Rolf Harris 86
Roof Gardens 149
Rose Theatre 86
Rose Theatre Kingston 105 & 123
Rosemarie Trockel: A Cosmos 88
Roundhouse 56, 86, 104, 117 & 163
Royal Academy of Arts 72, 105, 118, 150, 165, 192 & 206
Royal Academy Summer Exhibition 150
Royal Air Force Museum London 72 & 125
Royal Albert Hall 70, 73, 92, 102, 115, 117, 124, 126, 133, 136, 138, 140, 141, 148, 151, 166, 192, 193, 214, 215 & 221
Royal Ascot 153
Royal Ballet: The Nutcracker 223
Royal College of Art 133
Royal Court Theatre 71, 107 & 117
Royal Hospital Chelsea 138 & 157
Royal Observatory Greenwich 59 & 110
Royal Opera House 74, 94, 100, 102, 104, 110, 117, 120, 122, 132, 137, 139, 154, 157, 164 & 223
Royal Parks Foundation Half Marathon 202
Royal Philharmonic Orchestra Resident Season 57
Royal Philharmonic Orchestra: Film Music Gala 136
Royal Philharmonic Orchestra: Leonard Bernstein Evening 151
Royal Society of Portrait Painters Exhibition 133
Run to the Beat 206
Rushes Soho Shorts Festival 2012 167
Rutherford and Son 105

S

Saatchi Gallery 60, 63 & 133
Sadler's Sampled 155
Sadler's Wells Theatre 56, 88, 104, 116, 118, 132, 135, 142, 149, 153, 155 & 178
Salgado's Genesis 119
Salif Keita 88
Saloua Raouda Choucair 101
Santa Run 222
Sarah Lucas 200
Sarah Millican: Home Bird 213

Savoy Theatre 55
Scala 153
Scandinavia Show 203
School of Life Sunday Sermon: Hussein Chalayan on Fitting In 87
School of Life Sunday Sermon: Jon Ronson 137
Schumann: Under the Influence 132
Schwitters in Britain 78
Science Museum 64, 71, 158 & 213
Science Night 71
Scoop at More London 158
Scoop at More London Free Festival 158
Scotch Egg Challenge 193
Scream and an Outrage 133
Script 107
Seagull 142
Season in the Congo 164
Seduced By Art: Photography Past And Present 55
Serpentine Boating Lake 224
Serpentine Gallery 88 & 172
Serpentine Gallery Pavilion 172
Seven Dials 202
Shaftesbury Theatre 101 & 194
Shakespeare's Globe Theatre 126
Shard 83
Shepherd's Bush Empire 73, 94, 101, 103 & 124
Ship 193
Shoreditch Park 194
Shoreditch Town Hall 221
Shunga: Sex and Humour in Japanese Art 201
Sigur Ros 131
Silence of the Sea 70
Silent Opera 75
Silver Age of Hollywood 54
Simon Boccanegra 157
Sinead O'Connor 73
Singin' In The Rain 102
Sir John Soane's Museum 90
Ski & Snowboard Show 206
Snowman 215
Soho Theatre 75, 77, 91, 103, 108, 115 & 123
Somerset House 56, 57, 61, 77, 89, 115, 125, 149, 151, 164, 179, 189, 190 & 191
Somerset House Summer Series 164
Sound of Music 170
South West Four Weekender 180
Southbank Centre 71, 74, 86, 87, 88, 100, 107, 118, 119, 122, 132, 133, 135, 139, 152, 193, 202, 211, 215 & 223
Southbank Centre: Queen Elizabeth Hall 84 & 121
Southbank Centre: Royal Festival Hall 100, 139 & 205
Specials 142
Spirit of Christmas Fair 212
Spitalfields City Farm 110
Spitalfields Music Summer Festival 155

Spitalfields Winter Festival 222
Spring Real Bread Festival 133
St George's Church Hanover Square 103
St George's Day 123
St James's Park 141 & 177
St Pancras International Station 99
St Paul's Cathedral 156 & 223
St Paul's Covent Garden 135
Stand Up For Women 72
Steadman at 77 103
Steve Reich: Radio Rewrite 100
Stone Roses 148
Stranglers: Feel It Live Tour 104
Sundance London 124
Sunken Garden 119
Sweet Bird of Youth 149
Symphony in C 139
Syon Park 215

T
Taming of the Shrew 123
Tango Fire: Flames Of Desire 77
Tanztheater Wuppertal Pina Bausch: Two Cigarettes in the Dark | Vollmond 88
Taste of Christmas 222
Taste of London 154
Tate Britain 54, 59, 60, 61, 63, 78, 87, 104, 131, 148, 156 & 200
Tate Britain Commission: Simon Starling 104
Tate Modern 55, 57, 59, 62, 63, 84, 92, 120, 131, 193 & 203
Taylor Wessing Photographic Portrait Prize 59
Taylor Wessing Photographic Portrait Prize 213
Tea & Coffee Festival 139
Theatre Royal Drury Lane 156
This House 93
Thousand Slimy Things 75
Three Birds 106
Three Cane Whale 102
Tiger Territory 110
Tiger Tracks 99
Tim Walker: Storyteller 57
Times BFI London Film Festival 202
To Kill a Mockingbird 136
Tobacco Dock 203
Tomorrow: Elmgreen & Dragset at the V&A 200
Tosca 100
Tower Bridge 147 & 192
Traditional Crafts Weekend 169
Trafalgar Square 119, 123 & 178
Trafalgar Studios 70 & 87
Treasure 151
Treasures of the Royal Courts: Tudors, Stuarts and the Russian Tsars 165
Trelawny of the Wells 90
Tri Together 187

Trinity Buoy Wharf 75 & 116
Trooping the Colour 153
Tullet Prebon London Boat Show 71
Turn Of The Screw 73
Turner and the Sea 216
Twelfth Night 123
Twickenham Stadium 84, 93, 103, 134, 140, 153 & 224
Two Door Cinema Club 86

U
Ubu Roi 118
UEFA Champions League Final 2013 140
Uncle Vanya 59
Unexpected Pleasures 60
Unicorn Theatre 75
Union Chapel 92 & 135
United Micro Kingdoms (UmK) - A Design Fiction 78

V
V&A Museum of Childhood 63
V&A Illustration Awards 158
Vaccines 131
Vaisakhi on the Square 119
Valentino: Master of Couture 61
Vaudeville Theatre 59
Vauxhall Fashion Scout 190
Veolia Environnement Wildlife Photographer of the Year 61
Vermeer and Music: The Art of Love and Leisure 156
Very Old Man With Enormous Wings 69
Victoria and Albert (V&A) Museum 53, 56, 61, 63, 64, 105, 108, 136, 158, 171, 190, 192, 199, 200, 205 & 223
Victoria Park 140 & 168
View From The Shard 83
Village Underground 205
Virgin London Marathon 2013 122
Visions of the Universe 158
Vogue Festival 121
Voice Of The BBC: 90 Years Of Public Broadcasting 64
Vortex 86

W
Wagner Anniversary Concert 139
Walk Through British Art - BP British Art Displays 131
Wallace Collection 85, 154 & 204
Walpole Park 172
Weir 121
Wellcome Collection 60
Wembley Arena 102, 125, 134 & 139
Wembley Stadium 84, 93, 108, 117, 119, 132, 134, 137, 140, 141, 142, 152, 158, 178, 180, 187, 190, 194, 202, 203 & 206
West End 182

West End VIP Shopping Day 216
West Side Story 178
Westbourne Studios: Under the Westway 181
Westminster Abbey 151
Westminster College Garden 150
Whistler in London: Battersea Bridge and the Thames 203
White Cube Bermondsey 58
White Cube Mason's Yard 54 & 74
Whitechapel Gallery 61, 64, 73, 106 & 200
Wigmore Hall 132
Wildlife Photographer of the Year 206
William Hill Winter Festival 224
William Kentridge: I Am Not Me, The Horse Is Not Mine 55
William Klein/Daido Moriyama 57
Wilton's Music Hall 91
Wimbledon Bookfest 202
Wimbledon Finals Weekend 164
Wimbledon Lawn Tennis Championship 157
Wimbledon: The All England Lawn Tennis and Croquet Club 157, 164 & 165
Windsor Castle 62
Winslow Boy 102
Winter Fine Arts & Antiques Fair 212
Winter Tea and Coffee Festival 211
Winter's Tale 157
Women in Focus 59
Women of the World Festival 100
Wonder: Art and Science on the Brain 100
World Cup Qualifier: England v Moldova 187
World Cup Qualifier: England v Montenegro 202
World Cup Qualifier: England v Poland 203
World Photography Awards Exhibition 125
World Travel Market 212
Wozzeck 135
Written on Skin 102
WWT London Wetland Centre 169
Wyndhams Theatre 76, 120, 136 & 188

Y
Young Durer Drawing The Figure 205
Young Vic 76, 101, 116, 133, 164 & 190

Z
Zoo Lates 158
ZooNation Dance Company: Some Like It Hip Hop 132
ZSL London Zoo 110 & 158
Zucchero 138

Bye Bye

LondonTown.com
18 years as the number one internet site for London

Editor
Steven Potter
SP@LondonTown.com

Assistant to the Editor
Laura Sharps
Laura@LondonTown.com

Events Editor
Vicki Forde
Vicki@LondonTown.com

Feature Writers
Francesca Young, Felix Lowe, Tessa Edmondson, Rachel Halliburton, Omer Ali, James Mullinger, Crinan Potter and Peter Watts

Venues & Events Team
Marianne Antoine, Yasmine Bendjoudi, Sophie Mezei, Paul Johnson, Jessica Heili, Adam Ganne, Deborah Tyrer, Melissa Piggott, & Gal Oren

Design, Photography & Art Direction
Troy, Ana Potter, Gabriel Solomons, Mike Coopey & John Paul Dowling

Information Systems & Mapping
Guy Middleton, Kersten Bepler, James Holden, Robin Charisse, Seb Tranchand & Kieran Kerrigan

LONDONTOWN.COM
90 Long Acre, Covent Garden, London WC2E 9RZ

Booking Department
Contact us, seven days a week:
hotels - tickets - tours
020 7437 4370
0800-LONDON
Assistance@LondonTown.com

'London 2013 from LondonTown.com'
Published by:
London Marketing Corporation Limited

Every effort has been taken to ensure the accuracy of the information provided. However the publisher cannot be held liable for the consequences that may arise from any inaccuracies. Event information is also likely to change - *double check before travelling.*

LondonTown.com

"**Love it, love it, love it - where can one get more copies of the amazing 'London 2013' book?**"

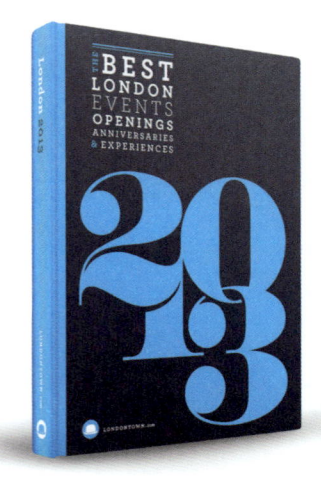

For further copies of **'London 2013 from LondonTown.com'** including free editions for iPad, Kindle Fire and Android tablets go to:

www.LondonTown.com/London2013